ORGANIZATIONAL COMMUNICATION

ORGANIZATIONAL COMMUNICATION
A Managerial Perspective
Second Edition

JANE WHITNEY GIBSON
Nova University

RICHARD M. HODGETTS
Florida International University

HarperCollins*Publishers*

Sponsoring Editor: Debra Riegert
Project Editor: Ellen MacElree
Art Direction/Cover Coordinator: Heather A. Ziegler
Text Design: Kay Wanuos
Cover Design: Delgado Design Inc.
Cover Photo: Copyright © 1989 Comstock
Production: Paula Keller

Organizational Communication: A Managerial Perspective, Second Edition
Copyright © 1991 by HarperCollins Publishers, Inc.

Library of Congress Cataloging-in-Publication Data

Gibson, Jane W.
    Organizational communication: a managerial perspective/Jane Whitney Gibson, Richard M. Hodgetts. — 2nd ed.
        p.   cm.
    Includes bibliographical references.
    ISBN 0-06-042315-3
    1. Communication in management.   2. Communication in organizations.   I. Hodgetts, Richard M. II. Title.
HD30.3.G52   1990   90-33629
658.4′5 — dc20   CIP

90 91 92 93 9 8 7 6 5 4 3 2 1

To our beloved fathers, Frank Whitney and Harold Hodgetts. And to the "children" in our lives, Sharon, Ingrid, Craig, Greg, Chip, Steven, and Jennifer.

Contents

Part Three

GROUP AND INTERGROUP COMMUNICATION

Part Five

APPLICATIONS FOR MANAGEMENT

Part Six

EMERGING CHALLENGES

Preface

Communicating effectively in the information age is no easy task. In organizations, lack of employee motivation, lower than desired productivity, and disharmony among supervisors and subordinates are frequently the result of poor communication. Although most of us are doing the best we can, our opportunities for learning how to be more effective communicators are quite limited.

This book provides such an opportunity for every interested management student or practitioner. Management is communication; effective managers are effective communicators. The second edition of *Organizational Communication: A Managerial Perspective* is designed to provide both a conceptual base and practical applications to bridge theory and real-world growth opportunities. The book is written at a level that is equally appropriate for undergraduates, graduate students, and practicing managers. Our underlying premise is that *no* skill is more important to the manager than effective communication.

ORGANIZATION OF THE BOOK
From our experience in teaching organizational communication to both undergraduate and graduate students, we have found that the most successful approach presents interpersonal communication first, group communication next, and finally organization-wide concepts. We have followed this organization in our book, prefacing it with a general overview of communication theory and following it with more specific communication applications. Therefore, the book is divided into six parts.

- Part One is an overview of organizational communication. Chapter 1 presents the nature of the communication process and the communication needs of managers, and Chapter 2 provides a historical perspective of the field.

- Part Two focuses on interpersonal communication. Specific chapters address such areas as effective listening, barriers to interpersonal communication, and nonverbal communication.

- Part Three addresses group communication. Included in this section are group dynamics, group decision making and leadership, and communication.

- Part Four deals with organization-wide communication. In this section, attention is focused on formal organizational communication, informal organizational communication, and organizational communication barriers.

- Part Five discusses applications for management, including such important areas as power, persuasion and negotiation, the management of conflict and change, interviews, and the management of meetings and conferences.

■ Part Six treats emerging challenges in organizational communication. Chapter 15 is a new chapter on international communication, and Chapter 16 looks at communication audits and communication training programs.

FEATURES AND WHAT'S NEW IN THIS EDITION

The second edition has been thoroughly updated through the use of the most recent research in the field. It incorporates the suggestions and ideas of many of the instructors who used the first edition and our reviewers who worked on the second edition. It also addresses emerging topics and the hot issues of the day in the field of organizational communication.

Content

Although the comprehensive content of the first edition has been retained, some changes have been made. In the second edition, the material on transactional analysis has been deleted, and the discussion of self-disclosure which was in Chapter 6 has been moved to Chapter 4, on barriers to interpersonal communication. A totally new chapter, Chapter 15, on international business communication has been added. This addition reflects the growing interest of business schools around the country in integrating international topics into the curriculum. It provides the student with material that will surely be relevant in almost any work environment of the 1990s.

Pedagogy

This book has been written with the student in mind; it is therefore practical in focus and applications oriented in its style. Each chapter has a number of distinctive pedagogical features designed to make the text more relevant to the student's present and future work environment. First, each chapter is supplemented with *Objectives* to focus the student's thinking and *Self-Assessment Quizzes* to help students put themselves "into the chapter." *Questions for Discussion and Analysis* review the text material, and *Exercises* provide applications for students to do individually or in groups. End-of-chapter cases called *You Be the Consultant* provide a realistic scenario and ask the student to provide advice about the case. The *Implications for Management* sections in each chapter highlight key points for managers. These in-text supplements are designed to increase awareness of current communication performance and of potential communication improvement.

Some pedagogical additions have been made in the second edition. Suggestions from our colleagues centered around adding cases and other self-assessment quizzes to the already applied pedagogy. The second edition, therefore, introduces an opening *Case in Point* for each chapter. The Case in Point is used as a starting point for discussion, and it is revisited at the end of each chapter where it is used as a review. In addition, a *second Self-Assessment Quiz* has been added to most chapters to provide students with another opportunity to immediately apply what they have read to their own experience.

Finally, each new chapter has a brand-new boxed feature. There are three types of boxes. First, *Communication Technology boxes* illustrate the ways in which changing technology has affected all types of organizational communication. An example is "Communication Technology: Brainstorming Electronically," which discusses how microcomputers provide an environment for creative group brainstorming when a face-to-face meeting is neither available nor advisable. Second, *International Communication boxes* carry the international theme throughout the text. One example is "International Communication: Cultural Assimilators Can Be Good for Business," which deals with the use of programmed learning designed to expose members of one culture to the basic concepts, attitudes, role perceptions, customs, and values of another culture. A third type of box, *Ethics in Communication*, is illustrated by a box entitled "Big Brother Is Listening." This box examines the ethics involved in listening to confidential information or even overhearing someone's conversation. The ethics boxes are a timely response to the growing concern that business schools should be doing a lot more in training people to be ethical professionals.

SUPPLEMENTS
A number of supplements are available to the instructor upon adoption of this textbook.

■ A comprehensive *Instructor's Manual/Test Bank*, written by us and Charles W. Blackwell of Nova University, contains chapter summaries, chapter outlines, and lecture notes as well as suggested solutions to all exercises and applications. The Instructor's Manual also contains a complete test bank of true/false and multiple-choice questions that may be used in preparing quizzes and exams and transparency masters which illustrate key concepts in the text.

■ The test bank is also available on *Harper Test*. This highly acclaimed test generation system allows instructors to create fully customized tests. It features full word-processing capability, "help" screens, and a password option to protect data. It is available free to adopters on request for the IBM and most compatibles.

ACKNOWLEDGMENTS
We didn't do it alone. Our gratitude goes to the many reviewers who have provided us with valuable input that was incorporated into the final manuscript. These include the following people:

■ **Robert Boren**
Boise State University
■ **Susan Hellweg**
San Diego State University
■ **Walter Hill**
Green River Community College
■ **Robert Insley**
University of North Texas

■ **Robert J. Myers**
Baruch College, CUNY
■ **William Sharbrough**
The Citadel
■ **Larry Smeltzer**
Arizona State University
■ **John Waltman**
East Michigan University

We have also benefited greatly in the past several years from our association with the Academy of Management Organizational Communication Division, the IEEE Professional Communication Society, and the Association for Business Communication where we have had the opportunity to observe and participate in discussions about the current theories and practices in organizational communication.

On the production side, we wish to thank our most gracious editor, Debra Riegert, without whom this second edition would still be a twinkle in our eyes. We also are most appreciative to Suzy Spivey and Ellen MacElree for their enthusiastic support of this project. We continue to be grateful to our respective deans, Phil DeTurk at Nova University and Charles Nickerson at Florida International University, for their encouragement and support. Special thanks to our secretaries, Roma Hagler and Ruth Chapman, who take care of us, keep us on schedule, and provide moral support. Finally, we wish to thank our families for their continued patience and love. Writing a book means long hours of quiet work and isolation from those around you. They have settled for less of our communication time so that we could be free to study and write about the subject.

Jane Whitney Gibson
Richard M. Hodgetts

Part One

COMMUNICATION OVERVIEW

In Part One we will introduce the field of organizational communication. Organizational personnel do many things in their efforts both to convey and to receive information, and quite often the overall effectiveness and efficiency of an enterprise rest on the ability of these people to communicate well. This part of the book examines two important areas of organizational communication: the process itself and the role that is played by management theory.

Chapter 1 defines the term *communication* and describes the communication process. It also focuses on the needs that organizations have for effective communication. Factors that influence effective communication will be discussed: the nature of the industry, the goals of the enterprise, its organizational culture, the number of levels in the structure, and the quality of work life that exists in the workplace.

Chapter 2 explains the link between management theory and communication. The field of management has gone through several eras. Years ago downward communication was the most common form of communication. The main purpose of communication was to provide specific job instructions to employees so that they would know exactly what they were to do. This classical era of management eventually was replaced by a human relations era in which formal lines of communication were supplemented with informal lines. The purpose of communication was expanded from that of providing specific work instructions to also making the employee feel needed and satisfied. Upward communication began to complement downward communication. Today organizational communication is in a human resources era. Effective organizations use both formal and informal communication, and messages flow in whichever direction is necessary to ensure efficiency and effectiveness: upward, downward, horizontal, or diagonal. In the process, employees are regarded as human resources that are of more importance to management than its machines and equipment. As management moved from one era to the next, a number of important changes took place in managerial thinking and management theory; these developments will be explained in the chapter.

When you have finished reading all the material in Part One, you will know how the communication process works. You will also understand why the most effective organizations operate within the confines of a human resources philosophy of management.

CHAPTER 1

The Communication Process

"Communications has proven as elusive as the Unicorn. The noise level has gone up so fast that no one can really listen any more to all that babble about communications. But there is clearly less and less communicating. The communication gap within institutions and between groups in society has been widening steadily — to the point where it threatens to become an unbridgeable gulf of total misunderstanding."

Peter Drucker, *An Introductory View of Management* (New York: Harper and Row, 1977), p. 408.

Objectives

1. To define the term *communication*.

2. To describe how the communication process works, with particular emphasis given to coding, transmission, feedback, and noise.

3. To define the term *organizational communication*.

4. To relate some of the major factors that influence managerial communication needs.

C A S E   I N   P O I N T

A Joint Misunderstanding

Sometimes when Paul Prandon finds himself getting behind in his work, he delegates the least important parts to his assistant, Jane Draff. Jane has worked for Paul for three weeks, and during this time period has come to realize that if Paul needs things done in a hurry, he will typically leave a note on her desk telling her what he would like done. Paul often works until 7:00–9:00 P.M. but sometimes does not show up for work until 10:00 or 11:00 A.M.

Two days ago Paul left a pile of papers on Jane's desk. The note on top read, "Please take care of all of this as soon as you can." Most of the material was a product proposal report that Paul had handwritten with references regarding where various figures and charts were to go. Jane read the entire report, carefully made a series of comments on a piece of paper regarding additional changes that should be made in the report to put it in final form, and then sent if off to the typing pool with a note that said, "Please return to me the original handwritten report along with the typewritten one."

When the person in the typing pool received the material, she read the note and then put the material under a large pile of other reports and manuscripts that were to be typed. The typists in the pool have always followed a rule of "first in, first out" in deciding what to type next. So when a typist has completed an assignment, he or she takes the next batch of material off the top of the pile.

When Jane arrived at 8:30 this morning, Paul was nervously pacing the office. Upon seeing her he breathed a sigh of relief. "Ah, there you are. I've looked everywhere for my report but couldn't find it. Where did you put it?" Jane explained that she had

not received the report back from the typing pool but would check on it immediately. "Great," said Paul. "The meeting for new product proposals is at ten o'clock and we're still going to have to get fifteen copies of the proposal run off."

It took Jane a couple of seconds to get through to the typing pool. The head of the department informed her that Paul's report was scheduled for typing some time after lunch that day. Paul heard the comment and immediately bolted for the door. Along with Jane, he entered the typing pool area and immediately began to explain his dilemma to the supervisor. She listened carefully and then told him that she would reschedule his work immediately. However, it would take until around 9:45 A.M. before the report would be finished. "That's fine," said Paul. "Just as long as I can get it before ten." On the way back to the office, Paul expressed his concern to Jane over her not getting the report finished on time. Jane was surprised. "What do you mean by 'on time'?" she asked. "You never said anything about deadlines. Let me show you your note." Paul looked over his memo and said to her, "Here it is. The last part of the note says 'as soon as you can.'" Jane looked at Paul for a minute and then said, "I think in the future you and I had better work on improving our communication. Quite obviously you feel I made a mistake, while I think you failed to communicate properly with me.

Exactly what did go wrong? Who made the mistake? How could it have been prevented? Write down your analysis of the situation and then put it aside. We will return to it later.

INTRODUCTION

Communication is a word that has many meanings. Even among communication theorists, the term has gone through an evolutionary process. Early definitions tended to focus on the dynamics of stimulus – response. For example, in 1950 one author offered the following definition: "Communication is the discriminatory response of an organism to a stimulus." [1] A decade later many authors were defining the word with a process orientation. Berelson and Steiner referred to communication as "the transmission of information, ideas, emotions, skills, etc., by the use of symbols — words, pictures, figures, graphs, etc. It is the act or process of transmission that is usually called communication." [2]

In recent years definitions have become more inclusive. Today no communication theorist would likely define communication without giving consideration to the sender, the receiver, and the need for an "understanding" of the message. At the same time, it is helpful if the definition can be presented in a brief statement. For our purposes, we define communication as *the process of transferring messages between sender and receiver*. Notice that we have included the three most important parts of any effective communication process: a sender, a receiver, and a successful transmission of meaning.

> **The communication process requires a transfer of messages between sender and receiver.**

THE COMMUNICATION PROCESS

The *communication process* involves a message moving from the creation stage (the sender conjures up the idea(s) that is to be transmitted) to the feedback stage (the receiver indicates that he or she understands the communique or requests further information on the matter). If the process is carried out effectively, the receiver knows what the sender wants him or her to know. If the process is not carried out effectively, the receiver lacks this information, which indicates a breakdown somewhere in the process.

Figure 1.1 illustrates the communication process in action. Notice that there are seven steps in the process: (1) the sender must have an idea, (2) this idea must be put (encoded) into some form (letter, memo, conversation) so that it can be sent, (3) the idea must be transmitted, (4) the message must be received, (5) the receiver must interpret (decode) the message, (6) the message must be correctly understood, and (7) the receiver must provide feedback where necessary.

Also of importance in understanding the communication process is "noise," a term standing for the environment in which the process takes place. In the chapters that follow, we discuss these elements in more depth. For the moment, however, we want to focus our attention on the three most critical steps in the communication process: coding, transmission, and feedback, as well as the role played by noise.

Coding

Before transmitting an idea to a receiver, the sender must organize his or her thoughts into a coherent package, This is called *encoding*. In this step the sender selects the words, phrases, and sentences so as to convey the correct meanings. During this process, the individual will be guided by how the receiver is most likely to interpret or "decode" the message. Thus coding involves two major areas of consideration: (1) what the sender wants to convey and (2) how this individual believes the message will be understood by the receiver.

> **Senders encode messages; receivers decode them.**

Figure 1.1

The communication process.

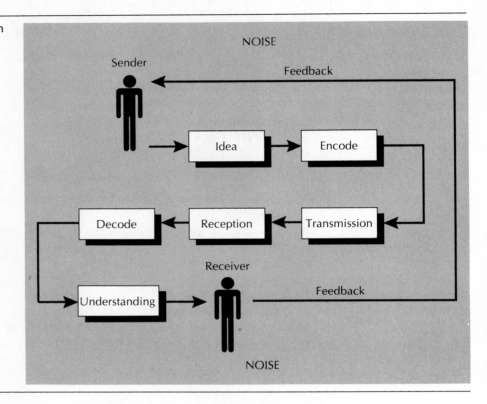

In coding the message, the receiver relies heavily on his or her "code of past experience." Everyone carries within themselves a unique code of past experiences that represents an accumulation of everything they have seen, heard, and otherwise experienced during their life. This accumulation of memories, both consciously and unconsciously, directs their coding of the message. In turn receivers' codes affect their decoding of the transmission. When a breakdown of communication occurs because what the sender "said" is not what the receiver "heard," it is often a result of different codes of past experience.[3] For example, assume you are driving along the highway and intend to get off at Exit 11. One hundred yards ahead of you is a sign that says, "Exit 11 Next Right." Where should you turn off the highway? Most people would take the next right. However, many people from the Northeast section of the country, especially New York City, will drive past this exit and take the next one. To them "next right" means "two more rights." If you want them to take the *very* next right, the sign should read, "Exit 11 This Right."

Parallel examples exist for all parts of the country. Unless the sender is aware of how the receiver has been taught to interpret certain words or phrases, communication breakdown will often occur. Another example is provided in the case of words that either are misinterpreted or are technical and beyond the understanding of the average employee. Some of these examples are provided in Self-Assessment Quiz 1.1: What Do These Words Mean? Take the quiz and check your answers at the back of the book before continuing.

SELF-ASSESSMENT QUIZ 1.1

What Do These Words Mean?

One of the most difficult coding problems for managers is using words that receivers understand. Many times bosses will use technical terms or words that are unfamiliar to the average employee. Some of the following underlined words are technical in the sense that they have specific meanings in the business world. Others are understood by many employees providing they have had exposure to the words. Identify the meaning of each underlined word by circling the appropriate alternative. Answers can be found at the back of the book.

1. In this firm, we have biweekly meetings.
   a. once a week
   b. twice a week
   c. every other week
   d. every four weeks

2. A college education is mandatory for vice presidents.
   a. possible
   b. difficult
   c. financially rewarding
   d. required

3. The chairmain of the board will relinquish her position next week.
   a. give up
   b. expand
   c. explain
   d. diminish

4. They have a very liquid cash position.
   a. lots of cash on hand
   b. long-term cash receivable
   c. unstable
   d. no cash

5. He was tardy today.
   a. sick
   b. absent
   c. fooling around
   d. late

Continued next page

6. The <u>bears</u> dominated the stock market yesterday.
   a. sellers
   b. financial institutions
   c. brokers
   d. money market specialists

7. He was told to <u>burn</u> the blueprints.
   a. photocopy
   b. number
   c. file
   d. destroy

8. She has excellent <u>conceptual</u> skills.
   a. ability to make quantitative decisions
   b. ability to make short-run decisions
   c. ability to make production-oriented decisions
   d. ability to make strategic planning decisions

9. The two companies have a <u>tacit</u> agreement.
   a. brief
   b. financially profitable
   c. unspoken or implied
   d. written

10. From everything she could find, the firm was <u>solvent</u>.
    a. maximizing its profits
    b. able to pay its bills
    c. in financial straits
    d. out of cash

Transmission

An effective means of transmission must be found.

After coding the message, the sender must choose a method for transmitting it. How will the message be sent: written or orally? Will it be conveyed in a letter or a memo, or will a telephone or conference call be used?[4] When will it be transmitted: now or later? If later, exactly when? Of particular importance is the timing. Many well-thought-out communications have been inadvertently sabotaged by inappropriate timing. The sender is ready to send but the receiver is not ready to receive.

For example, George feels that he is entitled to a larger-than-average raise. Where and when should he make this request? Both location and timing are critical. The request should be made in the boss's office. This is where his superior makes important decisions, and, at least in George's mind, this matter is as important as most things the boss will take care of this week. It is also important that George make the request after the proper groundwork supporting the decision has been laid. For example, if George can bring his latest sales figures or show the boss that his performance ratings have been consistently higher than anyone else's in the department, the timing may be right. Better yet, if George can get in to see the boss just after he has been given some good news, he may get his request. The boss should be in a very good mood, and George may find his timing to be excellent. In any event, there are times when the boss is more likely to agree to requests and this is when George should ask.

Feedback

Both receiver and sender can provide feedback.

Feedback is information provided about messages that have been received. Both receiver and sender can provide feedback. The receiver's feedback takes the form of asking for additional information/clarification or relating personal opinions/impressions regarding the overall value of the communique. An example of asking for additional information is, "These data do not contain the annual sales forecast. Would you please send it to me at your earliest convenience?" or "Could you tell more about why this problem exists?" In a case of relating overall value, the feedback message may be "I don't think this is a good idea" or "I like your approach but have you considered bringing the vice president in on your plan?" Feedback from the receiver is designed to continue the flow of information between the two parties.

When the sender receives feedback, the individual will use this information to guide further communiques. By providing additional information and clarification, the sender may get the receiver to act in the desired manner. The most important thing to keep in mind is that without feedback the communication process is likely to break down. This is particularly true when the receiver does not adequately understand the message and cannot get additional input, or when the individual is a poor listener.[5] Conversely, when an individual learns how to get feedback, the person's communication skills often improve.[6]

Noise

Noise is anything that interferes with message transmission and/or reception.

All communication takes place within an environment. The term *noise* refers to anything in this environment that interferes with the content of the message being transmitted or received. In its literal sense, noise interferes with communication and the sender must work to overcome this environmental interference. If the individual is speaking, he or she will have to talk louder. If listening, the individual will have to concentrate on the speaker's words, trying very hard to screen out external distractions.

Implications for Management

1. Remember that communication involves the transfer of messages. Regardless of how the message is coded or sent, the important thing is that the subordinate understands what you want him or her to understand.

2. When coding messages, keep in mind the value of the code of past experience. Be sure that the individual understands what you are transmitting. Do not use words with which the individual is unfamiliar. Do not say or write anything that is in direct conflict with the person's values and is likely to elicit a negative response. Work to warm the individual to your point of view.

3. When transmitting messages, be aware of two important considerations: how to send the message and when to send it. If at all possible, use face-to-face communication since this tends to be most effective. However, if this approach is not possible or advisable, make your message brief and understandable, and present it in such a way that the other party is likely to agree with your point of view. Also remember that when the person receives the message is sometimes as important as what the person receives. Learn about your receiver and rely on this information to help you decide the best time to present the message.

4. Encourage feedback from your people. If they do not know what you want done or need some additional information, be available to them. Likewise, if you are unsure of what they are saying, ask questions. Make sure both of you are on the same wavelength before moving on to other matters. Be sure that you give them your undivided attention and that they do the same. Do not allow noise to creep into the communication environment. Your willingness to spend time preventing communication problems will provide big dividends later on.

Yet noise does not have to be loud. If the individual next to you is slowly turning the pages of a report as you present your findings to the board of directors, that individual is creating noise. So is the person in the back of the room who is quietly talking to the individual in the next seat.

USING THE COMMUNICATION PROCESS EFFECTIVELY

The basic communication process is helpful in understanding how messages are conveyed from sender to receiver. The process is also useful in learning how to communicate effectively. When the sender is carrying out the process, he or she should take three important steps: (1) plan the communication, (2) remember that meanings are in people, not in words, and (3) select the best method for transmission.

Planning the Communique

An effective communication begins with a plan. This plan should help the manager answer three questions: What do you want to communicate? To whom will the message be directed? What do you want to happen as a result of this message?

Effective communication begins with a plan. The manager should begin by examining all three questions as a composite. It is seldom possible to plan a communication by focusing exclusively on one of the questions because there is too much overlap between them. Suppose a senior-level manager decides to send a memo to the credit department because the average customer is now paying his or her bill every 37 days, and all sales contracts require payment within 30 days. The manager knows that, on average, customers are paying late and wants to tell the people in the credit department that they have to do a better job of determining who is to be given credit and who is to be denied.

The message that the senior-level manager wants to convey is now clear: Tighten up the granting of credit. The manager also knows that the message is to be sent to the credit department. Who in this department should receive the message? Assume it is the head of the department. Now the manager must decide how formal or informal the communication should be. If the two individuals know each other, the manager will use a more informal tone. If they are not well acquainted or the manager wants the communication to be regarded as highly serious, the individual will use a more formal tone.

The action that the manager wants to result from the communication is also clear. Current customers who do not pay on time are to be denied further credit, and new customers who are unlikely to pay on time are to be turned down for credit.

Meanings in People Not Words

Now the senior-level manager has to decide the proper way to convey the message. How is the credit manager likely to view this communication? Will the individual feel that he or she is being called incompetent, or will the manager regard the message as an objective evaluation of the current situation and a recommendation for future action?

It is important to understand meaning is in people.

In tailoring the message to the audience, the sender must remember that meanings are in people. What one person intends to convey is not always what the other person receives. If the sender says "this situation has gone on far too long," how is this message likely to be viewed? Is the competence of the credit manager being challenged? Or is the credit manager likely to agree and to welcome the fact that someone else is also interested in eliminating the problem of late payment by credit customers? The answer to these questions will be based on how the senior-level manager reads the situation. This is typically accomplished by the sender "getting into the other person's shoes" and trying to interpret the message the way the receiver will. To the extent that the senior-level manager can effectively empathize, the message will carry the intended meaning. However, this will be determined not by the sender but by the receiver for, as noted above, meanings are in people.

Selecting the Best Method of Transmission

How should the message be conveyed? The answer will depend on the overall goals that the senior-level manager wants to attain. For example, if the individual wants to convey the basic message in a personal, face-to-face way, a brief meeting might be held. If the manager does not have time for such a meeting, the individual might telephone the credit manager and talk to him or her about the matter. If the manager feels that the issue should be conveyed in writing, the credit manager might follow up the meeting or telephone conversation with a memo, or the individual might use only a memo and forgo direct, personal contact.

Think carefully how the message should be transmitted.

In selecting the best method of transmission, the manager must remember three things. First, direct, personal contact allows the other party to respond to the message and when feedback is important, this communication medium is useful. Second, if a record of the communication is needed, a memo or letter should be written. In fact, the more important the message, the more likely it is that the manager should put it in writing. Third, time is money. If no one form of communication is regarded as any better than any other, the fastest, most direct route should be chosen. For example, if the senior-level manager is in the office, he or she might place a call to the credit manager. If the manager is away from the office, he or she might dictate a memo to be transcribed and sent to the credit manager through interoffice mail. In choosing the best method of transmission, the sender must weigh the time involved and the cost associated with this choice. Surprisingly, perhaps, many managers have found that brief face-to-face meetings and telephone conversations are usually highly cost effective because they save the organizational time spent in dictating, typing, and routing internal messages or mailing external ones. The cost to write and send a first-class letter is now around $7.[7] So the careful choice of a method of transmission is extremely important and can directly affect organizational efficiency and effectiveness.

ORGANIZATIONAL COMMUNICATION NEEDS

Organizational communication is the transfer of information and knowledge among organizational members for the purpose of achieving organizational efficiency and effectiveness. In this book, we look at organizational communication at the individual, group, and total organizational levels. We also examine how management can improve each type of communication.

The Nature of the Industry

Some organizations operate in very placid environments, that is, very little changes. Most function under turbulent conditions where change is common. The airlines are a good example. Today it is common to find one airline cutting its fares and starting a price war in an effort to generate more passenger traffic for its own routes. This action is then met by counter price moves by the competition, resulting in an even more turbulent environment. The banking business provides another example. Today interstate banking is a reality. Large banks are looking to acquire well-positioned, well-managed smaller ones. Citicorp, Bank of America, and Chase Manhattan currently are seeking acquisitions and mergers in growing states like Texas and Florida. Yet we do not need to confine our attention to industries where government deregulation has occurred over the last decade. Many industries have faced fierce competition for a long time. The computer field is one of the best examples, with personal computers providing the most recent case history. Ever since IBM entered the personal computer market in the early 1980s, this market has seen one major development after another. By the late 1980s it was obvious that IBM was beginning to dominate; Apple had dropped to second place and was trying to maintain its position; and AT&T, fresh from the divestiture of its local operating companies, was trying to decide the precise nature of its own attack on the field.

> Dynamic industries have a greater need for information.

Developments such as these require organizations to have a well-formulated, efficiently functioning communication network. The enterprise cannot afford to misread a competitor's moves; it also cannot afford to maintain the status quo. The organization must have a strategy in place that it can use to capture and maintain market share. This strategy involves two communication phases: acquisition and transferal.

The *communication acquisition* phase entails investigating the external market, studying conditions, analyzing competitive strategies, and combining all of this information in a form that can be readily transmitted.

The *communication transferal* phase involves passing this information to those managers in the organization who are charged with acting on the data. Most communication textbooks discuss only internal flows of information. However, external data collection must precede these internal transmissions. Every organization exists to provide a good or service. By knowing what competitors are doing, an enterprise is in the best position to judge its own offerings and strategic countermoves. Quite clearly managers in competitive industries must rely heavily on communication to ensure the survival and growth of their own enterprises.

> **Communication acquisition and transferal are vitally important.**

Organizational Culture

Organizational culture encompasses the norms, attitudes, values, beliefs, and philosophies of an enterprise.[8] Every organization has its own culture. Table 1.1 provides a general description of the four basic types of organizational cultures. A close look at these cultures reveals that each has different communication needs. For example, in the "tough-guy macho" culture the top manager makes all important decisions. The enterprise revolves around this individual who is a "one-person show." He or she expects to be kept abreast of what is going on and, once a decision has been made, expects subordinates to carry it out without asking a lot of questions. The "work hard/play hard" culture places a great deal of emphasis on teamwork and short-run results. Managers want information, and they want it now. The "bet-your-company" culture focuses on the long run. Although these managers want information that helps them make decisions and allows them to check (and recheck) their thinking, communication feedback tends to be very slow. The "process" culture is one in which the personnel are cautious and protective of their position. A large percentage of the communications are designed to ensure that things get done according to regulations; individual initiative and effort are downplayed, and bureaucratic rules and regulations carry the day.

> **Every organization has its own culture.**

In recent years a number of organizations have shown the importance of organizational culture in the success of their operations. Wal-Mart, the fastest growing retailer in America, is a good example. Founded by Sam Walton, the company now dominates the retail business in rural America and is moving into urban areas. By using a work hard/play hard philosophy that is heavily personnel- and customer-oriented, Wal-Mart has achieved a phenomenal sales growth. In Wal-Mart stores there are no subordinates; everyone is an "associate." In addition, customers are greeted upon entering the store, and anyone who wants to return merchandise can do so without question. At Wal-Mart everyone follows the philosophy "the customer is always right," and the culture that it creates has proven successful for both the company and the buying public.

AT&T is another example of how the creation of the right organizational culture has led to success. When the firm was government regulated, it did not have to be concerned with competition. Now that the industry has been deregulated, AT&T has made tremendous changes in its corporate culture and has become much more responsive to customer needs and desires. As a result of its ability to adjust to its environment,

Table 1.1

ORGANIZATIONAL CULTURE PROFILES

	Tough-Guy/Macho Culture	Work Hard/Play Hard Culture
Type of risks that are assumed	High	Low
Type of feedback from decisions	Fast	Fast
Typical kinds of organizations that use this culture	Construction, cosmetics, TV, radio, venture capitalism, management consulting	Real estate, computer firms, auto distributors, door-to-door sales operations, retail stores, mass consumer sales
The ways survivors and/or heroes in this culture behave	They have a tough attitude. They are individualistic. They can tolerate all-or-nothing risks. They are superstitious.	They are super salespeople. They often are friendly, hail-fellow-well-met types. They use a team approach to problem solving. They are not superstitious.
Strengths of the personnel/culture	They can get things done in short order.	They are able to produce a high volume of work quickly.
Weakness of the personnel/culture	They do not learn from past mistakes. Everything tends to be short term in orientation. The virtues of cooperation are ignored.	They look for quick-fix solutions. They have a short-term time perspective. They are more committed to action than to problem solving.
Habits of the survivors and/or heroes	They dress in fashion. They live in ''in'' places. They like one-on-one sports such as tennis. They enjoy scoring points off one another in verbal interaction.	They avoid extremes in dress. They live in tract houses. They prefer team sports such as touch football. They like to drink together.

AT&T is still the major company in the long-distance telephone market, and it is making major headway in the computer field as well.

Levels and Goals

Communication needs vary by organizational level.

Organizational levels and goals also help determine managerial communication needs. In general terms, there are three managerial levels in an organization: top, middle, and lower. Top managers are most interested in developments in the external environment and the ways in which these can be used to formulate strategies for the enterprise.

Table 1.1 *(Continued)*

Bet-Your-Company Culture	Process Culture
High	Low
Slow	Slow
Oil, aerospace, capital goods manufacturers, architectural firms, investment banks, mining and smelting firms, military	Banks, insurance companies, utilities, pharmaceuticals, financial-service organizations, many agencies of the government
They can endure long-term ambiguity. They always double check their decisions. They are technically competent. They have a strong respect for authority.	They are very cautious and protective of their own flank. They are orderly and punctual. They are good at attending to detail. They always follow established procedures.
They can generate high-quality inventions and major scientific breakthroughs.	They bring order and system to the workplace.
They are extremely slow in getting things done. Their organizations are vulnerable to short-term economic fluctuations. Their organizations often face-cash-flow problems.	There is lots of red tape. Initiative is downplayed. They face long hours and boring work.
They dress according to their organizational rank. Their housing matches their hierarchical position. They like sports where the outcome is unclear until the end, such as golf. The older members serve as mentors for the younger ones.	They dress according to hierarchical rank. They live in apartments or no-frill homes. They enjoy process sports like jogging and swimming. They like discussing memos.

SOURCE: Adapted from Terence E. Deal and Allen A. Kennedy, *Corporate Cultures: The Rites and Rituals of Corporate Life* (Reading, Mass.: Addison-Wesley, 1982), Ch. 6.

Middle managers are most concerned with taking top management directives and seeing that they are translated into specific actions. Lower managers are most concerned with seeing that particular goods and services are produced. As a result, each has a need for specific types of information. (See International Communication in Action: Vive Le Bureaucracy.)

At the upper levels, information is often general. Aware that one of its competitors, Company A, is designing a new laptop computer, the top management may feel that the firm should also produce an offering for this market. Communication with the middle managers will take the form of "let us design and produce a laptop that is better than

INTERNATIONAL COMMUNICATION IN ACTION

Vive Le Bureaucracy

Communication seems to be a fairly straightforward process. However, the logic and reasoning behind the process often vary from country to country. For example, in the United States organizational communication is viewed as a process for getting things done, and when managers communicate down the hierarchy, they are interested in attaining results. For this reason they sometimes jump over hierarchical boundaries and encourage their subordinates to do so also. In France, however, hierarchical communication is much more social and power oriented. French managers believe that the hierarchy should not be bypassed in transmitting information up and down the line. They also believe that they should be in control of the situation at all times and that subordinates should obey orders without asking a lot of questions. Here are some results from a study that compared the ways in which American and French managers viewed organizational communication and the hierarchy.

PERCENTAGES OF AMERICAN AND FRENCH MANAGERS AGREEING WITH STATEMENTS RELATED TO STRUCTURAL ISSUES		
	USA (n = 90)	France (n = 219)
1. The main reason for having a hierarchical structure is so that everyone knows who has authority over whom.	26	45
2. No organization could ever function without a hierarchy of authority.	50	73
3. The notion of subordination always has a negative connotation.	31	43
4. In order to maintain his or her authority, it is important for a manager to be able to keep a certain distance vis-à-vis subordinates.	50	28
5. Most managers seem to be motivated more by obtaining power than by achieving objectives.	36	56
6. It is desirable that management authority be able to be questioned.	80	69
7. The subordinate should submit to all of a superior's demands if the superior has legitimate authority.	10	19
8. It is important for a manager to have at hand precise answers to most of the questions that his or her subordinates may raise about their work.	23	53
9. An organizational structure in which certain	52	83

PERCENTAGES OF AMERICAN AND FRENCH MANAGERS AGREEING WITH
STATEMENTS RELATED TO STRUCTURAL ISSUES *(Continued)*

	USA (n = 90)	France (n = 219)
subordinates have two direct bosses should be avoided at all costs.		
10. In order to have efficient work relationships, it is often necessary to bypass the hierarchical line.	68	53

SOURCE: Giorgio Inzerilli and Andre Laurent, "Managerial Views of Organization Structure in France and the USA," *International Studies of Management & Organization,* Spring-Summer 1983, p. 104.

Quite obviously, the French and Americans have very different views regarding the role and nature of the hierarchy. This difference undoubtedly helps account for the problems French managers sometimes encounter when they are assigned to American subsidiaries and vice versa. Each treats the subordinates in a way that is quite different from the methods employed by local managers. The result is that American subordinates often view the French manager as autocratic, whereas French subordinates view the American manager as overly lenient. In fact, each is carrying out the job the way he or she is accustomed to doing it without taking into consideration that the subordinates are not used to being treated this way. International differences can have an important effect on the communication process.

anything on the market currently, and one that will help us offset the new product that will be coming out of Company A." This directive will then be translated into action by managers from the research and development, manufacturing, and marketing departments. Working together, they will design and produce the most up-to-date piece of equipment for that market niche. The planning part of the task will fall to the middle managers. The production phase will be under the direct control of the lower-level managers. As the plan is pushed farther down the line, it will become more and more specific. A directive of "let us do this" from the top will eventually result in a laptop computer being manufactured, assembled, tested, and shipped by lower-level personnel.

The communication needs of the three levels of management can also be differentiated on the basis of objectives. At the upper levels of the hierarchy, management focuses on overall enterprise objectives such as share of the market, return on investment, and growth. At the middle levels of the hierarchy these goals are translated into shorter range objectives such as the establishment of sales territories and sales quotas, purchase of machinery and equipment, and financing of operations. At the lower levels of the management hierarchy, typical objectives include daily output quotas, maintenance of machinery, and control of tardiness, absenteeism, and turnover.

The Size of the Organization

Another factor affecting managerial communication needs is organizational size. As enterprises grow, the managers' need for information tends to increase. More customers must be served, and the manager needs to know what goods and services these individuals want, how much they are willing to pay, and what problems they are encountering in their use of them. At the same time, the firm now needs to do more marketing research, hire more salespeople, and increase the amount of administrative support for facilitating operations. In the process, dramatic changes in both the nature and scope of communication take place.

When the firm is quite small, most managers communicate directly with one another. Informal channels are widely used in both sending and receiving information. As the enterprise increases in size, however, more formal channels begin to evolve. The chief executive officer can no longer allow managers to drop by at their leisure. Too many things have to be done, and the executive's daily calendar is filled with meetings, conferences, and top-level decisions. Rules, policies, and procedures are now developed in an effort to keep everyone working in the same direction. Written communication in the form of memos and reports begins to replace the informal face-to-face discussions. Major decisions that used to be handled by one person are now checked and rechecked by three or four managers. Committees are now more common. In this growing organizational network, a proliferation of levels often develops as managers strive to build empires by increasing the number of their subordinates. More and more of the manager's day is spent cutting through the resulting red tape.

This does not always happen, of course, but as the size of the enterprise increases, bureaucratic rules begin to replace informal channels and organizations have to step back, review their organizational design, and work to restructure it so as to facilitate the flow of effective communication.

The Need for Autonomy

Not all managerial communication needs are related directly to the organization and its objectives. Many are a result of the individual manager's personal needs for such factors as growth, a feeling of accomplishment, and the need to socialize with others in the workplace. Most managers like their jobs because it gives them a feeling they are doing something important. This psychological satisfaction is highly motivational.[9] As the manager makes decisions and sees the results of his or her actions, the individual achieves a feeling of confidence and self-fulfillment. This is usually more easily achieved in small organizations than in large ones. However, large organizations do not continually lose managerial personnel because managers feel their psychological needs are not being satisfied. Recent research reveals that many enterprises are well aware of the manager's need for autonomy and growth, and they work to provide it. As a result, today managerial employment stability is at a high and increasing level. Tuckel and Siegel have found that from the turn of the century to the present time, the percentage of chief executive officers (CEOs) of major corporations who have worked for only one employer has continued to rise.[10] In 1900 it stood at approximately 8 percent; by the end

Organization size affects communication needs.

Autonomy is psychologically rewarding for many people.

of the 1970s it had risen to almost 36 percent. In addition, research reveals that the largest firms have had the greatest employment stability in terms of chief executive officers. Of the top 100 industrials in the United States, 53 percent of the CEOs have worked for only one company.

The Quality of Work Life

Closely related to the need for autonomy is the desire for an improved quality of work life. Everyone who works would like their job to be interesting, challenging, and psychologically rewarding. Many firms are attempting to fulfill this desire by improving the quality of life at work. This is being done in many ways. Autonomy, mentioned above, is one of the most important. Others include

- *Variety of skill.* The degree to which a job allows the individual to perform a wide range of operations and/or the degree to which the person uses a variety of different procedures in his or her daily work.

- *Task identity.* The extent to which the individual can do an entire piece of work and can clearly identify with the results of that effort.

Common qualities of work-life characteristics.

- *Task significance.* The degree to which the job has an impact on the lives or work of others.

- *Feedback.* The degree to which the job allows the individual to receive information regarding how well he or she is doing; if this feedback is built into the job in some way, it is a more effective motivator than if the individual must be told by others how well he or she is doing.

- *Dealing with others.* The degree to which a job allows the individual to deal with others in getting things done; this job characteristic is particularly important among individuals with a strong need for social interaction.

- *Opportunity for friendship.* The extent to which a job allows the individual to talk to others on the job and establish informal relationships with them.

Implications for Management

1. Remember that the communication needs of your managers are going to vary for both external and internal reasons. Externally, the more dynamic the environment the more these managers will need to be kept apprised of what is going on so that they can generate the proper counter-response from the organization. Internally, the managers need to be able to interact with other members of the organizational staff and meet their psychological needs for autonomy and high quality of work life.

2. The organizational culture is going to have a dramatic impact on how managers communicate. If you are operating in a process environment, do not expect everyone to share information openly with everyone else. This environment lends itself to lots of red tape and cautious action. On the other hand, if you are operating in a work hard/play hard environment, you must insist on high teamwork and interaction. Match the communication patterns to the organizational culture. Each reinforces the other.

3. Don't underestimate your staff's desire for psychological rewards on the job. Autonomy, feedback, variety of skill, task identity, and the opportunity for friendship are all important. If the organization's efficiency will not suffer, see how communication patterns can be changed so as to promote these elements. However, do not be surprised if some people do not want psychological rewards and tell you they work for the money only; there are many of these people in modern organizations. Do not assume that just because their philosophy is different from yours that they are not hard workers. Let people be themselves while you focus on trying to help improve their quality of work life.

Communication plays a key role in redesigning jobs so as to build in the appropriate characteristics, and we know that enriched, meaningful jobs are important to the success of modern organizations. The Japanese have proved that they can produce high-quality goods at competitive prices. Since many American firms have the same degree of technology and the same basic machines, why are we often unable to compete effectively? Part of the answer rests with the morale and desire of the workers to do the best possible job. Redesigning jobs to improve the quality of work life promises to bring together the workers and the work. Many firms are now beginning to realize that communication is a significant part of this strategy.[11]

C A S E   I N   P O I N T
Revisited

Now that you have had a chance to read this introductory chapter, you realize that the problem in this case was one of communication of meanings. What Paul meant by the phrase "as soon as possible" was not what Jane understood. Paul encoded one message but Jane decoded another. Yet the entire problem is not Paul's alone. Remember that a few days elapsed between the time he asked for the report to be typed and the time it was due. In the interim, Jane could have told him what she had done with the report. She also should have considered asking the typing pool people when the report would be ready and conveyed this information to Paul. In this instance, she failed to provide him feedback on the status of the project.

Taken as a composite, the case shows how communication problems can be caused by both the sender and the receiver. Each failed to follow up to see that they were on the same wavelength. The two areas where the communication process broke down were in coding and feedback.

YOU BE THE CONSULTANT

A Question of Promotion

When Jacqueline Frances learned that the regional manager of the eastern sales division had resigned to take a job with a competing firm, she made it a point to drop by and talk to her boss. As the number-one salesperson in her territory, Jackie was very well thought of by the firm; however, she had her sights set on being more than just a salesperson for the rest of her career. Here is how part of her conversation with her boss went.

Jackie: I heard that Pete resigned as head of the eastern sales division. Is that right?

Manager: Yup. It's effective the first of next month. Why do you ask?

Jackie: Well, I've been a salesperson here for five years and I certainly don't want to be one for the rest of my life. I think I'd like to be a regional manager. I watch what you guys do all day long, and it seems to me that it's not a bad life. You've got a guaranteed salary, a good retirement program, excellent fringes, and you don't have to be on the road more than a few days a month.

Manager: Heck, you wouldn't want a job like this. My salary is less than yours and I've got to be here from 9 to 5 every day. And a lot of my time is spent listening to salespeople's problems. Believe me, this job is a big headache. You're in a much better position as a salesperson.

Jackie: I don't know. I think I'd like it. I'm certainly going to apply for it and I want you to go to bat for me in helping me get it. I'm the number-one salesperson in this region and one of the best in the entire company. I'm entitled to consideration for that job.

Manager: Okay, I'll see what I can do. But I think you're making a big mistake.

A few weeks later there was a meeting to decide who should get the opening in the eastern sales region. Jackie's boss pointed out that she had expressed interest in the job. When pressed on the matter, however, he admitted that he did not think that she would really like the position. "She's a salesperson, not a manager," he said. "She will be disappointed within a couple of months and want her old job back. However, the fact that she is one of our best salespeople, and we do try to promote from within, is a major plus in her favor." The committee listened carefully and decided that one of the other candidates was better qualified for the job. This individual was given the offer and she took it.

Last week Jackie went to see her boss. She told him that she would be leaving effective the end of the week. She was going to become the head of the eastern sales division for the firm's major competitor. Her boss was stunned. "You're going to be sorry. It's nothing like you think." However, Jackie was having none of it. "That's pure nonsense and you know it. You guys are just trying to hold me back. You want to slot people into pigeon holes and not let them move ahead. There's a lot better quality of work life at the top of the organization than at the bottom, but you were afraid that if I got that job you would have stiff competition for your next promotion. Well, friend, it's all yours, if you can keep this company afloat. Because I'm going to be with the competition, spending most of my time drawing away old clients. You guys didn't know a good thing when you had it. Next time you'll understand the importance of hanging on to your valuable resources."

Act as a consultant to Jackie's boss. What did he do wrong? What should he have done? What communication lessons can be learned from this experience? In your answer also be sure to explain what is meant by quality of work life and what Jackie was looking for in her work. Be as complete as possible in your answer so as to ensure that this problem does not recur.

Key Points in This Chapter

1. Communication is a term that has been defined in many different ways. In this book, we define it as the transfer of messages between sender and receiver.

2. The communication process entails the steps involved as a message moves from the creation of the idea to be conveyed by the sender to the reception and interpretation of that idea by the receiver. The three most critical steps in the communication process are coding, transmission, and feedback. Noise, which is anything that interferes with the content of the message, is also of vital importance.

3. Organizational communication is the transfer of information and knowledge among organizational members for the purpose of increasing organizational efficiency and effectiveness. From the manager's perspective, some of the major factors that dictate specific communication needs include the nature of the industry, organizational culture, levels and goals, size of the enterprise, personal need for autonomy, and desire for increased quality of work life by the personnel.

4. Quality of work life can be enhanced by making the workplace more interesting and enjoyable. Numerous factors are involved in improving work life. Some of the most important include variety of skill, task identity, task significance, feedback, dealing with others, and the opportunity for friendship on the job.

Questions for Discussion and Analysis

1. In your own words, what is meant by the term *communication?*

2. The communication process has three critical steps: coding, transmission, and feedback. What does this statement mean? Be sure to include in your answer a discussion of each of these three steps.

3. How does noise interfere with the communication process? Provide an example in your answer.

4. What does a manager need to know about using the communication process effectively? Identify and describe two guidelines that would be useful to the individual.

5. In your own words, what is meant by the term *organizational communication?*

6. In what way does the nature of the industry affect managers' communication needs? Explain.

7. What is meant by communication acquisition and communication transferal? Explain.

8. What is meant by the term *organizational culture?* How does this culture affect managerial communication needs? Explain.

9. How do organizational levels affect managerial communication needs? How do organizational goals affect managerial communication needs?

10. Does organizational size have any effect on managerial communication needs? Explain.

11. In what way does quality of work life play a role in organizational communication? Be complete in your answer.

Exercises

1. Ask five different people for a definition of organizational communication. Choose a cross section of business people as well as a student not enrolled in this class. Are people very sure of their definitions? What commonalities do you find in their definitions? Finally, formulate your own comprehensive definition of organizational communications.

2. Chapter 1 has proposed that organizational culture influences communication patterns. Choose one organization that you know well and describe both its corporate culture and its apparent communication patterns. How are they interrelated?

3. Assume that you have been assigned to a corporate committee to improve the quality of work life at your organization. Specifically, you are to prepare a report on how effective communication can lead to improved quality of work life.

References

1. S. S. Stevens, "A Definition of Communication," *Journal of the Acoustical Society*, 1950, p. 689.

2. Bernard Berelson and Gary A. Steiner, *Human Behavior* (New York: Harcourt, Brace & World, 1964), p. 254.

3. Pauline E. Henderson, "Communication Without Words," *Personnel Journal*, January 1989, pp. 22–29.

4. Markus B. Zimmer, "A Practical Guide to Videoconferencing," *Training and Development Journal*, May 1988, pp. 84–89.

5. C. Glenn Pearce, "Doing Something About Your Listening Ability," *Supervisory Management*, March 1989, pp. 29–34.

6. Gordon E. Mills and R. Wayne Pace, "What Effects Do Practice and Video Feedback Have on the Development of Interpersonal Communication Skills," *Journal of Business Communication*, Spring 1989, pp. 159–176.

7. Jane W. Gibson and Richard M. Hodgetts, *Business Communication: Skills and Strategies* (New York: Harper & Row, 1990), p. 8.

8. Terence E. Deal and Allan A. Kennedy, *Corporate Cultures: The Rites and Rituals of Corporate Life* (Reading, Mass.: Addison-Wesley, 1982).

9. John J. Trombetta and Donald P. Rogers, "Communication Climate, Job Satisfaction, and Organizational Commitment," *Management Communication Quarterly*, May 1988, pp. 494–514.

10. Peter Tuckel and Karolynn Siegel, "The Myth of the Migrant Worker," *Business Horizons*, January-February 1983, pp. 64–70.

11. Roger L. Kirkham, "Communicating to Influence Others More Effectively," *Personnel*, December 1987, pp. 52–55.

Annotated Bibliography

Deal, Terence E., and Allan A. Kennedy, *Corporate Cultures: The Rites and Rituals of Corporate Life* (Reading, Mass.: Addison-Wesley, 1982).

> This very interesting book discusses the elements of corporate culture including heroes, rites and rituals, and core values. The four general organizational culture types described in this chapter are fully developed: tough-guy/macho; work hard/play hard; bet your company; and process.

Peters, Tom, *Thriving on Chaos* (New York: Alfred A. Knopf, 1987).

> This is a practical, hands-on book for dealing with the changes that business will be facing during the 1990s. Strong emphasis is given to the importance of communicating with customers, listening to their needs and wants, and taking effective action. Many managers consider this a "must read" book for dealing with the challenges of the coming decade.

Sathe, Vijay, *Culture and Related Corporate Realities* (Homewood, Ill.: Richard D. Irwin, 1985).

> This well-organized, comprehensive book has a dual focus: teaching managers how to analyze and fit into a corporate culture as well as how to change that culture when necessary. Cases and readings complement the text.

CHAPTER 2

Management Theory and Communication

"With the coming of large organizations, talk was no longer trivial. It became essential for such organizations to cultivate the art of communication."

Roger D'Aprix, *Communicating for Productivity* (New York: Harper and Row, 1982), p. 37.

Objectives

1. To describe the basic management philosophy of the classical managers.

2. To explain the status of communication in the classical management era.

3. To understand the basic management philosophy of the human relations managers.

4. To note the contributions made to the field of communication as a result of the Hawthorne Studies.

5. To explain the status of communication in the human relations era.

6. To compare and contrast the philosophy of human relations with that of human resources.

7. To set forth the specific contributions to organizational communication theory by individuals such as Frederick Taylor, Henri Fayol, Mary Parker Follett, George Elton Mayo, Fritz Jules Roethlisberger, Chester Barnard, Herbert Simon, Douglas McGregor, and Rensis Likert.

8. To explain the role and importance of the systems approach and the contingency approach to modern organizational communication theory.

9. To be able to apply the ideas and concepts presented here to real-life cases that are provided at the end of the chapter.

C A S E I N P O I N T

Cliff's Approach

When Cliff Dandridge learned of the job opening at Garrett Laboratories, he was sure they would not be interested in him. Cliff knew nothing about research and development (R&D), yet the newspaper ad said that the firm was looking for an office manager with administrative experience. Cliff had been the sales manager for an insurance firm and then moved up to head the entire office. He therefore had administrative experience and had worked with white collar employees. Hoping that this might be enough to get him an initial interview, Cliff applied for the job. After two interviews and a short meeting with the R&D staff, Cliff was hired.

The job proved to be just what was promised. Most of Cliff's time has been taken up with paperwork or office matters. For example, Cliff is responsible for seeing that all the scientists who are presenting a paper or traveling to another city have their airline tickets delivered to them, and reservations for both hotel and transportation are taken care of before they leave. Cliff also looks over their receipts when they return and makes sure that everything is in order before filing their expense forms.

Another key aspect of Cliff's job is the budget. He is responsible for seeing that all the personnel have all the equipment and support help they need. A good portion of his time is spent talking to suppliers and equipment manufacturers and checking with the scientists to see exactly what equipment they feel will best meet their needs. Typically, Cliff, the equipment manufacturing representative, and a group of scientists will sit down and discuss laboratory needs and product offerings. Then Cliff and his people will put their heads together and decide what to buy. Cliff is the one who makes the final purchase decision, so the scientists are shielded from the hard sell of the sales representatives. In fact, when Cliff took the job, his boss told him, "Keep these guys happy. Take the heat for them. Clean up after them. They'll do all the rest. Remember, you're the coach here, but you've got a group of super athletes. Stay out of their way

and they'll win for you every time. This is the best R&D lab in the company."

Another key responsibility is salary raises. Although Cliff initially did not know anything about the scientists' work assignments, except that they were concerned with developing new processes and patents for the corporation, he is responsible for recommending raises. Cliff usually does this by relying heavily on the most senior-level scientist in the room, who advises him as to how well each person is doing. Cliff can also review personnel folders and see how many new processes or patents each scientist has been responsible for during the past year.

For the first six months, everything appeared to be going smoothly. Cliff indicated on his personnel evaluation forms that every single member of the lab was doing an excellent job. At the same time, the members indicated on their respective "rate the boss" forms, that they thought Cliff was doing an excellent job. During the last six months, however, things seem to have taken a turn for the worse. Perhaps it all began when Cliff attended a managerial workshop discussing the value and benefits of management by objectives (MBO). During the workshop, the speaker discussed the value of setting specific, measurable objectives for each of the personnel and then following up closely to make sure that everyone does what he or she is supposed to do.

Cliff liked this idea and decided to try it out at the lab. He began during his six-month review with each of the scientists. In each case, Cliff noted the particular patent or process on which the individual was working. He then put together a timetable for the person. For example, in one case the scientist told him that it would take about six months to design and develop a prototype of the product he was working on. Cliff assigned the man six months to finish the prototype. At the same time, Cliff began restructuring some of the work, putting people into teams to handle some of the more difficult processes and breaking them into individual units when he felt that a group approach would be too time consuming. However, Cliff did not let this work-oriented approach dull his behavioral sensitivities. Twice a day, he would walk through the department talking to the personnel, urging them to keep up the good work. Also, when salary recommendations were made three weeks ago, Cliff brushed off the suggestions of the senior scientist and recommended that everyone receive much more money. The average recommendation throughout the firm was 8 percent, while in Cliff's department it was 13 percent.

Nevertheless, something seemed to be wrong. During his annual review of each scientist's performance, Cliff learned that 6 of the 20 employees will be leaving within three months. Although most of them were reluctant to explain why, one of them told him, "I want a more creative environment. Perhaps business-related R&D isn't my thing. I don't know. I just know that I want more personal freedom. I don't think I'm going to get that here." This surprised Cliff since the man had been with the lab for more than ten years. Cliff tried to get to the bottom of the problem by talking to the senior scientist, but she offered him little information. Not realizing what the problem was, Cliff believed that his next step should simply be to get on with day-to-day business and start looking for replacements for the six scientists who would be leaving.

What did Cliff do wrong? In your answer, sketch out Cliff's basic beliefs regarding how to manage and lead people. Then examine those that are not correct and note what changes are necessary. Be as realistic as possible in your evaluation. Then put your analysis to the side. We will return to it later.

INTRODUCTION

The way managers communicate is a direct reflection of their philosophy regarding worker behavior and motivation. If a manager believes that the subordinates are lazy, unintelligent, or deliberately uncooperative, the manager will adopt an appropriate leadership style: close control, little delegation of authority, quick use of sanctions to punish those who do things wrong. Conversely, if the manager believes that the subordinates are hard working, intelligent, and determined to perform their assignments right the first time, the manager typically will adopt a style that encourages such behavior: loose control, heavy delegation of authority, and a reward system designed to promote initiative, creativity, and high job performance.

Today we find some managers who fall into the first and many who fall into the second of these two categories. Over the last century, there has been a gradual transition from the first category to the second. The management philosophy of many currently successful administrators reveals a basic understanding and appreciation of employee ability and effort. Yet it was not always this way. In this chapter, we examine the evolution of management and its relevance to communication theory by looking at the three major eras of management thinking: classical, human relations, and human resources. As we move along this time continuum, you will see the relationship between management philosophy and communication theory and practice. Many of our current communication practices are a result of decades of evolution. The way managers communicated 80 years ago is markedly different from how they communicate today. Back then, managers were operating within what is known as the classical management era.

THE CLASSICAL MANAGEMENT ERA

The beginning of the twentieth century saw managers throughout the industrialized world struggling with the goal of maximizing productivity. These individuals fell into two main groups: scientific managers and administrative managers. The two created what today is called the classical management era.

Scientific Management

The scientific managers believed that all jobs should be studied in order to develop the most efficient procedures for carrying them out. These procedures should then be taught to the workers. The ranks of the scientific managers included such distinguished contributors as Frederick Taylor, Frank Gilbreth, and Henry Gantt. These managers viewed the workers as economically driven; money was the ultimate motivator. As a result, they conducted time and motion studies to identify the most efficient methods for doing work and offered incentive pay to the highest producers. The basic managerial philosophy of the scientific manager was that:

1. Work is inherently distasteful to most people.

Basic philosophy of scientific management

2. What workers do is less important than what they earn for doing it.

3. Few workers want, or can handle, work that requires creativity, self-direction, or self-control.[1]

The best known member of the scientific management group was Frederick Winslow Taylor. Born in 1856 in Pennsylvania, he received a mechanical engineering degree from Stevens Institute. Over the next 30 years, Taylor started with the Midvale Steel Corporation and worked his way up to chief engineer. Later he joined the Bethlehem Steel Corporation, conducted important time and motion studies, and began writing in the field of scientific management. In his most famous book, *Principles of Scientific Management*,[2] he established a principle of cooperation between management and the workers.

Although the idea of cooperation seems to imply that effective communication was an integral part of scientific management philosophy, actually Taylor and his associates saw communication as a formal means of giving orders and monitoring productivity. Channels of communication were strictly designed by the organizational hierarchy and rigidly adhered to, the emphasis being on one-way, downward communication.

Administrative Management

The administrative managers were less concerned with operations at the lower levels of the hierarchy than they were with those at the middle and upper levels of the structure. The most famous administrative manager was Henri Fayol. Born in France in 1841, he worked his way up to president of a giant mining combine in 1888. For the next 30 years, he skillfully managed the firm. As many of the administrative managers who followed him, Fayol was interested in management principles and functions. In 1916, in his book *General and Industrial Administration*,[3] he set forth 14 administrative princi-

COMMUNICATION TECHNOLOGY

Fred Taylor Would Have Loved It

If there is one word that characterized the classical management era it was "efficiency." The scientific managers were interested in finding ways of doing things faster and cheaper. Today communication technology accounts for a great deal of organizational efficiency. We can cite many examples.

One that is becoming increasingly popular is the cellular phone that allows people to make calls from their car. Business executives can save their companies thousands of dollars every year by conducting business on their way to the office or during working hours. Salespeople find that the car phone allows them to call ahead to confirm sales meetings with clients or to let customers know that they are stuck in traffic and will be late. The phone also gives them flexibility so that if a meeting is canceled they can try to arrange a replacement sales call.

A second example is electronic mail that lets people send messages via a microcomputer. These messages are left in the person's electronic mailbox, and the individual can retrieve them whenever he or she wants. This communication technology eliminates the time that is wasted trying to reach someone by phone. Moreover, the receiver can read the message, remove it from the mailbox or leave it there for future reference, and send back a reply within a matter of minutes. If the individuals have to communicate interactively with each other, they can do so by sending written messages back and forth on the computer monitor. Each individual can read the other's message and then respond. Although they cannot see each other, they can communicate via the written word.

A third technological development is the facsimile machine that allows written messages, documents, and photos to be sent telephonically. Some of the latest "fax" machines are so efficient that the materials being received are almost as letter-perfect as those that are transmitted. In addition, in some cases faxed legal documents are allowed as temporary substitutes for the original. Thus, if a contract requires a company to provide a client with an original document and the material has been inadvertently left at the home office 1,000 miles away, the document can be faxed and the deal can be closed. The original can then be sent by overnight delivery and put into the file the next day.

Communication technology is making it easier to convey information between people. It is also saving companies a great deal of time and money. Frederick Taylor and the scientific managers would have been very pleased to learn about these developments.

Figure 2.1

Following the hierarchy.

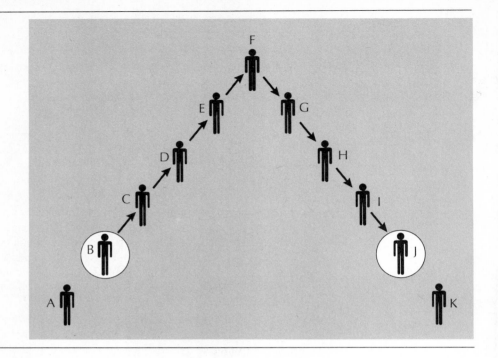

Figure 2.2

Fayol's "Gangplank."

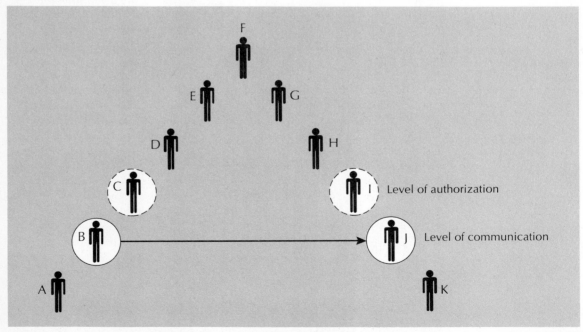

ples. Principle number nine, having to do with the organizational hierarchy, holds the most interest for communication students. Fayol recognized the organizational hierarchy as establishing the rightful progression of communication but saw in it an inherent impasse when people at the same level needed to communicate. According to the theory of the time (see Figure 2.1), person B needing to talk to person J would have to proceed up the hierarchical ranks to the top and then back down. The implications are clear. Not only was the process time consuming, but the multiple levels helped assure that distortion would occur in the communication itself.

Fayol's gangplank theory   As a result, Fayol developed his now famous gangplank theory, which partially bypassed these problems. According to this theory, person B would be allowed to speak directly to person J providing each had permission from their immediate supervisor to do so and with the condition that they apprise these supervisors of the results (see Figure 2.2). At last, there was some formal recognition of the need for horizontal communications!

Overall, with the exception of Fayol's bridge, classical management did little to develop the importance of communication in organization. The prevailing notion of communication was limited to one-way, vertical, formal channels. Take Self-Assessment Quiz 2-1 to see if your management style matches classical thinking.

SELF-ASSESSMENT QUIZ 2.1

Are You a Classical Management Person?

Answer each of the following true/false statements by underlining your response. Compare your answers to those given at the back of the book. For each one you have correct, score one point.

1. Face it, money is the primary reason why people work. True/False

2. Most employees work best under loose (as opposed to close) control. True/False

3. The primary function of communication is to give orders and monitor results. True/False

4. An open door is widely used by effective managers. True/False

5. The primary function of the union is to undermine management's efforts. True/False

6. The most important communication channel is downward from superior to subordinate. True/False

7. Increased work autonomy or self-control will result in a highly motivated worker increasing his or her output. True/False

8. Under the right conditions, most workers could do a much better job than they are doing now. True/False

9. Face it, if given the opportunity, most workers would goof off. True/False

10. Most workers are willing to assume responsibility for their own work. True/False

Status of Communication in the Classical Management Era

1. Communication was formal and written, and channels were structured by the organization chart. The one exception was Fayol's gangplank theory, which allowed for limited horizontal communication.

2. Communication direction was basically downward from managers to employees.

3. The purpose of communication was to provide specific instructions to employees as to exactly what to do and how to do it. As Taylor put it: "The work of every workman is fully planned out by the management at least one day in advance, and each man receives in most cases complete written instructions, describing in detail the task which he is to accomplish, as well as the means to be used in doing the work."[4]

4. Upward communication consisted basically of progress reports and answers to specific requests from management.

5. Feedback channels were formal and related to tasks.

6. The communication system assumed a need for secrecy. This was to prevent employees from manipulating or subverting objectives and measurements. All planning and control information was carefully guarded, and members had access only to that information required for their immediate duties. Meanwhile, feedback on performance was provided only as necessary for corrective action.[5]

The Bridge to the Human Relations Era

Not everyone interested in maximizing productivity at the turn of the century subscribed to classical management beliefs. Some individuals were much more oriented to human relations. Perhaps the most famous of this group was Mary Parker Follett.

Born in 1868, Follett graduated from Radcliffe in 1898 with a major in political science. Although she lived during the era of the classical managers, her writings illustrate a much deeper understanding of human relations in organizations than most possessed.[6] Her two main contributions to the field of communication were the concepts of one universal fact and one universal goal.

The one universal fact — circular response

The *universal fact* was called circular or reciprocal response. Follett believed that the traditional stimulus – response reaction was an oversimplification that simply did not exist in interpersonal relations. Instead, she said, people have a mutual, interacting influence on each other, thus recognizing the feedback loop critical to communication theory today.[7]

The one universal goal — integration

Her *universal goal* was the goal of integration, which Follett sometimes called coordination and which seemed to foresee the systems approach to management so popular today. This consisted of managing people in an organization to meet common purposes. Follett admitted, however, that integration was not always possible. "Prejudice, ignorance, unwillingness to change, reluctance to entertain expressions of differences, geographical or social barriers to communication — all these can block the process."[8]

Follett's leader was a coordinator.

Yet the contribution for which Follett is best known is that of coordination. In her view, a manager's primary job was that of coordinator. This was a far cry from the autocratic philosophy of scientific management.

Although Follett did not explicitly spell out the importance of effective communication, it is the shadow behind both her principle of reciprocal response and her goal of integration. The emphasis on coordination likewise could only be operationalized through adequate, systemwide communication. Follett's importance, then, remains in her prophetic visions of future management beliefs — human relations, participative management, contingency management, and the belief in a systems approach.

Effective communication was implicit in her work.

THE HUMAN RELATIONS MANAGEMENT ERA

During the 1920s and 1930s, the guiding principles of classical management were increasingly called into question. Developments such as the rise of the American labor movement helped challenge classical philosophy and bring about a new era known as human relations. Management now began to realize the importance of treating workers more as people and less as appendages of machines. The basic assumptions of this new era were as follows:

1. People want to feel useful and important.

2. People desire to belong and to be recognized as individuals.

3. These needs are more important than money in motivating people to work.[9]

Assumptions of human relations management

Mary Parker Follett anticipated this changing philosophy. However, it was left to the famous Hawthorne Studies officially to open the era of human relations.

Hawthorne Studies

The Hawthorne Studies took place at the Western Electric plant in Cicero, Illinois. They lasted from 1924 to 1932 and consisted of four phases: (1) the illumination experiments, (2) the relay assembly tests, (3) a massive interviewing program, and (4) the bank wiring observations. Originally, the Hawthorne Studies were designed to show the effect of increased environmental lighting on worker productivity. Instead, they pointed out the importance of social and group influences on productivity. A new emphasis emerged — that of "social man." It was now becoming obvious that social networks and personal interaction were important determinants of individual and group behavior. This was in contrast to the "economic man" model of the classicists in which money was viewed as the primary motivator. The guiding lights during the Hawthorne Studies turned out to be two Harvard professors, George Elton Mayo and Fritz Roethlisberger.

The Hawthorne Studies started out as a productivity study.

George Elton Mayo was born in Australia in 1880 and moved to the United States where he joined the faculty at the Wharton School. He moved to Harvard in 1926 as an Associate Professor of Industrial Research. The Hawthorne Studies made him famous, to the point that he is often called the father of human relations.

Mayo came to be called the father of human relations.

Roethlisberger
joined Mayo at
Hawthorne.
Fritz Jules Roethlisberger was a native American. Born in 1898, he studied at Columbia University and the Massachusetts Institute of Technology before earning his master's degree at Harvard University. He was in the Industrial Research Department at Harvard when Mayo arrived in 1926.[10]

Mayo and Roethlisberger were not involved in the initial illumination experiments in which worker output continued to rise despite changes in the illumination variable. Looking back at this period of time, however, Mayo postulated that the explanation was to be found in a remarkable change of mental attitude in the group.[11] He believed that the social situation of the group had been manipulated in such a way that the social needs of the people had been addressed.

Another major part of the study occurred after Mayo and Roethlisberger became active in the project. A massive interviewing program was begun for the purpose of engendering an open, concerned supervisory relationship with the employees. Mayo explained the guidelines that each interviewer was to follow in this way:

1. Give your whole attention to the person interviewed and make it evident you are doing so.

2. Listen — don't talk.

3. Never argue; never give advice.

Interviewing
guidelines
4. Listen to:
    a. What he wants to say.
    b. What he does not want to say.
    c   What he cannot say without help.

5. As you listen, plot out tentatively and for subsequent correction the pattern (personal) that is being set before you. To test this, from time to time summarize what has been said and present for comment (e.g., "Is this what you are telling me?") Always do this with the greatest caution, that is, clarify but do not add or twist.

6. Remember that everything said must be considered a personal confidence and not divulged to anyone.[12]

Here, in Mayo's own words, we have one of the early pioneers of effective listening techniques telling supervisors to be empathetic, nonevaluative, active participants in the listening experience.

Informal networks
were studied.
In the last stage of the Hawthorne Studies, the bank wiring experiments, the Harvard researchers went even further and anticipated the coming emphasis on network analysis of informal cliques. Within the formal structure of the bank wiring room, two cliques or informal groups were discovered. These cliques cut across the formal structure. Members of the same informal group were found to engage in intragroup activities such as games, trading jobs, and helping one another even though company policy forbade these activities. The groups also adhered to certain norms such as not telling a supervisor anything that would prove detrimental to a fellow worker.

In summary, the Hawthorne Studies taught managers the need for a new mix of managerial skills that emphasize the importance of understanding human behavior and exhibiting good interpersonal skills in listening, motivating, counseling, and leading.

Chester Barnard

Barnard was a
practicing manager.

Whereas Mayo, Roethlisberger, and the Hawthorne Studies are widely recognized as the names synonymous with human relations, another contemporary, Chester Barnard, is equally deserving of credit. His classic text, *Functions of the Executive*, was written after he had retired as president of the New Jersey Bell Telephone Company.

Barnard recognized
the importance of
communication.

Barnard's book marked the beginning of a growing emphasis on the importance of communication in organizations. He identified the primary functions of all executives, with communication being the most important one.

He discussed the importance of formal communication systems and set forth a series of communication principles.

1. Channels of communication should be definitely known.

2. Objective authority requires a definite formal channel of communication to every member of an organization.

Barnard's
communication
principles

3. The line of communication must be as direct or short as possible.

4. The complete line of communication should usually be used.

5. The competence of the persons serving as communication centers, that is, officers, supervisory heads, and the like, must be adequate.

6. The line of communication should not be interrupted during the time when the organization is to function.

7. Every communication should be authenticated.[13]

Most of these principles tied directly into Barnard's now-famous "acceptance theory of authority," which said that the amount of authority a person has depends entirely on how willing the workers are to accept his or her orders. Noting that established authority is essential for the leader, Barnard explained that every manager must understand the four conditions necessary for an employee to accept another's authority.

**Status of
Communication
in the
Human
Relations Era**

1. Communication was still basically formal, but informal systems of communication were recognized as inevitable and important to the creation of employee satisfaction.

2. Communication for direction and control was still basically downward from managers to employees, although upward mechanisms such as suggestion boxes and complaint systems were operationalized. These were mainly cosmetic but were in keeping with the slogan of the day, "A happy worker is a productive worker."

3. The purpose of communication was expanded from that of providing specific work instructions to also making the employee feel needed and satisfied. The interview process at the Hawthorne plant was a good example of this desire to promote open

communication for establishing an environment more conducive to satisfied workers.

4. Upward communication now included cosmetic additions such as the suggestion box and indirect routes such as supervisors listening to workers. Out of the latter came a great deal of unexpected input as to the real concerns of employees.

5. Horizontal communication gained ground with the establishment of cross-department committees and liaisons.

6. Communication was now seen as relatively more important than during the classical era. Organizational communication started to be perceived as not just a means for management to talk to the workers, but for management to listen to what the workers were saying.

Conditions for acceptance of authority

1. The employee must understand the communication.

2. The employee must believe the request, order, and the like, is not inconsistent with the goals of the organization.

3. The employee must believe the communication is not inconsistent with his or her own personal beliefs and goals.

4. The employee must be mentally and physically able to comply.[14]

Barnard also opened up the study of the informal organization system and its concomitant influence on organizational communication. He identified functions of this organization as maintaining (1) communication, (2) cohesiveness, and (3) individual feelings of integrity, self-respect, and independent choice.[15]

In the evolution of communication thought, then, Barnard was one of the first to identify the importance of communication as the critical factor for management. He also explained its role in both formal and informal organizations.

How about you? Are you a human relations manager? Take Self-Assessment Quiz 2.2 before continuing.

SELF-ASSESSMENT QUIZ 2.2

Are You a Human Relations Management Person?

Answer each of the following true/false statements by underlining your response. Compare your answers to those given at the back of the book. For each one you have correct, score one point.

1. People want to belong and to be recognized as individuals more than they want to earn money. True/False

2. A happy worker is a productive worker. True/False

3. Open-door policies seldom make much sense. True/False

4. Personal achievement is more important to an employee than is social interaction. True/False

5. People want to feel that they are useful, important members of a team. True/False

6. Social networks and personal interaction are important determinants of individual and group behavior. True/False

7. The need to succeed is more important than the need to belong. True/False

8. Most workers simply want to be treated well. True/False

9. The informal organization, if at all possible, should be eliminated. True/False

10. Suggestion boxes are a waste of time and should be done away with. True/False

The Bridge to the Human Resources Era

During the 1920s and 1930s, not everyone subscribed totally to the human relations philosophy. Some people were ahead of their time, being much more interested in a human resources approach to managing people. One of these individuals was Joseph Scanlon.

As with many significant theorists, Scanlon is not easily categorized. A steelworker, union official, and later professor at the Massachusetts Institute of Technology, Scanlon saved the near-bankrupt La Pointe Steel Company by forging a participative management/union productivity plan. In a nutshell, this plan established a system that encouraged workers to file suggestions for productivity improvement. If the suggestions were accepted (and many were), all employees shared in the profits from those that were implemented.

Scanlon believed in creative employee participation.

Scanlon foresaw the importance of *meaningful*, *creative*, worker participation. The suggestion box was used not as a human relations instrument to assuage the workers, but as a valuable source of creative input, which was the cornerstone of the human resources movement.

THE HUMAN RESOURCES MANAGEMENT ERA

Beginning around the end of World War II and continuing through the 1950s, management thinking started to move beyond a human relations philosophy. Both theorists and practitioners began to realize that people work for more than just money (classical thinking) or the opportunity to belong and feel wanted (human relations thinking). People are also interested in meaningful and challenging jobs, and quality of work life is a major motivational force. Upper-level need satisfactions cannot be ignored. This line of thinking eventually resulted in the emergence of the basic assumptions that were to form the foundation of the human resources movement.

1. Work is not inherently distasteful. In fact, if people are given a say in setting job-related goals and determining how the work is to be done, they will be motivated to do the best possible job.

Foundations of the
human resource
movement

2. Most people are far more creative than they are given credit for being. This creativity can be unleashed if the right work environment is created.

3. If people are properly motivated, they will assume responsibility and exercise self-direction and self-control in carrying out their jobs.[16]

Human resources thinking is quite different. It rejects the simplicity of past philosophies, recognizes the innate ability of the employees, and urges management to take these people and use them well! Not only must management change the basic philosophy toward the workers, but also it must alter its old style. The benevolence of human relations must give way to the participatory, free-rein approach of human resources management.

At the heart of the human resources approach is that of participative management, which is the process of involving subordinates in the decision-making process. This process stresses active involvement of the personnel and draws on their expertise and creativity in solving important managerial problems. Participative management rests on the concept of *shared authority* and decision making between managers and subordinates.

The benefits of this participation are numerous. Some of the most commonly cited are increased productivity, improved morale, decreased absenteeism, and reduced waste.

Communication is
central to
participative
management.

Central to the entire concept of participative management is that of communication. Under a human resources approach, open communication becomes a reality. Such techniques as an open-door policy, brainstorming, the use of management by objectives, and the effective use of group decision making are characteristic of this approach.

Many theorists can properly be put into the developmental history of the human resources era. We will focus our attention on the distinctive contributions of three of the most important: Herbert Simon, Douglas McGregor, and Rensis Likert.

Herbert Simon

Herbert Simon, currently of Carnegie Mellon University, has published a number of important books in the field of administration. His two most famous are *Administrative Behavior*[17] and *Organizations*.[18] Simon's contributions have spanned the fields of economics, management, organizational behavior, sociology, political science, and psychology. The impact of his writings and theories have proved so significant that he was awarded the Nobel Prize in economics in 1978.

Simon won the
Nobel Prize.

One of Simon's major contributions was his expansion of Barnard's ideas by examining and writing about communication as an integral part of the decision-making process. In addition, he addressed informal communication networks, noting that formal channels are always augmented by "an equally important informal network of communications based on social relations within the organization." [19] These informal channels are important in conveying gossip, information, and advice and often reflect

Simon addressed
informal networks.

more adequately than the formal channels the true relationships of people within the organization.

> . . . the grapevine is valuable as a barometer of "public opinion" in the organization. If the administrator listens to it, it apprises him of the topics that are subjects of interest to the organization members and their attitudes toward these topics.[20]

Simon also wrote of "natural leaders" in the informal system, and noted how important it was for managers to understand the informal system and strive to promote cordial relationships within that system.

Simon analyzed formal communication.

Nor did Simon overlook the value and benefit of formal communication. He noted that formal channels of communication carry the extra weight of official authority. On the other hand, he realized that only certain types of information are likely to be channeled upward by employees, and they will do so only under certain conditions. Three of the conditions for such communication are (1) the transmission will not have unpleasant consequences for the person sending the message; (2) the boss is going to hear about it anyway, so it is better to get the news to him or her as quickly as possible; and (3) the boss needs this information in dealing effectively with his or her own superiors and will be displeased if it is not transmitted up the line.[21]

Simon helped shape a human resources philosophy.

Overall, Simon's main contribution to the field of communication is his expansion of Bernard's ideas and the emphasis he gave to the relationship of decision making and the communication process. His writings on cliques and communication networks also helped expand understanding of how organizational communication worked. Simon's ideas reveal a basic understanding and appreciation for the human resources philosophy of management. Although his major writings appeared during the 1940s and 1950s, he helped shape the thinking of human resources managers of the 1970s and 1980s, many of whom acknowledged his influence on their thinking.

Douglas McGregor

The essence of participative management is perhaps best captured by Douglas McGregor in his famous Theory X, Theory Y dichotomy. Holder of a Ph.D. from Harvard, McGregor taught at Harvard, MIT, and Antioch College; he also served as president at Antioch. His book, *The Human Side of Enterprise*,[22] introduced his theory of managerial assumptions about workers. Theory X presents the conventional model of managerial assumptions, which underlies both the classical and the human relations approaches. (See Table 2.1 for a comparison of these two theories.) In implementation of management style, the classicists took what McGregor called a "hard approach . . . involving coercion and threat, close supervision, tight controls over behavior."[23] The human relationists employed a "soft" Theory X approach. They believed managers should be more permissive, try to help satisfy employee needs, and work to achieve harmony. If this were done, they believed the employees would accept direction. The human relationists extended the classical philosophy to make it more humanistic. However, they still basically believed in a Theory X approach to management.

McGregor formulated Theory X and Theory Y.

Human resources management subscribes to the participative theory espoused by

Table 2.1

THEORY X AND THEORY Y ASSUMPTIONS ABOUT WORKERS: A CONTRAST

Theory X	Theory Y
1. The average worker is lazy.	1. The average worker is not lazy.
2. The average worker shirks responsibility and wants to be led.	2. The average worker is not by *nature* passive or resistant to organizational needs.
3. The average worker is self-centered and uninterested in organizational needs.	3. The capacity to accept responsibility and work toward organizational goals is present in *all* workers
4. The average worker is resistant to change.	4. Managers must seek to develop the total potential of the employees.
5. The average worker is not very bright and, quite often, is guillible.	5. In the typical work environment, the creativity, imagination, and ingenuity of the average worker go basically untapped.
6. Managers must persuade, reward, punish, and control employee behavior in order to ensure goal attainment.	6. Management must arrange work conditions so that the employees can achieve their personal goals while also attaining organizational objectives.

SOURCE: Adapted from Douglas McGregor, *The Human Side of Enterprise* (New York: McGraw-Hill, 1960), Chs. 3 and 4.

Theory X. Many people believe this theory is too soft or wishy-washy. McGregor disagreed totally with this view. He felt Theory Y was

> . . . a process primarily of creating opportunities, releasing potential, removing obstacles, encouraging growth, providing guidance. It is what Peter Drucker has called "Management by Objectives" in contrast to "management by control." It does *not* involve the abdication of management, the absence of leadership, the lowering of standards of the other characteristics usually associated with the "soft" approach under Theory X.[24]

In McGregor's view, the assumptions managers make about their workers dictate how they will seek to communicate and lead the employees. Under Theory X, communication flows are basically vertical with most of them involving orders coming down from the top. The manager's job is one of controlling the workers so as to ensure that they do not goof off. Under Theory Y, management does not try to control the workers. Rather, it seeks to establish an environment in which the employees can participate and contribute to both personal and organizational goals. Management, realizing that a large percentage of employee creativity, ingenuity, and imagination often go untapped in a work setting, employs a philosophy designed to help the workers use all their abilities. The result is an open environment in which communication is used for personal and organizational goal attainment.

Theory Y fosters a creative environment.

Rensis Likert

Likert is well known for his work on participative management, leadership, and the management of organizational conflict. For many years, he was head of the prestigious Institute for Social Research (ISR) at the University of Michigan. He also wrote three books: *New Patterns of Management* (1961),[25] *The Human Organization* (1967),[26] and *New Ways of Managing Conflict* (1976),[27] all of which offer empirical data supporting the practical value of a human resources philosophy.

Likert's early writing recognized the fragile nature of organizational communication systems. In addition, it addressed the need to promote a communication climate of openness and trust.

> Distrust and lack of confidence lead members of an organization at all levels in the hierarchy to "play it close to the chest," to share a minimum of information with others, and to look with suspicion at the information passed on by others. Distrust leads to communication failures. Reciprocal confidence and trust on the part of the members of the organization seems necessary if the communication process is to function effectively.[28]

Communication and performance are related.

Likert also reported that empirical research by the ISR found that good communication and high performance were highly correlated. With this in mind, and his observation that current management practices were woefully deficient, he developed four basic management systems for describing leadership behavior. They were

- System 1 — Exploitive authoritative

- System 2 — Benevolent authoritative

- System 3 — Consultative democratic

- System 4 — Participative democratic

These systems presented management on a continuum ranging from highly autocratic (exploitive) to highly democratic (participative).

Likert reported that in an optimal System 4 organization:

> High levels of reciprocal influence occur, and high levels of totally coordinated influence are achieved. Additionally, communication is both efficient and effective. There is a flow from one part of the organization to another of all information necessary for decision making and action. The leadership in the organization develops a highly effective social system for interaction and mutual influence.[29]

When applied to communication, System 4 offers a marked contrast to that of the other systems. Table 2.2, showing the portion of the Likert research profile that addresses communication, clearly illustrates this contrast. Notice that as one moves across each continuum from System 1 to System 4, management's trust and confidence in the employees increase.

Likert's research showed the benefits of a System 4 approach.

Likert's contribution to human resource management was extremely important. His research, showing that a System 4 approach offered better long-run results than any other system, did much to support and encourage participative management. Using the detailed profile he developed (of which Table 2.2 is but a part), he was also able to show how organizations could measure which system they were operating under and take any corrective action necessary to move them toward a participative management approach.

Table 2.2

Operating Characteristic	System of Organization			
	Authoritative		Participative	
	Exploitive Authoritative	Benevolent Authoritative	Consultative	Participative Group
2. Character of communication process				
a. Amount of interaction and communication aimed at achieving organization's objectives	Very little	Little	Quite a bit	Much with both individuals and groups
b. Direction of information flow	Downward	Mostly downward	Down and up	Down, up, and with peers
c. Downard communication				
(1) Where initiated	At top of organization or to implement top directive	Primarily at top or patterned on communication from top	Patterned on communication from top but with some initiative at lower levels	Initiated at all levels
(2) Extent to which communication is accepted by subordinates	Viewed with great suspicion	May or may not be viewed with suspicion	Often accepted but at times viewed with suspicion. May or may not be openly questioned	Generally accepted, but if not, openly and candidly questioned
d. Upward communication				
(1) Adequacy of upward communication via line organization	Very little	Limited	Some	A great deal
(2) Subordinates' feeling of	None at all	Relatively little, usually communicates "filtered"	Some to moderate degree of responsibility to initiate	Considerable responsibility felt and much initiative.

Table 2.2 (Continued)

Operating Characteristic	System of Organization			
	Authoritative		Participative	
	Exploitive Authoritative	Benevolent Authoritative	Consultative	Participative Group
responsibility for initiating accurate upward communication		information but only when requested. May "yes" the boss	accurate upward communication	Group communicates all relevant information
(3) Forces leading to accurate or distorted information	Powerful forces to distort information and deceive superiors	Occasional forces to distort; also forces for honest communication	Some forces to distort along with many forces to communicate accurately	Virtually no forces to distort and powerful forces to communicate accurately
(4) Accuracy of upward communication via line	Tends to be inaccurate	Information that boss wants to hear flows; other information is restricted and filtered	Information that boss wants to hear flows; other information may be limited or cautiously given	Accurate
(5) Need for supplementary upward communication system	Need to supplement upward communication by spy system, suggestion system, or some similar devices	Upward communication often supplemented by suggestion system and similar devices	Slight need for supplementary system; suggestion system may be used	No need for any supplementary system
e. Sideward communication, its adequacy and accuracy	Usually poor because of competition between peers and corresponding hostility	Fairly poor because of competition between peers	Fair to good	Good to excellent
f. Psychological closeness of superiors to subordinates (i.e., how well does superior know and understand problems faced by subordinates?)	Far apart	Can be moderately close if proper roles are kept	Fairly close	Usually very close

Table 2.2 *(Continued)*

Operating Characteristic	System of Organization			
	Authoritative		Participative	
	Exploitive Authoritative	Benevolent Authoritative	Consultative	Participative Group
(1) Accuracy of perceptions by superiors and subordinates	Often in error	Often in error on some points	Moderately accurate	Usually quite accurate

SOURCE: Rensis Likert, *New Patterns of Management* (New York: McGraw-Hill, 1961), pps. 226–227.

Table 2.3 provides an overview of communication in the three management eras. You have already assessed your personal similarity in beliefs to classical and human relations thinking. Now, take Self-Assessment Quiz 2.3 and see how you compare with the human resources philosophy.

Table 2.3

AN OVERVIEW OF COMMUNICATION IN THE THREE MANAGEMENT ERAS

	Classical Management Era	Human Relations Era	Human Resources Era
Purpose	To provide specific instructions to employees	To provide direction but also to make employees feel needed	To coordinate activities and tap the full creative resources of all employees
Direction of communication	Almost exclusively one way, downward	Predominantly downward. Some cosmetic upward communication. Recognition of horizontal communication	Multidirectional, open communication
Nature of emphasis	Exclusively on formal communication	Formal communication predominates. Recognition of informal communication	Formal and informal communication are in wide use

SELF-ASSESSMENT QUIZ 2.3

Are You a Human Resources Management Person?

Answer each of the following true/false statements by underlining your response. Compare your answers to those given at the back of the book. For each one you have correct, score one point.

1. Most workers find work to be inherently distasteful. True/False

2. Properly motivated people exercise self-direction and self-control. True/False

3. Most workers are given credit for being far more creative than they are. True/False

4. If people have a say in setting job-related goals, they are often motivated to do a better job. True/False

5. The average worker is basically self-centered and uninterested in organizational needs. True/False

6. Democratic leadership styles are usually superior to autocratic leadership styles. True/False

7. Most employees dislike participative management practices. True/False

8. Money is the prime motivator for most workers. True/False

9. The average worker likes to be led. True/False

10. Most workers need to be managed through the use of close control and threats of punishment. True/False

---

Status of Communication in the Human Resources era

1. Communication is both formal and informal in nature. Both are recognized as necessary to the proper functioning of the organization.

2. Communication takes whatever direction is necessary to ensure efficiency and effectiveness. This includes upward, downward, horizontal, and diagonal flows.

3. Communication is used for more than just control purposes. It also supports participative planning, organizing, and directing efforts.

4. Decision making is decentralized, and in many cases authority based on knowledge replaces authority of the position.

5. The informal organization is identified as an important part of organizational life, and its support and assistance are encouraged by management.

6. The purpose of communication is designed to tap the full potential of all individual members. Employees are regarded as human resources who are of more importance to management than its machines and equipment.

MANAGEMENT COMMUNICATION THEORY TODAY

Management communication theory today still reflects elements of the thinking of the three eras discussed in this chapter (see Table 2.3). Two new trends are affecting the way communication occurs in modern organizations. These trends are a systems approach to management and communication and the contingency theory of what is appropriate managerial behavior.

A systems approach looks at the total organization.

Borrowed from the world of physical sciences, the systems approach sees the organization as a set of interrelated component parts. A problem in one area cannot be treated as an isolated event, but must be dealt with in the framework of the total organization. Systems theory stresses the importance of open communication and healthy interaction with the external environment. Indeed, the role of communication is now seen as of prime importance.

A contingency approach urges flexibility.

The contingency approach formalizes the realization that there is no one best way of always doing something. What works well in one instance will not always work well under other circumstances. A Theory X approach, for example, might work quite nicely with one employee or group of employees and fail miserably with another. Effective communicators must bear in mind the necessity of first recognizing the variables that call for certain types of behavior and then being able to adapt to the required behavior.

In this text, we are going to approach the study of communications from a human resources standpoint. We will also be integrating systems and contingency ideas into our analysis and discussion of this subject. In this way, we will be reinforcing the importance of participative management in effective communication.

C A S E   I N   P O I N T

Revisited

What did Cliff do wrong? Pulling together the information in this chapter, you should have noted that Cliff was using a human relations approach to managing a group of highly skilled, highly motivated professionals. He should have been using a human resources approach. If you take the basic philosophies of both groups, human relations and human re-

sources, and compare them, you will see why Cliff fits into the human relations category. Notice his emphasis on money and work restructuring coupled with verbal encouragement of the personnel. Although you might think he was a classic management era type, remember that the human relations approach uses the classic style plus an emphasis on social need satisfaction. Everyone is encouraged to be a member of the team, and the manager tries to turn the environment into a "nice place to work."

The scientists are undoubtedly accustomed to being managed via the human resources approach. Using Likert terminology, Cliff was employing a System 2 approach when he should have been using a System 4. This is particularly clear when approached from the standpoint of communication. Compare the information contained in the Likert profile in Table 2.2 with the information in the case.

Notice how much Cliff's approach to introducing and using MBO was System 2 in nature. Communication was mostly downward; there was limited upward flow of ideas. The psychological closeness of Cliff and the scientists was moderate at best.

What can Cliff do? He needs to recognize his shortcomings and revert to his old approach. Remember that the scientists are not going to change. Their need for a human resources manager is tied directly to personal values and lab progress. It is Cliff who must change!

YOU BE THE CONSULTANT

Fred's Place

The Wilshire Academy is a private educational facility that offers classes from kindergarten through high school. In the local community, Wilshire has a very good reputation. It is regarded as one of the best private schools in the area. A recent public opinion poll put it fourteenth out of 127 private and public schools in the region.

The owner of the school is Fred Wilshire who, with his wife Susan, built the academy from a one-room first grade to its current state. Wilshire is located on 15 acres of land on the edge of a major eastern metropolis. A series of connected cottages house the kindergarten and grammar school classes. The school has a large building for the junior high school and another one for the senior high school. The academy's auditorium is large enough to accommodate all the students and teachers and 150 guests, an Olympic swimming pool, a track field, and ten tennis courts. Wilshire's advertising promises students a "well-rounded education."

Fred is principal of the entire system and his wife is the associate principal. They are assisted by a large administrative staff that takes care of tuition billing, purchases all books and equipment, and oversees general maintenance. Fred directly supervises the teaching personnel and does all hiring and firing of these people.

The editor of the large local paper was intrigued by the results of the recent public opinion poll mentioned above. His son attends one of the other private schools in the area, and the boy has often told his dad that the students at Wilshire are "not that hot." The editor has heard this criticism numerous times before, sometimes from other students at his son's school and sometimes from members of the school board. This made the man think about a story related to which schools in town really are the best. As a result, last month he sent a team of four reporters into the community to interview graduates of the 15 "best" (based on the public opinion poll) private schools in the area. The reporters also asked to talk to students at these schools and to members of the faculty and administration of the respective educational institutions. The latter two groups were asked about admission requirements, faculty standards, status of the students on nationally scored exams, number of students who go on to college, where they go, and so on. This week, the editor got a firsthand report from those who were covering Wilshire Academy. It is a very interesting story. Here are the facts as gathered by the reporting team:

1. The admission requirements at Wilshire are much lower than the general public believes. Actually, just about anyone with the tuition money can secure entrance.

2. The owner, Fred Wilshire, runs the whole show himself. His basic philosophy appears to be one of increasing enrollments and keeping them high.

3. Fred spends a great deal of time interacting with the students and faculty. Everyone refers to him as a nice guy, and the students admit that without him the school would lose some of its appeal for them.

4. Fred is well educated, having earned an Ed.D. from a major university. However, he shows very little interest in curriculum development. The faculty or the outside review team he brings in once a year advise him on curriculum changes.

5. The faculty are evenly divided on Fred. The older people, most of whom have been there for five or more years, like him a lot. The younger ones think he lacks tact and understanding. For example, they report that Fred hates controversy, and during faculty meetings he either ignores or refuses to listen to any advice that does not fit with his view of things as they should be. The younger faculty feel Fred lacks academic rigor in the program and puts pressure on them to teach to the lowest students in their class. Fred also dislikes outside tutoring and urges the faculty not to engage in this practice. The young faculty believe this is because Fred is ill equipped to deal with the demands of the advanced student. Fred sent formal letters to two faculty members who were tutoring students from other classes, demanding that they stop. When the parents who were paying for the tutoring learned of this order, they wrote him blistering letters. Fred ignored the letters; he appears unable to face irate parents. However, he did back down on his demand that these faculty stop their tutoring.

6. The most academically qualified faculty, in terms of classroom performance and academic degrees (master's degree or work toward the doctorate), typically leave Wilshire. Interviews with five of these people indicated that Fred was a pleasant person but was too interested in running a friendly school than in pushing for an academically oriented one.

7. Contrary to public opinion, most students who stay at Wilshire for two years or more are unable to pass the entrance exams for admission to most of the other "better" private schools in the area. Not one Wilshire student has been able to gain admission to any of the other 14 schools ranked in the top 15 by the public opinion poll, although the reverse is not true. Students leaving Wilshire almost always go back into the public school system.

8. Only three students in Wilshire's graduating class of 130 seniors last year were accepted into a university rated as difficult or extremely difficult. Most of the

students went into junior colleges or state schools where admission requirements, as identified by a national testing agency, were average or less. The class valedictorian was rejected by every Ivy League, Big Ten, Pacific Ten, and Big Eight school to which he applied. Like the valedictorian before him, he opted for a large city university where admission is open to anyone who finishes in the top half of the high school graduating class.

The editor read and reread these findings. He could hardly believe it. Since he is unwilling to make the newspaper story look like a smear of Wilshire, he wants to add some positive facts to the report. So he sent the reporters back to confront Fred with the story and to ask for an explanation. Fred admits that the facts are basically true, although he disagrees about the statements related to academic quality. "Every school is getting better and better. Maybe we're not moving up as fast as others. However, we are still an excellent academic institution. Of course, there is still a lot more that we need to do. For example, referring to your comments about the way I manage things around here, I'll admit that I may be a little too social in my orientation but I think it's important that people in academia not fight with each other. We work best in a pleasant, friendly environment. I'm surprised that some of my prior teachers say that they left because they feel the academic goals here are not high enough. I think that many of these problems will be addressed in the near future. I've hired a management consulting firm to come in, analyze us from top to bottom, and tell us what's wrong and what we ought to do about it. They'll be here in three weeks. How about coming back next year and taking another look? I think you'll have a lot of changes to report to your readers."

Assume that you are a member of the consulting team that is coming into Fred's academy. Based on your reading of the case, what is Fred's philosophy of management? In which era would you place him: classic, human relations, or human resources? How does he communicate with his people? What is he doing wrong? What recommendations would you make to him? Be sure to show him how a human resources philosophy can be of value in running a first-class academic institution.

Key Points in This Chapter

1. The classical management era was characterized by an interest in finding ways of maximizing productivity. The two important groups in this era were scientific managers and administrative managers.

2. Scientific managers were interested in conducting time and motion studies and identifying the most efficient methods for doing work. They also offered incentive pay to the highest producers. Their basic philosophy was that work was inherently distasteful to most people, money was the primary motivator, and few workers wanted work that required creativity, self-direction, or self-control. The most famous of their group was Frederick Taylor who set forth four principles of scientific management: (a) determine the way the work ought to be done; (b) scientifically select the workers; (c) train and educate the workers in how to do their jobs, and (d) develop cooperation between management and the workers so that each works in accord with the other.

3. The administrative managers were interested in developing management principles and techniques. The most important member of this group was Henri Fayol who set forth 14 administrative principles and developed the now-famous gangplank theory of communication.

4. Mary Parker Follett was a bridge to the human relations era. Her two main contributions to the field of communication were the concept of one universal fact and one universal goal.

5. The human relations era was characterized by individuals who believed that (a) people wanted to feel useful and important, (b) they desired to belong and to be recognized as individuals, and (c) these needs were more important than money in motivating them.

6. The Hawthorne Studies provided important human relations insights. The two individuals who were most important during these studies were George Elton Mayo and Fritz Roethlisberger. Another important contributor during this time period was Chester Barnard who incorporated his business experience into a book and set forth the now-famous acceptance theory of authority. He also identified and described a series of communication principles.

7. Joseph Scanlon was a bridge to the human resources era. His participative management/union productivity plan encouraged workers to file suggestions for productivity management. This emphasis on meaningful, creative, worker participation went far beyond the human relations emphasis of the day.

8. The human resources era is characterized by beliefs such as (a) work is not inherently distasteful, (b) most people are far more creative than they are given credit for being, and (c) if properly motivated, people will assume responsibility and exercise self-direction and self-control in carrying out their jobs.

9. Some of the major contributors to the human resources management era have been Herbert Simon, Douglas McGregor, and Rensis Likert. Simon wrote widely about communication as an integral part of the decision-making process. McGregor set forth his Theory X and Theory Y tenets and explained why the Theory Y philosophy was preferable to Theory X if one wanted to be a successful manager. Likert showed that a System 4, participative management approach resulted in improved communication and increased efficiency and effectiveness in organizations.

10. Modern communication theory is currently in a human resources era. It is also typified by a concern for both the systems approach and the contingency approach.

Questions for Discussion and Analysis

1. What was the basic managerial philosophy of the scientific managers? How did this philosophy influence their approach to organizational communication? Explain.

2. Of what value is Fayol's gangplank theory to the field of communication? Be complete in your answer.

3. In what way is Mary Parker Follett a bridge to the human relations school? How did her work add to a growing understanding of organizational communication?

4. How did the Hawthorne Studies contribute to an improved understanding of organizational communication? Be specific in your answer, being sure to include a general discussion of the techniques used during the interviewing program.

5. What human relations findings emerged from the Hawthorne Studies? How did this help increase our understanding of communication in organizations?

6. What communication principles did Chester Barnard set forth? How accurate were these principles? Are they of value to today's managers? Explain.

7. According to Barnard, under what conditions will a person accept orders from a superior? Include in your answer a brief discussion of the acceptance theory of authority. Of what value is this information to a manager seeking to improve his or her communication skills?

8. How did the Scanlon plan work? In what way does this plan show that Scanlon himself was a human resources manager? How does the plan have value to those interested in effective communication? Describe the causal link.

9. How does human resources management differ from human relations management? Compare and contrast the philosophies of both.

10. Are any benefits associated with participative management? What are they?

11. Of what value have Herbert Simon's contributions been to the field of communication? Explain.

12. In what way does a Theory X philosophy differ from a Theory Y philosophy? Compare and contrast the two.

13. Are human resources managers Theory X or Theory Y advocates? Defend your answer.

14. What is the basic philosophy of a System 1 manager? A System 2 manager? A System 3 manager? A System 4 manager?

15. In what way does an understanding of the four systems of management help improve a person's communication ability? Explain your answer.

16. How does an understanding of the systems approach help one become a more effective manager? How does the contingency approach help one become a more effective manager? Explain.

Exercises

1. Choose three people to have a debate. Each one is assigned a role as a classical manager, a human relations manager, or a human resources manager. Debate one of the following topics:
   a. The importance of feedback.

    b. The purpose of managerial communication.

    c. The "open-door" policy.

    d. Participative management.

2. Role play the following situation from the point of view of first a classical manager, then a human relations manager, and finally a human resources manager.

    Situation: An employee is having a problem with his supervisor. He feels the supervisor is unfair and unrealistically demanding. Furthermore, the supervisor does not communicate with her employees except to give direct orders and to criticize productivity. You, the manager, are now speaking with the employee who has made an appointment to see you.

3. Have various students play the roles of the following theorists:

    a. Frederick Taylor

    b. George Elton Mayo

    c. Chester Barnard

    d. Mary Parker Follett

    e. Rensis Likert

    f. Herbert Simon

Each person should speak to the group about his or her view of the function and importance of management communication. Remember to stay in role!

References

1. Raymond E. Miles, *Theories of Management: Implications for Organizational Behavior and Development* (New York: McGraw-Hill, 1975), p. 35.

2. Frederick W. Taylor, *Principles of Scientific Management* (New York: Harper & Brothers, 1911).

3. Henri Fayol, *General and Industrial Management*, translated by J. A. Coubrough (Geneva: International Management Institute, 1930).

4. Taylor, *op. cit.*, p. 39.

5. Miles, *op. cit.*, p. 100.

6. Elliot M. Fox and L. Urwick, eds., *Dynamic Administration: The Collected Papers of Mary Parker Follett* (New York: Hypocrene Books, 1973).

7. *Ibid.*, p. xxiii.

8. *Ibid.*, p. xxvii.

9. Miles, *op. cit.*, p. 35.

10. The biographical data on Mayo and Roethlisberger come from Daniel A. Wren, *The Evolution of Management Thought*, 3rd ed. (New York: John Wiley, 1987), pp. 240–247.

11. Elton Mayo, *The Human Problems of an Industrial Civilization* (New York: Macmillan, 1933), pp. 71 – 72.

12. Elton Mayo, "Hawthorne and the Western Electric Company," as found in Louis E. Boone and D. D. Bowen, eds., *The Great Writings in Management and Organizational Behavior*, 2nd ed. (NY: Random House, Inc), p. 82.

13. Chester Barnard, *Functions of the Executive* (Cambridge, Mass.: Harvard University Press, 1938).

14. *Ibid.*, pp. 165 – 166.

15. *Ibid.*, p. 122.

16. Miles, *op cit.*, p. 35.

17. Herbert A. Simon, *Administrative Behavior*, 3rd ed. (New York: The Free Press, 1976).

18. James G. March and Herbert A. Simon, *Organizations* (New York: John Wiley, 1958).

19. Simon, *op cit.*, p. 157.

20. *Ibid.*, p. 162.

21. *Ibid.*, p. 163.

22. Douglas McGregor, *The Human Side of Enterprise* (New York: McGraw-Hill, 1960).

23. Douglas M. McGregor, "The Human Side of Enterprise" in Jane W. Gibson and Richard M. Hodgetts, eds., *Readings and Exercises in Organization Behavior* (Orlando, Fla.: Academic Press, Inc., 1985), p. 29.

24. *Ibid.*, p. 33.

25. Rensis Likert, *New Patterns of Management* (New York: McGraw-Hill, 1961).

26. Rensis Likert, *The Human Organization* (New York: McGraw-Hill, 1967).

27. Rensis Likert and Jane Gibson Likert, *New Ways of Managing Conflict* (New York: McGraw-Hill, 1976).

28. Likert, *op. cit.*, *New Patterns of Management*, p. 45.

29. Rensis Likert, "An Integrating Principle and an Overview," as in Boone and Bowen, *op. cit.*, p. 219.

Annotated Bibliography

Barnard, Chester I., *Functions of the Executive* (Cambridge, Mass.: Harvard University Press, 1974).

Whether you read the 1938 original or this 1974 edition, Barnard's contributions to management thought are unmistakable. The book is ponderous, but classic and full of the commonsense conclusions of an experienced chief executive.

Fox, Elliot M., and L. Urwick, *Dynamic Administration* (New York: Hypocrene Books, 1973).

This compilation of the speeches of Mary Parker Follett clearly shows her advanced thinking in the areas of management and communication. The roots of the human relationists and even systems theory can be found in her work.

Miles, Raymond E., *Theories of Management: Implications for Organizational Behavior and Development* (New York: McGraw-Hill, 1975).

Miles fully develops the classical, human relations, and human resources models used in this chapter. He explores the model's use not only in the field of communication but also in job design, organizational design, leadership style, personnel practices, and organization development.

Simon, Herbert A., *Administrative Behavior*, 3rd ed. (New York: The Free Press, 1976).

This latest edition of Simon's classic work adds substantially to his initial work on decision making. Of interest to communication students is the information on processing technology and its impact on organization design.

Wren, Daniel A., *The Evolution of Management Thought*, 3rd ed. (New York: John Wiley, 1987).

This highly readable book documents the historic development of management theory. It is full of details on the major theorists and their contributions. It is an excellent resource book for anyone interested in managment theory.

INTRODUCTION

Before beginning our study of effective listening, we would like you to answer Self-Assessment Quiz 3.1. After recording your answers and checking how well you did, continue with the material below. Regardless of how well you did on the quiz, you now have an initial understanding of what the area of effective listening is all about.

Forty-five percent of time is spent listening.

Research studies have shown that while white collar workers devote approximately 45 percent of their time to listening, they listen with only a 25 percent rate of efficiency. That is, a short period of time after they are done listening, they are able to accurately recall only about one-quarter of everything they heard.[1]

On the other hand, sadly, our school systems, from kindergarten through college, devote very little time and effort to teaching people to listen effectively. This is rather startling given the fact that listening researchers like Hulbert have found that

> In business, the list of problems caused by poor listening is endless. Because of ineffective listening, letters have to be retyped, appointments have to be rescheduled, orders have to be reprocessed, products have to be remanufactured, and shipments have to be rerouted. Because of poor listening, employees cannot understand and satisfy customers' and clients' desires; and managers cannot understand and satisfy employees' needs. As a result, customers and clients are alienated; and unnecessary employee-employer conflicts disrupt operations and decrease productivity.[2]

In this chapter, we are going to try to help you overcome any listening deficiencies you may have.

SELF-ASSESSMENT QUIZ 3.1

What Do You Know About Listening? An Initial Inquiry

Respond to each of the following by placing a true (T) or false (F) answer before it.

_____ 1. Listening accounts for about 45 percent of the average manager's communication time.

_____ 2. People who hear well are usually very good listeners.

_____ 3. There is a high positive correlation between intelligence and effective listening.

_____ 4. Learning to listen is largely automatic and does not need to be taught.

_____ 5. Listening carefully to someone can be both physically and psychologically stressful.

_____ 6. To show you are listening carefully to someone, you should ask appropriate questions when the individual pauses.

_____ 7. Studies show that people remember only about 50 percent of what they hear.

Continued next page

_____ **8.** The best listeners at a lecture or conference are those who outline the talk for later review.

_____ **9.** Proficiency in reading leads to proficiency in listening.

_____ **10.** Listening is easy if you know how to do it; it requires almost no effort.

Before continuing, check your answers at the back of the book.

THE LISTENING ENVIRONMENT

Listening can take place in virtually any kind of environment from a quiet office to a noisy street corner. This environment can be broken into two subenvironments: the psychological and the physical. The psychological environment is that which exists within the people who are listening. The physical environment is that which exists around the listeners. Of the two, the psychological environment is the more important. Regardless of how much noise there is in the external environment or what kind of time demands the listener is under, if that person wants to listen, then listening is going to occur. It may not be 100 percent effective, but it will take place. Conversely, if an individual does not want to listen, regardless of the surroundings, listening will not occur. Psychological environmental factors determine whether listening will occur; physical environmental factors help influence the degree of listening efficiency that results. The following examines both of these environments.

The Psychological Environment

The psychological environment consists of the mental variables internal to the speaker and the listener. Four of the most important are codes, value systems, education, and psychological set.

Past experience is important.

CODES   In Chapter 1 we noted that the encoding and decoding processes are central to the transfer of meaning. As we then explained, codes of past experience are unique compilations of everything the speaker or listener has gone through. It includes memories, values, and beliefs. The resultant attitude with which the listener and/or speaker approaches the communication determines, to a large extent, how successful it will be. For example, a manager, who has had an accumulated negative experience with union representatives, will often approach a conference with the shop steward with preconceived ideas and mindblocks. Effective listening can still occur but *only* if the manager recognizes the mindset and works hard to be open minded.

Values influence listening.

VALUE SYSTEMS   The operating value systems of the speaker and the listener help determine what is said and what is heard. These systems are a result of the early life experiences of the individual. To a large degree, each of us is what we were at the age of twenty. In fact, of this period the first ten years are the most significant. For example, people now in their sixties were developing their value systems during the 1930s when the Great Depression was in full swing. As a result, for many members of this group, job security and the importance of hard work are key values. Many children of the 1950s, on the other hand, grew up in a period of affluence and abundance. For many of them, an entirely different attitude exists about work. How does this affect listening? Consider the following.

Foreman (age 55) to employee (age 22): We've got to get this shipment out tonight or we'll lose this account. We're all going to have to pitch in and work until midnight.

Employee: You've got to be kidding — count me out! I've got tickets to the soccer game.

How can an understanding of values have helped this encounter? Consider the following.

Foreman: I know you've got better things to do but we're in a real bind. If you can help me out tonight and stay until this order is out, I'll owe you one.

Employee (Scenario One): I know you're really desperate, but I've promised to take my kid brother to this soccer game. Let me see if I can get Joe to stay back and help you out.

Employee (Scenario Two): I know how important this is to you, so I'll give you a hand. Maybe Joe will buy my soccer tickets.

Taking time to recognize the other person's values can greatly help in the listening and communication processes — but it cannot be one-sided!

EDUCATION Education level has a major impact on the listening experience. Although formal education in no way implies formal training in listening, the educated person has a better chance to listen effectively to another educated person because they "speak the same language." Two high school dropouts speaking "street language" will likewise be more able to listen effectively to each other. As with values and age, *similarity* in educational background is the key to more effective listening. Lacking this commonality, the communicators must recognize the differences and compensate for them.

Education also influences listening.

PSYCHOLOGICAL SET The psychological makeup of the listener and speaker also impact on the results. Is one or the other defensive in some way? Aggressive? Hostile? Is he or she repressing part of the conversation or projecting onto the listener? Psychological set will be discussed further in Chapter 4.

The Physical Environment

The physical environment includes the setting in which the speaker and listener find themselves. Five of the most important physical environmental elements are physical acuity, age, place, time, and noise. The first two are internal to the person and virtually beyond the control of the listener. The last three are external to the person and can be manipulated to create a more effective listening environment.

PHYSICAL ACUITY   Hearing ability and speech ability are major factors in listening effectiveness. This is easily seen if you try to speak to a deaf person who does not read lips. Hearing and speaking ability are fundamental skills that become critical whenever they are not well developed.

Physical ability affects listening.

AGE   Age is a correlate to the value issue discussed earlier under the psychological environment. Similarities and differences intrude on the listening environment. Children are taught to "listen to your parents," which actually means doing as you are told, not listening for meaning. Adults, in turn, sometimes fail to listen to their children and miss the opportunity for understanding and mutual growth. Between these two groups are teenagers who often fail to listen to adults because they believe adults have nothing worthwhile to say. We are much more likely to really listen to someone near our own age — someone we suspect will say something of interest to *us*.

Age also affects listening.

PLACE   Although we spend a great deal of our communication time listening, sometimes the place is neither appropriate nor optimally effective. The corporate cafeteria may be all right for casual banter, but serious listening can usually be enhanced by a move to a more private, comfortable spot.

Where the communication takes place can affect listening.

TIME   How often have you had someone say to you, "Let's talk about that later," or "I'd like to resolve this issue before Wednesday," or "Give me your analysis, in a five-minute summary, right now." Statements such as these are time related. The big problem, of course, is that you may find that when you do get to talk, the other person is not ready to listen.

Time is a key variable in effective listening.

NOISE   Noise is a very common environmental variable. Typical examples include the ringing of a telephone, the clacking of a typewriter, and the loud conversation of those seated nearby. Noise often impedes the listening process. When there is a great deal of it in the immediate environment, listening becomes very difficult and often impossible. On the other hand, some kinds of noise can enhance communication. Soft music is an example. Many firms pipe in music so that the employees can work in an environment more conducive to productivity.

Noise can reduce listening effectiveness.

Finally, noise made by the speaker personally will affect the listening process. Voice intonation, pauses, and the rapping of one's hand on the table all influence the listener's interpretation of what is *really* being said. So does lack of noise. Consider the manager who tells the subordinates "I just don't understand how you could have made a mistake like this," and then says nothing. Is the individual waiting for the subordinate to respond? Maybe not. The manager may be using silence to add weight to his statement. These pauses help accentuate the message and give it more importance than would otherwise be the case.

LISTENING HABITS: INEFFECTIVE VERSUS EFFECTIVE

A knowledge of the listening environment provides important insights regarding factors that influence listening effectiveness. Another key dimension is listening habits. Some people, regardless of their efforts, always seem to have trouble listening. Others have no problem at all. What accounts for the difference? Nichols, after studying 100 good listeners and 100 poor listeners, found ten basic differences. These ten, along with our explanations and illustrations of each, are presented below.[3,4]

1. Deciding in advance that the subject is uninteresting.

- *Poor listeners.* Before the speaker ever reaches the podium, poor listeners have made up their minds that the subject of the talk is the last thing they want to hear. The decision, and the resulting negative mindset, gives the listener an excuse for daydreaming, writing letters, or engaging in other nonlistening-related activities.

Accept the challenge to find something interesting.

- *Effective listeners.* Effective listeners may find the subject boring but decide to accept the challenge by making the most of the situation. Instead of finding alternative activities, they focus on the speaker's message, determined to derive something from the encounter.

2. Focusing on the poor delivery of the speaker.

- *Poor listeners.* Poor listeners quickly concentrate on the negative mannerisms of a mediocre speaker. The person's clothes are not in style; he needs a haircut; her accent is difficult to understand; he repeats himself too often; she says "OK" after every other sentence. The listeners thereupon conclude that this person could not possibly say anything that is worth listening to.

Focus on what is being said.

- *Effective listeners.* Effective listeners also recognize the poor delivery of the speaker. However, they quickly put it in the back of their mind and focus on what is being said rather than how it is being delivered. One of the authors attended a freshman biology class which clearly illustrates this situation.

  > The instructor was a 30-year veteran who had been delivering the same lecture in the same monotone for longer than he could remember. Worse yet, he paced back and forth in front of the class with his hands locked behind his back. Never did he look at the class. The pacing stopped only when the professor needed to write something on the board. Never had the students been faced with a less effective delivery! However, the fact that it was a required course taught only by this professor resulted in the early conclusion by many students to dig in and get all the information possible. As it turned out, the man was brilliant and the material was stimulating. However, the students had to focus long enough to get past the poor delivery.

3. Becoming overexcited and anxious to make your own point.

- *Poor listeners.* Poor listeners hear just a brief part of what the speaker is trying to convey and interrupt at the first pause. When they are finished, the speaker will often say, "Well, if you had waited, I was about to make that point" or even worse, "I *just* said that a minute ago." Ineffective listeners do not hear it, of course. They are too busy putting together their own comments.

Hear the person out.

- *Effective listeners.* Effective listeners practice the cliche, "Hear the person out." These listeners are easily spotted in a meeting. They are often the ones quietly arguing to the compulsive interruptor to "Let him finish what he is saying." These listeners do not jump to conclusions about what the speaker is saying. They wait for the entire presentation to conclude before beginning their overall evaluation.

4. Focusing only on facts.

■ *Poor listeners.* Invariably, poor listeners try to remember specific facts presented. In so doing, they usually miss the main idea. Consider, for example, the following recent case.

> An accounting professor announced to his students that the final exam would consist of ten problems. In each case, the student would be expected to show how they would handle the specific problem in terms of journal entries and then would be expected to explain the logic behind the entries. Fully one-third of the class stopped listening the minute the professor made the comment about journal entries. They concentrated on memorizing format and procedures for the exam. On the test they were able to address the mechanical parts of the problems but were unable to explain the logic behind their entries. No one in this group received more than a 70 on the exam.

Listen for the main ideas.

■ *Effective listeners.* Conversely, good listeners look for the main ideas — the theme that keeps coming back again and again during a presentation. Without it, isolated facts do not make any sense. Once the sense of the talk is internalized, the facts will be remembered as logical supporting evidence.

> As applied to the above case, the two-thirds of the students who did listen long enough to hear the professor relate the importance of explaining the logic behind the entries did well on the exam. They looked at the "big picture" in relating why the particular entries were being made. When the exam tests were returned, the professor referred to those who did poorly on the exam as bookkeepers, whereas those who did well on the exam were called potential accountants. "As in all things," he noted, "You have to listen for more than just facts. You have to seek meaning. Accountants may have technical ability but the best ones know that accounting is more than just number crunching."

5. Outlining everything.

■ *Poor listeners.* Put poor listeners in a situation where they must assume responsibility for what is being said, and they start to take copious notes. We recently observed a class of 40 students who were told they would have to write a summary of a videotaped talk on comparative analysis as a research methodology. Unfortunately for the students, the speaker was talking extemporaneously and not from an outline. Those students who outlined everything found it almost impossible to transcend their notes and summarize the main points.

Listen before taking notes.

■ *Effective listeners.* In the above classroom example, a smattering of good listeners sat back and listened. Eventually they wrote down the main points, but for each point written down they listened for two or three minutes.

6. Pretending to pay attention.

■ *Poor listeners.* This is one we professors see all too often! Poor listeners are often tired, lazy, bored, or preoccupied. They pay the speaker the courtesy of an attentive posture — such as leaning forward in the chair, chin resting on hand. From this position, however, they proceed to ponder their personal problems or compose that memo that needs writing. Often you can look at these people and see them drifting away — eyes glazed. Even worse, some poor listeners do not even fake attention. They proceed to sign letters, read mail, and make notes as you talk to them.

Stay alert and attentive.

■ *Effective listeners.* Listening is hard work. It is not a passive encounter at all but requires energy and attention: The heart beats faster and the temperature rises. The good listener not only hears effectively but also observes the nonverbal signals of the speaker — tone of voice, gestures, and facial expression — all of which add up to a *real* understanding of what is being said.

7. Allowing distractions to interfere.

■ *Poor listener.* There are a million distractions — all part of the "noise" in our original communication model that was presented in Chapter 1. These distractions cover a wide gamut from actual noise, which interferes with your ability to hear the speaker, to visual distractions that attract your attention away from the speaker. Equally upsetting is noise caused by a speaker who talks too loudly or too softly. The poor listener does nothing about these distractions, allowing them to sidetrack his or her attention.

Screen out distractions.

■ *Effective listeners.* Effective listeners try to control their environment by screening out distractions. They choose a quiet place to listen, refuse phone calls, and close their office doors to avoid intruders. If they are at a conference, and the speaker talks too low, they ask him or her to speak up or give the nonverbal hand-behind-the-ear cue for "louder please."

8. Avoiding difficult material.

■ *Poor listeners.* Time after time we shake our heads at students who avoid certain classes because "that stuff's too hard to follow." This is the sign of a lazy listener as well as an inexperienced one. For those who have been brought up on television cartoons and situation comedies, a good lecture on economic forecasting techniques will seem hopelessly complex. The poor listener does not fight this difficult feeling; rather, the individual avoids anything that is the least bit challenging, quickly tuning out what he or she does not easily understand.

Occasionally, listen to difficult presentations.

■ *Effective listeners.* The good listener, on the other hand, occasionally seeks out the difficult subjects to challenge his or her listening skills. These individuals are determined not to let a complicated presentation get the better of them.

9. Responding emotionally to certain words or phrases.

■ *Poor listeners.* Certain terms, phrases, and words affect us all in an emotional way; derogatory ethnic references are a good example. In business, certain other terms tend to make some people block out the rest of the conversation. For example, consider the department head who, pleading her cause for a new employee, may suddenly become irate when she hears her boss give her a counterargument about "budget constraints." We can all think of instances where in the middle of a conversation our blood began to boil. At that moment, we are all poor listeners.

Keep your emotions under control.

■ *Effective listeners.* Effective listeners examine those words and phrases that tend to have an emotional effect on them. By doing so, they usually become more adept at controlling their emotions. In a one-on-one or small-group situation, they may discuss this problem frankly, even asking the other person to refrain from these terms. Above all, the awareness of this problem helps the good listener to conquer it as a listening barrier.

10. Daydreaming because of the difference between speech speed and thought speed.

■ *Poor listeners.* Studies show that the average person speaks at about 125 words a minute while thinking at 400 to 500 words per minute. That means that, while listening, you have a lot of potential words per minute sitting in your head waiting to be used. The poor listener employs them on a completely different subject such as where to go for lunch or when to call a staff meeting. At first, the poor listener tunes in and out, loosely keeping track of the speaker's progress. All

---

Table 3.1

INEFFECTIVE AND EFFECTIVE LISTENERS: A COMPARISON OF STYLES

Ineffective Listeners	Effective Listeners
1. Call the subject uninteresting	1. Find interest in every subject
2. Focus on how the speaker looks and talks	2. Focus on what the speaker is saying
3. Become overexcited and anxious to interrupt	3. Hear the speaker out
4. Focus on facts	4. Focus on main ideas
5. Try to outline everything	5. Listen first and, if appropriate, take notes
6. Pretend to pay attention	6. Work at listening
7. Allow distractions	7. Control distractions
8. Avoid difficult listening	8. Seek out challenging listening
9. Get overemotional at certain words	9. Understand and overcome emotional reactions
10. Daydream because of the difference between speech rate and thought rate	10. Use extra thought time to summarize, anticipate speaker's next point, and read between the lines

Table 3.2

LISTENING FACTORS IN WORK ENVIRONMENTS

Category Description the Listener . . .	Total
1. Did (or did not) follow my directions or suggestions	33
2. Did (or did not) maintain eye contact	32
3. Was (or was not) attentive	25
4. Did (or did not) give nonverbal feedback that showed he was listening	23
5. Did (or did not) seem interested in helping me	15
6. Did (or did not) seem interested and concerned about me	15
7. Did (or did not) stop physical movements that interfered with listening	15
8. Did (or did not) remember what I had said in the past	15
9. Did (or did not) ignore my message or did not react to it	14
10. Asked me questions	13

SOURCE: Marilyn A. Lewis and N. L. Riensch, Jr., "Listening in Organizational Environments," *The Journal of Business Communication,* Summer 1988, pp. 49–65.
These human relations factors point out the need for what is called active listening.

too often, however, he or she becomes too involved in an interesting daydream and forgets to tune back in — thereby missing large portions of the talk. This habit is not just poor listening; it is nonlistening, probably the worst pitfall of all.

Stay tuned in to the speaker.

■ *Effective listening.* Effective listeners also find something to fill in the extra time, but they remain tuned in to the speaker and spend their extra thoughts on material related to the talk. They may make mental summaries of key points or try to read between the lines. They may anticipate the speaker's next point or reflect on the evidence when drawing a conclusion. Any way you look at it, the effective listener mentally reinforces what the speaker is saying and causes a more lasting memory to form.

Table 3.1 provides a summary of these good and bad listening behaviors that were described here. Look them over and see if you can recall what was said about each. How well were you "listening" to what we were saying?

Recently, some researchers have suggested that Nichols' prescription for better listening is more appropriate for the classroom than for the board room. More specifically, these studies suggest that classroom listening is based mainly on absorbing facts and being able to recall them at a later date, whereas business listening seems to be more oriented toward human relations. One such study by Lewis and Reinsch used a critical incident technique which asked participants to cite an example of effective listening and another of ineffective listening. Table 3.2 shows the top ten listening factors in work environments that resulted from this study.[5]

Implications for Management

1. If you expect someone to listen to you, phrase your message in terms of the listener's values. Show the individual how what you have to say will benefit him or her.

2. As you listen to subordinates, stay alert for signs of common defense mechanisms such as repression, denial, projection, and/or aggression. These indicate frustration and can result in communication breakdown.

3. Remember that where you communicate is often as important as how or what you communicate. Pick the right setting for listening or you will find yourself distracted by too many outside elements. You will never become a good listener if you have to spend as much time screening out noise and other disturbances as you do trying to follow the message.

4. When someone asks you "Is this a good time for me to tell you about this?" be honest. If the timing is bad, say so. Some managers are basically morning people; other managers are more effective during the afternoon. During which time period are you alert and able to do your best listening? Whichever one it is, schedule important meetings or conversations for this period. Remember that if you are not at your best, your listening effectiveness is going to suffer.

5. Keep the four steps in the communication process in mind. Listening is involved at each step whether it is by your subordinate or both of you. Remember that listening is not over until the action step is completed and everything has been done in accord with management instructions.

ACTIVE LISTENING: THE KEY TO EFFECTIVENESS

Effective listening involves more than just paying attention. It also includes active, empathic, and supportive behaviors that tell the speaker, "I understand, please go on." This mode of response is called active listening.

Of course, not all speakers are active listeners. Many fall into one of the other four response modes. The following is a brief description of all five, beginning with the directing orientation.

Some listeners lead the speaker.

1. *Directing.* The "directing listener" leads the speaker by guiding the limits and direction of the conversation. Consider an employee telling the supervisor of his inability to get along with a co-worker. The directing supervisor would make a reply such as, "If I were you, I'd just ignore him" or "Don't worry about it — everybody thinks he's a pain in the neck."

Others inject personal values or opinions.

2. *Judgmental.* The "judgmental" listener introduces personal value judgments into the conversation. The listener tends to offer advice or make statements regarding right or wrong behavior. In responding to the employee plight described above, the judgmental listener might say, "You'll just have to learn to get along with your co-workers" or "You're absolutely right, Tom is impossible to get along with."

Some ask a lot of questions.

3. *Probing.* The "probing" listener asks a lot of questions in an attempt to get to the heart of the matter. This individual tends to lead the conversation and satisfy his or her personal needs rather than those of the speaker. A probing listener might answer the above employee as follows: "Exactly what has this person done to you so that you can't get along?" or "When did all this start?" or even "What do you want me to do about it?"

Others urge conflict resolution.

4. *Smoothing.* The "smoothing" listener tends to pat the speaker on the head and make light of his or her problems. The underlying belief here is that conflict is bad and should be avoided at all costs. The smoothing listener would tell the employee in our example "You and Tom just had a bad day; don't worry — tomorrow it will all be forgotten."

Effective listeners create an encouraging environment for the speaker.

5. *Empathic/Active.* The "empathic/active" listener tries to create an encouraging atmosphere for the speaker to use in expressing and solving the problem. Active listeners tend to feed back to the speaker *neutral summaries* of what they have heard in order to (a) establish that understanding has occurred and (b) allow the speaker to continue. The active listener might respond to the employee in our example as follows: "It seems you are troubled by the fact that you and Tom can't seem to get along." Take Self-Assessment Quiz 3.2 and identify your typical response style.

SELF-ASSESSMENT QUIZ 3.2

Identify Your Response Style

Carefully read each of the following ten speaker comments. In each situation, check the response you would most likely make to each of these comments.

1. "It's so hot out today; I just can't think about mowing the grass."
   A. "If I were you, I'd get the job over with."
   B. "You're just looking for an excuse not to do the grass."
   C. "When will you mow it if you don't do it now?"
   D. "It will probably cool off later."
   E. "The heat really bothers you, doesn't it?"

2. "I am really tired of studying. For the last two weeks, I have spent all my free time hitting the books. I don't think I can retain anything else at this point."
   A. "Why not take a break and go back to it later?"
   B. "If you didn't let all your studying go to the end of the term, you wouldn't have this problem."
   C. "Why have you had to study so hard the last two weeks?"
   D. "Everybody feels that way sometimes."
   E. "You sound concerned that your studying may not be effective at this point."

3. "I don't know what to do first. John has given me two special projects to do on top of everything else. There just aren't enough hours in the day."
   A. "How about asking John what he wants done first?"   Continued next page

    B. "You always worry unnecessarily about things."
    C. "What exactly do you have to do?"
    D. "We all get real busy sometimes; things will calm down."
    E. "You're frustrated by the workload and need someone to help you set priorities."

4. "The Dean just assigned me to teach a new course in organization theory and it starts next week. I'll never be ready for it."
    A. "You'd better start right now and prep that course."
    B. "You never should have accepted it."
    C. "Haven't you taught this course before?"
    D. "It will only seem tough for the first few weeks. By then, you'll have the time to get fully prepped for the course."
    E. "You sound anxious because you weren't prepared for a new course."

5. "The word from the home office is that 10 percent of our sales force is going to be laid off because of overall failure to make a quota. This would be the worst possible time for me to lose my job."
    A. "Why don't you ask the branch manager if you're likely to be one of the 10 percent?"
    B. "You're a good person and they know it. They'd never lay you off."
    C. "Why do you think you might be one of the 10 percent laid off?"
    D. "Don't worry. Chances are you won't be affected."
    E. "You seem nervous about the possibility that you might be one of the 10 percent to go."

6. "That clerk we fired last week is threatening to bring a discrimination suit against us. She says she was fired solely because she was a woman. This could be a real messy situation. You know how the boss hates lawsuits."
    A. "You'd better call the lawyer now."
    B. "She couldn't be that foolish—it will never happen."
    C. "What could she base her suit on?"
    D. "If she does, nobody can say it's your fault."
    E. "You appear concerned that this situation could become messy."

7. "Darn! Now I've got to go to Los Angeles. I've been away from the family every weekend for a month. Pretty soon I won't have a family."
    A. "Why don't you take them with you one of these times?"
    B. "A manager's family has to realize that traveling is part of the deal."
    C. "Why do you have to travel so much?"
    D. "Next month you'll probably be able to stay home and make it up to them."
    E. "You sound concerned about the effect your traveling is having on your family life."

8. "If I take the promotion, I'll have to move to Pittsburgh. If I refuse it, the company probably won't offer me another one. I just don't know what to do."
    A. "Let's look at the pros and cons of living in Pittsburgh."
    B. "You'd better take this offer while you can."
    C. "What's so bad about Pittsburgh?"
    D. "This seems a big problem now, but in the long run everything will work out."
    E. "You sound in conflict over whether to accept this promotion or not."

9. "Jerry is a constant complainer. If he isn't griping to me about the rest of the group, he's complaining about his salary. He's really getting on my nerves."
   A. "Complaints often point to larger general dissatisfaction."
   B. "That's because you always lend a shoulder for people to cry on."
   C. "Why do you think he's so unhappy?"
   D. "Don't let that bother you. Every office has a Jerry."
   E. "You seem aggravated because Jerry complains to you so often."

10. "I'm delighted I got this new job, but I'm scared I won't be able to learn quickly enough to keep up with everyone else."
    A. "I'm sure your supervisor will help you learn quickly."
    B. "You should just be grateful you got the promotion."
    C. "What new things do you need to learn?"
    D. "Everyone feels that way about a new job."
    E. "You sound both happy and nervous about your new job."

Answers are in the Answer section at the back of the book.

Here is another example of the five listening responses mentioned earlier. Read it carefully so as to develop a working knowledge of the five response pattern modes.

Employee: I know I'm late again this morning, and I really tried to get here on time. But something always seems to happen to delay me in the morning.

Manager Responses

Directing: Just get up a half an hour earlier and you'll have plenty of time to cope with anything unexpected.

Judgmental: Being late so often really looks bad for you. You'd better find a way to get here on time.

Probing: Well, what happened this morning to make you late?

Smoothing: We're all late sometimes no matter how good our intentions are.

Active Listening: You sound frustrated that you were late again this morning.

Table 3.3 provides a detailed summary of these response patterns. Read it carefully and note how the listener acts and the speaker reacts in each of these modes.

The Nature of Active Listening

According to Fisher, four components underlie active listening behavior: empathy, acceptance, congruence, and concreteness.[6] *Empathy* is the quality of trying to understand the speaker from his or her own viewpoint rather than from any external criterion, such as the listener's past experience or personal preference. *Acceptance* is the quality of deep concern for the other person's welfare along with a respect for the other's individuality and worth as a person. *Congruence* is the quality of openness, frankness, and genuineness on the part of the listener, which tends to encourage the same pattern in the

Table 3.3

LISTENING RESPONSE PATTERN IDENTIFICATION

Pattern	Listener's Focus	Response Mode	Responds to	Listener's Attitude and Posture	Speaker's Reaction
Directing	Listener's own ideas	Limited to the listener's way of looking at the problem	Speaker's content	Superior attitude	Speaker's focus lost as the listener pursues his or her own track
Judgmental	Listener's own ideas	Gives the verdict of what to do or not do	Speaker's content	Superior attitude	May feel defensive, resentful and/or misunderstand
Probing	Speaker's ideas or listener's ideas	Directing and/or leading by asking questions	Speaker's content	Impatient; wants to get to the point	Must focus on listener's questions even if they go away from the central problem
Smoothing	Speaker's feelings	Ignores the problem; feels it is not important	Speaker's content and emotion	Healing and encouraging	Compromising at best; frustrating at worst
Active empathic	Speaker's ideas and feelings	Encouraging and accepting behavior	Speaker's emotion	Attentive, forward leaning, good eye contact	Must look more closely at own problem; free to continue talking

speaker. *Concreteness* is the quality of focusing on specifics and avoiding vagueness by helping the speaker concentrate on real problems and avoid generalities such as "they say" or "everyone knows." Active listeners develop and nurture these four components.

Active listening offers a number of important benefits to managers who want to increase their effectiveness. In particular the process

1. Encourages the individual to speak his or her mind fully.

2. Provides the speaker with a sounding board in solving problems.

Benefits of active listening
3. Offers a motivational benefit to the speaker, who feels important in the eyes of the listener.

4. Encourages the speaker to think through his or her problem thoroughly and not be quickly diverted.

5. Encourages the speaker to become more open and less defensive in communication, thus fostering emotional maturity.

6. Makes the speaker feel his or her ideas are worthwhile and can be helpful in stimulating creative thinking.

7. Makes the speaker listen to his or her own ideas more carefully.

8. Provides the listener with a wealth of information on facts, attitudes, and emotions that were previously unexpressed.

9. Provides a growth experience for both the speaker and the listener.

On the other hand, active listening is not without drawbacks. In particular, the activity

Potential drawbacks to active listening

1. Is time consuming and takes both a physical and psychological toll on the listener.

2. Frequently results in people hearing things with which they do not want to cope. (The average listener has a multitude of defense mechanisms for dealing with undesired comments, ranging from denial to simply tuning out. The active listener does not have this luxury because the very process of active listening requires that such defense mechanisms be set aside.)

3. Can cause an involuntary change in the listener. (Most people are quite pleased with the way they are; active listening forces individuals to see the world from someone else's perspective and, in so doing, often presents the possibility that these people may be wrong and need to change.)

Implications for Management

1. Remember that there are five different types of listening response styles. You use all five types and so do your subordinates. So in addition to trying to develop your own use of the empathic/active style, keep an eye on how your subordinates listen. You can use this feedback as a guide in helping them improve their own listening styles.

2. Keep in mind that many managers, especially at the lower levels of the hierarchy, tend to make heavy use of the directing response style. They want to tell the other person how to do it. They feel that subordinates want to be led, and this is the best way of meeting this need. Work with these managers to show them that the directing response style tends to be overused. Remember from Chapter 2 that the directing style tends to be more classic management-oriented than any of the other four response styles. It is also the one that, in the long-run, is least useful in developing the personnel as human resources.

3. Remain alert for the overuse of the judgmental response style. Many subordinate managers use this approach because they think that it is important to fashion the opinions and values of their subordinates. However, in many cases all they end up doing is making their people angry through the use of ineffective or uncalled-for advice. Overuse of the judgmental response is typically the result of a large ego. Urge your staff to use this style judiciously.

4. Remember that the smoothing style is sometimes the sign of a manager who is more concerned with everyone being a member of one big family than it is the sign of a manager who knows how to be an effective manager. Excessive emphasis on smoothing is typical among individuals with a high affiliation need. They want to be

ETHICS IN COMMUNICATION

Big Brother Is Listening

Listening is an important management activity, but sometimes it can go too far. For example, over the last decade many employers have gained the ability to monitor worker performance through the use of computers and phones. Sometimes this monitoring is done to check whether the individual is busily working or is instead socializing. Other times, however, it is done to listen into conversations or gain confidential information about the person. For example, some firms have their employees' telephone conversations monitored on a random basis to ensure that the calls are not being used for personal purposes. In the process, the listener sometimes stays on the line and becomes privy to information that is none of his or her business.

Another example of such interference is the boss who learns that one of her employees has AIDS and then relates this information to other members of the work group. This is a violation of the individual's right to privacy and can result in a major lawsuit for the firm. In fact, AIDS victims have sued employers over this failure to maintain confidentiality and have won out-of-court settlements. Sometimes effective listening involves hearing what is being communicated but *not* passing it on to others.

A third common listening-related problem involves hearing what is going on and not taking any action because it is not related to company business. An example is the employee who dates individuals who work for competing firms. Unless the company can prove that its employee is passing on business-related information that is detrimental to its competitive position, the relationship is none of the company's business. Yet some firms have demanded that their employees break off these relationships or be terminated. As a result, such employees have successfully sued the company for interference in their personal life.

These examples illustrate that, whereas listening is an important managerial activity, it can be taken too far. Managers need to be good listeners, but they also need to learn to respect their employees' right of privacy. Failure to know when to stop listening can be as detrimental as failure to know when to start. The effective manager maintains a careful balance between the two.

SOURCE: John Hoerr, "Privacy," *Business Week*, March 28, 1988, pp. 61–68.

liked more than they want to be regarded as effective. When you see someone making too much use of this style, you need to have a conference with the individual. Remember that, like it or not, conflict is sometimes a part of effective management. Anyone who does not like the heat simply has to stay out of the kitchen.

5. Remember that the empathic/active listener is the most effective of all. Yet remember that no one operates out of this style in all instances. Sometimes you will find one of the other response styles to be more effective. When it comes to listening, however, this is the best one. Do not confuse a humanistic approach to management with the best approach to listening to your subordinates.

Becoming an Active Listener

Now that you know that active listening is a worthwhile tool, what habits or techniques do you need to develop to build your base skills?

1. Listen for total meaning. This means being receptive to both the message and the accompanying emotional content.

2. Respond to feelings. Remember that the emotional content often is far more important than the verbal message.

3. Note all cues. Keep in mind that the entire nonverbal behavior of the speaker must be observed in order to get the total picture.[7]

Robert Bolton, an expert in human relations skills, has suggested a series of useful guidelines for building active listening skills. His recommendations include the following:

1. Do not fake understanding. Admit when you lose track of what the speaker is saying and ask him or her to explain further.

2. Do not tell the speaker you know how he or she feels. This is often seen as patronizing and phony.

3. Vary your responses. There is no single "right" response to every communication situation. Depending on the environment, paraphrase, remain silent, or give an encouraging word such as uh-huh, to let the speaker know you are paying attention.

4. Focus on feelings. Do not ignore the emotional content of the message; be aware of the speaker's attitudes, values, and opinions.

5. Choose the word that most accurately reflects the feeling intended. Try to be specific in identifying the emotion, and the degree of that emotion, appropriate to the situation. Degrees of the word "sad," for example, can be expressed as "very sad," "distraught," "despairing," and "heartbroken."

6. Develop a vocal empathy. No matter how empathic your words, if your voice is cold and clinical, the speaker will not feel comfortable. Also have your tone of voice and its rate, rhythm, and volume reflect the speaker's emotional state.

Some ways to build active-listening skills

7. Strive for concreteness and relevance. Help the speaker come to the point rather than continue in generalities by making your responses specific and, if necessary, asking clarifying questions such as "How did you feel when that happened?"

8. Provide nondogmatic but firm responses. State these responses in such a way that the speaker feels comfortable in disagreeing with your paraphrasing.

9. Reflect the speaker's resources. Often, the speaker will become so involved with his or her problem that the individual focuses on negative points and neglects strengths. The active listener will highlight these strengths when he or she hears them and thus provide a bit of encouragement to the speaker.

10. Reflect the feelings that are implicit in questions. When a speaker asks you directly what you would do in his position, it becomes difficult not to give advice. A truly skilled active listener, however, can reflect the feeling of the direct question back at the speaker. For example,

   Employee: Jones is sure messing up my production quota — what would you do with him?"

   Manager: This really has you troubled, hasn't it?

11. Accept the fact that many interactions will be inconclusive. Few listening incidents will come to closure. The active listener often must settle for the knowledge that he or she has left the speaker with a sounder basis for further thought.[8]

Hope on the Horizon

Fortunately, many sectors have come to the realization lately that listening is indeed a neglected but necessary skill. In 1978 the federal government issued a directive to public school systems to include listening in their basic competencies.

> Now the historical neglect may be ending. The states that have already included listening on their lists of required skills are increasing. Professional organizations, such as the International Listening Association, universities, and organizations are providing increased training materials, and listening centers have been established.[9]

Business also seems to be giving much more attention to effective listening as an important business skill. Perhaps business has finally realized the cost of poor listening.

> Inefficient and ineffective listening is extraordinarily costly . . . simple listening mistakes result in letters having to be retyped, appointments rescheduled, shipments rerouted. With more than 100 million workers in America, a simple $10 mistake by each would total $10 billion wasted.[10]

Many corporations have demonstrated their new commitment to listening training by instituting formal listening training programs. These companies include Sperry, Xerox, Pfizer, 3M, Pitney Bowes, AT&T, GE, Western Electric, General Motors, and the U.S. Steel Company. The Sperry Corporation, now part of UNISYS, has probably carried its training further than others. During the early 1980s, Sperry became known for its advertisement "We understand how important it is to listen." By 1983, 10,000 Sperry employees had been trained in listening and 80,000 others had received training materials.[11]

C A S E   I N   P O I N T

Revisited

At this point, review your notes on the Case in Point. This chapter presented a great deal of new information. Where possible, take this chapter information and revise, expand, or add to your analysis. When you are finished, continue reading.

We can size up this case in a number of ways and determine what went wrong. The two best ways are by looking at mistakes Willie made in terms of ineffective listening habits and then by identifying and describing his listening style.

In terms of ineffective listening habits, where did Willie go wrong? Several items merit consideration. First, to Willie, the subject of the discussion did not appear very interesting. He did not really seem to feel that Rita had a problem in the first place. Second, although he did not interrupt her, he certainly did not focus on her main idea. Rather than investigate exactly what her problem was, he simply responded to what she was saying. He made no attempt to get more information or to work out a plan of action regarding an acceptable solution. We are also left to wonder how much the meeting he was supposed to be attending was weighing on his mind and competing with Rita's message. You may have found other ineffective listening habits in the case, but these are the main ones you should have identified.

Willie's listening response pattern is also worthy of analysis. Let us see Table 3.3 to help identify how he conducted himself during the meeting. Notice that Willie used a number of different styles. First, he offered Rita advice (do not leave the firm, we will find something for you), which is the directing style. Second, he used the judgmental style by letting his personal values enter the picture. Bits of the probing and smoothing styles are also in evidence, but not too much. However, virtually no empathic/active listening is being used. Notice that Willie never fed back to Rita what she was saying, allowing her to explain why she felt as she did. Far from being neutral about the matter, Willie took a very positive stance and indicated that he felt Rita was making a mistake.

So in summary, what we have here is not effective listening, but an attempt at effective persuasion. Sometimes we can persuade people to take certain actions through the effective use of listening. However, in Willie's case this was not true.

YOU BE THE CONSULTANT

Take the Rest of the Day Off

Mary Kenway is a middle manager in a large insurance firm. About a year ago the company hired an outside consulting firm to examine its overall operations and recommend ways of improving the efficiency and effectiveness of the managerial staff. One of the most successful techniques recommended by the consultants, and then implemented, is the "in-house observer." This technique involves putting one of the consulting firm's people in a manager's office. From this vantage point, the consultant watches the manager in action. As the president of the insurance firm put it, "It lets the consultant get a look at how our managers really do things. The individual gets a real-life picture of how our people work."

Last month, Mary was told that one of the consultants would be spending a day with her in the near future. When she met the consultant, Alan Greenberg, she was somewhat nervous. However, it took Alan only a few minutes to calm her down. "I'm not going to be following you around for the purpose of telling you what to do, or looking for problems that I can report back to your boss," he told her. "My job is to stay in the background, watch how you do things, and then discuss with you how you can improve your management style for dealing with both problems and people. If I do a good job, you'll have a chance to tell your boss. If I do a poor job, you'll also be able to tell him this. So the person who is really on the spot is me. I have to be both helpful and tactful." Mary laughed. "I'll try to be a fair grader," she told him.

During the day Alan was with Mary, he sat in the back of her office and before long, she forgot he was there. Occasionally, he would take notes, but for the most part, he would simply look out the window or leaf through a book he had in his lap. Alan went out of his way to fade into the woodwork, and he was successful.

During this day, Mary got involved in many different matters. Of particular importance were two extended conferences in her office that took up about an hour each. One dealt with a problem employee; the other was related to a cost control report that had to be filled out by one of Mary's subordinates. The communication approach that Mary used was the same in both cases. Part of the exchange that occurred during the cost control report discussion went like this:

Mary: Bill, I'm sorry that I haven't had time to get with you about that report until now, but I've really been snowed under with work. How can I help?

Bill: Well, I've filled out this report three times over the last year and its never been too difficult. However, this time the accounting people called over and they want a whole lot more information than we sent them the last couple of times. In particular, they want data related to absenteeism, turnover, photocopying and typing expenses, and receipts related to some of the travel of the junior executives who were assigned to us six months ago.

Mary: Heck, that shouldn't be too hard. Have you asked Jim to provide you with the information? Also, Dennis should be able to give you input.

Bill: I already talked to them, but the data that the accounting people want can only be obtained by actually going through some of our monthly expense forms and analyzing them carefully. This could take a couple of weeks. If you ask me, those accounting people are going out of their way to make trouble.

Mary: Oh, c'mon Bill, they're really nice guys over there. We've been able to help them out in the past and when possible, they've always tried to reciprocate. Don't get down on them. They're an important part of our team here at headquarters.

Bill: Well, I don't mean that they're not helpful. But why do we need to generate all of this information? I really think it's a waste of time. If you want it done, of course, I'll get it done. But there are two favors I'd like. First, I need to have at least two people assigned to me for three days to help dig out what I need. Second, I need to have you go over some of the figures and decide what needs to be put into the report.

Mary: Oh sure, if I can help just let me know. I'm always glad to lend a hand. And if you need any help, I want you to call on Jim or Dennis for assistance.

Bill: No, I don't mean general help. I mean I need some people who are going to be doing nothing but helping me finish the report. This is a lot more difficult than it looks. Believe me, I'm not just crying wolf.

Mary: Of course you're not. You always do good work. And I know you'll get this report done on time and in the form that accounting wants. However, don't you think you're asking for more resources than you really need? If you have Dennis and Jim help you pull the files, that'll take around an hour, I'd guess. Then you can go through them and get whatever you need.

Bill: I don't know. I feel like I'm being left at the station while everyone else is on the train. I'm getting more and more nervous about this report. I even woke up last night thinking about it. It's beginning to drive me crazy and I'm not half done gathering all the information I need.

Mary: Gee, you really seem to be getting yourself worked into a frenzy about this. I'll tell you what. Take the rest of the day off, come in tomorrow morning and you can get started at that point in time.

Bill: I don't know if that's a great idea. I think I'd probably just walk around for the rest of the day and worry about the report. Don't you think I'd really be better off getting on the report right away?

Mary: Hey, don't worry. Tomorrow you'll feel a lot better and be ready to tackle the report. Wait until then.

From where he was sitting in the room, Alan could see that Bill was not very satisfied with Mary's decision. However, he did not argue with it. He simply got up and went out. Later that afternoon Alan and Mary went upstairs to the cafeteria to get a cup of coffee. On the way, they passed Bill hurrying down the hallway with some papers. He smiled at them sheepishly. "Just getting some stuff together for tomorrow. I'm leaving in a few minutes." They smiled back and continued toward the elevator. When they got their coffee and sat down, Mary said, "Tell me, do you think I handled that one right? It seems to me that what Bill really needed was someone to calm him down. Tomorrow he'll feel a lot better and be ready to get to work on that report." Alan looked at her for a moment and asked, "How effective do you think you are as a listener? Do you think you identified Bill's problem and responded in a way that will help him solve them?" Mary thought for a moment and said, "I have a feeling that I did something wrong. How could I have handled the situation better?"

Assume you are Alan. Put yourself in his shoes and play the role of the consultant. Tell Mary how she could have done a better job in helping Bill out. In your answer, be sure to identify Mary's listening response style(s). Then compare those styles to the one(s) she could have used in talking to Bill. Finally, make recommendations to Mary regarding how she can improve her listening effectiveness. In your answer, be as practical and helpful as you can.

Key Points in This Chapter

1. Research studies show that while white collar workers devote approximately 45 percent of their time to listening, they listen with only a 25 percent rate of efficiency. Yet of all the sources a manager has by which he or she can come to know and accurately size up the personalities of the people in the department, listening to the individual employee is the most important.

2. The listening environment consists of two subenvironments: psychological and physical. On the psychological side some of the most important variables include codes, value systems, education, and psychological set. On the physical side, some of the most important variables include physical acuity, age, place, time, and noise. Both sets of factors play important roles in determining the effectiveness of the listener.

3. A series of listening habits can help differentiate ineffective and effective listeners. The ineffective listeners tend to have the following ten ineffective habits: they (a) call the subject uninteresting, (b) focus on how the speaker looks and talks, (c) become overexcited and anxious to interrupt the speaker, (d) focus on facts, (e) try to outline everything, (f) pretend to pay attention, (g) allow distractions, (h) avoid difficult listening, (i) get overemotional at certain words, and (j) daydream because of the difference between speech rate and thought rate.

4. The five basic listening style responses are (a) directing, which is characterized by the speaker guiding the limits and direction of the conversation; (b) judgmental, which is characterized by the speaker introducing personal value judgments into the conversation; (c) probing, which is characterized by the listener asking a lot of questions; (d) smoothing, which is characterized by the listener trying to play down the problem or issue; and (e) empathic/active, which is characterized by the listener using neutral summary feedback to establish understanding and allow the speaker to continue.

5. The four components of active listening behavior are empathy, acceptance, congruence, and concreteness. In addition, many steps can be used to improve one's ability to listen actively. The latter part of the chapter explained these components and steps.

Questions for Discussion and Analysis

1. What key variables constitute the psychological listening environment? Identify and describe them.

2. What key variables constitute the physical listening environment? Identify and describe them.

3. A number of listening habits characterize ineffective listeners. What are the most common ten habits that fall into this group? Identify and describe each briefly.

4. How do each of the following listeners behave: directing, judgmental, probing, smoothing? Identify the behaviors of each.

5. How does the empathic/active listener behave? Give an example.

6. Four components underlie active listening behavior: empathy, acceptance, congruence, and concreteness. What is meant by this statement?

7. Are any benefits associated with active listening? Are any drawbacks associated with active listening? Identify and describe three benefits and the drawbacks of each.

8. How can a manager become a more empathic/active listener? Offer at least five recommendations or suggestions that the individual should follow.

Exercises

1. In pairs, practice active listening responses to the following comments.
   a. "I wish Frank would stop borrowing my tools. He never returns them unless I go and ask for them."
   b. "I'm really counting on a six-month raise. With my mortgage payments and the new baby, I can barely keep up with the bills."
   c. "I can't stand how Jim takes us for granted. He assumed I'd be willing to work overtime again tonight after I stayed late two nights in a row. It's not like we get paid overtime."
   d. "Helen seems to think she's better than everyone else. She never socializes with the rest of us. She'd rather bring a sandwich than go out to lunch with us."
   e. "Just how important is this test? I know it's worth 50 percent of the grade, but my class participation should count for something."
   f. "Harry never really listens to me. He pretends he hears and then goes on as if I hadn't said anything."
   g. "I don't know what I'll do with my secretary on vacation. I can't find anything without her and this is such a busy time of the year."
   h. "Sam really makes me mad when he changes every letter I write before it goes out of the office. The changes are so small, I think they're to let me know who's boss."
   i. "I don't care what statistics say about how safe flying is, I feel a lot safer in a car."

2. Practice paraphrasing: in pairs discuss a controversial issue such as those mentioned below. Take opposite sides of the issue. After the first person states his or her position, the partner must paraphrase back what he or she has heard until the first person is satisfied. Only then does the partner proceed to state his or her own position. Continue in this way, each time paraphrasing what the other person has said before stating your side.
   a. Legalizing marijuana.
   b. Smoking.
   c. Equal Rights Amendment.

References

1. Ralph Nichols, "Listening is a 10-Part Skill," *Nation's Business*, July 1957, p. 56.

2. Jack E. Hulbert, "Barriers to Effective Listening," *The Bulletin*, June 1989, p. 3.

3. Ralph Nichols, "Listening Is a 10-Part Skill," *op. cit.*, pp. 56–60.

4. Nichols, "Listening Is Good Business," *Management of Personnel Quarterly*, Winter 1962, pp. 2–9.

5. Marilyn H. Lewis and N. L. Reinsch, Jr., "Listening in Organizational Environments," *The Journal of Business Communication*, Summer 1988, pp. 49–65.

6. Dalmar Fisher, *Communication in Organizations* (New York: West, 1981), pp. 330–331.

7. Carl R. Rogers and Richard E. Farson, "Active Listening," in Richard C. Huseman, Cal M. Logue, and Dwight L. Freshley, eds., *Readings in Interpersonal and Organizational Communication*, 3rd ed. (Boston: Holbrook Press, 1977), p. 561.

8. Robert Bolton, *People Skills* (Englewood Cliffs, N.J.: Prentice-Hall, 1979), pp. 90–99.

9. Judy C. Nixon and Judy F. West, "Listening: Vital to Communication," *The Bulletin*, June 1989, pp. 15–17.

10. Lyman K. Steil, "How to Communicate by Listening," *Credit and Financial Management*, October 1983, p. 17.

11. John Lewis Degaetani, "The Sperry Corporation and Listening: An Interview," *Business Horizons*, March–April 1983, pp. 34–39.

Annotated Bibliography

Banville, Thomas, *How To Listen — How to Be Heard* (Chicago: Nelson-Hall, 1978). An entertaining, easy-to-follow book that builds chapter by chapter to a "total listening" package of skills. Practical for the manager or aspiring manager.

Brownell, Judi, *Building Active Listening Skills* (Englewood Cliffs, N.J.: Prentice-Hall, 1986). This experiential, skill-building book focuses on how to be an active listener. It does this by coaching us on six approaches to listening: Hearing messages, understanding messages, remembering messages, interpreting messages, evaluating messages, and responding to messages.

Nichols, Ralph G., and Leonard A. Stevens, *Are You Listening?* (New York: McGraw-Hill 1957).

> Nichols is the best known author in the listening field. This famous work details all of his research and gives practical guidelines for more effective listening in a variety of situations. Written in an easy-to-follow, interesting manner, it is as applicable today as when it was written.

Wolvin, Andrew D., and Carolyn Gwynn Coakley, *Listening*, (Dubuque, Iowa: William C. Brown, 1982).

> This book takes a very thorough approach to studying the various types of listening, namely, appreciative, discriminative, comprehensive, therapeutic, and critical listening. It ends with an interesting discussion of the listener's responsibilities to others as well as to himself or herself.

CHAPTER 4
Barriers to Interpersonal Communication

"We can make ourselves a place apart behind light words that tease and flout. But oh, the agitated beast till someone really finds us out."

Robert Frost, "Revelation"

Objectives

1. To define the term *perception*.

2. To compare and contrast sensory perception with normative perception.

3. To describe the three critical elements of perception.

4. To explain some of the most important factors that make perception a difficult process.

5. To explain what is meant by the following terms: *projection*, *denial*, *repression*, and *rationalization*, and relate their relevance to the perception process.

6. To define the term *semantics* and explain some of the most common kinds of semantic problems that face communicators.

7. To discuss the importance of general semantics to the field of communication.

8. To relate the importance of self-disclosure to open, honest communication.

9. To discuss the value of the Johari Window in understanding interpersonal and group communication and the ways to improve one's effectiveness when using each type.

C A S E   I N   P O I N T

A Satisfactory Rating

When Julie Kraluskie started working at the Highland Corporation she promised herself that if she did not receive a 10 percent raise the first year, she would leave. Julie has a five-year plan: 10 percent increases in salary each year and a middle management position by the end of five years. Highland is a subcontracting firm in the electronics industry. Over the past five years it has grown at an annual rate of 22 percent. Most of the personnel have averaged annual 7.5 percent increases in salary, although some, especially those who have been promoted into middle- and upper-level management, have averaged 18 percent. When Julie interviewed at Highland and learned these statistics, she knew this was the type of firm that would help her attain her five-year objectives.

Julie started with the firm six months ago. During this time she has done quite well. However, an incident happened two weeks ago that has had an important impact on her first six-month performance evaluation. Julie had been working overtime to help her boss complete a detailed market analysis report. The data for the report were being compiled from sales information being sent in by the company's salespeople. Highland has a 50-person sales force that covers all 48 contiguous states. The firm had also hired a marketing research organization to help with the market analysis report. Julie's job was to take the information she was receiving from these sources and condense it into a series of tables and charts. Her boss was writing the textual part of the report that would refer to and elaborate on data.

One day while Julie was working very hard on one of the most complicated tables, her boss put his head into her office and said, "There's a file out here with some incompleted pages. Would you mind getting the data and finishing the file?" Julie asked, "When do you need it?" The reply was, "As soon as you can get to it." Julie dropped everything and began work on the file. It took her almost three days

to complete it because it was much more difficult than her boss had indicated.

The day after she completed the file, her boss called her into his office. The two of them started going over the marketing research report. "You should be all done with those charts and tables by tomorrow," he said. "And none too soon. The entire report is due on the president's desk by the day after tomorrow." Julie was shocked. Her boss had never told her when the report was actually due; she thought it was scheduled for completion some time the following month. Surprised by her boss's comments, Julie explained to him that she needed another three days to finish her work. "I spent three whole days finishing that incompleted file. I only got back on the report yesterday." Her boss's face turned a deep red. "You mean that you took time away from this report for that silly file? You could have gotten to that work when you were finished with this report! What's the matter with you anyway?" Julie was not certain how angry he really was. However, she found out when he called her in two days later to discuss her semiannual performance appraisal. The boss seemed to have forgotten how hard Julie had worked on the market analysis report. All he kept harping on was the fact that he had to bring in two extra people to ensure that the report was completed on time. Julie received an overall rating of "satisfactory." This means that her annual raise will be somewhere between 3.5 and 6.8 percent. Without an overall "superior" rating, there is no chance of her getting more than a 7.5 percent increase. Realizing that she will be unable to reach her five-year objective if she stays with Highland, Julie submitted her resignation yesterday.

What happened? Why did Julie make the mistake she did? Who was to blame? In your own words describe the situation and then offer your analysis as to how it could have been avoided. When you are finished, put your answers to the side. We will return to them later.

INTRODUCTION

We might have called this chapter "Why What I Said Is Not What You Heard." How many times have you felt you did a fine job of communicating only to discover that the other person has completely missed your message? Oh, he or she heard you all right, but the meaning derived was not the meaning you intended. Consider the following:

> John called his wife Linda to tell her he had to stay late at the office and prepare for the next day's meeting. He was tired and frustrated and looking for some sympathy. Instead, Linda heard him out and said "Have fun!" just before slamming down the phone. John was hurt at being misunderstood. Linda was furious that John thought he could get away with spending another night with the boys by giving her such a flimsy excuse.

The above clearly illustrates the intrusion of the "code of past experience," which was described in Chapter 1. John's past experience had been that Linda was an understanding and sympathetic wife. He had every reason to expect that she would give him the sympathy he sought. Linda, on the other hand, was tired of spending so many evenings alone at home. She was feeling neglected and miserable. Instead of hearing John with a sympathetic ear, she interpreted his message as but another excuse to spend time away from her. The desired communication had not occurred.

Every day, at home, at work, and in our business and personal relationships, much of our communication activity misses the mark. Even more alarming is the fact that much of the time we are unaware that our message has been understood. In Chapter 3 we discussed effective listening, one of the major communication requirements. This chapter identifies and discusses three of the most common barriers to effective *interpersonal* communication: perception, lack of self-disclosure, and language.

PERCEPTION

Perception is a person's view of reality.

Perception is *a person's view of reality*. This reality can either be sensory or normative.

Sensory perception is physical reality. It refers to how we see concrete, visible phenomena. We can probably all agree that at this moment you are reading a book. We might call the book by a different name if we speak a different language, but basically we all have a similar idea of what we are talking about. When dealing with sensory reality, communication breakdown is not very great.

Normative perception is interpretive reality. It deals with matters of opinion or personal preference. Someone who is "beautiful" to one person may be totally unattractive to another. Figure 4.1 illustrates this idea. Look at the figure for a moment and then answer the following questions.

1. Is this person physically attractive?

2. Approximately how old is this woman?

3. From what socioeconomic class does this woman come?

Figure 4.1

Old lady — young
lady.

4. Would you want to have a conversation with this woman?

5. Does this woman work? If so, what does she do for a living?

Share your perceptions of Figure 4.1 with some of your classmates. How many different answers did you get? Are any of them totally correct or are they all matters of opinion and judgment?

Figure 4.2 presents other pictures open to perceptual interpretation. Look at each and determine whether it illustrates normative or sensory perception. (See the answers at the back of the book.)

Critical Elements of Perception

We as students of communication need to be aware of the three main elements of perception: figure/ground, selective perception, and psychological set.

FIGURE/GROUND   The concept of figure/ground is illustrated by the famous vase/face drawing in Figure 4.3.

Do you see the faces first or the vase? If you choose the vase, then the vase is the **Figure/ground** figure and the black area is the background. If instead your eye focuses on the black areas **determines focus.** showing faces in silhouette, the black area is the figure and the white area is the background. It is up to each of us in the communication situation to decide on what to focus — what to consider the figure and what to consider the background. Consider the

Figure 4.2

Sensory and normative reality: some examples.

(a) Is the above circle lopsided or round?　(b) Which of the center circles is larger, the left or the right?　(c) Which is longer, the length of the hat or the width of the hat?

(d) What do you see?　(e) What do you see here?

Figure 4.3

The Peter–Paul goblet.

following case. A 63-year old supervisor is conducting a performance appraisal of a 25-year old employee. The employee produces as much as anyone in the department but has long hair and wears jeans to work. He also chews gum and generally looks like a bum to the supervisor. Chances are, the appearance of the employee will become the focus or the "figure" in their relationship, whereas the productivity reports will fade into the "background." In the case of a different supervisor, however, the employee's dress would probably be insignificant and form part of the ground, whereas the relatively high production rate would become the figure. *What* we choose to focus on in any particular communication sequence can be of paramount importance.

SELECTIVE PERCEPTION *Selective perception* is the personal filtering of what we see and hear so as to suit our own needs. Much of this process is psychological and often unconscious. Consider again the performance appraisal example described above. The 63-year old supervisor may "selectively" see or hear the employee in question owing to a great variety of external factors. The individual may be tired or full of energy, happy or sad, angry or feeling ill. All of these things will have an effect on what he selects to perceive about his subordinates.

Selective perception involves filtering.

PSYCHOLOGICAL SET A third basic component of perception is *psychological set*. This ties in most closely with the code of past experience discussed in Chapter 1. Because of past patterns of behavior and experiences, we have fairly well-defined ideas about how things are supposed to happen and how people are supposed to act. Any differences in actual occurrences cause us stress until we either reconcile them with our expectations or cause the differences to disappear.

Past experience helps shape perceptions.

Everything we perceive in the office is done through a set of expectations. We expect the boss to act in certain ways; we expect our daily routine to be somewhat consistent; we expect the secretary to answer the telephone and open the mail, and so on. Many male managers have recently had to seriously alter their office "sets" to the changing sets of their female employees. It is no longer appropriate to expect the woman to make the coffee and take notes — a departure from the past that is still very difficult for some men to accept. Communication may freeze when a woman tells such a man that she does not make coffee!

What we expect in terms of ethical behavior also influences our behavior. See "Ethics in Communication: Is It Ethical?"

Factors Making Perception More Difficult

Perception results in different people getting different meanings from the same stimulus or experience. Four factors that cause this difference are the steel trap syndrome, stereotyping, the halo effect, and defense mechanisms.

THE STEEL TRAP SYNDROME The *steel trap syndrome* refers to the fact that our thinking tends to get more and more rigid as we get older. The more past experiences we have, the more narrowly we tend to perceive the world. Whatever the stimulus, we tend to tie our memory and preconceived perceptions to it. Years ago, as a student, one of the

Rigid thinking increases with age.

Is It Ethical?

Sometimes ethics is a matter of perception. What may be ethical to one individual may not be so regarded by another. For example, an individual receives a phone call from a broker who relates, "I've got inside information that Stock XYZ is going up. I think you should buy 1,000 shares at $6 right away." If the individual purchases the 1,000 shares and the stock rises from $6 to $18 over the next month, was the investor's decision unethical? The Securities and Exchange Commission says that it was and the individual must give back the profits. In addition, the stock broker will be barred from ever again working in the securities business. Insider trading, which is knowledge about what is going to happen to the price of a stock, cannot be used for financial gain.

If instead of getting this information from a stockbroker, what if the individual was walking down Wall Street and came across a piece of paper on the ground which revealed that Company A would soon make an offer to buy Company B. Could the individual use this information, buy 1,000 shares of Company B, and keep the profits that would result when the price went up? The Securities and Exchange Commission has ruled that the individual can keep the money because the person did not get the information as a result of an illegal tip. In fact, the person really did not know that the piece of paper had accurate information. So the individual was just acting on what appeared to be useful information.

Here is a third case. Suppose an individual is watching a Little League ball game when he suddenly spots a friend from high school. Since they have not seen each other in over ten years, he decides to switch seats and move just behind his old schoolmate. As he sits down, the man realizes that the friend is in the middle of a conversation with his spouse and decides to wait until they are finished talking. Suddenly he hears his friend say, "So when the boss asked me to put together the merger between Company A and Company B, I was just delighted." Aware that he has heard a confidential discussion, the man is embarrassed and decides not to announce his presence to his friend. The following Monday this man buys 10,000 shares of Company B and the stock triples within a month. Is this transaction legal or does the man have to give back the money? The transaction is legal because the investor did not get the information through insider trading.

In comparing the above three examples, some individuals have trouble understanding exactly what constitutes insider trading. They also have trouble understanding why it is not all right to use this information regardless of how it is obtained. For them, insider trading is a matter of perception and they perceive it to be all right.

SOURCE: Gary L. Tidwell and Abdul Aziz, "Insider Trading: How Well Do You Understand the Current Status of the Law?" *California Mgmt. Review*, Summer 1988, pp 115–123.

authors was much impressed when a professor asked the class to add one line to the following figure and make a 6. The figure he wrote on the board was

IX

Can you do it? Think for a moment before reading on. In that particular graduate class, only two of some 30 students came up with the right answer. It was simply to add an "S." Why is this so difficult for us to see? Because rigidity has set in and we focus on the Roman numeral configuration and try to continue along that line of thinking. We also tend to read "straight" when we read "one line." Experiments with children age 7 to 12, however, show a much higher correct response. One nine year old startled the authors with a unique but totally correct answer: 1×6.

STEREOTYPING *Stereotyping* is a process whereby we categorize people or events according to similarities that we perceive them as having.

Stereotyping consists of three steps. First, we identify categories by which we will sort people (race, religion, sex). Next, we associate attributes with those categories (athletic ability, speech patterns, occupations). Finally, we infer that all people in certain categories take on the attributes we have decided on (all blacks are athletic; all people from Boston talk funny; all secretaries are women: all people pursuing an MBA are aggressive and career-oriented.) Needless to say, stereotypes are almost always inaccurate.[1]

Stereotyping simplifies reality.

Much of the recent research on stereotyping has been concerned with age stereotyping and sex-role stereotyping. Age stereotypes include the view that older workers are less productive and less committed than younger workers.[2] Sex-role stereotyping of women is a continuing problem. Many still perceive women as being more emotional and less competent in a business situation than men. One recent study, for example, showed that male MBA students over a ten-year time period continued to have negative attitudes about women executives, whereas female MBA students held generally positive attitudes.[3]

THE HALO EFFECT The halo effect refers to judging or evaluating a person, place, or event by a single trait or experience. This overall impression can be good or bad but will prejudice our further involvement with the stimulus. Each of us can remember making a snap judgment about someone based on a first impression. Often we try to perceive further interaction with the individual based on this first impression, regardless of whether it was positive or negative. If this impression is incorrect, it often takes considerable pressure to concede this fact and break the halo effect.

The Halo effect prejudices judgment.

Examples are plentiful in business. A plush office convinces us someone is an important person in the organization and must be taken seriously. A sloppily typed letter by our new secretary proves to us the individual is going to be an unsatisfactory employee. The halo effect often shows up most conspicuously on performance appraisals where our overall good or bad opinion of the workers interferes with our ability to evaluate weaknesses or strengths accurately on individual job functions.

DEFENSE MECHANISMS Defense mechanisms are individual responses to anxiety-producing situations. Anxiety, within limits, keeps people alert and stimulated. Beyond an optimal amount, however, anxiety interferes with the communication process.

Everyone uses psychological defenses.

Most people have well-developed self-protective defense mechanisms to handle these situations. These devices shield the ego from a sense of failure or defeat. Typically, these responses are unconscious and are used in combination with an individual's response to anxiety. Four common defense mechanisms are projection, denial, repression, and rationalization.

■ *Projection.* Projection occurs when we assign our own feelings or impulses to another person. For example, Tom dislikes Judy and believes that Judy dislikes him. It is especially interesting to note that people rated high on characteristics such as stubbornness, sloppiness, and stinginess have a great tendency to rate others high on these traits. People often see others in more negative terms because they project their own characteristics onto them.

Common defense mechanisms

■ *Denial.* Denial is a conscious refusal to acknowledge a thought, feeling, experience, or unpleasant fact. It may take the form of an outright denial, for example, "That never happened," or a decision to postpone looking at the facts, for example, "I don't have time to think about that now." This mechanism, sometimes called perceptual defense, effectively filters out disturbing information. It helps explain why people "hear" data that support their thinking and fail to hear conflicting information.

■ *Repression.* Repression is an unconscious suppression of feelings that are unacceptable to the individual. For example, a manager may suppress her anger at an incompetent subordinate because she believes it to be unprofessional. In both cases, repressed feelings are influencing the perception capabilities of the individuals involved.

■ *Rationalization.* People rationalize by finding a convincing reason for otherwise unacceptable behavior. This behavior is explained in terms of "good intentions," whereas the real reasons remain unknown to themselves and/or others. Rationalization is the most common defense mechanism. The following are typical examples: A high school student explains he could not do his algebra homework because he had to babysit for his sick sister. A secretary reports that she could not finish typing a report because the telephones were particularly busy. A salesman says he did not meet his sales quota because his entertainment budget was too small.

✓

Implications for Management

1. Be aware that perception is a highly individual matter. Do not assume that other people will "see" things your way. Particularly watch out for confusion when normative perception is involved. People often come to vastly different conclusions after being exposed to essentially the same stimuli.

2. Do not let your perceptions trick you into making snap judgments about people. Just like the old woman/young woman drawing, things are not always as they first seem. Remember that your mind tends to get less flexible as it becomes tied to past experiences. Slow down in your evaluations and take a second look!

3. Be aware of your own psychological set. What are your preconceived ideas about

the way things are at the office? About the way employees think and act? The stronger your expectations, the more likely you will miss the mark. Remember, "what you see depends on what you are set to see."

4. Watch out for stereotyping. The manager who stereotypes quickly loses the respect of his or her employees. Statements such as "Accountants never see the whole picture" are easy to make but hard to prove. Intelligent listeners will resent your simplistic interpretation of reality.

5. When supervising others, be very careful about the halo effect. Do you always give Sam the choice assignments because he's a nice guy? Stop and think, does he actually do the best job?

6. Take stock of your system of defense mechanisms. Which tend to interfere with effective communication? Are you apt to be defensive when anyone criticizes you? Do you avoid unpleasant situations until they build into a crisis? Realistically appraising your reactions will help you communicate better.

SELF-DISCLOSURE

One of the often overlooked prerequisites for successful communication is the ability comfortably to engage in self-disclosure, which is

Self-disclosure defined

. . . a process, whereby an individual voluntarily shares information in a personal way, about his or her "self" that cannot be discovered through other sources.[4]

Often our natural tendency is to say as little as possible about ourselves and to keep all knowledge and feelings inside.

Reasons for Nondisclosure

The tendency for nondisclosure can commonly be tied to a host of reasons. The following examines four of the most typical.

First, childhood experiences have proven to many people that "silence is golden" and one's place is to be "seen but not heard." Many individuals act out these life scripts by being unassertive, passive adults. "Mind your own business" is the guideline for their behavior.

Second, through past experience and observation, many people have reached the conclusion that knowledge is power, especially in an organizational setting. "Keep them guessing" is their motto. At the same time, however, they try to learn as much as possible about other people. This obviously gives them an advantage in the competitive arena in which they choose to play.

Third, and perhaps more serious, many individuals are so wrapped up in their personal problems that they are unable to share thoughts and emotions with others. A person caught in this frame of mind usually needs professional help to unravel the problem.

Finally, related to the above reasons but without their serious psychological complications, many people see themselves as loners. They truly enjoy the independence of doing things on their own and being responsible for their personal success or failure. High achievers are typical of this group in that they love nothing better than to work on their own, bearing the ultimate responsibility for their efforts. To these individuals, self-disclosure by others is important because they want concrete feedback on how their efforts are being perceived.

For reasons such as these, large numbers of people have grown up without feeling the need for self-disclosure. Have you? Find out by answering the questions for Self-Assessment Quiz 4.1.

Self-Disclosure and You

Perhaps the major reason why people practice nondisclosure is to prevent themselves from being hurt. Jouard explains the typical cause and effect:

> We camouflage our true being before others to protect ourselves against criticism or rejection. This protection comes at a steep price. When we are not truly known by the other people in our lives, we are misunderstood. When we are misunderstood, especially by family and friends, we join the "lonely crowd." Worse, when we succeed in hiding our being from others, we tend to lose touch with our real selves.[5]

Many people hide their feelings.

How many times do you go through life playing the various roles of spouse, parent, employee, and/or group member without really letting your feelings show or without knowing the other people with whom you deal? A story by John Powell illustrates the remorse of wishing we had known how others felt. He was in the hospital and had just witnessed the death of his father. Afterward, his mother told him how proud his father had been of him and how much he had loved him. As Powell started to cry, he realized,

> I'm not crying because my father is dead. I'm crying because my father never told me that he was proud of me. He never told me that he loved me. Of course, I was expected to know these things. I was expected to know the great part I played in his life and the great part I occupied in his heart, but he never told me.[6]

Many of us have shared this experience in reverse. A loved one has died and we think of all the things we wish we had said. Of course, this can be a productive lesson if we reform our behavior in dealing with others, but too often it is a fleeting, but traumatic, part of our grief and we go back to our entrenched ways of keeping others at arm's distance. In our culture men in particular find it difficult to be open in their feelings. Again, this is a result of past programming. Boys are supposed to be tough. "Take it like a man" and "Don't be a sissy" are hard to erase.

The Johari Window

One of the most effective models for describing self-disclosure and its importance to interpersonal and group communication is the Johari window. Created by Joseph Luft and Harry Ingham[7] the model has a great deal of practical value, allowing us to look at how we relate to other people. This model, shown in Figure 4.4 consists of four areas, or quadrants, which together reveal all possible combinations of knowledge people possess.

SELF-ASSESSMENT QUIZ 4.1

How Do You Feel about Self-Disclosure?

Respond to each of the following by placing a true (T) or false (F) answer before it.

_____ 1. It is usually better not to tell your employees more than they need to know to do their specific job. This minimizes office politics and gossip.

_____ 2. A manager who is open and friendly with his or her employees is often seen as a soft touch.

_____ 3. Open sharing of goals and attitudes by the manager will help the employee to be more productive.

_____ 4. A manager should be careful how much personal information he or she discloses to employees. Workers who know you too well tend to lose respect for you as a supervisor.

_____ 5. In personal relations, the more open and candid you can be, the healthier the relationship will be.

_____ 6. Openness in personal relationships is fine, but sometimes it's better to maintain your privacy on certain issues. You can avoid a lot of disagreements this way.

_____ 7. If telling others what you really think, especially when you know they do not agree, is very uncomfortable for you unless the topic is of extreme importance, you should not mention it.

_____ 8. Consistently disclosing information to employees at work is extremely time consuming. The motivational value that might be gained is lost due to the amount of time and effort consumed in the process.

_____ 9. Being open with others and sharing things with them, like everything else, has its time and place. For example, it is appropriate at home with family and friends. However, it has no place in the office.

_____ 10. Being open and sharing with superiors at work can cause many problems. They may see you as pushy or egotistical, if not a little eccentric in your behavior.

An interpretation of this quiz can be found at the back of the book.

Quadrant 1 consists of all behavior, knowledge, attitudes, and values that a person recognizes in himself or herself and that is also known to others. This area is the location of self-disclosure behaviors and open communication. There are no secrets here. For this reason, it is commonly called the open area.[8]

The Johari window described

The second quadrant is called the "blind area." Material in this area is not known to oneself but is generally recognized by other people. This is an uncomfortable area to be in. Here, people know something about you that, for whatever reasons, you do not know.

Figure 4.4

The Johari window.

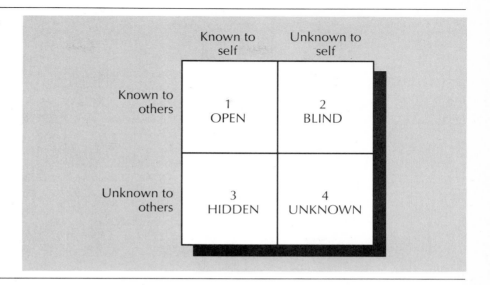

The third area is known as the "hidden quadrant." This is the opposite of Quadrant 2 in that we now have knowledge of ourselves that we do not share with others. This area is the one most affected by the lack of self-disclosure of which we spoke earlier.

The fourth and final quadrant is the "unknown area." In this quadrant is information unknown both to oneself and to others. All data in this part of the window are secret, although it sometimes can be released by temporary inducements such as drugs, hypnosis, illness, or a high fever. Projective personality instruments such as the Rorschach and the Thematic Apperception Test also can bring about a new awareness of self.

Practicing Self-Disclosure

In the 1980s open communication became synonymous with effective management. *In Search of Excellence* authors Thomas Peters and Robert Waterman found that excellent companies are characterized by intense attention to communication. Here is an example of what they found:

> We've had the opportunity to observe senior managers in action at both companies. The difference between their behavior and that of their competitors is nothing short of astonishing. They make a presentation, and then the screaming and shouting begin. The questions are unabashed; the flow is free; everyone is involved. Nobody hesitates to cut off the chairman, the president, a board member.[9]

Studies show open communication is very important.

William Ouchi, author of the best-selling *Theory Z*, also spoke of open communication and participation in a trusting environment as the key to effective organizations.[10] Similarly, Harold Geneen, CEO of International Telephone and Telegraph, instituted a corporatewide system of open communication because

The free flow of information is so essential in any business enterprise, for it is only by knowing the realities of one's own business and the realities of the marketplace that management can hope to manage satisfactorily.[11]

Organizational research, however, shows that most organizations still have managers who do not follow open communication and self-disclosure. In 1982 the International Association of Business Communicators, along with Towers, Perrin, Forster, and Crosby, surveyed 32,000 employees in 26 U.S. and Canadian organizations to assess the effectiveness of organizational communication. Some of their relevant findings included:

Only about 50 percent of the 32,000 respondents rated their organizations' communications as "candid and accurate," and 67.8 percent felt that "official communication doesn't tell the full story."[12]

A study by Allan Frank revealed another alarming aspect of the lack of candor found in organizations. From his sample of 416 members of the American Society for Training and Development came the following conclusion:

The most striking statistic . . . is the 78 percent probability that subordinates will not give feedback to their superiors concerning superiors' mistakes. In terms of Luft's Johari Window, managers' blind areas are likely to balloon in such situations to the point where managers are "flying blind."[13]

What benefits can managers expect from practicing self-disclosure? First, the effective use of self-disclosure should improve the communication climate by reducing secrecy and nurturing confrontation and mutual problem solving. (For guidelines on what constitutes effective self-disclosure read the box, "Guidelines for Meaningful Self-Disclosure.") Second, the manager will enhance cooperative teamwork if he or she sets a good example in lessening the feeling of information ownership. Third, the effective manager not only engages in self-disclosure and sets a good example, but also invites feedback which will help employees have a better understanding of their manager. Finally, the manager and employee will ultimately begin to have more mutual understanding and respect for each other as human beings and as co-workers.

Implications for Management

1. Remember that most people are not accustomed to engaging in self-disclosure. They are afraid that the revelation of any information may be used against them. They prefer to remain relatively closed-lipped.

2. Be aware that the two most important dimensions of the Johari Window may well be exposure and feedback. Unless you can get subordinates to open up and be candid in their expression of feelings and feel comfortable requesting feedback from others, they are likely to communicate from defensive positions.

Guidelines for Meaningful Self-Disclosure

Most managers need to increase their self-disclosure. As this is done, the openness of the communication climate in the organization as a whole increases and further stimulates more openness. Yet, not all situations are equally appropriate for self-disclosure. The following guidelines can help you along the way.

1. DO self-disclose when the situation under discussion is of mutual concern. DON'T self-disclose when the situation is extraneous to the other person. Letting your employees know how badly you want the department to meet quota next month is both honest and goal-directed. Discussing with them how happy you are that another department is way off their quota makes you look petty and unprofessional. Your people will wonder what you say to others about them!

2. DO self-disclose when the sharing of one's concerns and feelings is reciprocal. DON'T self-disclose beyond some first attempts when the other person is closed-mouthed and obviously unreceptive. Few things are more rewarding than sharing with others who respond in an equally open fashion. Few things are more sobering than baring your soul to someone who fixes you with an icy stare and says nothing.

3. DO proceed slowly to engage in self-disclosure with a group that is not used to open communication. DON'T plunge full steam ahead into self-disclosure in an attempt to change the organizational environment quickly. Approaching self-disclosure in a step-by-step, gentle fashion will provide lasting benefits for your communication system. If you move too fast, however, any short-term gains (and there may be none!) will likely be of a temporary nature. Worse than this, actual harm may occur to your image, and people may become more closed-mouthed than ever.

4. DO self-disclose when the information is timely and pertinent to the current situation. DON'T self-disclose when your information is stale or irrelevant to the situation at hand. It is appropriate that the manager openly discuss either good or bad employee performance or behavior *when* it happens. Too often, however, we gloss over incidents, especially unpleasant ones, and then at a later crisis point blurt out all our past observations. This practice, called "gunnysacking," typically occurs at performance appraisal time. Understandably, it usually results in employee puzzlement and resentment.

5. DO self-disclose within a confronting, problem-solving environment. DON'T self-disclose in an effort to emotionally dump your frustrations on others.

SOURCE: Jane Whitney Gibson and Richard M. Hodgetts, "Self-Disclosure. A Neglected Management Skill," *IEEE Transactions on Professional Communication*, Vol. PC-28, No. 3, September 1985, p. 45.

3. Keep in mind that as research reveals, most people are reluctant to engage in self-disclosure. Managers can work to change this attitude by exhibiting a healthy, enlarged, open quadrant 1 and promoting a trusting, sharing work environment. Fostering an open first quadrant will serve to lessen information ownership and increase problem solving and cooperative teamwork.

4. When talking with and counseling subordinates, think about which quadrant of the Johari Window they use most often. If you find them to be reluctant to increase exposure or feedback, discuss the matter with them. A large portion of open communication is a function of management's ability to convince subordinates that the willingness to be open and honest will not result in their being punished for candor. As long as the personnel believe anything they say can and will be used against them, they will prefer to operate in quadrant 3, showing only that face which they want everyone else to see. Research results show that managers alter their exposure and feedback to fit the individual(s) with whom they are speaking. This practice can be overcome only if people feel there is no danger in engaging in open communication. Your role in helping to create this environment is important.

LANGUAGE

After perception, language is the second greatest barrier to interpersonal communication. Words are often misleading and misunderstood. The term *biannually*, for example, is understood by some to mean twice a year and by others once every other year. A new employee who learned at orientation that pay raises are given biannually might expect her first raise in six months only to discover she has a year and a half left to wait.

Language problems can be divided into two areas: semantics and general semantics. *Semantics* refers to the study of meaning, whereas *general semantics* postulates a theory of behavior based on language patterns.

Semantics

Words are symbols. Communication problems result when the words we use evoke the wrong symbol or picture in the mind of the listener. This problem can easily be understood when we realize that each of the 500 most frequently used words has, on the average, 28 different meanings.[14] Even when we are lucky enough to communicate the appropriate definition of our word, understanding can still be elusive.

The most important lesson to be learned from semantics is that *meaning is not in words; meaning is in people*.

Meanings are in people not words.

If meaning is a private affair, so that my experience in a situation cannot be the same as your experience in that situation, by what magic can we ever get meaning from one to the other of us? *We must accept the disheartening probability that neither of us can ever completely grasp a meaning as the other has experienced it*. However, we can achieve some degree of success in our speech communication efforts if we create messages and stimuli that relate as much as possible to the nature of the other person's experience and response system.[15]

Multiple meanings of words are not the only kinds of semantic problems. Four other major ones are contextual meanings, regional variations, word coinage, and confusion of inferences for facts.

CONTEXTUAL MEANINGS In an attempt to distinguish among the multiple meanings of words, we have to look at the context of the situation. One word can mean different things depending on its context. You can *charge* a purchase at the department store. I can *charge* my battery if it is dead. He might get a *charge* out of a joke. Her *charge* might be a nine-year-old boy. The policeman *charges* the suspect with a felony. Custer probably should not have *charged* into the Little Big Horn.

The verbal context, that is, the position of the "word" among other words, is not the only context to keep in mind. A nonverbal context and an environmental context must also be considered. The nonverbal context is particularly important when it contradicts the verbal context. For example, if John is telling Mary, "I really like you a lot" while slamming his hand on the desk and looking angry, the nonverbal context will signal that the verbal context is not to be believed.

The environmental context refers to the external and internal conditions under which the statement is made. External factors include such things as noise, timing, and place. For example, if John says to Mary, "Would you like to have something to eat?" at 5 P.M. after just picking her up, she will likely take it as an invitation to dinner. If this same statement is made coming out of a movie at 11 P.M., Mary will likely think it is an invitation for a snack.

Internal environmental conditions include such things as being tired, bored, impatient, or angry. Other internal barriers are lack of interest and lack of fundamental knowledge. Lack of knowledge occurs when either the speaker or the listener does not have the same knowledge necessary to place the message in the proper context. A physicist talking about nuclear reactors at a social party will likely be met with yawns or puzzlement, unless the other guests are part of the peer group.

REGIONAL VARIATIONS Regional variations in speech are another reason for misunderstanding. In a country as big as the United States, variations in speech patterns abound. Pronunciation patterns alone can make communication difficult. The Southern "you all" has irritated many a Yankee, whereas the Bostonian practice of dropping r's has puzzled many westerners.

Meaning can differ with region. Individual words or names for things vary from place to place. When ordering a Coca Cola in New England, you ask for a tonic; in other parts of the Northeast, a soda; and in some other regions of the country, a pop.

New words are always being coined. **WORD COINAGE** Coining new words is an ongoing process. It explains why the English of today varies so greatly from the Middle English of our high school classics. It explains why *thee* and *thou* have been replaced by *you*. In terms of barriers to communication, the category of word coinage can be further divided into jargon, buzz words, and revised meanings.

■ *Jargon*. Unshared vocabulary can be a problem in communication transactions. One specific reason is the use of professional jargon. Psychologists become used to speaking about neurotics and anal-compulsives; organizational development consultants speak of OB Mod and change agents; lawyers casually mention writs and torts; computer specialists speak of bytes and floppy disks. Words like these can be totally perplexing to the uninitiated.

■ *Buzz words*. Each generation seems to have its own popularized, special words. "Cool," "hip," and "laid back" were all popular cliches of the 1960s and 1970s and are all now passé. In the early 1980s, some of the common buzz words were I can *relate to* . . . , Are you *into* . . . , I try to *facilitate* . . . , The *bottom-line* is . . . , You've got to *bite the bullet*, I'd like to *share* my thoughts on. . . .

At the time this chapter was written, the current favorite buzz words of teenagers were "grody," "to the max," and "awesome," whatever they mean.

■ *Revised meanings*. Revised meanings occur when standardly used words acquire new meanings over time. Some examples are listed below.

ORIGINAL WORD	"NEW" MEANING
juice	electricity, liquor
bread	money
sauce	liquor
acid	LSD
speed	PCP
dog	ugly woman
pig	policeman
fuzz	policeman
fox	attractive woman

Being sensitive to jargon, buzz words, and revised meanings helps us to avoid misunderstanding. We should also be careful when using these words, being sure that we have a "shared vocabulary" with those with whom we are trying to communicate.

CONFUSION OF INFERENCES FOR FACTS "New Jersey is a state consisting of 7,836 square miles" is a fact. "New Jersey is a small state" is an inference. "Small" compared to what? Texas? Rhode Island? New York?

Confusing facts and inferences is one of the most dangerous pitfalls to effective

An inference is an assumption.

communication. An *inference* is an assumption based, at least partially, on fact.

Recall that an inference is based on the known but makes a statement about the unknown. These statements can be based on a wide background of related experiences, or they may be made on gut feeling alone. Sometimes they are close to the truth; more often they are not. Hayakawa tells us:

We may *infer* from the handsomeness of a woman's clothes her wealth or social position; we may *infer* from the character of the ruins the origin of the fire that destroyed the building; we may *infer* from a man's calloused hands the nature of his occupation; we may *infer* from a senator's vote on an armaments bill his attitude toward Russia; we may *infer* from a halo on an unexposed photographic plate that it has been in the vicinity of radioactive materials; we may *infer* from the noise an engine makes the conditions of the connecting rods.[16]

An inference can be valid or invalid depending on whether a logical connection exists between the facts and the conclusion. For example, note the following.

- Fact: The weatherman said it will rain tomorrow.

- Invalid Inference: It will rain tomorrow.

- Valid Inference: It may rain tomorrow.

- Fact: New Jersey is a state consisting of 7,836 square miles.

- Fact: Rhode Island is a state consisting of 1,214 square miles.

- Invalid Inference: New Jersey and Rhode Island are small states.

- Valid Inference: Rhode Island is smaller in square miles than New Jersey.

Much of the information we receive or send is in the form of inferences. The danger is in mistaking inference for fact or in assuming that your listener can tell one from another. Test your understanding of inferences by taking Self-Assessment Quiz 4.2.

SELF-ASSESSMENT QUIZ 4.2

Fact or Inference?

Directions: Label each sentence F for fact or I for inference.

_____ 1. "I am 23 years old."

_____ 2. "Ralph makes a good salary as a mechanic."

_____ 3. "Roger ran 5 miles after work today."

_____ 4. "My husband always comes home early."

_____ 5. "Sally liked my chocolate cake."

_____ 6. "She is a middle-aged woman."

_____ 7. "It snowed yesterday in Philadelphia."

_____ 8. "It's going to be a sunny day tomorrow."

_____ 9. "In the winter, the water is too cold for swimming."

_____ 10. "Sam always does well on his math test."

Answers are in the Answer section at the back of the book.

General Semantics

General semantics is a field apart from semantics. It was first developed by a Polish mathematician and engineer Alfred Korzbyski whose work, *Science and Sanity*,[17] presented the basic tenets of the field. In essence, general semantics deals with the relationship between language and how people think and act. Some of the underlying principles of the field are the following:

1. Human beings differ from other animals in that they are "timebinders." This means they can accumulate knowledge and pass it down from one generation to another. Language is the element that makes this growth possible.

2. Just as a map of New York City is not New York City, a word is not the object it names. General semanticists believe that we too often confuse the symbol with the real thing.

3. Inherent in the concept of language is the phenomenon of abstraction. "The notion of abstracting states simply that there are limitations upon our ability to 'see' the world around us, and that our language restricts us even further when we attempt to communicate our observations to others." [18]

Some underlying principles of general semantics

ABSTRACTION   Abstraction consists of verbal and preverbal components. Table 4.1 provides an illustration.

The verbal level is an abstraction of what we are able to see at the preverbal level. Our eye sees a dog; we call it Rover (specific), a dog (more abstract), or an animal (still more abstract). Yet to a listener who does not know Rover, the word "Rover" may be hopelessly abstract. The listener may think of a vicious Doberman pinscher, a tiny yapping Chihuahua, or a loveable, medium-sized, russet-colored cocker spaniel. The

Table 4.1

	LEVELS OF ABSTRACTION	
		Etc.
Verbal	Inference level # 2	"Animal"
	Inference level #1	"Dog"
	Labeling	"Rover"
Preverbal	Macroscopic level	What one can see with the naked eye
	Microscopic level	What one can see with a microscope
	Submicroscopic levels	What lies beneath microscopic vision

symbol, Rover, cannot only "look" different to the listener but also evoke different feelings in terms of such things as size, color, and temperament.

At the first inference level, we have replaced the word "Rover" with the word "dog" and Rover has lost his identity in so doing. At inference level 2, his "dogness" is lost in the word animal. The Etc. at the top of Table 4.1 shows that abstraction can always be continued another step. Hatch and Myers present the key lesson about abstraction.

There are degrees of abstraction.

> Messages are more interesting and communicate better when they avoid high-level abstraction and use specific, concrete words instead. Specific words create vivid images in the audience's mind and are more likely to stimulate the audience to visualize your message. . . . It's almost impossible to be too specific: of course, some objects are more abstract than others, and it would be impractical to rule out all higher level abstractions. But in most cases, try to use the most specific word you can. Specific is vivid.[19]

To better understand the problems inherent in the area of general semantics, we must examine extensional versus intensional meanings and emotion-laden words.

EXTENSIONAL VERSUS INTENSIONAL MEANINGS What lessons can be gained from this knowledge of general semantics and especially that of abstraction? One is that we should be aware that words have extensional as well as intensional meaning. Extensional meaning refers to the concrete meaning of a word, a meaning that can be verified by observation of the physical item. Intensional meaning is the abstract image the word produces in the mind of the listener.

Words are used in many different ways.

If a person had an extensional orientation, he or she tends to examine the territory first and then draw the map or pick the right word. "Extensional knowledge operates on perceptions and uses names, statistics and descriptions from actual observation which can be verified by someone else.[20] Those who have intensional orientations, however, tend to find the word first and then "see" the reality in terms of the already-arrived-at map. Extensional and intensional orientations are roughly equivalent to deductive and inductive logic, respectively.

> *Deductive logic* might be described as reasoning from the general to the particular, from a given premise to its necessary conclusion (i.e., from generalizations to names). *Inductive logic* is reasoning from a part to a whole, from the individual to the universal (i.e., from names to generalizations).[21]

EMOTION-LADEN WORDS Emotion-laden words often serve to halt communication. This emotional or affective use of symbols can result in complete loss of meaning. Name-calling is a particularly negative use of affective symbols. What difference in meaning do you attach to the following three words describing the same person?

policeman   cop   pig

Both the second and third words are more emotionally laden than the first one.

Many names about peoples' preferences and beliefs are used in damaging ways to interrupt communication. These include sentences such as "He/she is a ———— (note that deceptive use of the word "is"):

rabble rouser	high roller
radical	fast tracker
fascist	loose woman

right winger	Casanova
communist	playboy
capitalist	wheeler-dealer
Holy Roller	troublemaker
drunk	weak sister
junkie	sissy
Jesus freak	feminist
Moonie	male chauvinist pig

Two other categories of affective symbols, and ones that are particularly likely to arouse emotions, are ethnic slurs and name-calling that refer to the physical characteristics of people, such as "skinny" or "weakling." Racial and ethnic humor is also potentially emotion-laden. Some people think such humor is funny; others are very offended. The best guideline is to avoid all humor that may be offensive.

There is another group of misleading words, however, which differs dramatically from these negative symbols. They are *euphemisms* or positively loaded words, which cast the territory in a particularly good light. A used car, for example, might be called a "pre-owned vehicle." Here are some examples:

NEUTRAL WORD	EUPHEMISM
little girl	little angel
house that needs work	handyman's special
car	luxury automobile
economy class	special coach
juvenile delinquent	misguided youth
bathroom	powder room
lot on a canal	waterfront property

A final category of emotion-laden words is sexist language. Consider the following excerpt from a memo a supervisor wrote to the personnel department regarding a job vacancy.

The successful applicant will have experience in telephone sales. He should be willing to work long hours, be aggressive, and have a wife who won't mind him working evenings and Saturdays.

This supervisor clearly is not acknowledging the fact that there may be female applicants! Here's another example. Why are the following objectives so often applied to males versus females?

MALE CHARACTERISTICS	FEMALE CHARACTERISTICS
Aggressive	Pushy
Inquisitive	Nosey
Articulate	Talkative
Forceful	Domineering

Sexist stereotyping is rooted deeply in American business culture. Men are men and women are girls. Men are managers; women are secretaries. Men give the orders; women make the coffee. Today these stereotypes are rapidly crumbling, but the sexist language that supports them is harder to eradicate.

Sexist and other emotion-laden words are an unnecessary barrier to communication. We should attempt to eliminate them from our own speech as well as to identify these words in others' speech. Once they have been analyzed or anticipated, we can greatly diminish their emotional effect on us.

Implications for Management

1. Keep in mind that managers should strive to develop an extensional orientation. Examine the territory first, before picking your words. Above all, remember that the map is not the territory it represents. Also remember that maps tend to change more slowly than territories. Be sure that you are not using old words to describe new situations.

2. Remember that words do not contain meaning; meaning is defined by the individual. Do not assume that *your* meaning has been received. Use feedback to find out if you have been understood.

3. Watch out how you use the word "is." It can be a culprit unless used as a helping verb such as "She is preparing the agenda." Often the word "is" can be used to equate two things as if they were one and the same. "Anne is crazy." "Winter is cold," "Brian is a Republican." The listener evaluates Anne, winter, and Brian based on his or her abstract understanding of the words crazy, cold, and Republican.

4. Avoid the "allness" trap, that is, the tendency to speak as if you are saying all there is to be said about a subject. Add "etc." to all messages to remind yourself and your employees that one can never say *all* that is to be said about any subject.

5. Avoid fixed conclusions about people, places, things, and events by being aware of dates. Your employee benefit plan in 1975 might have produced rave reviews from the employees. But employee benefits of 1991 are not employee benefits of 1975 any more than ABC Co., 1991 is identical to ABC Co., 1975. Everything changes. To often we freeze our evaluations not only of things, but also of employees, judging them to be the way we found them years ago. Employee, 1991 is not employee, 1975.

6. When defining words, try to use examples. Producing Rover, or at least a picture of Rover, is far more accurately descriptive than trying to use words to portray the dog. The old adage "a picture is worth 1,000 words" is true. In a business setting, take the following example. Have your personnel director spend some time on the line, directly observing the tasks to be done. He or she will then have a much better understanding of the job to be filled. Likewise, encourage the personnel department to take applicants for a tour of the plant. Let them see the job and talk to other employees. Realistic job expectations result in decreased turnover!

7. Understand the difference between directive and informative statements. Informative statements simply describe things as they are whereas directive statements relate to how things should be, tentative maps of developing territories. A statement such as "Managers in our company are loyal and hardworking" is really a goal statement

(directive) and not an actual account of how every single manager acts. Yet, if we accept that statement as informative, we will be puzzled and in conflict when we meet Joe who constantly talks badly about the company.

8. Beware of the two-value orientation, that is, things are either good or bad, right or wrong, hot or cold. Instead of assuming a statement to be true or false, one should assume it has a truth value somewhere between 0 and 100 percent. Do not tell your employee she did a good job; tell her exactly what was good about it. Do not force people into yes or no answers; you'll get better information and make more effective decisions if you recognize the great continuum between yes and no, good and bad.

C A S E   I N   P O I N T

Revisited

You should have noted a number of things in your analysis. One is that there was a perception problem when the boss told Julie that she should get to the file as soon as she could. Quite obviously, "as soon as you can" meant one thing to Julie and quite another to her boss. This problem helps illustrate the comment in the case regarding "meanings are not in words; they are in the people who use them."

A second point you should have noted is that Julie used selective perception. She filtered the boss's message to fit her code of past experiences. When someone says "as soon as you can" she interprets this literally. For his part, the boss should have been more careful of the way he communicated with her. She was new on the job and trying very hard to make a good impression; he should have anticipated her response.

A third point relates to Julie's resignation. She quit because she could not reach her five-year objectives if she stayed with Highland. She had already fallen too far behind. It is the boss who has caused this situation because he allowed the halo effect to prejudice his evaluation. If he had looked at her overall work performance, Julie would have gotten a much higher rating.

You may have included other parts of the case in your analysis, but these three points should have been observed.

YOU BE THE CONSULTANT

The Unexpected Promotion

When George Saunderson graduated from State University he had 15 job offers. They ranged from a sales position with a large manufacturing firm to a lower-level management job with a nationally known finance/insurance company. He eventually settled on the management job and began working there a year ago.

George was put through a rigorous management training program. During this time he learned the company's philosophy of management and how he was expected to act. The firm put a great deal of emphasis on management efficiency. "We are in the financial planning business," the president told the trainees, "and that means low profit margins. This industry has become so competitive that in many cases we are forced to sell insurance programs at a loss with the hope that during the second year the policies are in force we can raise our rates and recover our money. This is why efficiency is so important to us. Every dollar we can cut from our operating expenses means another pretax dollar at the bottom of the income statement."

When the training program was completed, George was assigned to one of the largest branches. Located in a major metropolitan area, the branch actually occupied an entire building. Over 7,500 employees worked here. Every day George would marvel at the stream of people flocking into the building, jamming the lobby, and cramming the elevators. The same thing happened on the way out at quitting time.

Throughout the day every floor bustled with busy people. Well, maybe not busy but at least taking up space. This is one of the first things that struck George during his first week in the building. It seemed to him that a lot of the people were either sitting around talking to their neighbors or doing things unrelated to their job. For example, on one occasion he walked past a group of young men who were in the midst of starting a football pool. Apparently everyone in the department was in on the betting since he heard reference made to "selling everyone in the department only one ticket." On another occasion George had to go to the photocopying room to have some copies made of a financial report. Three full-time people were running the operation. One was writing down what the individual wanted copied; the second was feeding originals into the machine and collating the output; the third was simply watching what was going on. George assumed that the third person was the manager. George waited in line behind a young man who had five books in his arms. When it was the man's turn, he told the photocopy person, "I'd like two copies of each, please." As they were placed on the table, George was able to see their titles. They were all from the best-seller list. The conversation that ensued between the young man and the photocopy employee indicated that one of the upper-level executives had bought these five books at a nearby bookstore and intended to return them after they had been copied. In this way the individual would get a refund and still have a personal copy.

On another occasion George was sent across town on an errand. Realizing that he could not get back to the office before noon, he decided to drop into a small nearby restaurant for a fast bite to eat. Just as his order was placed on the table, he looked up and saw some of the middle managers from his department come through the front door. Since it was 11:50 A.M., he guessed that they must have left the office around 11:30 A.M. and caught a cab. The room was beginning to fill up rapidly; George figured that they could not possibly eat and be back to the office before 1:45 P.M. On the way out, he stopped by their table to say hello. They greeted him warmly, asked him to join them and, when they found that he had already eaten, offered him an invitation for the next day. "We always come over here for lunch," one of them told him. "Join us in the lobby at 11:30 A.M. tomorrow. We leave from there." George smiled and said goodbye.

Later that day there was a meeting of senior-level managers and five of the new trainees who had started with the firm at the same time as George. The purpose of the meeting was to determine ways of increasing efficiency in the branch. The manager talked in general terms, but, based on what he said, George believed that the types of things he had been seeing around the building were not going unnoticed by management. Apparently there was going to be a crackdown. The manager asked each of the trainees to come up with a handful of suggestions that could be used to improve efficiency. "We know that you have not been around here a long time," he said. "Nevertheless, sometimes it's those who are new on the scene who are best able to pick out the problems that exist. Keep your eyes open and write down any changes you think would help improve efficiency. Then send them to me in a memo. We'll meet again in two weeks. My secretary will send you a followup reminder as well as the room for the meeting." With that, the meeting adjourned.

Over the next three days, George thought long and hard as to what he should put into his memo. When he constructed the final draft, he recommended three things: (1) all managers are to closely monitor lunch times; no one is to leave before noon and everyone is to be back by 1:00 P.M.; (b) excessive socializing on company time is to be discouraged and there is to be no wagering of any type, including football pools; and (c) all managers are to look over their operations to see where they can reduce the number of current personnel. Accompanying the memo, George sent along a personal note to the manager in which he outlined some of the practices he had witnessed on the job. The next day there was a brief note in the mail. It was from the manager and read, "I have received your report and read it with great interest. You will be hearing from me." George was delighted. During the next two days he had the opportunity to talk to some of his friends who had been at the meeting with him. None had completed their memo to the manager. However, from what he could glean from the conversations, none had any cost savings ideas similar to his.

On Friday afternoon his own manager called George in and talked about how delighted the company was with George's performance. He even made reference to the memo, which he said was "being circulated to some of the key managers in the branch." He then told George that the company was so happy with his performance that he was being promoted to a job at one of the other major branches. It was located in a major city 1,200 miles away. The promotion called for a salary raise of 16 percent, a cost-of-living adjustment, and what his boss called "increased responsibility." George is scheduled to leave by the middle of next week, assuming that he will accept the promotion. If he does not, he can stay in his current job, but his boss has "strongly recommended" that he take the promotion. "It's in your own best interest, if you know what I mean," he told George. Somehow George is not sure whether this is a promotion or a means of getting him out of the way. He has checked around and found that none of the other trainees has been offered a promotion.

On his way home that evening, George thought about what had happened. He then called up one of his best friends in the company. The individual concluded the conversation by jokingly telling George, "Now you know what is meant by kicking troublemakers upstairs." George sat back in his chair and stared out the window. He was not sure whether what he did was right or wrong. More to the point, he is concerned about how he should act on his new assignment.

Assume that you are George's personal friend. Evaluate his actions on the job. How might he have misinterpreted the desire of management to increase efficiency. Why are they sending him to another office? What is their logic? How can George find out if he is being promoted on the basis of merit or simply kicked upstairs? In what way would an understanding of the material in this chapter be of value to him? Explain.

Key Points in This Chapter

1. Perception is a person's view of reality. This reality can be either sensory or normative. The normative is more likely to cause communication breakdown.

2. There are three main elements of perception. figure/ground, selective perception, and psychological set. All three can influence the way people "see" things.

3. Numerous factors make perception more difficult. Four of the most important are the steel trap syndrome, stereotyping, the halo effect, and defense mechanisms. Included in defense mechanisms are projection, denial, repression, and rationalization.

4. Self-disclosure is a process whereby an individual voluntarily shares information about his or her self that cannot be discovered through other sources.

5. One way of examining the area of self-disclosure is through the use of the Johari Window model. The model has four quadrants that measure information that is known or unknown both to oneself and to others.

6. Semantics refers to the study of word meanings. Since words are symbols, their meanings can differ depending on the person who is receiving the message. This is why communication experts are so quick to point out that meanings are not in words but in people.

7. In addition to the multiple meanings of words, four other major semantic problems are contextual meanings, regional variations, word coinage, and confusion of inferences for facts. Examples of each were provided in the chapter.

8. General semantics is a field apart from semantics. It deals with the relationship between language and how people think and act. The lessons to be learned from a knowledge of general semantics relate to abstraction. One should be aware that words have both extensional and intensional meaning. There are emotion-laden words and words with revised meanings.

Questions for Discussion and Analysis

1. In your own words, what is meant by the term *perception*? How does sensory perception differ from normative perception? Explain.

2. There are three critical elements of perception. What does this statement mean?

3. In what way is each of the following a perception problem: the steel trap syndrome, stereotyping, the halo effect? Be sure to describe each in your answer.

4. How do each of the following defense mechanisms work: projection, denial, repression, rationalization? In your answer, be sure to describe each.

5. What are some important guidelines that managers should keep in mind in overcoming perception barriers to communication? Identify and discuss three.

6. What is meant by the term *self-disclosure*? What value does it have to effective communication? Explain.

7. In your own words, what is the Johari Window? Explain with an illustration.

8. What is meant by the term *semantics*? How does this term differ from *general semantics*?

9. Three of the major semantic problems are contextual meanings, regional variations, and word coinage. What does this statement mean? Be sure to include a discussion of the three problems in your answer.

10. What is an inference? How does it differ from a fact? In what way are inferences semantic problems? Explain.

11. What are some of the underlying principles of the field of general semantics? Identify and discuss three of them.

12. How does racial humor or sexist language interfere with effective communication?

Exercises

1. Role play the following situation. The President, Mr. Simms, of ABC Corporation is telling the Sales Manager, Mrs. Locke, that the figures show sales have been slowly but steadily declining each month for the last six months. As different people play Mrs. Locke, have each show a different defense mechanism: projection, denial, rationalization, and repression.

2. Study the following figure for two minutes and count the total number of triangles. When time is called, go around the room quickly and have each student call out the "answer." Was there much variation in the numbers called? Do you think this variation would be smaller if more time was given? What type of perception does this illustrate?

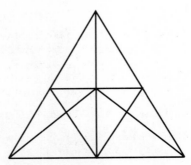

3. In groups of three to five people, discuss the pros and cons of self-disclosure. Take turns revealing something to the group that they have probably not known about you. Start with disclosing something nonthreatening and very comfortable to you such as your favorite TV program and why you like it. In rounds, progress to topics that are more personal such as your attitude toward group exercises and having to work with other students or your views on life after death or abortion.

References

1. Gregory Moorhead and Ricky W. Griffin, *Organizational Behavior* (Boston: Houghton Mifflin Co., 1989), p. 61.

2. For further information on age stereotyping, see Benson Rosen and Thomas H. Jerdee, *Older Employees: New Roles for Valued Resources* (Homewood, Ill.: Dow Jones-Irwin, 1985); Susan R. Rhodes, "Age-Related Differences in Work Attitudes and Behavior: A Review and Conceptual Analysis," *Psychological Bulletin*, March 1983, pp. 238–267; and David A. Waldman and Bruce J. Avolio, "A Meta-Analysis of Age Differences in Job Performance," *Journal of Applied Psychology*, February 1986, p. 36.

3. Peter Dubno, "Attitudes Toward Women Executives: A Longitudinal Approach," *Academy of Management Journal*, March 1985, pp. 235–239.

4. Stewart L. Tubbs, *A Systems Approach to Small Group Interaction*, 3rd ed. (Reading, Mass.: Addison-Wesley, 1988), p. 224.

5. Sidney Jouard, *The Transparent Self*, revised ed. (New York: Van Nostrand Reinhold, 1971). p. viii.

6. John Powell, *The Secret of Staying in Love* (Niles, Ill.: Argus Communications, 1974), p. 68.

7. Joseph Luft, *Of Human Interaction* (Palo Alto, Calif.: National Press Books, 1969), p. 5.

8. Joseph Luft, *Group Processes: An Introduction to Group Dynamics* (Palo Alto, Calif.: Mayfield, 1970), p. 11.

9. Thomas J. Peters and Robert H. Waterman, Jr., *In Search of Excellence* (New York: Harper & Row, 1982).

10. William G. Ouchi, *Theory Z: How American Business Can Meet the Japanese Challenge.* (New York: Avon Books, 1982).

11. Harold Geneen, *Managing* (New York: Doubleday & Co., 1984).

12. June Foehrenbach and Karn Rosenberg, "How Are We Doing?" *Journal of Communication Management*, 1982, pp. 3–11.

13. Allan D. Frank, "Can Water Flow Uphill?" *Training and Development Journal*, May 1984, pp. 118–128.

14. Philip V. Lewis, *Organizational Communication: The Essence of Effective Management*, 3rd ed. (Columbus, Ohio: Grid, 1987), p. 118.

15. John W. Keltner, *Interpersonal Speech Communication: Elements and Structures* (Belmont, Calif.: Wadsworth, 1970), p. 69.

16. S. I. Hayakawa, *Language in Thought and Action (New York: Harcourt, Brace & Co., 1949), p. 42.*

17. Alfred Korzbyski, *Science and Sanity* (Baltimore, Md.: Institute for General Semantics, 1980).

18. Richard W. Budd, "General Semantics: An Approach to Human Communication," in R. W. Budd and B. D. Ruben, editors, *Approaches to Human Communications* (Rochelle Park, N.J.: Hayden Book, 1972), p. 102.

19. *Ibid.*, p. 112.

20. Lewis, *Op. cit.*, p. 120.

21. *Ibid.*, p. 121.

Annotated Bibliography

Alston, William P., *Philosophy of Language* (Englewood Cliffs, N.J.: Prentice-Hall, 1964).
> This is a short and sweet examination of the concept of meaning. Alston provides a thorough examination of how meanings are derived and the problems inherent in their derivations.

Hayakawa, S. I., *Language in Thought and Action* (New York: Harcourt, Brace & Co., 1949).
> Hayakawa is one of the foremost writers in the field of semantics. This is a classic text on the subject — easily understood and full of practical advice on how to avoid the pitfalls found in semantics.

Keltner, John W., *Interpersonal Speech Communication: Elements and Structures* (Belmont, Calif.: Wadsworth, 1970).
> An in-depth treatment of speech communication. At least half of this book focuses on how to make interpersonal speech more effective. This book is well documented and easy to read.

Luft, Joseph, *Of Human Interaction* (Palo Alto, Calif.: National Press Books, 1969).
> This is the single most important work on the Johari Window, easily read and understood. Luft guides the reader through his underlying assumptions, the basic Johari Window model, and applications for interpersonal intragroup and intergroup dynamics.

Luft, Joseph, *Group Processes: An Introduction to Group Dynamics* (Palo Alto, Calif.: Mayfield, 1970).

This general treatise on group dynamics is well organized and flowing. It contains a well-written chapter on the Johari Window, which will give the casual reader a sufficient overview of the subject.

Nierenberg, Gerald I., and Henry H. Calero, *Meta-Talk (New York: Simon & Schuster, 1981).*

Nierenberg and Calero are an unbeatable combination for informative, entertaining communication books. Like their earlier *How to Read a Person Like a Book*, this offering outlines their ideas and gives lots of interesting examples. The elements of *Meta-Talk* are further used to examine a variety of interpersonal relationships.

CHAPTER 5

Nonverbal Communication

"'Tis not my speeches that you do mislike, But 'tis my presence that doth trouble ye."

Shakespeare, *King Henry VI*

Objectives

1. To understand the critical importance of nonverbal communication in the transfer of meanings.

2. To study the role of body language such as facial expressions, gestures, and posture in communicating with others.

3. To investigate the rapidly expanding area of proxemics by studying the role and importance of physical space and its relationship to the communication process.

4. To become familiar with the area of paralanguage, the vocal aspect of nonverbal behavior that relates not what is said but how it is said.

5. To be able to apply the ideas and concepts presented here to real-life cases, which are provided at the end of the chapter.

C A S E   I N   P O I N T

Now It's Up to Them

Jack Dalton's father could hardly wait for Jack to graduate from college. The company was expanding very rapidly, and Jack's dad was finding himself spending more and more time on the road. He wanted someone at headquarters whom he could count on to get things done. Oh sure, there was a large staff of personnel responsible for the day-to-day work, but he and Jack had always been very close; he felt that with Jack around things would go well while he was gone. All of this was six months ago.

Since assuming the position of assistant to the president, Jack has been given a number of important tasks by his father. One of these is to serve as a link with the workers in the production area. These workers have been quite vocal in the past; when they were displeased with something down on the line, they would not hesitate to come up to the president's office and tell him. Jack has been filling in for his father in dealing with this kind of problem.

Two months ago Jack announced that he was establishing an open-door policy for all employees. A week later he received a visit from three production workers. They were quite angry. Jack immediately invited them in, came around from his large desk, and joined them at the conference table located on the side of the room. They talked for over 30 minutes about problems on the line. During this period Jack was continually interrupted by his secretary, and on three occasions he had to go back to his desk to handle long-distance calls. He also found himself becoming irritated by some of the comments made by the workers and, at one point, caught himself becoming angry as he addressed one of their questions. Never-

theless, when the meeting was over Jack promised to look into their complaints and see what could be done. When they left, he jotted down some random notes about the meeting and instructed his secretary to have their foreman drop by for a visit the next morning.

During this visit Jack learned that the workers felt he had not paid much attention to their complaints. He also learned that they were not very impressed by his open-door policy. This upset Jack because he felt he had done his very best. How could the workers expect him to stop everything just because they had dropped by for a visit? He felt he had listened to their problems and had been able to carry on business at the same time. The foreman agreed that Jack was right, but also told Jack not to expect the production workers to take advantage of his open-door policy in the future. This really made Jack angry, and he closed his discussion with the foreman by saying, "Well, I don't know what those guys are crying about now, but I've done my part. Now it's up to them if they want this open-door policy to succeed. Heaven knows I've tried."

Based on your first impressions from the case, what did Jack do wrong? What are the workers upset about? Concentrate your attention not on what you think Jack might have said, but on his nonverbal behavior. Make a list of the things he did that turned off the workers. Be as complete as possible. Then put this list aside until you have finished reading the chapter. We will return to it at that point.

INTRODUCTION

Many times you may walk away from a conversation convinced that you have made a very good impression and can expect positive results. Other times just the opposite may be true. Yet when you think back over the conversation at a later time, you may find yourself unable to identify those words that caused your impressions to form. You may have then become uneasy and wondered if you read something into the conversation that was not there. Only then do you begin to focus on the signs and signals the other person was sending you, apart from the actual verbal content of the conversation. Perhaps you felt good because of an especially warm handshake or the fact that the other person stepped around the desk and sat on the couch next to you during the meeting. On the other hand, perhaps something in the tone of the individual's voice warned you that all was not well or you remembered that the person did not smile the way he or she normally does at the end of a meeting.

These and countless other examples help present the phenomenon of *nonverbal communication*. Individuals unfamiliar with nonverbal cues and actions are often ineffective communicators; those familiar with such phenomena are typically quite effective in communication. In this chapter you are going to learn what nonverbal communication is all about and how to be more effective in using it. Particular attention will be directed to the three major components of nonverbal communication:

1. *Kinesics*. Also called body language, which includes facial expressions, gestures, and posture.

2. *Proxemics*. The study of the use of space and its relationship to the communication process.

3. *Paralanguage*. The vocal aspect of nonverbal behavior, which relates not what is said but how it is said.

We will begin our study of nonverbal communication with the subject of kinesics.

KINESICS

Of all the areas of nonverbal communication, kinesics has received the greatest amount of attention. Coined by Ray Birdwhistell in 1955, *kinesics* refers to *the study of communication* through body movement and facial expression. The underlying assumptions that encompass the area of kinesics are the following:

1. Body movements and facial expressions transfer meaning to others. This meaning is just as important as verbal activity.

Underlying assumptions regarding kinesics

2. These body movements and facial expressions can be regarded as forming patterns and can be interpreted according to their context.

3. On a larger scale, these body movements and facial expressions must be analyzed in light of the culture and environment surrounding the sender.

The study of kinesics became popular in 1971 with the publication of Julius Fast's *Body Language*.[1] Since then general public awareness of this important area of communication has increased dramatically. Explore your understanding of kinesics by taking Self-Assessment Quiz 5.1.

SELF-ASSESSMENT QUIZ 5.1

What Do You Know About Kinesics?

Answer each of the following true/false statements by underlining your response.

1. The hands are the most important conveyor of kinesic messages. True/False

2. When an employer scolds an employee while smiling at the same time, the employee is apt to take the scolding very seriously. True/False

3. A single body movement may be correctly interpreted in most cases, providing the interpreter is a serious student of nonverbal behavior. True/False

4. Unlike verbal behavior, most sign language is universally understood; for example, the up and down shaking of the head always means "yes." True/False

5. Like verbal behavior, nonverbal behavior is usually calculated and therefore is not truly indicative of a person's attitude. True/False

6. Men tend to engage in more eye contact than women. True/False

7. Being on time is an important value the world over. True/False

8. Men tend to be more adept at facial signaling of emotions than do women. True/False

9. A very relaxed posture means that the person likes his or her companion a great deal. True/False

10. A smiling face is the best indicator of approval and/or happiness. True/False

Answers are in the Answer section at the back of the book.

You can improve your understanding of kinesics with a careful study of the material to follow. Attention is devoted to the four most important subcategories of kinesics: the face, the eyes, posture, and gesture. The following examines each.

The Face

The face is the most important nonverbal communicator.

In terms of relative kinesic importance, the face carries the most communication messages. In their studies, Ekman and Friesen found the face to be the best nonverbal conveyor (and the feet/legs the worst) in terms of "sending capacity" as measured by visibility, average transmission time, and the actual number of signals it can portray.[2] They discovered three component parts of the face that were capable of independent movement: "the brow/forehead; the eyes/lids, and root of the nose; and the lower face, including the cheeks, mouth, most of the nose, and chin."[3] As a result, they identified six universal facial expressions that can be combined into 33 modifications or blends. The six are happiness, sadness, surprise, fear, anger, and disgust.

There are six universal facial expressions.

Although Ekman and Friesen believe these six facial expressions are universal, variations can occur in two ways. First, basic emotions are produced by different events in different cultures. Second, different cultures impose emotional restraint or masks to hold back true feelings. The cultural contradictions of nonverbal behavior were clearly illustrated in the dealings one of the authors had with a Harvard MBA from India. She was most uneasy when every time they engaged in a conversation, her Indian friend would punctuate her best comments with a shake of his head from side to side. How could he be so rude, and all the while smiling? It was some time before she realized that the positive up and down nod of our culture is expressed as a side-to-side gesture in India!

A related study by Buck and colleagues examined the communication of feeling through facial expression. Interestingly, female pairs were significantly more successful in the correct sending and receiving of emotional signals than were male pairs. Buck postulates that this may be a result of our societal insistence on boys "being men" and hiding or masking their feelings.[4]

Smiles mean many things.

When we go from the overall face to specific facial features, we discover that the eyes and the smile have received the most attention by students of kinesics. Smiles, for example, can be broad or narrow, open or closed, wholehearted, polite, or phony. They convey everything from embarrassment to an apology. A smile at the lips, however, can be betrayed by unsmiling eyes. Recent research by Ekman, Friesen, and O'Sullivan confirmed "subtle differences among forms of smiling when subjects were truthful and when they lied about pleasant feelings."[5] In fact, research shows that *nonverbal leakage*, the involuntary expression of emotion, is particularly evident in the face and that careful observation of the face provides clues of deceptive behavior.

The Eyes

Of all body expressions, the eyes seem to hold the most significance. To gauge a person's mood, probe the individual's eyes. The successful manager knows at first hand the power carried by effective eye contact. Studies and observations have also provided insights about eye contact useful for effective management, including:

1. Speakers tend to perceive those who look at them as being more instrumental to their goals than those who do not.

2. Eye contact is generally perceived as a sign of honesty, interest, openness, and confidence.

3. People will avoid eye contact when embarrassed or nervous.

Generalities about eye contact

4. Eye contact is easier to maintain at a social or public distance than at closer range.

5. If distance is held constant, an employee will have less eye contact with others of a higher status and more eye contact with subordinates.

6. Eye contact varies by culture. Some Latin American cultures, for example, teach children not to look directly in the face of an adult. A newly appointed overseas American manager could erroneously interpret this as a deceptive signal.

Recent research shows that eye movements may indicate whether an individual is telling the truth. Thus observation of the eyes may provide clues to deception. The St.

Paul Insurance companies have been teaching their people to use the "eye truth test" in loss prevention programs and in handling claims. The test is based on the belief that when people are recalling information, they glance to the left. When they are thinking of a new thought, they glance to the right. Thus, the theory goes, if clients are looking to the right, they may be trying to deceive or stall the listener. Note, however, that the same research shows that some lefthanders reverse this pattern of eye movement.[6]

Posture

Posture is something we hear a great deal about. From the time we are very young we are given advice regarding posture, such as stand up straight, hold in your stomach, keep your shoulders back, and walk erect.

Posture provides immediate clues about the attitude of the bearer. For example, it can portray confidence, superiority, aggressiveness, fear, anxiety, or rejection to name but six characteristics. Consider the way a salesperson tries to close a sale, leaning forward and assuming a command presence. Or what about a boss who reprimands a subordinate by standing up and leaning over the desk, peering down at the employee? These individuals use posture to put them in charge.

Other people use posture to indicate that they are confident. A person who sits back expansively, arm over the back of the chair and legs stretched out in front is telling everyone else that he or she is quite confident. Another strides to the front of the room, ready to assume the podium; the individual is telling us, "I'm ready to go."

Still other times posture reveals a person to be insecure or nervous. Slouching, biting one's nails, looking down, or hanging back in the crowd are all examples of individuals who are not feeling sure of themselves.

Researchers have provided us with some interesting empirically based information on posture. Mehrabian, for example, conceptualized a two-dimensional model for studying posture. The two variables were (1) immediacy, which indicates nearness, for example, forward leaning of the body, possible touching, and eye contact, and (2) relaxation, which indicates a loose posture. His studies produced the following findings in relation to immediacy and relaxation:

1. A high degree of relaxation generally indicates a lack of respect or a dislike of the other person, whereas a lesser degree of relaxation indicates a liking for the person.

Findings regarding posture

2. An absence of relaxation or increased postural tension occurs when a person addresses someone of higher status.

3. Subjects are more "immediate" with people they like than with those they dislike.

4. Relaxation is also related to status, with higher status people being generally more relaxed than their lower status counterparts.[7]

A last word regarding posture — a shift in posture means that something is happening. It does not always tell us what is happening. To find that out we must study the shift in relation to the entire incident.

INTERNATIONAL COMMUNICATION

Cultural Assimilators Can Be Good Business

Nonverbal communication can be particularly troublesome for Americans because they are accustomed to explicit language. When Americans set objectives, for example, they typically relate what is to be accomplished, by when, and how progress will be measured. This approach is not universal, however. In the Far East, for example, communication is often heavily implicit. Individuals are not directly told what they are to do. The manager offers general suggestions and guidance, and it is up to the individual to decide how to follow through on this advice.

As international trade increases and nations begin to buy and sell more goods throughout the world, communication training will gain in importance. Americans are going to have to learn how to be more implicit when dealing with Orientals, and business people from the Far East are going to have to learn to be more explicit when dealing with Occidentals. How can this objective be accomplished? One way that is proving particularly helpful is the cultural assimilator.

A cultural assimilator is a programmed learning technique that is designed to expose members of one culture to some of the basic concepts, attitudes, role perceptions, customs, and values of another culture. This commonly is done through the development of a series of written situations in which the manager is confronted with a typical day-to-day problem or occurrence and is asked how he or she would handle the matter. Frequently, a series of alternative answers are provided, and the individual is asked to choose the best one. If the choice is correct, the person then goes on to the next episode. If the response is incorrect, the trainee is asked to reread the episode and choose another response. In this way, the manager receives a wealth of experience in the local customs and culture.

How effective are cultural assimilators? Research shows that, properly designed, these program learning kits are extremely useful training tools. They can be worth thousands of dollars to the organization because the managers are more effective in conducting business in their overseas environment. No wonder so many enterprises are now developing assimilators and requiring managers to use them prior to leaving for their new assignments. It's just good business.

Gesture

Gestural language ties together the facial expressions and posture. Like the aforementioned areas, gestures are culturally bound and very susceptible to misinterpretation by the casual observer. The serious student, however, will find a wealth of useful information in the gestures of a sender.

Ekman and Friesen have also shed light on the area of gestures, distinguishing among four types of nonverbal behavior — emblems, adaptors, regulators, and illustrators.[8] These four cover the subject of gestures quite completely.

Emblems are those signals given specific meaning by the culture at large and therefore readily understood. In America, the "O.K." sign is an emblem as is the waving of a good-bye hand or the "quiet sign" of the index finger in front of pursed lips.

Adaptors are primary learned movements related to satisfying bodily needs and desires. In adulthood, these motions are triggered by a long-ago memory flash. Adaptors are almost completely habitual and automatic. Learned behavior such as the method of using a knife and fork is an example of an adaptor.

Regulators are gestures that serve to control the conversation. Forward leaning encourages the speaker; fidgeting in the chair does not. A pat on the back encourages a child to air his or her story; a clenched fist does not.

Illustrators are those actions most closely related to what is being said and serve to complement or extend the words. Pointing while telling someone how to find the exit is an example.

Types of gestures include emblems, adaptors, regulators, and illustrators.

✓

Implications for Management

1. Remember that many people use kinesics to help clarify power relationships among employees. Informal opinion leaders may be found, for example, by observing who talks to whom and who interrupts whom.

2. Observe gesture clusters and how well they fit in with facial expressions and verbal messages. When verbal messages differ, give primary consideration to the nonverbal messages.

3. When observing gestures, do not generalize or jump to conclusions too quickly. Remember the impact of cultural context and pay special attention to the nonverbal habits of your foreign-born and -raised employees.

4. Keep in mind that observation of kinesics is hard work. You need to educate your eye and to exercise your new awareness. If you do, the payoff can be great!

PROXEMICS

Proxemics deals with the way we use physical space and what that use says about us. The importance of this concept is easily illustrated. Think of how you would feel if you walked into class midway through the term and someone was sitting in "your" seat. Your space is being invaded, and it is likely that you will find yourself becoming angry and/or nervous. This is because space, and its use, have communicative importance. They say something to us and we respond in some way. Today, the field of proxemics is receiving increased attention in the quest for a deeper understanding of human behavior.

Humans are territorial animals.

Proxemics was founded as a field of study in the late 1950s by Edward T. Hall and is based on the concept of the human being as a territorial animal.[9] Territoriality is best defined as the behavior of laying claim to an area and defending it against intruders. The concept of the human being as an instinctively territorial animal has not been easy for everyone to accept. In 1966 Robert Ardrey came out strongly behind this belief in his provocative book, *The Territorial Imperative*, saying the human species "is as much a territorial animal as is a mockingbird" . . . "and [this] behavior is as much a mark of our species as is the shape of a human thigh bone."[10] Others such as George N. Gordon have disagreed, attributing territorial display to behavior learned from the culture.[11] Perhaps the best explanation is that of Hall himself who saw territoriality as instinctual but modified by cultural expressions. Without any doubt, space needs do vary by culture or subculture. For example, think of what a city dweller would consider a large "yard" as compared to what a suburban commuter or a rural farmer would think.

We do not know how much space a person needs, but it does seem to differ by culture. Cultures can be divided into two categories: contact and noncontact. Contact cultures interact at a closer range, engage in more touching and eye contact, and face each other more directly. The United States' general culture falls in the noncontact category.[12] Whichever the case, however, persons seek to extend their territory in many ways and thus to attain power or intimacy.

To experiment with this concept of territoriality, Mehrabian suggests the following.

> Sometime if you care to risk an episode of unpleasantness, appropriate the favorite lounge chair of a friend whom you visit at home. Note her reactions, if she reveals them and any change in her behavior toward you. I suggest this as an informal experiment that could be fun to discuss afterward with a good (and forgiving) friend, but I would be very reluctant to suggest such recurrent experiments with your family at home.[13]

Space equates with power.

How we handle space, guard our zones, and intrude on another person's zones is an integral part of how we relate to other people and to the world. People often use space to say things they are unaware of and as we become aware of this language, we become more skillful in both personal and professional relations. One of the most effective ways of studying proxemics is in terms of (1) *fixed feature space* (permanent structures and boundaries), (2) *semifixed feature space* (moveable objects), and (3) *informal feature space* (spatial relationships between people).[14] Before reading on, however, take the Self-Assessment Quiz 5.2 to learn how territorial you are. You may be surprised.

Fixed Feature Space

Have you ever noticed how the design of a room or building can make you feel either comfortable or uneasy? Hospitals, for example, are generally disliked, not only because of their association with illness, but because of their built-in impersonality and coldness.

SELF-ASSESSMENT QUIZ 5.2

How Territorial Are You?

Instructions: Circle a number for each question as follows:
        1 = strongly agree, 2 = agree, 3 = not sure,
        4 = disagree, 5 = strongly disagree

1. If I arrive at my office/desk and find a co-worker sitting in my chair, I am annoyed if he/she does not at least offer to get up immediately.

        1 . . . . . 2 . . . . 3 . . . . . 4 5

2. I do not like anyone to remove anything from my desk or office without asking me first.

        1 . . . . . 2 . . . . . 3 . . . . . 4 5

3. If a stranger puts his/her hand on my shoulder when talking to me, I feel uncomfortable.

        1 . . . . . 2 . . . . . 3 . . . . . 4 5

4. If my suit jacket is lying on the back of a chair in my office and a co-worker comes in and chooses to sit in that chair, I feel she/he should ask to move my jacket or choose another chair.

        1 . . . . . 2 . . . . . 3 . . . . . 4 5

5. If I enter a classroom and "reserve" a chair with a notebook, I am annoyed or offended to find upon my return my book moved and someone sitting in "my seat."

        1 . . . . . 2 . . . . . 3 . . . . . 4 5

6. If a person who is not a close friend of mine gets within a foot from my face to talk to me, I will back off or uncomfortably stand my ground.

        1 . . . . . 2 . . . . . 3 . . . . . 4 5

7. I do not like strangers walking across my lawn.

        1 . . . . . 2 . . . . . 3 . . . . . 4 5

8. If I lived in an apartment, I would not want the landlord to let himself into the apartment for any reason without my permission.

        1 . . . . . 2 . . . . 3 . . . . . 4 5

9. I do not like my friends or family borrowing my clothes without asking me first.

        1 . . . . . 2 . . . . . 3 . . . . . 4 5

10. If I notice someone staring at me in a restaurant, I become annoyed or uncomfortable.

        1 . . . . . 2 . . . . . 3 . . . . . 4 5

Add up the numbers you have circled for all ten statements. The interpretation of this Self-Assessment Quiz is provided at the back of the book.

Fixed feature space refers specifically to those permanent components of a building or room such as walls, ceilings, partitions, and windows. A modern production department where workbenches are surrounded by half partitions severely limits the communication among workers. What may be gained in productivity can be lost through a lower quality of working life and subsequent dissatisfaction by employees.

Partitions create fixed feature space.

Windows can also play an important part in fixed feature space. In many cases, an employee who has an office without a window will consider it a promotion to get an office with a window. The same situation in reverse can add up to a demotivated employee unless compensated for in other ways — a larger, though inside, office nearer the boss.

Windows also create fixed feature space.

Semifixed Feature Space

In the area of semifixed feature space, considerable communication versatility can be witnessed by merely observing layouts of various rooms.

Consider the difference in communication dynamics in a traditional classroom with rows of students facing a teacher as opposed to a classroom where the students form a circle. Without doubt, the circle arrangement makes it easier to communicate but harder to take a nap!

Classroom seating is an example of semifixed feature space.

Office layout is another area where special arrangements can speak louder than words. Layouts (a) and (b) in Figure 5.1 are fairly traditional and formal. The existence of the desk between the resident officeholder and the visitor creates a barrier and an atmosphere of formality. The desk guarantees that conversations will take place at a safe distance. Layouts (c) and (d) are more participative and almost always create a more favorable environment for open communication.

Office layout has many implications.

Informal Feature Space

Although both fixed feature space and semifixed feature space have led to considerable study in office arrangement and decor, this last division, informal feature space, has been most widely pursued. This is the space that we carry around with us — the invisible boundary we put between ourselves and others.

Edward Hall has helped shed additional light on informal feature space, which he described in terms of four personal space categories.[15]

The first zone is *intimate distance*, where you are within 18 inches of your partner. This distance is reserved for the closest of family and friends, although cultural variations do exist. For example, contact of this sort is cause for awkwardness and uneasiness between two men in the United States but acceptable in Arab cultures. This same intimate zone for a man and a woman can be natural on one hand but embarrassing on the other; for example, between husband and wife it is natural, but between a man and a woman pressed together in a crowded subway or elevator it is not.

Intimate distance is up to 18 inches.

The second zone is *personal distance* and can range from 1½ to 4 feet. This closeness is usually reserved for friends and family. How the other person reacts to your intrusion into his or her personal space can be nonverbal language telling you whether you are being accepted or rejected.

Personal distance is 1½ to 4 feet.

Figure 5.1

Office layout.

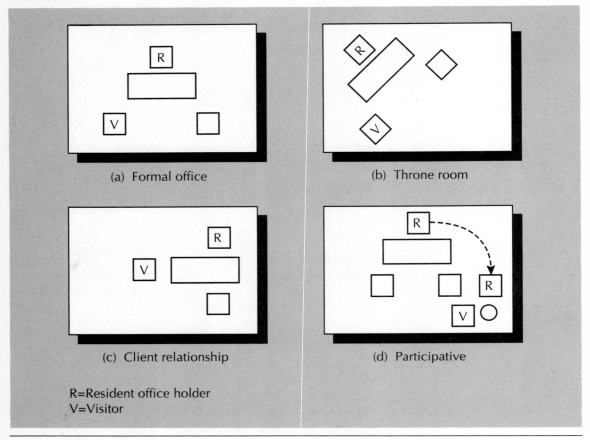

(a) Formal office

(b) Throne room

(c) Client relationship

(d) Participative

R=Resident office holder
V=Visitor

Social distance is 4 to 12 feet.

The third zone is *social distance* and is usually from 4 to 12 feet. It is the distance at which most business is transacted. Although this distance can indicate closeness or acceptance, it can also be just far enough to satisfy one's protective instincts.

Public distance is 12 to 25 feet.

The fourth zone is *public distance*, which extends from about 12 to 25 feet. It is about the farthest distance at which we can effectively communicate face to face, but it seems ideally suited to student–teacher lectures or speechmaking.

Space ownership also includes such items as briefcases, books, and purses. (Consider your answers to Questions 2 and 9 on Quiz 5-2 as evidence of this.) In short, how we handle space, guard our zones, and intrude on another's area is an integral part of how we see ourselves in relation to them. It is also an important part of communication.

Status Messages

Control of space
indicates status.

The study of proxemics also extends into the area of status messages. In organizations in particular, continuous fighting for status takes place. The control of space typically constitutes an extension of one's personal power and territorial ownership. Invasion of territory can be an important indicator of rank: how far a person will intrude into another's office, for example, and how the officeholder reacts are related to relative status. Other research findings include:

1. The size of offices exemplifies that "more is better than less." Status can often be determined by how much space a person occupies.

Some status
research findings

2. "Private and higher" is better than "public and lower" space. Corner offices on the higher floors are usually reserved for top officials. Then come center offices with windows, offices without windows, partitioned cubicles, and then open space. A smaller, private office near the president may be more desirable, however, than a larger office in a more remote location.[16]

3. Persons enjoying higher status will have more territory than others.

4. Persons with higher status have more protection of their territory than those of lower status.

5. The more status a person has, the easier it is for him or her to invade the territory of someone with lower status.[17]

**Implications
for
Management**

1. Be aware that territoriality is a strong individual motive.

2. Realize that in many cases the motive is largely automatic and perhaps subconscious.

3. Respect your employee's space. Don't barge in and interrupt a person who is speaking to another or someone who is on the telephone. If an immediate audience is needed, make yourself seen and back off until the person can gracefully finish. An immediate interruption makes your employee look unimportant to whomever he or she is speaking. (On the other hand, if you want to place stress on someone, maintain the high ground. Sit on the edge of your desk or stand over them. Use the technique of invading personal space to make the person nervous — a good approach to employ in ending a lingering meeting!)

4. If it is teamwork you want, minimize the status difference between yourself and your employees. When individuals show up for a meeting in your office (unless it is a discipline talk) be informal. Get up from your desk and come around and sit on the other side with your people.

5. Respect the privacy of your employees' office or desk. Some bosses make a habit of going through desks, in-boxes, and mail that do not belong to them. This causes resentment. Ask for what you want. Employees know you are the boss; you should not have to coerce anyone.

These assumptions, of course, are relative. Although a large corner office may seem desirable, a smaller private one next to the "top dog" may actually be better. All aspects have to be considered. An interesting example of space and location as status indicators was noted in a *Newsweek* article on the resignation of Secretary of State Alexander Haig.

According to some Haig partisans, the secretary's enemies in the White House tried to hasten the process (his resignation) by deliberately offending the touchy Haig on Reagan's recent European trip — consigning him to the back of Air Force One and assigning him hotel rooms far away from the boss.[18]

PARALANGUAGE

Paralanguage deals with how things are said.

The last of the three major components of nonverbal communication, paralanguage, is most closely associated with verbal communication. Whereas language deals with what is said, paralanguage deals with how things are said. How often do you remember either being told or hearing the phrase, "It's not what you say, but how you say it"? The most harmless phrase or sentence can be given the opposite shade of meaning by varying the intensity or intonation with which it is spoken.

Emphasis affects meaning.

Take the simple sentence, "It's two o'clock." A radio announcer might be simply stating the time, "It's two o'clock." A listener who had no idea how late it was might react with surprise, "It's two o'clock!" Another who doubts the accuracy of the radio announcer might react with doubt, "It's two o'clock?" A person reiterating the lateness of the hour because something has not been done on time might react in anger, "It's two o'clock!" These same words could be used with many additional nuances such as delight, secrecy, sadness, teasing, and so on. At times, we have to do no more than vary the inflection of the voice to produce these changes. We might also vary the loudness, the pitch, the rate, the rhythm, the voice tension, or the pacing to produce still new meanings.

Loudness also affects meaning.

Loudness, for example, can do much by way of producing a listener effect. As a person raises his or her voice, we automatically assume the individual is excited or angry. Different levels of voice volume are the norm for different cultures. It has been established, for example, that in Latin cultures, the noise level is generally higher than what might be acceptable in parts of our society, and our noise level would be considered too soft in South American countries. Many North Americans, for example, find it difficult to concentrate on what a person is saying once the volume has gone beyond what we consider comfortable, and we focus instead on the emotions that the speaker is perceived as projecting. At other times, pure volume can be offensive. Fast relates an incident in a restaurant where two wealthy-looking women were talking so loudly that everyone in the restaurant could overhear their conversation. The interpretation he gave was that the women considered everyone else very unimportant (as nonpersons), and therefore they spoke with no concern of being overheard.[19] Here, pure volume portrayed an impression of the speakers—whether accurate or not.

Rate of speech can also tell us about a speaker's mood or intentions. Charismatic speakers are normally forceful, louder than the norm, and quick in their speech pattern. We are pulled along as much by the feeling they stir within us as by what they say.

Rate of speech is important.

Collectively, these qualities of speech identify what paralanguage is, and without doubt the whole area adds much to the communicated language we perceive. Paralanguage is, in fact, an additional component to the verbal content of expressed messages. Along with kinesics and proxemics, paralanguage provides us audible clues regarding the intent and feelings of communicators.

Is paralinguistic content more important than verbal content? Some studies report that it is at least as important (if not more so) in selected circumstances.[20] Generally, the voice often gives us a better picture of how the person really feels than the actual words he or she is saying in his speech.

Paralanguage can be as important as verbal content.

Sometimes paralinguistic communication is unintentional; in other cases it is entirely premeditated. During the Nixon administration, Robert J. McCloskey, a member of the State Department, was known to communicate different messages by varying this nonverbal voice quality. He was specifically known to have three different ways of saying, "I would not speculate." *Newsweek* explained it this way:

Paralanguage may be unintentional or premeditated.

> Spoken without accent, it means the Department does not know for sure; emphasis on the "I" means "I would not, but you may," and with some assurance; the accent on speculate means that the questioner's premise is probably wrong.[21]

Perhaps the most complete study of the area of paralanguage has been provided by Trager. He divides paralanguage into four parts: voice qualities, vocal qualifiers, vocal characteristics, and vocal segregates.[22]

Vocal qualities include such factors as volume of the voice, rate of speech, and pitch. When any of these is used in amounts different from the norm, the listener rapidly perceives that something unusual is occurring. Voice quality is of two different kinds—those that are not controllable by the speaker and those that are. Some of the components that are outside the speaker's control are inborn, such as the size of the tongue, shape of the palate, and size of the vocal chords. Other uncontrollable components of voice quality, not innate, include such things as temporary medical problems that may arise from a common cold, laryngitis, tonsilitis, or other physical developments. Controllable components are more useful in drawing conclusions regarding what the speaker is saying. Much of this segment of voice quality is derived from the adjustment in muscular tensions maintained by the speaker while talking. These tensions are acquired through learning but can become such a habit that the speaker is not aware of them. Although there is no basis for a scientific classification of voice qualities, they can be described by adjectives such as cracked, dry, flat, hollow, husky, raucous, thin, melodious, or tinny.

Voice qualities can be voluntary or involuntary.

Voice qualifiers refer to temporary variants in pitch and volume.

Vocal qualifiers refer to temporary variations in pitch and volume as well as the emphasis we put on certain words, which changes the meaning of the entire sentence. Our earlier example of "It's two o'clock" is an excellent illustration.

Vocal characteristics are verbal conditions such as laughing, coughing, throat clearing, and sighing. Laughing often gives special significance to what the speaker is saying. It can mean that the individual does not take what he or she is saying too seriously; it can mean that the person is simply relating a story that is personally amusing; or it may simply mean that the speaker is nervous or ill at ease. Coughing or throat clearing can, of course, be physically caused. However, it can also signal a desire for attention or nervousness. Sighing, on the other hand, often shows a dissatisfaction, sadness, or weariness about what is being communicated.

Vocal characteristics give special significance to what is being said.

Vocal segregates consist of filler words.

Vocal segregates consist of those little filler words we use when we are unsure, stalling for time, or nervous. Words such as "ah," "er," "um," as well as silent pauses, all tell the listener something, regardless of the fact that they seem to be content-free.

Implications for Management

1. Be aware that your tone of voice — your total paralinguistic delivery — is at least as important as what you actually say.

2. Remember that lack of congruence between verbal and paralinguistic content will result in your words being doubted and perhaps even disregarded.

3. Observe carefully the paralinguistic content of your employees' conversations with you. It will help you judge their openness, honesty, and intentions. You may easily remember their words later, but without paralinguistic observations you will often come to the wrong conclusions.

4. Monitor your own use of paralanguage. Much of your nonverbal delivery is unconscious. You may be delivering messages that you do not wish to send. Be sure this is not the case.

C A S E   I N   P O I N T

Revisited

Having completed a study of nonverbal communication, let us now return to the case at the beginning of the chapter. First, before reading on, review your list of things that Jack did wrong. Based on the chapter information, revise your list appropriately. Remember to be as complete as possible.

What kinds of things did Jack do wrong? Basically, your list should contain three major areas re-

lated to kinesics, proxemics, and paralanguage. In the section on kinesics, you should have noted some of the nonverbal messages Jack was sending with his body language. (Remember how he became angry during the discussion? Can you guess how he must have looked and acted at this point?) In the section on proxemics, did you notice the way Jack's office was laid out and how he continued to move from the conference table back to the desk? He was abandoning the warm, participative atmosphere of the conference setup and going back to the superior-subordinate atmosphere as soon as other business called. Quite obviously, Jack was as interested in other matters as he was in listening to the production workers.

Finally, in the section on paralanguage, you should have noted some points regarding how Jack must have sounded (voice intonation, emphasis, loudness, etc.) as he responded and talked to the workers. Remember that what he said is not the important issue; how he said it is!

YOU BE THE CONSULTANT

Too Big for Her Britches?

When Margaret Muldoon was hired as head of art and design for a large publishing house, she was delighted. The staff was highly motivated and extremely talented. During the previous year they had won 19 awards for excellence in design and layout. One of their books, a chemistry text for the high school market, was awarded first prize in a nationwide textbook art exhibit.

Margaret's boss has told her to concentrate her attention on the actual management of business-related matters and to leave the art and design work to her people. As a result, most of Margaret's day is spent dealing with budgets, office expenses, and annual plans designed to coordinate the art and design work with actual book production.

About a month after Margaret took over she realized that a great deal of her time was being spent on the telephone or pouring over paperwork. The amount of reading was astounding, and it seemed that from the time she came in until she went home, her desk was cluttered with reports, forms, memos, and other associated materials. During this time she also began to see that she was having trouble working at top speed. At first Margaret thought it might be her unfamiliarity with the company's policies and procedures and the need to learn shortcuts for dealing with paperwork. However, she eventually came to realize that she was spending a large amount of her time (about an hour a day) listening to conversations in the room and being distracted by ringing telephones.

Margaret's desk was located at the far end of a very large room. Although the desk was bigger than that of anyone else in the department and she had far more floor space allocated to her, everyone was within earshot of each other. The previous department head, who had been with the firm for over 40 years, had determined that all the personnel should be located in one geographic area. She also decided that if there were no separate offices or barriers dividing the employees, it would be possible to communicate more openly and easily. The result would be higher morale and esprit de corps.

After giving the matter some thought, Margaret decided to change this arrangement. Since all the other people in the department were directly involved in art and design, they could all remain where they were. Their ability to interrelate and communicate with each other would not be affected at all. Margaret went to her boss and asked to have an office built for her. Using just the space she had currently, workers could erect walls on both sides, thereby screening out all the noise in her end of the room. This would allow her to work at a faster pace. Inside the office would be two windows, so she would not feel trapped in the corner. In addition, Margaret intended to personally tell all the workers in the department that they should feel free to interrupt her at any time. She would be in the office working on financial and management matters but would always have time for art and design problems. Moreover, the weekly meetings she had with the three main people in the department would be held in her office so as to give these meetings an aura of increased importance. Margaret was having a conference desk and some chairs put into the room. All of this sounded just great to her boss, who gave her the go ahead.

The office was built in just one day, a Saturday. When everyone came to work on Monday, Margaret called a meeting and told them what had happened. She also explained to them her reasons and closed the meeting by assuring them that she always had time for them so "drop by whenever you have a problem."

During the last two months 3 of the 17 people in the department have quit. Four others have transferred to other departments. Margaret's boss happens to know one of the men who transferred to another area and asked him why. The individual talked about a number of different things including a chance for more creative work and increased responsibility. However, the man also mentioned that Margaret had changed dramatically since taking over the department. "In the beginning she used to be quite open and easily accessible. Now she holes up in that office and no one gets to see her any more. Apparently she is trying to create an image of an up-and-coming female executive. In any event, I'm sure she'll have no trouble getting to the top. However, if you ask me she just doesn't fit in. There are a lot of complaints about her behavior by other members of the department. She seems to have gotten too big for her britches." The boss was surprised to hear this. He has worked with Margaret on a daily basis and has noticed no change in her behavior. Nor has anyone else outside the department had a bad word to say about her. Nevertheless, he intends to call Margaret in and have an extended discussion with her. Things might be ready to get out of hand, he feels, and now is the best time to ensure that they do not.

Assume that you are a personal communication consultant to Margaret's boss. Using all the information in the case as well as your knowledge of the communication area, what exactly is the problem? How did it come about? What should now be done to deal with it? Be as practical as you can in your recommendations to the boss.

Key Points in This Chapter

1. Nonverbal communication is often more important than verbal content when conveying meanings from sender to receiver. The three most important areas of nonverbal communication are kinesics, proxemics, and paralanguage.

2. Kinesics refers to the study of communication through body movement and facial expression. The four most important subcategories of kinesics are the face, the eyes,

posture, and gesture. The six universal facial expressions are happiness, sadness, surprise, fear, anger, and disgust. Yet of all body expressions, the eyes seem to hold the most significance. In gauging a person's mood, the eyes often provide the best clues. Posture helps convey how a person is feeling and what the individual is thinking. Gestures tie together facial expressions and posture. The four major types of gestures are emblems, adaptors, regulators, and illustrators.

3. Proxemics deals with the way we use physical space and what that use says about us. One of the most effective ways of studying proxemics is in terms of: (a) fixed feature space, which consists of permanent structure and boundaries; (b) semifixed feature space, which is made up of moveable objects; and (c) informal feature space, which consists of the spatial relationships that exist between people. The role and importance of each was discussed in the chapter. So was the value of proxemics in conveying status messages, since where people sit and stand and how they decorate their office are often used as means of conveying their personal importance and power.

4. Paralanguage deals with how things are said. The emphasis given to words often affects their interpretation by others. In fact, the way something is said can be more important than what is actually said. The four parts of paralanguage are voice qualities, vocal qualifiers, vocal characteristics, and vocal segregates. Each was described in the chapter. In short, how something is communicated is often given greater weight than what is being communicated.

Questions for Discussion and Analysis

1. How can knowledge of the six universal facial expressions help a manager more effectively communicate with subordinates? Give examples covering at least three of these expressions.

2. In what way does culture affect the way a person uses facial expressions? Of what value would your answer be to a manager who is supervising individuals born and raised in a foreign country?

3. How does eye contact affect the nonverbal communication process? What types of conclusions do people tend to draw regarding the other party if there is no eye contact on the latter's part? Explain your reasoning.

4. In what way do people use posture to communicate messages? Choose a particular posture (slouching, standing tall, etc.) and give an interpretation of what the person is conveying with this posture.

5. Have there been any research findings regarding people's posture and what it means? Identify and describe three of these findings.

6. In studying gestures, one should look for gesture clusters rather than isolated gestures. What does this statement mean? Of what value is this advice for managers?

7. How would managers who want to convey an aura of importance or authority organize their offices? If these same managers decided to rearrange their offices so as to convey a feeling of closeness and/or participation, how would they do so? Use office diagrams to illustrate your answer.

8. How do effective managers use personal space (intimate distance, personal distance, social distance, public distance) to convey messages? What happens when someone comes too close or moves too far away? How does this upset the communication efforts of the manager? Explain.

9. In what way do managers attempt to use control of space to communicate status messages? Use two examples in your answer.

10. How can an understanding of paralanguage help a manager be a more effective communicator?

11. The way something is said can be more important than what is actually said. What does this statement mean?

12. What value does the study of paralinguistics have for modern managers? Be specific in your answer.

Exercises

1. Draw a diagram of three of your co-workers' offices. What do their offices tell us about their personalities? How does their use of space impede or facilitate effective communication?

2. Your instructor will assign each of you one other person in class to observe. During the next class period, observe your subject in terms of his or her nonverbal behavior. Notice how the person communicates nonverbally in terms of gestures, facial expression, eye contact, and so on. Keep notes as you will meet with this person at the end of the period and discuss your observations.

3. The instructor will choose five students to hold a group conversation in front of the class. A controversial subject such as legalizing marijuana will be discussed. Each participant will be assigned an "emotional set" out of which he or she should act for this discussion. The rest of the class will observe the nonverbal behavior and attempt to guess the assigned emotions.

References

1. Julius Fast, *Body Language* (New York: Pocket Books, 1971).

2. Paul Ekman and Wallace V. Friesen, "Nonverbal Leakage and Clues to Deception," *Psychiatry*, February 1969, p. 94.

3. Paul Ekman and Wallace V. Friesen, *Unmasking the Face: A Guide to Recognizing Emotions from Facial Clues* (Englewood Cliffs, N.J.: Prentice-Hall, 1975), p. 28.

4. R. W. Buck, V. J. Savin, R. E. Miller, and W. F. Caul, "Communication of Affect Through Facial Expressions in Humans," in *Nonverbal Communication*, Shirley Weitz, ed. (New York: Oxford University Press, 1974), p. 60.

5. Paul Ekman, Wallace V. Friesen, and Maureen O'Sullivan, "Smiles When Lying," *Journal of Personality and Social Psychology*, Vol. 54, No. 3, March 1988, p. 414.

6. Kerry L. Johnson, "How to Interview for the Truth," *Broker World*, July 1988, pp. 124–129.

7. Albert Mehrabian, *Silent Messages: Implicit Communication of Emotion and Attitudes* (Belmont, Calif.: Wadsworth, 1981), pp. 23, 61–62.

8. Ekman and Friesen, "Nonverbal Leakage and Clues to Deception," *op. cit.*, pp. 96–97.

9. Edward T. Hall, *The Silent Language* (New York: Doubleday, 1959).

10. Robert Ardrey, *The Territorial Imperative* (New York: Atheneum, 1970), p. 5.

11. George N. Gordon, *Persuasion: The Theory and Practice of Manipulative Communication* (New York: Hastings House, 1971).

12. Judee K. Burgoon, "Nonverbal Signals," in *Handbook of Interpersonal Communication*, Mark L. Knapp and Gerald R. Miller, (eds.) (Beverly Hills, Calif.: SAGE Publications, 1985), p. 362.

13. Albert Mehrabian, *Silent Messages: Implicit Communication of Emotions and Attitudes* (Belmont, Calif., Wadsworth, 1981), p. 70.

14. E. T. Hall, *The Hidden Dimension* (Garden City, N.Y.: Doubleday, 1982), pp. 103–112.

15. *Ibid.*, pp. 113–129.

16. Harvard Business School. "Communication: The Use of Time, Space and Things" (Intercollegiate Case Clearing House, 1974), pp. 46–50.

17. Gerald M. Goldhaber, *Organizational Communication* (Dubuque, Iowa: William C. Brown, 1986), pp. 204–206.

18. "The Resignation That Took," *Newsweek*, July 5, 1982, p. 18.

19. Fast, *op. cit.*, pp. 59–60.

20. See, for example, Albert Mehrabian and Morton Weiner, "Decoding of Inconsistent Communications," *Journal of Personality and Social Psychology*, May 1967, pp. 109–114. Also Bella M. DePaulo et al., "Decoding Discrepant Nonverbal Cues," *Journal of Personality and Social Psychology*, March 1978, pp. 313–323.

21. *Newsweek*, October 5, 1970, p. 106.

22. G. L. Trager, "Paralanguage: A First Approximation," *Studies in Linguistics*, Vol. 13, 1958, pp. 1–12.

Annotated Bibliography

Ardrey, Robert, *The Territorial Imperative* (New York: Atheneum, 1970).
    This fascinating sequel to *African Genesis* examines the natural science studies of territorial behavior and their potential impact on our study of humans.

Ekman, Paul, and Wallace V. Friesen, *Unmasking the Face: A Guide to Recognizing Emotions from Facial Clues* (Englewood Cliffs, N.J.: Prentice-Hall, 1975).
    This interesting book explores the realm of facial expressions and concludes that there are 6 universal expressions (surprise, fear, disgust, anger, happiness, sadness) and 33 blends of emotions. Many pictures illustrate their research findings.

Fast, Julius, *Body Language* (New York: Pocket Books, 1971).
    Although this book purports to deal predominantly with kinesics, it also has several fascinating chapters on proxemics. Easy to read and full of anecdotes, *Body Language* is probably the most popular book on the subject.

Hall, E. T., *The Hidden Dimension* (Garden City, N.Y.: Doubleday, 1982).
    This thorough study of the use of space by animals and humans presents the divisions of fixed feature, semifixed feature, and personal space. An excellent bibliography on the subject is also provided. Cross-cultural dynamics are examined, and guidelines are offered for effective design of office space.

Hall, E. T., *The Silent Language* (New York: Doubleday, 1959).
    This major work on time and space focuses on the cultural implications of both. It is dedicated to the hope that more international understanding will occur if awareness in these areas is heightened. Easy to read, it is a classic in the literature of communication.

Mehrabian, Albert, *Public Places and Private Space: The Psychology of Work, Play and Living Environments* (New York: Basic Books, 1976).
    This book takes a look at six human-controlled environments and how to make them more satisfying to the needs and desires of humankind. These environments include intimate environment, residences, work, therapeutic environments (e.g., hospitals and prisons), play environments (e.g., movies) and communal environments (e.g., city planning). A thorough bibliography is also provided.

Mehrabian, Albert, *Silent Messages: Implicit Communication of Emotions and Attitudes* (Belmont, Calif.: Wadsworth, 1981).
    This book is dedicated to increasing our awareness of the overlooked importance of nonverbal behavior in everyday communication. In turn, Mehrabian investigates nonverbal behavior as it relates to liking, dominance, social style, and environment and social interaction. Like his 1976 book, *Silent Messages* includes a detailed bibliography.

Part Three

GROUP AND INTERGROUP COMMUNICATION

This part of the book examines group and intergroup communication. Although a great deal of organizational communication occurs on a one-to-one basis, intra- and intergroup communication also is widely employed in modern enterprises.

Chapter 6 focuses on group dynamics and group decision making and explains why people join groups. The chapter also discusses the potential benefits and problems that accrue from group decision making. Particular consideration is given to both groupthink and the risky-shift phenomenon. The last part of the chapter examines creativity and decision making with emphasis on how creative thinking techniques can be used to stimulate communication toward effective problem solving.

Chapter 7 addresses leadership and communication. After defining the term *leadership,* leader characteristics are described. Next the focus is on how leadership styles can be used to improve communication and increase organizational effectiveness. The chapter describes these styles and approaches in terms of managerial level: lower, middle, and upper.

When you have finished studying all the material in this part of the book, you will understand the benefits and problems associated with group decision making. You also will know how to use creative thinking processes to improve group decision making and will be aware of the types of leadership styles that are of most value in promoting effective communication at the lower, middle, and upper levels of the hierarchy.

CHAPTER 6

Group Dynamics and Group Decision Making

" . . . Our evolution as a species into tightly knit interdependent groups — families — is no accident. By combining the resources and skills of team members with the higher energy and motivation level that the group provides, employees can reach extraordinary levels of achievement."

Marc Bassin, "Teamwork at General Foods: New and Improved," *Personnel Journal*, May 1988, pp. 62–70.

Objectives

1. To be able to define what is meant by the terms *group dynamics* and *group*.

2. To understand the four stages that groups go through as they develop and how each stage affects the way the members will communicate.

3. To be able to compare and contrast formal and informal groups and describe the communication flows used by each.

4. To explain the three major reasons why people join groups and the communication flows associated with each.

5. To set forth some of the potential benefits of group decision making.

6. To discuss what groupthink is all about and to describe some of its major symptoms.

7. To explain how the negative effects of groupthink can be sidestepped and/or eliminated.

8. To define the term *risky-shift phenomenon* and explain the reasons for its existence.

9. To describe the four major types of creativity and the characteristics of creative people.

10. To explain how personal creativity can be developed and promoted.

C A S E   I N   P O I N T

Egg All Over Our Faces

When Jenny Barden was contacted by Greg Whistler, she thought he wanted to talk about his salary. The two met later in the day, and Jenny learned that Greg was upset over not being promoted to the new supervisory position that had opened up in his department. "I'm next in line in terms of seniority, and that position should have been mine," he argued. Jenny, though in charge of the overall department, does not make it a habit to overrule her managers. Nevertheless, she did promise Greg that she would check into the matter. Upon doing so she learned that, whereas Greg did have seniority, his boss had not recommended him for the position because he did not have the highest efficiency rating in his group. Another person, Bill Hunter, did have the highest rating and he was given the job. When Jenny asked about the seniority factor, the manager told her that Bill had three years less time on the job than Greg, but that still put him second in terms of seniority. "We let the efficiency factor outweigh the seniority factor," he told Jenny.

Jenny then called the firm's Labor Relations Manager and asked for some advice. The officer told Jenny, "You could have a real problem on your hands. If I were you, I'd put together a committee to investigate the situation and hope that they can find a justification for the promotion." Jenny thought that this was good advice and assigned seven people to the group. Three came from Jenny's area, three from other units around the plant, and one from the Human Resources department. The latter was a young man who had just graduated from college.

The committee listened to Greg's point of view. They then called in Greg's supervisor and talked to him. Finally, they reviewed the way in which promotions had been given out in the past. When they finished, they deliberated for approximately six hours and then put together a short report. In essence, the report backed up Greg's supervisor.

Upon hearing the news, Greg went to the union and instituted a grievance. The hearing was held five days ago. The decision calls for Greg to be promoted to the rank of supervisor and to be reimbursed for all back pay lost as a result of him not holding that position. The union has also sent the company president a formal letter charging the company with breech of contract and announcing that a close scrutiny would be made of all promotions over the last 18 months to determine whether any similar cases could be found.

Jenny received a call from the company president yesterday. The president shouted at her in anger. "What's wrong with your people down there? We have egg all over our faces! Have you seen the national news? They're laughing at us in every state in the union!" Jenny was devastated. She could not believe what had happened. She called in the chairperson who headed the committee and asked for an explanation. Here is what the individual told her.

I was against the decision. I knew we were in for trouble. However, some of those guys from outside the department kept saying that we couldn't let those union guys push us around. If we wanted to change the rules, we could do so. It was our company and we had to run it the way we thought was right. Besides, the decision had already been made, so why rock the boat? After two or three hours, most of us were beaten down and we went along. Even the young kid from Human Resources caved in. It was terrible, but we were all hoping for the best.

Jenny agreed with him on one thing: it was terrible. Now the question was how to explain it to top management. What happened? Why did it happen? How did this effort at group decision making bring about such a problem? How could it have been prevented? In answering these questions, reconstruct the way the meeting must have gone. Then try to explain why everyone in the group finally capitulated and agreed to support Greg's boss. After you have sketched out your answer, put it aside until you have finished reading the chapter.

INTRODUCTION

Group dynamics
defined

People in organizations often communicate on a one-to-one basis. However, many times they are representing not only themselves but also their work and/or informal group. For this reason, it is important to have an understanding of group dynamics. *Group dynamics* is the way in which people communicate and interact in groups. Before examining this subject, let us look at the nature of a group.

What Is a Group?

There is no universal answer to the question "what is a group?" However, groups do seem to share some characteristics as they pursue their collective objectives. The three most common are interaction, dependency, and satisfaction arising from mutual association.

A group is a social unit of two or more people who interact with each other. Tubbs describes this interaction as "verbal and nonverbal messages in an attempt to influence one another."[1]

Groups consist of interdependent, interactive individuals.

The group members, for whatever reason, are also dependent on one another. In addition, the members receive some form of satisfaction from the association. (Otherwise they would drop out of the group.) Pulling together these three characteristics, we can define a *group* as a social unit consisting of two or more interdependent, interactive individuals who are striving to attain common goals.

Group Development

When we are examining communication in a group setting, it is important to remember that groups experience various stages of development. A group that has just formed will have different communication patterns from one that has been in existence for a year. As a group moves through these stages, relationships among the members often change as expectations and behaviors are adjusted in such a way as to promote intragroup harmony and satisfaction. Groups typically go through four stages.[2]

Group development goes through forming.

The first stage is that of *forming*. During this period, group members discover those interpersonal behaviors that are both acceptable and unacceptable to others in the group. During this phase each member relies on the others to provide cues regarding acceptable behavior. During the forming stage group members get to know each other.

Then storming

The second stage of group development is called *storming*. This phase is often marked by some degree of intragroup conflict as members attempt to develop a special place for themselves in the group and to influence the development of its norms and roles. At this time, members also try to develop some form(s) of interpersonal relationships with others in the group. In the process each person tries to mark off certain domains of authority or power. This stage is often a period of jockeying for position.

Followed by norming

The third stage is called *norming*. During this stage, the infighting is basically over and group cohesion starts to develop. Most group members have now come to accept their fellow members. A unity of purpose has developed which serves to unite them. At this point the group's development has basically matured, and the members understand how they are to interact with each other. People joining the group at this stage often find themselves having to go back through stages one and two (forming and storming) in an effort to integrate themselves comfortably into the group's environment.

And finally by performing

The fourth stage of group development is called *performing*. During this phase, group members agree on the basic roles each is to play. This includes not only job behavior, but also the ways in which each will interact with the others in getting things done. During this stage task specialization and personal needs and desires are brought together. The formal needs of the organization are integrated with the informal needs of the member. As a result, group members are able to make their jobs more interesting and enjoyable.

Formal groups usually have an easier time with group development than do informal groups, because they have to follow the rules laid down by the organization. However, even formal groups have to adapt their organizational design so as to accommodate the specific needs of the members.

As groups move through these four phases their communication patterns change. The defensiveness and hostility that often characterize the early phases give way to feelings of trust, confidence, and openness. This is as true in formal as in informal groups.

TYPES OF GROUPS

Every organization has various types of groups. For purposes of analysis, they can be divided into two major categories: formal and informal.

Formal Groups

Formal groups are created by the organization.

Formal groups are created by the organization itself. The three most common are functional groups, project groups, and committees. The following examines each.

Functional group members perform the same basic tasks.

Functional groups are made up of individuals who perform the same job or tasks. Accountants located in an accounting department constitute a functional group. So do the lawyers in a legal department, salespeople in a sales department, and engineers in an engineering department. Functional groups, as seen in Figure 6.1, are usually quite easy to spot on the organization chart.

Project groups are temporary in nature.

Project groups are made up of people, usually from different functional areas, who have been brought together to pursue a particular objective after which the group is disbanded. A product planning group consisting of managers from the finance, production, personnel, and marketing departments is an example. So, too, is a quality control group made up of representatives from the engineering, production, purchasing, and quality control departments. Project groups go out of existence after their objective is attained. Unlike functional groups, they are temporary. For this reason, they are seldom represented on an organization chart.

Committees examine, analyze, and/or evaluate operations.

Committees are groups whose major responsibilities are to examine, analyze, and/or evaluate particular areas of organizational operations. Committees usually have only advisory authority. Recommendations resulting from their efforts are typically sent to managers who are responsible for implementing them. Most committees are *ad hoc*, in which case they go out of existence after they have finished their assignment. Some,

Figure 6.1

Groups and communication flows in a typical organization.

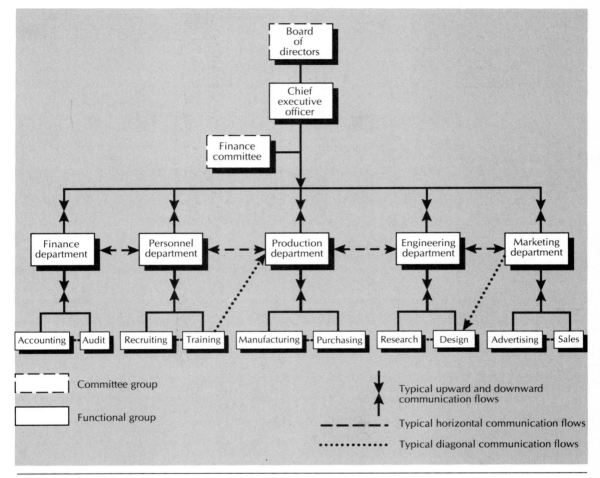

however, are *standing committees*, such as the board of directors, in which case they continue to exist indefinitely. As seen in Figure 6.1, it is sometimes possible to identify committees on the formal organization chart. This is particularly true for standing committees.

Downward, upward, and horizontal communication flows are used.

Communication, both within and between formal groups, tends to follow the chain of command: superior to subordinate and vice versa. The *downward* flow is used to carry information related to such things as objectives, work assignments, rules, policies, and procedures. The *upward* flow is employed in conveying information related to work progress and requests for clarification of directives and/or assistance and support. Wide use is also made of *horizontal* communication flows, which take place between groups at the same level of the hierarchy. These flows are employed by groups attempting to coordinate their efforts. An excellent example is provided by project groups whose members often come from the same level of the hierarchy and must coordinate their energies in accomplishing the specific objective that has been assigned to them. Figure 6.1 provides examples of all three of these communication flows. A further discussion of communication flows will be presented in Chapter 8.

☑️

Implications for Management

1. Remember that formal groups rely heavily on upward and downward communication channels. When communicating with and receiving information from these groups, use the formal chain of command whenever possible.

2. Realize that upward and downward channels support the hierarchical structure and convey a degree of importance and formality not possible through most other communication flows. When, in the role of a manager, you communicate with a formal group, make use of these channels.

3. If your group has to coordinate its efforts or activities with those of other groups, make use of horizontal communication. Work with your group and the manager(s) of the other group(s) in developing the most effective communication system possible. Remember that if you can smooth the way for horizontal communication flows, you will automatically improve the likelihood of effective coordination.

4. Keep in mind that informal groups use all four communication flows: downward, upward, horizontal, and diagonal. In getting things done, they are an excellent resource because of their contacts throughout the organization. Rely on them to supplement formal group efforts.

Informal Groups

Informal groups are created by the personnel.

Informal groups are created by the personnel themselves. These groups are a result of individual and collective self-interest, and so it is possible to describe their membership on this basis. For example, consider a group of five who are members of the company bowling team. Although the individuals may all come from different departments, they are members of the same group. Yet informal groups are not limited to social functions. Many of them spring up during the normal course of business. Consider the head of purchasing who is a close friend of both the accounting vice president and the head of computer operations. The purchasing head may contact these two managers to seek help in getting a purchase order delivered on time. By cutting across formal lines and using the informal network, many organizational personnel find they can speed things up and/or sidestep red tape.

Downward, upward, horizontal, and vertical flows are used.

Informal groups use all three of the communication flows we have described earlier: downward, upward, and horizontal. They also employ *diagonal* flows in which members in one department contact those at other hierarchical levels in other departments (see Figure 6.1). Diagonal flows are particularly important in informal communication because they help group members circumvent the often time-consuming formal channels.

WHY PEOPLE JOIN GROUPS

People join groups for a number of different reasons. These reasons help dictate whether the group is formal, informal, or a combination. A *combination group* is at least partly formal and partly informal. An example is a group of accountants who work together (formal) and also go to lunch together (informal). In carrying out their jobs, both their formal and informal relationships play a role.

The three major reasons why people join groups are propinquity, productivity, and personal satisfaction. The following discusses each of these reasons and also illustrates that the three reasons are interdependent; when we find one of them we may find the others as well.

Propinquity

Frequency of contact is important.

Propinquity means nearness. When used to explain why people join groups, *propinquity* means that those who come into frequent contact with each other are likely to belong to the same group(s). Propinquity is most useful in describing informal group membership. When it does, we find that the membership is usually small (five or fewer), and communication channels tend to be open, direct, and frequent, making wide use of all four communication flows. Propinquity can also be used to describe the communication interaction between members of a formal group. However, since these individuals are brought together by the organization and are directly assigned tasks, a large percentage of their communication is job related. The fact that they are near each other is more a function of organizational directive than of personal choice. Within formal groups, communication tends to flow upward and downward, following the chain of command, as well as horizontally.

Productivity

People also join groups in an effort to achieve productivity or to get things done.

> Any group interaction can be characterized in terms of the task(s) that the group is trying to carry out: giving (and receiving) a lecture or a sermon or a play; processing steel; assembling an auto; choosing a new vice president; deciding on a zoning variance; preparing a budget justification; arbitrating a grievance; enjoying dinner; having a good time at the nightclub, on the backpacking trip, or in the dump. The task, as you can see from those examples, involves informally assumed goals (e.g., having a good time) as well as assigned jobs (e.g., assembling an auto).[3]

The desire to get things done is equally evident in formal and informal groups. In formal groups, part of this process is handled by the organization itself. Using job descriptions and predetermined objectives, the enterprise assigns tasks to the personnel and makes wide use of rules, policies, and procedures in guiding their efforts.

People often join informal groups in order to get things done more efficiently. These goals can take many different forms, but when tied in with those of the organization, they often include a friendly environment (the work group is a nice place to be), harmony (everyone works in accord with each other), and less work effort (the informal group rearranges things so that the work gets done in the easiest way possible). Although the informal group can be very helpful in assisting an organization to attain formal objectives, a great degree of personal goal attainment also goes on. In fact, it is often impossible to separate the productivity objective from that of personal satisfaction. In any event, the communication flows will vary depending on the group. Formal groups make wide use of upward, downward, and horizontal communication flows. Informal groups make use of these three flows as well as diagonal flows.

The desire to get things done is important.

Personal Satisfaction

Although propinquity and productivity are important reasons why people join groups, in virtually every case at least some degree of personal satisfaction is present. How does this satisfaction come about? In answering this question, we have to examine the subject of motivation.

Personal satisfaction is important.

MOTIVATION *Motivation* is a force that directs a person toward an objective. This force has been described in many different ways. One of the most popular, and certainly easiest to understand, is that of need satisfaction. People do things (or refrain from doing them) because of certain needs they want to satisfy. For example, a hungry man is motivated to eat. A tired woman is motivated to sleep. A young executive with a need to succeed is motivated to work extra hard for a promotion. In each of these cases, an inner need drives or directs the person toward a particular objective. This approach to explaining motivation has been well presented by Abraham Maslow.[4]

Motivation directs people toward an objective.

Maslow contends that everyone is motivated by one of five needs: physiological, safety, social, esteem, and self-actualization. These needs can be presented in the form of a hierarchy (see Figure 6.2). Maslow argues that when a person is basically satisfied at

Figure 6.2

Maslow's need hierarchy.

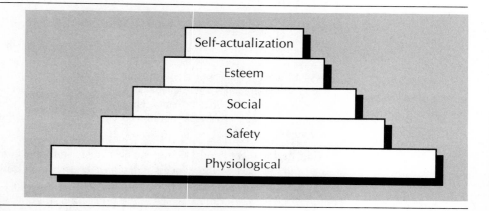

one level, he or she will move on to the next level. As one moves up the hierarchy, there tends to be less satisfaction of that need than there was at the lower levels. So upper-level need satisfaction is not as complete as lower-level need satisfaction.

> In actual fact, most members of our society who are normal are partially satisfied in all their basic needs and partially unsatisfied in all their basic needs at the same time. A more realistic description of the hierarchy would be in terms of decreasing percentage of satisfaction as we go up the hierarchy of prepotency. For instance, if I may assign arbitrary figures . . . it is as if the average citizen is satisfied perhaps 85 percent in his physiological needs, 70 percent in his safety needs, 50 percent in his social needs, 40 percent in his self-esteem needs, and 10 percent in his self-actualization needs.[5]

Physiological needs are the most basic.

Physiological needs are the most basic. They consist of such things as food, clothing, and shelter. People who join or remain with groups because they are concerned with these needs are usually most interested in money. The reason is quite simple. Few organizations directly provide food, clothing, and/or shelter to their members. However, most do provide money, which is a means of satisfying these needs.

Safety needs include survival and security.

Safety needs include both survival and security. Few people in organizational life join groups for survival. Security tends to be the most important safety need. The formal group often works to resolve this need by offering its members such things as accident, health, and life insurance, job security, and safety equipment. The informal organization tries to meet these needs by providing psychological support and, in the case of unions, bargaining power with the management.

Social needs include friendship and acceptance.

Social needs include friendship, affection, and acceptance. Both formal and informal groups go about meeting this need in the same way. They create a warm, friendly environment in which everyone feels "wanted." Praise, kindness, close interaction, and open communication typify the groups' attempts to help the members meet their social needs.

Esteem needs include self-importance and self-respect.

Esteem needs include self-importance and self-respect. People fulfill these needs when they feel good about themselves. Groups are important in helping members do this because as individuals are told, "you are really a nice person," "we enjoy having a person like you working here," and "you make a real contribution to this group," self-importance tends to go up. Remember that groups do not actually give these feelings of esteem, but they do create the environment in which members can satisfy this need. This is done to the degree that the group can create feelings of prestige and power among the members. *Prestige* is respect and status. *Power* is the ability to influence or induce behavior. When the group environment nurtures prestige and power among the members, esteem need fulfillment occurs. Remember, however, that no matter how much the group members tell someone, "We think you are really great," if the individual does not believe them, the esteem need is not satisfied. In contrast to physiological or safety needs, for example, esteem needs are heavily psychological and are satisfied only to the degree that the individual allows them to be satisfied.

Self-actualization needs reflect a desire for competence and achievement.

Self-actualization needs are a person's need to feel that he or she is becoming better and better at what he or she does and is. These needs are satisfied through feelings of competence and achievement. *Competence* occurs when the individual feels control over the environment, that is, the person can do the job without any outside help. *Achievement* is the accomplishment of objectives. In their efforts to self-actualize, people try to develop competence and attain objectives. To a large degree, self-actualization needs are important to those who want to feel that they personally are doing the best they can. These people want to be able to look at themselves and say, "You really have reached the top; you are certainly one of the best in your area of expertise." Groups can help members fulfill self-actualization needs to the degree that they allow the person to see his or her competence and to attain those objectives that the individual feels are important to self-development. Because so little is really known about the self-actualization need, it is easy to get it confused with self-esteem. The best way to differentiate the two is to realize that self-esteem needs revolve around prestige and power, whereas self-actualization needs are reflected by a concern for competence and achievement. Which of these needs is most important to you? How would your answer affect the type of group you would seek to join? Take Self-Assessment Quiz 6.1 to see how the need hierarchy relates to group membership choices.

Implications for Management

1. Remember that people who are located near each other are likely to be members of the same group. If you want indirectly to communicate with someone, choose an individual who works near the person. You can almost bet that the manager will soon receive the message.

2. On the other hand, do not tell people in the same group something you do not want other members to know. The closer the members are to each other socially, the most likely it is that your message will get around to everyone, including those you did not want to hear it.

3. Keep in mind that informal groups are important to organizational productivity. You are not going to get everything done through formal channels. So encourage the use of informal relationships in cutting across departmental lines and increasing efficiency. Informal groups are an excellent supplement to the formal structure.

4. Realize that people join and remain with groups because there is something in it for them. Quite often, this is the ability to satisfy their safety, social, and esteem needs. To the degree that you can help groups meet these needs, you will increase your effectiveness as a manager. Remember that although physiological and self-actualization needs are important, people spend more of their job time trying to satisfy needs in the middle of the hierarchy.

5. Whenever you see forms of defensive behavior (aggression, rationalization, compensation, regression) know that someone is having trouble meeting one or more of their needs. Try to reduce this defensive behavior by finding out what is wrong and, if at all possible, working with the individual to reduce the roadblock(s) causing this defensiveness.

SELF-ASSESSMENT QUIZ 6.1

What Type of Group Do You Prefer?

Assume that you are about to take a full-time career job. There are many things you may be looking for from this job. Below are listed ten possible "payoffs." Look the list over carefully and place a "1" next to the factor that would be most important to you when you are seeking a full-time, career job. Put a "2" next to the second most important factor on down to a "10" next to the least important factor. Then follow the instructions at the bottom of the page.

_____ **a.** Job security

_____ **b.** Chance for advancement

_____ **c.** Good wages

_____ **d.** Increased responsibility

_____ **e.** Good working conditions

_____ **f.** Opportunity to succeed

_____ **g.** Well-defined job descriptions and objectives

_____ **h.** Recognition for a job well done

_____ **i.** Good health care and retirement benefits

_____ **j.** Interesting work

Now take your answers (1–10) and match them up to the following key. Then add the total in both columns.

Column A	Column B
_____ **a.**	_____ **b.**
_____ **c.**	_____ **d.**
_____ **e.**	_____ **f.**
_____ **g.**	_____ **h.**
_____ **i.**	_____ **j.**
_____ Total	_____ Total

Answers are in the Answer section at the back of the book.

NEED HIERARCHY AND COMMUNICATION When groups help members attain need satisfaction, the communication flows are quite different than when members feel their needs are not being satisfied. In a well-motivated group there is open communication and trust. On the other hand, when an individual feels that his or her needs are not being satisfied, various forms of defensive behavior result. For example, if a group member has a need for self-importance and this need is blocked or denied, the individual will often turn against the group or those in the group responsible for the situation. Intragroup hostility or friction will develop, and this person's communications will be defensive and restricted to those he or she feels can be trusted. Likewise, if an entire group feels that its needs are being blocked, as in the case of a supervisor who structures work assignments in such a way as to reduce social interaction among the members, the outcome will often be one of reduced work output coupled with minimum communication between the members and the manager. The group will simply give the manager the cold shoulder or refuse to provide any feedback except that which is job related.

Of course, we could provide endless examples of blocked or denied need satisfaction and then attempt to describe the communication patterns that result. A simpler, more direct way to approach the subject is to look at the various forms of defensive behavior that accompany blocked need satisfaction. Some of these were referred to earlier in Chapter 4. These forms of behavior are a result of frustration and, in communication terms, take the following forms:

1. *Aggression* — which is a physical or verbal defensive behavior directed against the person(s) believed to be responsible for the failure to achieve need fulfillment. For example, when George finds out that the boss will not recommend him for a promotion, he begins to yell at his supervisor.

2. *Rationalization* — which is a defensive behavior that takes the form of blaming others for failure to attain need fulfillment. For example, Suzy tells Bob that she did not get a merit raise because "the boss doesn't like me," when the truth of the matter is that Suzy is a poor worker.

Typical forms of defensive behavior

3. *Compensation* — which is the exertion of an unusual amount of energy on an activity to make up for a deficiency in another. For example, Bill cannot get along with his fellow workers, and so social need satisfaction is denied to him on the job. Off the job, however, he is extremely active in company-related social and recreational activities.

4. *Regression* — which is a reversion to a less mature level of behavior. For example, when Tina finds out that she has gotten a poor performance evaluation from her boss, she changes her communication with the boss from an open, friendly one to a terse, highly task-oriented and/or temperamental one.

One of the topics of group dynamics which has been of most interest to managers is group decision making. With today's emphasis on participative management, many decisions are now being made by groups. This fact poses problems as well as benefits.

POTENTIAL BENEFITS OF GROUP DECISION MAKING

Several important benefits can be obtained from group decision making, particularly when it comes to problem solving. The following examines four of the most significant benefits.

Greater Total Knowledge and/or Information

Two heads are
better than one.

When knowledge or information is a prerequisite for problem solving, groups are often superior to individuals. Even if one member of the group is more knowledgeable than any of the others, other group members are often useful in filling in some gaps in knowledge. For example, a committee charged with choosing a new computer system and getting it implemented may have one member who is an expert on computers. The individual knows what the computer salesperson is talking about and is able to evaluate the various costs and benefits associated with each machine. However, the person may have a limited understanding of how well the new system will be accepted by the personnel and what human relations problems will have to be overcome during the implementation stage. Other members of the group may be needed to help develop a strategy for personnel acceptance.

Greater Number of Problem-Solving Approaches

Individuals often get into a rut regarding the way they think. Their approach to problem solving follows the same basic path and occasionally proves to be ineffective.

Different
approaches are
offered.

Since the individual members of a group often have different approaches, a group effort can be very beneficial because each gets to see and hear a different way of addressing the problem. The result of this interchange of ideas can be an original solution. In any event, the process often brings about a much better solution than any of the members working alone could have generated.

Participation and Implementation

When individuals are involved in the formulation of a plan or the analysis of a problem, their support for the project increases. Having had a hand in fashioning the outcome, they tend to get behind and support their own decision. These benefits were explained in some depth in Chapter 2 when human resources management was examined, that is, people want a chance to contribute to organizational goals and to play a role. Group members are also important in helping sell decisions to other organizational personnel. This is particularly true when a committee is formed for the purpose of analyzing a situation, recommending a course of action, and then seeing to its implementation. Once the decision is made, the primary function of the committee is to sell the solution. If the membership has been chosen carefully, this is often not too difficult. For example, a group that will make a decision affecting an entire department will typically have

Commitment can
be attained.

representatives from throughout that department. A group making a decision affecting the entire organization will often have membership drawn from all areas of the enterprise. In these cases, participation plays two important problem-solving roles: solution formulation and solution implementation. Individual managers are often unable to carry out both roles successfully; groups, on the other hand, can.

Quality circles
improve
communication.

One manifestation of this increasing employee desire for group participation is the growth of quality circles in the United States. Quality circles are "groups of workers (usually not more than eight to ten) who, along with their supervisor, meet on company time to discuss ways in which they can be more productive or can improve product quality."[6] Circle members suggest ideas that are passed up through the formal organizational communication channel for consideration and implementation. Quality circles not only satisfy employee needs to participate, but often result in improved productivity, cost savings, and quality improvement as well.

> Employees also reap personal and professional growth from participation . . . These areas of growth include improved lateral communication skills as well as upward communication access; better interpersonal skills in creative problem-solving, group dynamics, conflict resolution, and creativity.[7]

Comprehension and Analysis

In some cases, individuals are inferior to groups with regard to comprehension and/or analysis. A group is often better able to understand problems or issues. What one member of the group does not understand, another does. In addition, when the issue or problem is one with which the group members may be collectively unfamiliar, the group has several advantages over the individual executive including: (1) one or more members may be able to describe or present a tentative solution to the problem because they have some experience with, or knowledge about, the issue; or (2) by examining the problem or issue, the group may find that, collectively, it can generate solutions that are beyond the scope of the individual executive. This is particularly true when the members feel that individually they would be "in over their heads."

Analysis can be improved.

POTENTIAL PROBLEMS OF GROUP DECISION MAKING

Although numerous benefits are associated with group decision making, their use may also mean potential problems. During the heyday of scientific management, Frederick Taylor and his associates individualized the workers because they realized that less total work was done when people functioned in a group than when they worked alone. Numerous reasons can be cited for this lack of productivity including group norms, excessive time spent in socializing, and the possibility that group size was often too large given the nature of the task. Today the potential problems of groups are still a matter of concern. Two problems that have been given the most attention in recent years are groupthink and the risky-shift phenomenon.

Groupthink

Groupthink defined

The term *groupthink* refers to the need for individuals in a group to suppress dissent and go along with things. Irving Janis, famous for his writing on the topic, has defined groupthink as "the mode of thinking that persons engage in when they are deeply involved in a cohesive in-group, when the members, striving for unanimity override their motivation to realistically appraise alternative courses of action."[8] Many examples can be cited of groupthink in action. Perhaps the most famous is that of the Bay of Pigs incident in which the United States committed itself to a plan of action that was clearly erroneous. After the fiasco, President Kennedy remarked, "How could I have been so stupid!" Quite obviously, in the clear light of the day the President realized that he never should have gone along with his advisors who urged him to adopt the CIA plan. Overcoming these phenomena, the President was able to handle the Cuban missile crisis, which arose two years later, more effectively. Unfortunately, not all managers understand what groupthink is about, and they continually fall prey to its dysfunctional effects.

When groupthink begins to develop, members of the group start avoiding harsh criticism of the leader and their colleagues. There is a feeling of togetherness among the members, and bickering or conflict, which spoils this cozy feeling, is discouraged. The feeling also develops that those who oppose the aims of the group are totally wrong so it is all right to take action against them. The group sees its principles as being humanitarian and high minded and, if it is necessary to use immoral or unethical behavior to defeat those who oppose these principles, that is acceptable behavior. The greater the cohesiveness of the group, the greater the chance that groupthink will develop.

> In a cohesive group of policy-makers the danger is not that each individual will fail to reveal his strong objections to a proposal favored by the majority but that he will think the proposal is a good one, without attempting to carry out a critical scrutiny that could lead him to see that there are grounds for strong objections. When groupthink dominates, suppression of deviant thoughts takes the form of each person's deciding that his misgivings are not relevant, that the benefit of any doubt should be given to the group consensus.[9]

Naturally, not all highly cohesive groups suffer from groupthink. However, it is more likely to develop within these groups than those with lower levels of cohesion.

SYMPTOMS Janis reports that his studies of high-level governmental decision making, in both civilian and military settings, reveal eight main symptoms of groupthink. These symptoms can also be found within private, nongovernmental settings. The eight, along with a brief description of each, are the following:

1. *Invulnerability*. Most, if not all, members of the group believe that nothing bad can happen to them. For this reason they are willing to assume risks and dangers that they would otherwise avoid. As applied to a well-known historical case, consider the fact that when Admiral Kimmel, in December 1941, was informed by his intelligence chief that radio contact with Japanese aircraft carriers had been lost, he joked, "What, you don't know where the carriers are? Do you mean to say that they could be rounding Diamond Head (in Honolulu) and you wouldn't know it?" In fact, the Japanese were moving full steam toward the admiral's command post at that very moment. Another example of invulnerability is offered by the Cabinet meetings of Lyndon Johnson where many participants believed that if the United States indicated a willingness to use its power, the North Vietnamese would back away from an all-out confrontation. The group's confidence in its own position gave it a feeling of invulnerability.

2. *Rationale*. Victims of groupthink construct rationalizations in order to ignore warnings about the problems they face. Whenever they see something going wrong with their position, they recommit themselves even more strongly to their stand. They do not look at the situation through the eyes of the other party. Admiral Kimmel was convinced that the Japanese would never attack Pearl Harbor because

this would precipitate a war that the Empire could not win. The Johnson Cabinet was convinced that, as long as they kept up the bombing of North Vietnam, the enemy would be forced to back off. No one bothered answering the question: what if the other group does not act as we are predicting?

3. *Morality*. Victims of groupthink believe that they are unquestionably right. They have no doubt about the morality of their position. So no questions are raised regarding whether or not what the group is doing is "right."

4. *Stereotypes*. Victims of groupthink have stereotyped views of those who oppose them. They see these people as evil, weak, stupid, or untrustworthy. This stereotyped image not only encourages the groupthink people to continue with their line of action, but also discourages them from opening any form of dialogue with the opposition. After all, why talk or communicate with those you know are going to lie to you? As applied to the Bay of Pigs, Janis offers the following:

> Kennedy's groupthinkers believed that Premier Fidel Castro's air force was so ineffectual that obsolete B-26's could knock it out completely in a surprise attack before the invasion began. They also believed that Castro's army was so weak that a small Cuban-exile brigade could establish a well-protected beachhead at the Bay of Pigs. In addition, they believed that Castro was not smart enough to put down any possible internal uprisings in support of the exiles. They were wrong on all three assumptions. Though much of the blame was attributable to faulty intelligence, the point is that none of Kennedy's advisors even questioned the CIA planners about the assumptions.[10]

5. *Pressure*. Victims of groupthink apply pressure against any individual who expresses doubts about the group's position or who questions the validity of the arguments supporting their actions. This serves to reinforce loyalty among the members.

6. *Self-censorship*. Members of the group avoid doing anything that can be interpreted as breaking with group unity. If they have any misgivings about what is going on, they keep these doubts to themselves.

7. *Unanimity*. The members of the group share the illusion that everyone in the group is in agreement with what is going on. Those who speak up do so to voice their support. Those who say nothing are seen as being part of the silent majority. In either event, all members are convinced that everyone is in agreement on their plan of action.

8. *Mindguards*. Some people in the group appoint themselves as "mindguards," that is, individuals who protect the leader and fellow members from adverse information that might break the complacency they share about the effectiveness and morality of their position. These individuals single out those who seem to be having doubts and put pressure on them. For example, if one person is seen as doubting whether the current recommendations will really prove useful, the mindguard might say, "Look, Bob, we've all worked very hard on this matter. All it needs is a unanimous push from us and it's going to work. So how about getting behind the cart instead of in front of it?" These types of comments serve to diffuse opposition.

In the Watergate scandal, Janis suggests that John Ehrlichman, assistant to the President, and H. R. Haldeman, Nixon's chief of staff, could have spoken to Nixon about the threat of impeachment when Nixon still had a chance to change his course of action. They could have urged their boss

> . . . to discontinue to cover-up by openly revealing the gist of the truth along with plausible explanations that might have enabled Nixon and his men to survive in office despite public censure. By abstaining from any mention of the impeachment threat, Ehrlichman and Haldeman appear to have been functioning as mindguards; they were protecting the leader from distressing ideas he would not welcome, which might impair their relationship to the leader and lead to dissension within the group.[11]

These groupthink symptoms can obviously result in groups making the most grievous blunders. How can a group ensure that it is not becoming a victim of groupthink? The answer is, by examining the group decision-making process very closely and ensuring that certain anti-groupthink steps are taken. These remedies are discussed below.

Remedies to Groupthink

One of the most effective steps against groupthink is for the group leader to encourage each member to be a critical evaluator of the decision-making process and to voice objections and doubts when they appear. This practice can be reinforced by the leader showing an ability to accept criticism and learn from it.

A second remedy is to urge all group members to adopt an impartial stance in regard to what the group is doing. Instead of stating preferences and expectations during the first couple of meetings, members should stand back and become less personally involved. This allows the participants to be more open in their inquiry and impartial in their probing of group activities.

A third remedy is to have more than one group working on a problem or issue. This approach will eliminate the insulation that often occurs within the group. The first group may report recommendations significantly different from those of the second group.

A fourth remedy is to have each member discuss the group's deliberations with people outside the group. In this way they can pick up doubts, concerns, and questions that ought to be raised with the group at large.

Ways of overcoming groupthink

A fifth remedy is to invite in outside experts. Having someone come in, listen to what is going on, and then challenge the thinking of the group provides a much better chance that the final decision will mesh with reality rather than merely be a product of a closed environment.

A sixth remedy is to appoint one of the group members as the devil's advocate. Whenever an evaluation of alternatives is made, this person's job is to challenge the position of those who support the alternative. Such an approach forces the supporters to think through their position and be able to defend it against criticism.

A seventh remedy, useful when a group is working on a strategy designed to compete with other groups, is to answer the questions: How will the other group(s) respond to this? What are they likely to do in turn? How should we read their signals?

An eighth remedy is to divide the overall group into subgroups and have each work on the problem separately. Then they can come back together and discuss their different approaches. This remedy encourages diversity of opinion and action.

A ninth remedy is to hold a "second-chance" meeting after a preliminary consensus has been reached regarding how to handle a problem. During this second meeting each member of the group is given the chance to express, as vividly as possible, all of his or her doubts about the preliminary consensus. Then after everyone has had a chance to rethink their position out loud, efforts to formulate a final decision can be made.

Such remedies are useful because they encourage the group to rethink the logic and morality of its position. Having done so, should the group still feel it is right, then the members can go ahead with their planned action. However, the important thing to remember is that the members have taken time to question their vulnerability and logic. If a group can avoid becoming isolated, the chances that groupthink will occur are greatly diminished.[12]

The Risky-Shift Phenomenon

Risky-shift defined

The *risky-shift phenomenon* is the tendency of individuals to be greater risk takers when acting as members of a group than when acting alone. This phenomenon, which has long intrigued behaviorial scientists, is not necessarily bad. What accounts for it? Researchers have offered five explanations:

1. Making a decision in a group permits diffusion of responsibility in the event of a wrong decision.

2. Risky people are more influential in group discussions than are conservative people and so are more likely to bring others to their point of view.

3. Group discussion leads to deeper consideration of, and greater familiarization with, the possible pros and cons of a particular decision. In turn, greater familiarization and consideration lead to higher levels of risk.

Explanations for the risky-shift

4. Risk taking is socially desirable in our culture, and socially desirable qualities are more likely to be expressed in a group than alone.

5. According to a modification of the fourth explanation, our culture values moderate risk on certain kinds of issues and moderate caution on others. When a decision-making group is formed, members who discover that they are more conservative than the average will become riskier. Similarly, those discovering that they are riskier than the average will shift in a conservative direction.[13]

Implications for Management

1. Remember that it is sometimes difficult to determine when a group is suffering the dysfunction of groupthink. The best way to stop this phenomenon from occurring is to personally attend a couple of meetings or have one of your key subordinates sit in on them. No one is going to admit that their committee has become a victim of groupthink. This is something that has to be determined from the outside.

2. In an effort to prevent groupthink, be careful about going too far the other way. By

encouraging continual disagreement or questioning group findings, you could wind up creating a couple of in-group cliques who refuse to coordinate their efforts for the overall good. You will have prevented groupthink, but you will not have promoted effective group decision making.

3. Be aware that the manager is the most important person when it comes to preventing groupthink. For example, during the bombing of North Vietnam, President Johnson always used to greet one of the people in his group by saying, "Oh, here comes Mr. Let's Stop the Bombing." Quite obviously, everyone realized that the President did not want to hear this line of reasoning. He was encouraging groupthink, although he most certainly did not see this. If asked, President Johnson would have said, "I'm discouraging unnecessary conflict and getting these people together into a cohesive unit." There is sometimes a fine line between someone who is trying to act like a gadfly and provide constructive criticism and someone who is simply being a pain. The result is that the gadfly loses the respect and attention of the group and groupthink begins to set in.

4. If a group makes a decision that is too risky as far as you are concerned, follow up and find out if the decision really represents the overall will of the group. You can do this by talking to the individual members. If you hear some of them saying, "Well, I'm not so sure that we ought to go this far but the rest of the group thinks so, so I'm willing to go along," the committee may be falling prey to the risky-shift phenomenon. On the other hand, if the individual members also seem to be in agreement, do not be too hasty in deciding that the decision is overly risky. After all, they had a chance to discuss the matter among themselves and they may know a lot more about the situation than you do. In a group, individuals not only get support from their fellow members, but attain a much better understanding of the risks and dangers associated with the various alternatives. The better they know what is going on, the more likely it is that the members will be able to decide the best course of action. Do not confuse excessive risk taking with a sound understanding of the situation.

The great danger is that in group decision making the members will be influenced to take greater risks than they should. This is particularly the case when individual members can hide behind the group, thereby diffusing personal responsibility. Consider the following:

George could hardly believe his ears. The advertising program that had been launched last month was proving to be a major flop. Sales were running at 20 percent of expectations, and top management had already met and decided to pull the ads off the air as of this coming Friday. The committee, which had screened the ad agencies that had applied for the job, and then chose the one that it felt was the best, had nine members. George was one of them. Personally, he liked one of the other ad agencies better than the one that was chosen. However, since six of the committee members liked one of the others, George went along and agreed to hire this one. Fortunately for George, the minutes contained a comment he had made: "I think we should do more investigation before we hire this ad agency, despite the fact that most of you think this is the best one." Not recorded in the minutes was George's followup statement in which he said, "However, if you guys think this is the best one, I'm willing to go along." Upon hearing the disastrous news, George pulled out his copy of the minutes of that meeting and went in to see his boss. "Wow, Ralph," he said, "I'll bet someone is going to catch it for this decision. Thank heavens I didn't go along."

Notice that in the above case George managed to hide behind the shield of the group, disclaiming any responsibility for its poor decision. This is one of the greatest dangers of the risky-shift. The other is that the group, collectively, will make a decision that none of the members individually would have agreed to make.[14]

CREATIVITY AND DECISION MAKING

In some cases, group decision making can be improved through the use of creativity techniques. These techniques are helpful in generating new ideas or solutions and, under the right circumstances, can produce very effective results. Depending on the situation, the group may need to be highly innovative, whereas in other cases a moderate degree of creativity is sufficient. In all, there are four kinds of creativity.

Kinds of Creativity

Creativity comes in many forms. Sometimes an idea or solution is unique; other times it combines a number of old ideas in a new or different way. The four major types of creativity are innovation, synthesis, extension, and duplication.

Innovation is original thinking.

INNOVATION Innovation is original thinking. Some of the most important inventions of the twentieth century fit into this category. Edwin Land's Polaroid camera is an example, as are some of the latest technological breakthroughs related to communication satellites and computers.

Synthesis combines data into a new pattern.

SYNTHESIS Synthesis is the combining of information from many sources and integrating it into a new, useful pattern. The evolution of discount stores is one example, and the rise of national hotel and motel chains is another. People with foresight and financial backing might have been able to realize the potential profit in these business ventures, but it took a special type of creative person to bring them about. As Conrad Hilton, the founder of the Hilton Hotel Corporation, once said, "I never did anything other people couldn't do. The only difference is that they were looking in another direction and didn't see what I saw."

Extension expands the current boundaries of knowledge.

EXTENSION Extension is the expansion of current boundaries of knowledge, accomplished by taking ideas that worked in one area and using them in another. An excellent example is provided by Ray Kroc who bought McDonald's and expanded the organization internationally. The same is true for other fast-food franchise entrepreneurs. By extending the basic idea into other areas, these creative people were able to develop opportunities for themselves.

DUPLICATION There is a cliche, "If you can't be original, copy good ideas." This is a common approach used by committees. By finding out how other committees or groups have solved similar situations, they use a solution that heavily duplicates these past approaches. Duplication uses a "follow the leader" theme and can be very useful in saving both time and money.

Duplication uses a "follow the leader" theme.

Characteristics of Creative People

How intelligent do group members have to be in order to develop creative solutions? The answer is that many creative people are not geniuses; they are simply more intelligent than the average person. Commenting on the characteristics of creative people, Andrew DuBrin has described them as

1. Bright but not brilliant. Creativity is not directly related to extraordinarily high intelligence.

2. Good at generating a high degree of different ideas in a short period of time. These people can produce quantity.

3. Possessing a high positive image of themselves. They like who they are.

4. Sensitive to the world around them. Creative people are aware of their universe.

Characteristics of creative people

5. Motivated by challenging problems. These people like to achieve things by overcoming hurdles and barriers.

6. Tending to withhold decisions on a problem until they have collected sufficient data. They are thinkers as well as doers.

7. Valuing their independence. They do not have a strong need for group approval.

8. Leading a rich, almost bizarre, fantasy life. They daydream widely and in creative ways.

9. Flexible in their thinking and actions. They can change as situations require.

10. More concerned with the meaning and implications of a problem than with minor details. They look at the big picture.[15]

How creative are you? Take Self-Assessment 6.2 and see how word-creative you are.

Developing Creativity

Creativity can actually be developed. One way is by knowing how creativity actually works. There are four stages in this process: preparation, incubation, illumination, and verification. In the preparation stage, the decision maker gets mentally ready by gathering all the information available on the problem. Incubation consists of allowing the data

SELF-ASSESSMENT QUIZ 6.2

How Word-Creative Are You?

This quiz calls for word completion. Each of the rows below contains three words. The meaning of all these words can be altered or expanded by adding one word before or after them. The word that is added is the *same for all three* and either becomes part of the word or helps create a two-word cliche. For example, what word can be added to these three words to alter or expand their meaning?

plane	hot	line

Look at the words again. The answer is "air": airplane, hot air, airline.
Try another:

smith	ball	boot

The answer is "black": blacksmith, black ball (to reject for membership), and boot black.

Follow this same logic in completing these ten groupings below. You have only five minutes so time yourself. When you are finished, join with two of your colleagues, review all your answers, change any you feel are wrong, and then go on and collectively try to complete any that have you stumped. Do not use a dictionary, but do use freewheeling and imaginative thinking. You have ten minutes to complete this group effort. When the time is up, check your answers. (Answers can be found at the back of the book.)

1. _____	village	light	golf
2. _____	up	hard	book
3. _____	loose	club	ball
4. _____	flash	star	lime
5. _____	show	dance	ground
6. _____	game	high	fast
7. _____	blue	pressure	line
8. _____	sky	blood	point
9. _____	priest	proof	tide
10. _____	door	oven	cheese

to sit in the subconscious mind where the brain actually rearranges it in different patterns. Illumination is the stage when the answer to the problem occurs to the individual. Verification is the testing of the solution and the making of adjustments so that the solution works. Although individuals make use of creative thinking, groups can also profit from it. Two of the best examples of group creative thinking are brainstorming and the Gordon technique.

Brainstorming helps generate creative ideas.

Brainstorming is a group approach to problem solving in which the emphasis is placed on generating as many ideas as possible. At the beginning of the brainstorming session, the group leader tells the participants the problem that is under analysis and urges them to be as imaginative and creative as they can in formulating their ideas. The members can say whatever they want. Criticism is forbidden, but "freewheeling" is encouraged as members attempt to expand the ideas of others or piggyback on them to develop still other suggestions. Some ideas, of course, are superficial and others are too imaginative to be workable. However, those that remain are often very helpful.

So does the Gordon technique.

A second useful technique is the *Gordon technique*. This technique is used for handling technical problems. Though similar to brainstorming, under this method the participants are not told the problem under consideration. They are only given a hint or stimulus. For example, if they are working on designing air conditioning units, the key phrase might be "greater efficiency." From here it is up to the group to generate ideas that might result in greater efficiency. Table 6.1 presents a summary of rules and suggestions for group sessions using brainstorming and the Gordon technique.

Table 6.1

SUMMARY OF RULES AND SUGGESTIONS FOR GROUP SESSIONS	
Brainstorming	Gordon Technique
Rules	
1. Judicial thinking or evaluation is ruled out. 2. Freewheeling is welcomed. 3. Quantity wanted. 4. Combinations and improvements are sought.	1. Only the group leader knows the problem. 2. Free association is used. 3. Subject for discussion must be carefully chosen.
Suggestions	
1. Length: 40 minutes to one hour, sessions of 10 to 15 minutes can be effective if time is short. 2. Do not reveal the problem before the session. An information sheet or suggested reference material on a related subject should be used if prior knowledge of the general field is needed. 3. Problem should be clearly stated and not too broad. 4. Use a small conference table which allows people to communicate with each other easily. 5. If a product is being discussed, samples may be useful as a point of reference.	1. Length of session: two to three hours are necessary. 2. Group leader must be exceptionally gifted and thoroughly trained in the use of the technique.

Table 6.1   *(Continued)*

SUMMARY OF RULES AND SUGGESTIONS FOR GROUP SESSIONS

Brainstorming	Gordon Technique

General suggestions that apply to both techniques:

1. Selection of personnel: a group from diverse backgrounds helps. Try to get a balance of highly active and quiet members.
2. Mixed groups of men and women are often more effective, especially for consumer problems.
3. Although physical atmosphere is not too important, a relaxed pleasant atmosphere is desirable.
4. Group size: groups of from four to twelve can be effective. We recommend six to nine.
5. Newcomers may be introduced without disturbing the group, but they must be properly briefed in the theory of creative thinking and the use of the particular technique.
6. A secretary or recording machine should be used to record the ideas produced. Otherwise they may not be remembered later. Gordon always uses a blackboard so that ideas can be visualized.

7. Hold sessions in the morning if people are going to continue to work on the same problem after the session has ended; otherwise hold them late in the afternoon. (The excitement of a session continues for several hours after it is completed, and can affect an employee's routine tasks.)
8. Usually it is advisable not to have people from widely differing ranks within the organization in the same session.

SOURCE: Charles S. Whiting, "Operational Techniques of Creative Thinking." *Advanced Management Journal,* October 1955, p. 28. Reprinted with permission.

Increasing Personal Creativity

Creativity is often thought of as a gift you have or do not have. Recent research shows that this is not true. People can actually increase their creativity if they follow four important steps:

1. Loosen up emotionally and intellectually. Creative people give free rein to their emotions.

2. Discipline yourself to think creatively. Highly creative people try not to be bound by old ways of looking at problems; they go beyond the familiar.

Ways of developing your own creativity

3. When trying to formulate creativity in a group setting, use approaches like brainstorming. Encourage imagination; discourage criticism.

COMMUNICATION TECHNOLOGY

Brainstorming Electronically

Brainstorming can be a very useful technique for generating new ideas or building on the ideas of others. However, it can also be expensive to bring everyone together for a 60- to 90-minute brainstorming session. This is why some firms are turning to electronic brainstorming.

Rather than having everyone leave the workplace and come to a central locale, electronic brainstorming lets everyone stay in their workplace and communicate interactively via the microcomputer. The process is quite simple. Individuals are sent a memo describing a particular problem the company has and are asked to think about possible solutions. They are urged to be as creative as possible. Then, at a predetermined time, the members of the group boot up their microcomputers and link in with the rest. This is where the fireworks often begin.

Anyone with an idea of how to solve the problem can begin by typing out a solution to the problem. Then everyone else can join in by sending messages regarding how to modify the initial solution or explaining why the initial solution will not work and offering one of their own. Although the participants cannot see each other, they can read each other's messages and respond to them. Research shows that people who engage in this form of computer interaction are often more blunt, direct, critical, and analytical than those who meet fact to face. This approach can be particularly helpful in ensuring that the group does not passively agree to a particular solution. Instead, there is often vigorous disagreement followed by detailed explanations regarding why the proposed solution will not work.

As the group continues brainstorming, the same general pattern emerges as in face-to-face discussion: a general consensus arises on those ideas that are worth pursuing and those that seem to be too creative or too unlikely to have useful payoff. Then the group can meet and, working with a limited number of ideas, decide how to proceed.

Several important benefits are associated with electronic brainstorming. First, it minimizes the amount of time needed to bring the participants together. Second, it serves as an important catalyst in generating a large number of ideas. Third, even if the group insists on some face-to-face meetings, it can be used to supplement the brainstorming process.

4. Develop the right climate for creativity by employing a human resources approach to management. People are more creative under conditions of participative management than they are under conditions of autocratic management.[16]

Implications for Management

1. Remember that most people are a lot more creative than they are given credit for being. If you have a problem that requires a creative solution, consider a team approach. Get additional information on how to set up and use brainstorming and the Gordon technique. They are not very difficult approaches to use, and the results are often well worth the time and effort.

2. Give people time to be creative. Nothing is more difficult for a comedian than to be approached by someone on the street and asked to "be funny." Funny people are creative, but even they cannot always turn on their "funniness" the way they would a light bulb. If you have a problem that needs a creative solution, the participants may need time to think about it. During the first brainstorming session, the ideas may be only mediocre. People are becoming familiar with the technique and are learning to work as a group. Also, they may need some time to think about potential solutions. Remember that the incubation period often takes time. The subconscious mind may need a week or more to sort out a solution to a complex problem.

3. Be aware that a creative climate is nurtured and developed by management. You can help create this necessary climate by opening channels of communication to your people, showing trust in their judgment and ability, letting them know that you are receptive to new ideas and are willing to accept necessary changes, and rewarding those who generate the most original and successful ideas. By following these kinds of guidelines, you will soon find that creative people from other departments will want to work for you. Your reputation will get around, and you will be regarded as a creative manager yourself.

4. Keep in mind that creativity can be increased if someone is shown how to be more creative and/or encouraged for being creative. Remember McGregor's Theory Y tenet that holds that the creative abilities of most people go untapped in the world of work. These abilities are there; it is a matter of getting people to use them. So the challenge is squarely in management's corner. Lazy, uncooperative, and unimaginative employees often reveal more about management's ability than about the worker's ability.

C A S E   I N   P O I N T

Revisited

Before reading these suggested answers, make any changes you want in your current answers. Update your analysis based on the chapter material.

The problem in this case can be traced to a combination of groupthink and the risky-shift phenomenon. Quite obviously, the members who wanted the group to go along with the decision that had already been made were able to impose their will on the others. Undoubtedly, the human resources person told them the dangers involved in such action, but they ignored his advice. Why did the members finally agree? The answer might well be found in the fact that high risk takers are often able to sway more moderate group members; such risk taking is socially acceptable. Finally, somewhere in your answer you should have had a discussion of groupthink. Those members who did not go along may well have been encouraged to "get on the bandwagon."

No matter what your final answer was, it should have been geared toward identifying problems with group decision making. How could the problem have been prevented? The answer to this question requires use of some of the remedies for groupthink that were offered in the chapter. If you missed any of these points, you may want to review some of the chapter material.

YOU BE THE CONSULTANT

The Better Mousetrap

It seems these days that just about everyone wants a personal computer. At least, that is the way Paula Burke and her associates feel about it. Paula is a major partner in a midwestern computer firm. The company is not very large. It was started two years ago by Paula's husband, Paula, and five of their close friends. All of them had been working at a major university teaching in the hard sciences. On an almost-daily basis, they increasingly found themselves using the computer and writing their own programs to handle the various types of research and analysis they needed performed.

One day the seven professors were having coffee and talking. One of them suggested that they take their skills and start their own business. "We know a lot about computers," he said. "I'll bet we can build a small one for the average person and it wouldn't cost anything close to what Apple, IBM, or any of the other big companies in the field want." This got the group thinking. Over the next six months, they collectively designed and built a small personal computer. There were various problems, but as they went along the partners found they could work out the bugs in the machine. They then decided to pool their funds, build ten of these units, and see if they could sell them. They were surprised with the results. The chairman of the accounting department in the College of Business, an old friend, was given a demonstration, and he immediately got a downtown accounting firm to buy three of them for his department. The other seven were snapped up by other departments around the campus, including one that was purchased by the University Budget Office.

After stepping back and taking a look at what they had, the partners realized that their machine was smaller, easier to master in terms of learning the instructions, and could be sold for approximately $500 less than any similar machine on the market. This figure of $500 was based on manufacturing costs plus an allowance of $200 per machine for marketing. "If we can get the university to take all of our machines off our hands," remarked one of the partners, "then we can make an additional $200 of profit from each of our units."

The partners decided to start small. They hired a subcontractor who was familiar with the business and had him build 25 units. These were sold within a month of the time they were delivered. Over the next three months, the partners sold an additional 400 units.

Now their attention is turning to producing and selling these machines on a nationwide basis. The biggest problem they believe they have currently is that very few people know about their particular personal computer. The other day, Paula picked up a copy of *Fortune* magazine and leafed through it. She saw over ten ads for personal computers. She found this same pattern in other business-related journals such as *Business Week* and *Forbes*. This has convinced the partners that, unless they can advertise their product effectively, they will not be able to survive. The group believes that if it can secure sales of 20,000 personal computers a year, its market niche will be safe. With a production run this large, economies of scale will set in. The machines can be produced for approximately 50 percent less than now when, at most, 100 units are being produced at one time.

One of the things that Paula, who has been charged with doing an analysis of the personal computer industry and the competition, has learned is that over the next five years there will be a big shakeout in the industry. Apparently, many small manufacturers of personal computers will be unable to survive the onslaught of firms like IBM. More importantly, the latest articles in the area all point to marketing as the key subject for consideration. Paula thought it would have been manufacturing, but the experts in the industry argue that if a firm has a large enough market niche, production costs can be spread over many units, thereby allowing the company to reduce its price per unit and remain highly competitive.

Armed with this information, Paula urged the partnership to address the need for a marketing campaign. "We need to begin," she said, "with a strong advertising campaign. We have to let people know that we have a small personal computer that is better than anything else in the field. I think that all of us agree that most buyers do not really know the difference between the various machines. They are confused and depend on the advertisements and/or salespeople to help sell them the product. If we were to come up with interesting, catchy ads that introduced our product and explained why the reader would be wise to buy it, I think we would be ahead of the game."

The partners basically agree with Paula's ideas. they know that they cannot depend on local sales alone to get them through, and they realize that, at best, they will be able to sell only a few more units at the university. So they will have to go out into the marketplace and begin drumming up business.

The head of the accounting department was by to see them last week. He recommends that the group look into bringing in a consulting firm. "You need someone who has business experience and knowledge. You are all very technically skilled, but do you really know anything about selling? In particular, do you know how to conduct a really effective advertising campaign? Oh sure, you believe now that you have a better product, the world is going to beat a path to your door. However, that is a little premature. They will only beat a path to your door if they know you have the better mousetrap, or in this case, personal computer." The group agreed and with the help of the accounting chairperson had a meeting with a national management consulting firm. The head of the consulting group explained that the place to begin was with a vigorous advertising campaign in the local area. "As your sales increase, you can then open up retail outlets in other sections of the country or offer franchise units to entrepreneurs in those locales. However, for the moment, we have to let everyone know about your product. Now I personally know very little about personal computers, so with my staff, I want to spend a few days learning how your product works and what it can do for the buyer. After that we'll be ready to take a crack at an ad campaign."

Assume that you are a member of the consulting team and have been appointed the task of designing the ad campaign. How would you go about getting ideas for the ads? Would brainstorming be of any value? Would the Gordon technique help? How would you arrange the creative thinking sessions? How many people would be present? How long would the meetings last? What would you allow everyone to talk about or refrain from saying? Spell out your plan of action and offer it to your boss, the head of the consulting firm. Be as complete and realistic as possible in your approach.

Key Points in This Chapter

1. People in organizations often communicate with one another as members of formal or informal groups. The way in which they communicate and interact in groups is known as group dynamics.

2. A group is a social unit consisting of two or more interdependent, interactive individuals who are striving to attain common goals.

3. Groups often go through four phases or stages of development. The first is called "forming," during which time group members discover those interpersonal behaviors that are both acceptable and unacceptable to others in the group. The second is called "storming," and during this phase, individual members develop a special place for themselves in the group and attempt to influence the development of its norms and roles. The third phase, "norming," is characterized by the development of group cohesion and unity of purpose. During the fourth stage, "performing," the group members agree on the basic roles each is to play.

4. Formal groups are created by the organization itself. The most common types of formal groups are functional groups, project groups, and committees. Formal groups make wide use of downward, upward, and horizontal communication flows.

5. Informal groups are created by the personnel themselves. They are a result of individual and collective self-interest. These groups make wide use of downward, upward, horizontal, and diagonal communication flows.

6. People join groups because they are physically located near one another; because they need to coordinate their efforts with others in getting things done; or because of the personal satisfaction that results from group membership.

7. Motivation is a force that directs a person toward an objective. When examined in terms of Maslow's need hierarchy, we find that individuals are motivated to satisfy five basic needs: physiological, safety, social, esteem, and self-actualization. When

group members attain need satisfaction, the communication flows are quite different than when need satisfaction is blocked. When blocking occurs, a number of different types of defensive behavior can result, including aggression, rationalization, compensation, and/or regression.

8. Group decision making offers several potential benefits over individual decision making: (a) greater total knowledge and/or information, (b) usually a greater number of problem-solving approaches, (c) higher morale and help in implementing the decision throughout the department or organization, and (d) improved comprehension and analysis of the problem and of alternative solutions.

9. A number of potential problems are associated with group decision making. One of the most common is groupthink, a term that refers to the need for individuals in a group to suppress dissent and go along with others. Some of the most common symptoms of groupthink include invulnerability, rationalization, morality, stereotyping, self-censorship, unanimity, and mindguarding. The chapter describes nine ways to prevent or reduce the negative impact of groupthink.

10. The risky-shift phenomenon is the tendency of individuals to be greater risk takers when acting as members of a group than when acting alone. Numerous explanations have been offered for the occurrence of this phenomenon, including the fact that (a) the individuals in a group often feel they will not be personally responsible should the group's decision prove to be wrong and (b) risky people in groups tend to be more influential than conservative people.

11. In some cases group decision making can be improved through the use of creativity techniques. Creativity comes in many different forms, the four major ones being innovation, synthesis, extension, and duplication. In developing creative solutions, two of the most common techniques are brainstorming and the Gordon technique. Both make wide use of freewheeling and piggybacking on the ideas of others.

12. Individual creativity can be developed if people follow some basic rules. Some of the most important ways are by loosening up emotionally and intellectually, disciplining oneself to think creatively, using creative thinking techniques such as brainstorming and the Gordon technique, and developing the right climate.

Questions for Discussion and Analysis

1. In your own words, what is mean by the term *group?* What characteristics are common to groups? Be sure to include them in your definition and description of the term.

2. Groups undergo four stages: forming, storming, norming, and performing. What happens during each stage? Identify and describe each.

3. How does a formal group differ from an informal one? Compare and contrast the two. In your comparison include examples of both types of groups including

functional, project, and committees as examples of formal groups and whatever social groups you would like in your description of informal ones.

4. The four basic communication flows are downward, upward, horizontal, and diagonal. How does each work? Which is likely to be used by formal groups? Informal groups? Explain.

5. Three of the major reasons why people join groups are propinquity, productivity, and personal satisfaction. What does this statement mean? Put it in your own words.

6. How do motivation and need satisfaction affect the communication process? If need satisfaction is blocked, what is likely to happen? How will the resulting defensive behaviors manifest themselves? Be sure to put your answer in terms of communication patterns or behaviors.

7. What are three of the potential benefits of group decision making? Identify and describe each.

8. How does groupthink work? What are some of the most common symptoms of groupthink? Identify and describe six of them.

9. How can groupthink be overcome and/or prevented? Offer at least five remedies.

10. In your own words, what is meant by the term risky-shift phenomenon? Why does this phenomenon exist? Offer at least three explanations for its existence.

11. There are four major types of creativity. What does this statement mean? Identify and describe each of the four types in your answer.

12. What characteristics do creative people have in common? Identify and describe at least five of them.

13. How does brainstorming work? How does the Gordon technique work? How can each bring about creative results? Explain.

14. What can you do to develop your personal creativity? Identify and describe at least three steps that should be followed.

Exercises

1. Each person is asked to take five minutes and list all the groups to which he or she belongs. Then in small groups of three or four, members share their lists with others. In turn, they analyze their list by answering the following questions:
   a. Why do I belong to this group? (Propinquity, productivity, and personal satisfaction are three reasons.)
   b. Which groups give me the greatest satisfaction? Why?
   c. Which group(s) do I consider as reference groups, that is, those that influence my behavior the most?
   d. Are my group memberships voluntary or involuntary?

2. Try your hand at brainstorming. In groups of four or five, spend five minutes coming up with alternative solutions to the following problem. Have one person in each group record the answers to report back to the entire class. Remember that in brainstorming alternatives *every* idea is a good idea. The more creative, the better! *Situation:* You are a wholesaler whose warehouse has just burned down. Today's train has brought in 5,000 prepaid automobile tires of all sizes, but you have no place to store them. You must, however, accept these tires, stack them on your property, and come up with some quick scheme(s) to market them. To whom can you sell them and for what purpose?

References

1. Stewart L. Tubbs, A *Systems Approach to Small Group Interaction*, 3rd ed. (New York: Random House, 1988), p. 10.

2. Bruce W. Tuckman, "Developmental Sequences in Small Groups," *Psychological Bulletin*, June 1965, pp. 384–399.

3. Joseph E. McGrath, *Groups: Interaction and Performance*, (Englewood Cliffs, N.J.: Prentice-Hall, 1984), p. 14.

4. Abraham Maslow, *Motivation and Personality*, 2nd ed. (New York: Harper & Row, 1970).

5. *Ibid.*, p. 54.

6. Jane Whitney Gibson, *The Supervisory Challenge* (Columbus, Ohio: Merrill Publishing Co., 1990), p. 208.

7. *Ibid.*, p. 208.

8. Irving L. Janis, *Groupthink: Psychological Studies of Policy Decisions and Fiascoes* (Boston: Houghton Mifflin Co., 1982), p. 9.

9. *Ibid.*, p. 247.

10. Irving Janis, "Groupthink," *Psychology Today*, November 1971, p. 44.

11. Janis, *Groupthink, op. cit.*, p. 233.

12. For more on this subject of groupthink, see Clarence W. Von Bergen, Jr., and Raymond J. Kirk, "Groupthink: When Too Many Heads Spoil the Decision," *Management Review*, March 1978, pp. 44–49; Martin Lasden, "Facing Down Groupthink," *Computer Decisions*, May 6, 1986, p. 52(5); Glen Whyte, "Groupthink Reconsidered" *Academy of Management Review*, January 1989, p. 40 (7); and Gregory Moorhead and John R. Montanari, "An Empirical Investigation of the Groupthink Phenomenon," *Human Relations*, May 1986, p. 399 (12).

13. Steven Altman, Enzo R. Valenzi, and Richard M. Hodgetts, *Organizational Behavior: Theory and Practice* (Orlando, Fl: Academic Press, 1985), pp. 251–254.

14. For more on the risky-shift phenomenon, see Dorwin Cartwright, "Risk Taking by Individuals and Groups: An Assessment of Research Employing Choice Dilemmas," *Journal of Personality and Social Psychology*, December 1971, pp. 361–378; Russell D. Clark III, "Group Induced Shift Toward Risk: A Critical Appraisal," *Psychological Bulletin*, October 1979, pp. 251–270; Dean G. Pruitt, "Choice Shifts in Group Discussion: An Introductory Review," *Journal of Personality and Social Psychology*, December 1971, pp. 339–360; and Timothy W. McGuire, Sara Kiesler, and Jane Siegel, "Group and Computer-Mediated Discussion Effects in Risk Decision Making," *Journal of Personality and Social Psychology*, May 1987, p. 917(14).

15. Andrew J. DuBrin, *Human Relations: A Job-Oriented Approach* (Reston, Va., 1978), pp. 54–55.

16. Daniel Plunkett, "Intervention for Creativity: An O.D. Approach," *Training and Development Journal*, August 1988, pp. 68–71.

Annotated Bibliography

Barnard, Chester, *The Functions of the Executive* (Cambridge, Mass.: Harvard University Press, 1938).

A classic in the field, this book was originally published in 1938 but has gone through numerous printings since then. It provides an excellent in-depth look at what managers do. Specific consideration is given to communication and group dynamics. For the practicing manager, in particular, this book is a must.

Janis, Irving, *Groupthink: Psychological Studies of Policy Decisions and Fiascoes* (Boston: Houghton Mifflin Co., 1982).

Janis's famous groupthink paradigm was energized by his musings about the Bay of Pigs fiasco. In this well-known book, Janis explains his theory, analyzes various well-known political events according to the model, and suggests remedies to the groupthink syndrome.

Maslow, Abraham, *Motivation and Personality*, 2nd ed. (New York: Harper & Row, 1970).

This is Maslow's major work revised shortly before his death in 1970. Maslow's life work was spent conceptualizing a humanistic and holistic way of looking at motivation, personality, and life as a whole.

McGrath, Joseph E. *Groups: Interaction and Performance* (Englewood Cliffs, N.J., Prentice-Hall, 1984).

This book is about the study of groups. It documents many scientific studies of group behavior and is a comprehensive resource for people looking for information on many aspects of group dynamics.

Smith, Kenwyn K., and Berg, David N. *Paradoxes of Group Life: Understanding Conflict, Paralysis, and Movement in Group Dynamics* (San Francisco: Jossey-Bass, 1987).

This book is a collaborative effort to explore the nature of conflict and opposition in groups as well as the processes of group paralysis and movement. The book focuses on the many ways in which paradox manifests itself in group life.

Tubbs, Stewart L. *A Systems Approach to Small Group Interaction*, 3rd ed. (New York: Random House, 1988).

This book is written as a primary textbook for courses in group communication. Tubbs uses many exercises, cases, and applications to relate his model of group behavior to the real-world organizational setting.

CHAPTER 7

Leadership and Communication

"There go my people. I must find out where they are going so I can lead them."

Alexandre Ledru-Rollin

Objectives

1. To be able to define the term *leadership* and explain the importance of efficiency and effectiveness to leaders.

2. To compare and contrast Theory X managers with Theory Y managers, explaining how the communication patterns of the two differ.

3. To explain the role of the communication effectiveness triad in the exercise of leadership.

4. To describe the five most common personal characteristics possessed by successful leaders.

5. To compare and contrast the communication styles of authoritarian, paternalistic, participative, and laissez-faire leaders.

6. To relate the most useful leadership models for managers at the lower, middle, and upper levels of the hierarchy.

7. To introduce the concepts of transformational leadership and empowerment.

C A S E   I N   P O I N T

Fred's Reorganization

When Fred Jackson was hired as a supervisor and first-line manager at a manufacturing firm three months ago, he was determined to do the best possible job. The people who work for him do the assembly and packing of small units. There are six assemblers and three packers.

The work is not very difficult, and all the personnel have been on the job for at least a year. In a typical week an assembler can complete 400 units and a packer can do 800 units. The break-in period for new people is about ten working days. It takes two or three days to master the finer parts of the job and the other seven or eight days to increase speed up to expected levels. The company believes that every assembler should be able to put together 375 units a week, and every packer should be able to finish 750 units weekly.

When Fred took over, his boss told him, "I know this is your first experience as a supervisor. However, just take it nice and easy. Don't rock the boat. The workers know what is going on and can get the job done. Your role should be one of handling problems or unexpected situations. Otherwise, just stay out of their way. They have the highest output in the company, and they have been working together for over 14 months. Give them their head and let them run. They'll take care of everything else."

Fred appreciated his boss's interest. However, he found that the workers were not doing a lot of work. Approximately 20 percent of the time they were just sitting around talking. Fred realized that they could do a lot more work if they would just cut out all the socializing. As a result, he called them together and told them that he intended to reorganize the group for increased efficiency. During the first four days following the reorganization, output went up. Since then it has come down and people are complaining about the changes Fred has made. Last week it stood at 378 units for the assemblers and 752 units for the packers. Fred's boss does not like these latest developments and called him in for a talk. When Fred left the office, he was very upset. "I don't understand what I did wrong," he told a friend. "I tried to get in there and act the part of a leader rather than sit on the sidelines and do nothing; and all it's gotten me is a lot of trouble. I don't know. Maybe I don't understand what leaders are supposed to do."

What did Fred do wrong? What mistakes did he make as a leader? What should he have done? Write down your answers and then put them off to the side. We will return to them later.

INTRODUCTION

The objective of every communication is to convey meanings, although the purpose of the communique will vary. Sometimes the communicator will want to inform someone about a new development. Other times the individual will want the receiver to act on this information. Still other times the individual will want to influence or alter the receiver's point of view. Consider some of the most common verbal messages that managers deliver on a daily basis:

■ I'd like you to look at this.

- I've read your report and would like to talk to you about it when you have some time.

- I think you should consider acting on this.

- Have you decided whether or not you'll be attending the supervisory leadership program? I think you should.

Managers, in particular, need to communicate effectively in order to carry out their role as leaders. This can be done through actions, words, or both. Whatever approach is employed, the leader must use communication to influence others to accept his or her point of view. No study of communication would be complete without consideration of this important topic. We begin our study of the subject by examining the nature of leadership.

THE NATURE OF LEADERSHIP

Leadership defined

Leadership is the process of influencing people to direct their efforts toward the attainment of particular goal(s). This process by its very nature requires the use of effective communication skills. Of course, the effective manager must be more than just a communicator, but without the ability to convey meanings and without followup to see that the desired results are achieved, the manager will fail to fulfill his or her basic responsibility — getting things done through people.

Efficiency and Effectiveness

Efficiency is doing things right.

Leaders must be both efficient and effective. *Efficiency* is the ability to do things right. A manager who sees that all of her people are in the building and working by 8:30 A.M. is efficient. She is ensuring that the company's resources are being used to carry out the tasks and responsibilities assigned to them. Efficiency is typically measured by the equation: output/input. Consider the following example:

> Wilma Thompson has noticed that many of her people begin preparing to leave at 4:15 P.M. even though quitting time is 4:30 P.M. She also knows that the amount of work being done in the department is less than it should be. In order to kill two birds with one stone, Wilma has now begun assigning her people additional work at about 3:45 P.M. In most cases, she gives them jobs that will take approximately 45 minutes and tells them, "I need this done before you go home today." Over the last three weeks, Wilma has noticed that the amount of work output has increased dramatically, and there is less carried over to the next day. When her boss asked her about her new practice, she said, "Look, we pay people to work, not to get ready to go home. It should only take five minutes to prepare to leave and I never object if someone starts putting things away and cleaning off their desk at 4:20 P.M. However, I don't see why we should give them a half hour to prepare to leave. My new approach is both efficient and fair." Her boss nodded in agreement.

Notice in our example that Wilma increased the efficiency of her work staff by getting more done (increased output) with the same number of people (same input). Of course, there are other ways to increase efficiency. One is to cut the number of personnel by 5 percent and require all the remaining workers to make up the output of these people. In this case we would have the same output but a decreased input. Another way is to increase the amount of output by a greater percentage than the amount of input. For example, by putting in three new machines that increase input cost by 27 percent, total output is increased by 35 percent. Many combinations of the input/output ratio can be created. The important thing to remember is that effective leaders strive to increase efficiency by making changes in the input/output ratio. Communication is a vital part of this process. In the case of Wilma, she used it to give her people additional work assignments.

Effectiveness is the ability to do the right things. Notice that in contrast to our definition of efficiency, effectiveness is more encompassing. An organization can be very efficient but not very effective. It may have the lowest cost per unit in the industry (efficiency), but no one is willing to buy its products because they are technologically inferior (effectiveness). Effectiveness deals with absolute achievement of results when compared against some standard. For example, a top manager may decide that the marketing department should capture 10 percent of the market with its new product. Share of the market is a measure of effectiveness because it compares the company's performance against that of the competition. Remember that share of the market can be attained only at the expense of other firms. So if the company wins, the competition loses and vice versa.

> Templar Construction, a large construction firm in the Southwest, learned that the federal government was asking for bids on a series of bridge and dam contracts. After examining its own expertise and that of the competition, top management decided to bid on four of the seven major contracts with the goal of winning two. When the contracts were awarded last month, Templar got two of the major ones. Each of their largest competitors got one. In addition, because of their expertise, Templar will also receive subcontracts for approximately 10 percent of the work to be done by these competitors. The chairman of the board was overjoyed. "We got more than our share," he told the president. "Your people did an excellent job on this one."

Notice in our example that the company was interested in getting a specific share of the work. The emphasis was not on how to build a particular dam as cheaply as possible but on doing better than the competition did in obtaining contract work. Notice also that although our efficiency example involved a leader at the middle/lower level of the hierarchy, our effectiveness example involved top management. This is because the objectives of middle-/lower-level leaders are directed more heavily to efficiency, whereas those of middle-/upper-level leaders are geared more heavily toward effectiveness. (See Table 7.1 for a comparison of the two.)

When leaders deal with efficiency, they generally communicate in terms of objectives such as cost, productivity, and labor turnover. When they deal with effectiveness, they often communicate in terms of market share, growth rate, return on investment, and other criteria that can be used in comparing company performance with that of the competition. However, regardless of which is primary, there is *always* some concern for *both* efficiency and effectiveness. For example, although Wilma would like her people to be efficient, how would we be able to determine *ideal* efficiency? One of the easiest

Effectiveness is doing the right things.

Leaders are concerned with both efficiency and effectiveness.

Table 7.1

EFFICIENCY AND EFFECTIVENESS: A COMPARISON	
Efficiency	Effectiveness
Do things right	Do the right things
Decrease inputs and/or increase outputs	Gain the upper hand vis-à-vis the competition
Solve problems	Produce results
Manage today's challenges	Manage tomorrow's challenges
Lower costs	Increase profitability
Safeguard resources	Optimize resource use

ways is by finding out how much work people holding similar jobs in other companies are doing. Similarly, although the top management would like to increase its market share, this goal will be impossible unless the good or service can be delivered at a reasonable price. So internal efficiency will have to be affected if external effectiveness is to be achieved. The most successful leaders are interested in *both* efficiency and effectiveness (see Figure 7.1).

Personal Philosophy

Every leader has a philosophy of management. This philosophy incorporates the individual's beliefs regarding, among other things, why people work and how they should be motivated. These ideas were well presented by Douglas McGregor when he discussed Theory X and Theory Y, topics examined in Chapter 2. Before continuing, take Self-Assessment Quiz 7.1 and determine your own philosophy of leadership.

Figure 7.1

Successful leaders in action.

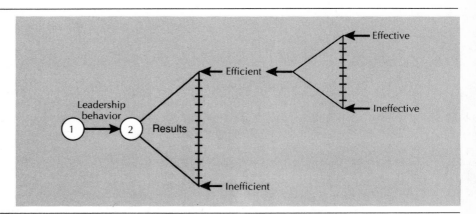

SELF-ASSESSMENT QUIZ 7.1

Identifying Your Personal Philosophy of Management

Read each of the following statements very carefully. After each write down a number from 0 to 10 depending on how strongly you agree with the statement. Use the following as your guide:

- 0 Totally disagree with the statement
- 3 Basically disagree with the statement
- 7 Basically agree with the statement
- 10 Totally agree with the statement

When you are finished total all of your numbers and put this number at the bottom of the page.

1. People hate to work. _____

2. People basically are lazy. _____

3. Money is the prime motivator for most workers. _____

4. Above all, workers want security. _____

5. Most workers shun responsibility whenever they can. _____

6. Most workers have very little ambition. _____

7. People like to be directed. _____

8. If you want people to do something right, you have to control them closely. _____

9. Unfortunately, to get people to attain organizational objectives it is necessary to use coercion and threats. _____

10. For the most part, work is so difficult that the average person has trouble mastering the job. _____

Total _____

An explanation of your philosophy is in the Answer section at the back of the book.

A leader who believes that workers are basically lazy and are interested only in money will attempt to motivate them in a much different manner than will a leader who believes that workers are interested in achieving upper-level need satisfaction and will respond enthusiastically to challenging jobs. The first leader is likely to communicate in very limited and job-oriented terms, putting the emphasis on what is to be done, how it is to be done, and by when it should be finished. If the individual does attempt to motivate the personnel, it is likely to be in terms such as, "If you do a good job, I'll see that you are mentioned for a raise" or "If you are finished with all of this by the close of business tomorrow, you'll get a 15 percent bonus for your performance." The second leader is likely to talk in terms of internal rewards to satisfactions for the personnel. Examples include, "You can choose your own approach to doing this, but I'd like you to be finished no later than tomorrow afternoon" or "I know how much you like this type of work because it gives you a chance to use your engineering skills. Go to it and give it your best shot. If you need any help, just let me know. Otherwise, the only limit is time. You have to be finished by tomorrow at 5 P.M."

The first type of leader is called a Theory X manager, and the second type is called a Theory Y manager. The differences between them are especially significant in terms of communication.

Communication Effectiveness Triad

Effective communication is a triad consisting of the leader, the members of the work group, and the environment in which the work is to be performed. See Figure 7.2.

THE LEADER The leader's job is to build an environment in which teamwork can be achieved. One of the leader's major objectives is to create and maintain credibility with the work group. Four factors influence this effort: drive, dependability, competence, and credibility. *Drive* is the physical and mental effort expended by the leader. Research reveals that individuals who are seen as having a great deal of drive have more influence with their peers and superiors. Because they walk, talk, and act with vigor, those around them assume they know what they are doing. Drive helps open doors for them. *Dependability* is the reliance people can place in the leader's word. Subordinates trust a highly dependable leader because they know that when the boss tells them something will happen, it will happen. They can depend on the individual to live up to promises. *Competence* is the ability of the leader to get a job done effectively and efficiently.

Leaders must protect their credibility.

Credibility is the degree to which a leader is believable. This is perhaps the leader's most important asset. It is directly affected by the perception people have of the individual's honesty, discretion, and ability. Credibility is influenced by the subordinate's perception of "why" the leader acts the way he or she does. A leader who tells a subordinate, "If you take this assignment and do well, I will recommend you for the promotion you wanted," and then follows through and makes the recommendation, adds to his or her credibility. On the other hand, if the subordinate finds out that top management has promised the

Figure 7.2

The communication effectiveness triad.

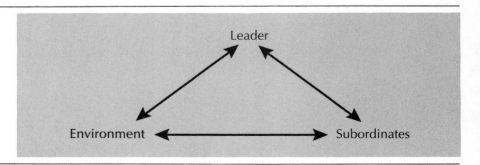

leader a large personal reward (a promotion, a big raise, etc.) if this particular job is carried out by one of his people, the leader's credibility will be jeopardized. If improper or self-serving motives are hidden from subordinates, the leader's believability declines.

THE SUBORDINATE The second critical element in the communication effectiveness triad is the subordinate. No matter how hard the leader tries to develop group

Teamwork is important.

teamwork, the support of the personnel is necessary. Group norms and feelings toward the leader and the organization must be positive. Sometimes events work against the manager. For example, if there has been a prolonged union–management contract dispute, the leader may find it difficult to create an efficient work team regardless of how credible the individual is with the members. They may like the leader but feel they are unable to go along with the individual's desires because of the pressure they are feeling from their peers. The situation may be one of us (the union) against them (the company). On the positive side, most workers do want to do a good job, and barring such mitigating circumstances as union–management difficulties, an effective leader can develop an efficient working team.

THE ENVIRONMENT The environment is the third major factor in the triad. We introduced it in the above paragraph in the form of union–management relations. However, the situation need not be as obvious as this example. Many times organizations have operating philosophies that, in and of themselves, create teamwork problems. For example, consider the fact that in many enterprises people are rewarded for attaining the objectives of their department without consideration of how these objectives fit in with those of other departments. The finance people are often rewarded for their conservativeness. They strive to ensure that the organization does not borrow too much money, can operate within its budget, and makes a reasonable return on its investment. The marketing people, on the other hand, are encouraged to be bold and daring. They must sell the company's goods and services throughout their country or region. They are much more optimistic about the future than their finance counterparts and seldom worry about how much money the company has borrowed. They are convinced that with a good sales program, these funds will be repaid and a high return achieved. The manufacturing people fall between the two extremes of finance and marketing. They want the finance people to increase the budget so that they can buy more plant and equipment and turn out more goods at a lower cost per unit. On the other hand, they believe that the marketing forecasts are too optimistic and demand will be less than the latter claim. Proceeding from different points of view, each of these three major departments will vie with the others. If the financial point of view wins out, the budget will be a conservative one and both marketing and production will lose. If the

The environment may need restructuring.

marketing people win out, they will get more money for advertising and personal selling efforts. If production wins out, more new plant and equipment will be purchased. Seldom does an organization have enough funds to satisfy both marketing and finance. Even if it does, this can be accomplished only at the expense of the finance department, which is urging conservativeness. In short, the system is set up to promote internal competition for resources. Teamwork can be achieved only by restructuring the priorities of the various departments. This is a job for top management.

Implications for Management

1. Determine whether it is important for you to be efficient or effective. Depending on your answer, communicate appropriately. Remember that lower-level managers have more of a need to be efficient while upper-level managers must place greater attention on effectiveness.

2. Work toward being a Theory Y manager. Sometimes you will need to exercise Theory X tenets, and some employees are best handled using a Theory X approach. However, in the main, Theory Y concepts are most useful for effective leadership. Over the long run personnel respond better to this style of leadership than to any other.

3. Work to build credibility among your personnel. Show them that you have drive and are dependable and competent. At the same time, keep in mind that there are three parts to the communication triad and to create the degree of teamwork needed to get the job done, you will have to focus attention on making the necessary changes in the personnel and the environment. The personnel need to be told what you expect of them and given continual encouragement and support in their work efforts. The environment sometimes needs to be modified so as to promote intragroup teamwork. Whenever you see conditions that reduce teamwork, change them or report them to your boss and encourage the boss to work with you in getting the necessary rules and regulations changed.

At the lower levels there are also environmental challenges to teamwork. One of the most common occurs when people in the work unit depend on others for assistance. Assembly-line work is an excellent illustration. If the individual who is assembling a widget is slow, those who are responsible for painting and testing the item must wait. In this case the leader must work with the informal group to induce the slow worker to increase the pace. Generally, the work environment cannot be redesigned, so the leader must focus attention on the subordinate(s) causing the problem. If this approach works, the problem is solved. If it does not work, then the leader must attempt to strike a wedge between the slow worker and the rest of the group. One human relations writer cites the reason:

> . . . until the manager is sure that the group's backing has been obtained, replacement of the slow worker should have a low priority. The leader needs to strike a wedge between this person and the group, to isolate the individual, and then to remove him. Teamwork depends on group support, and if the leader moves too fast, the group may feel that such action is not only inappropriate but also threatening. ("The manager might get rid of us just as fast. We'd better fight for [him] and protect our own jobs in the process.")[1]

LEADER CHARACTERISTICS

What characterizes an effective leader? This question continues to intrigue many scholars.

Leader characteristics

Literally thousands of empirical investigations of leaders have been conducted in the last seventy-five years alone, but no clear and unequivocal understanding exists as to what distinguishes leaders from non-leaders, and perhaps more important, what distinguishes "effective" leaders from "ineffective" leaders.[2]

Perhaps the biggest problem in examining leader characteristics is that there is no universal list. Some leaders are able to tolerate frustration and delay; others cannot. Some can make on-the-spot decisions; others are unable to do so. Some have tremendous physical stamina; others do not. Why then are both types successful? Because they carefully choose the environments in which they operate. A person who can put up with rules and regulations and not let them get him down may choose to work in a large government bureaucracy and do very well indeed. A person with a penchant for action will not accept a job in a slow bureaucracy where everything must go through channels; she will seek an organization where individual initiative and entrepreneurial skills are encouraged and promoted.

Yet all leaders have to be effective communicators. This can be seen clearly by examining the five most prevalent personal characteristics of the successful leader: superior intelligence, emotional maturity, motivation drive, problem-solving skills, and managerial skills.

SUPERIOR INTELLIGENCE Effective leaders tend to have superior intelligence. Certainly they are more intelligent than the average of their followers. They therefore have the mental skills needed to formulate and communicate information, process input from subordinates, and make decisions regarding work-related matters. If the leader were not as intelligent, on average, as the followers, he or she would have a difficult time influencing them. On the other hand, it is important to remember that the leader who is too highly intelligent may also have problems. This person may be too theoretical in his or her approach to a job.

Mental ability is important.

EMOTIONAL MATURITY Successful leaders are emotionally mature in that they have self-confidence and are able to direct their subordinates in a calm, conscientious manner. This is especially noticeable when a crisis or unexpected event occurs. Rather than losing their heads, screaming, or looking for scapegoats, they maintain their calm and try to figure out a course of action. They also know how to deal effectively with subordinates who have made mistakes. Rather than using the error as a basis for punishing or belittling the individual, they try to turn it into a lesson for future action. Consider the following:

Self-confidence is also important.

Paul Winslow was supposed to deliver a package to the president of the Bellow Corporation by 11 A.M. yesterday. The president was catching a plane to the East Coast and needed to take the material with him. However, Paul delivered the package to the president of the Rawlitt Company by mistake. The reason for the error was that Paul had delivered two packages to Rawlitt the day before and when he was given the latest package the head of the mail room said, "This one goes to the president, personally." Without looking at the name and address on the package, Paul signed for it and drove over to Rawlitt. The head of the administration department called Paul into his office to talk about the error. "I got a call from the president of Bellow. He's upset over not getting the package before he left for the coast. However, let's not start worrying about why the mistake was made. Let's look at what you can learn for future action. From now on, follow the rules. Read the name and address on the package before you leave the building. Okay?" Paul agreed.

Paul's boss exercised emotional maturity. He focused on the problem, not on the personality. If the problem occurs again, it may be necessary to reprimand Paul formally or dismiss him. However, for the moment the focus is on teaching Paul the importance of following rules and not lowering the boom on him.

Leaders need upper-level need satisfaction.

MOTIVATION DRIVE Effective leaders are highly motivated to get things done. They are most interested in upper-level need satisfaction. The chance to achieve power or control over a situation and to self-actualize by becoming the best person they can is particularly important. Even more interesting is the fact that they seek subordinates who feel the same way they do. As a result, successful leaders tend to work with, develop, and train other high-achieving people like themselves. Individuals who do not fall into this category soon find themselves being left behind and look for a chance to move to another department or organization where they can find a leader who is more to their liking. In managing their people, effective leaders make heavy use of participative management and open communication. This helps them delegate work and develop self-reliant subordinates.[3]

Good leaders know how to size up a situation.

PROBLEM-SOLVING SKILLS Effective leaders are problem solvers. They know how to size up a situation, figure out what is wrong, what needs to be done, and how it ought to be straightened out. They are able to differentiate between cause and effect and to focus their attention on cause. These leaders tend to be self-confident and able to learn from past experience. In this process they often involve their people, communicating what they want done and relying on the subordinates to do it. These leaders realize that they cannot singlehandedly solve all the group's problems. However, they can help focus on the important issues and see that the group is involved in the solution.

When Clara Betmer learned that top management was thinking about installing computers in her area, she knew that there would be problems with the personnel. In order to focus on the problem and ensure that any decision by top management met the least amount of resistance from the line, she called her people together and discussed how their workloads could be made easier. She then divided the group into four teams, each charged with determining what new types of technology could be used to do the job faster and easier. When all was said and done, the group had identified four major areas in which computers could be introduced to increase efficiency without causing unemployment. These happened to be the same four that management was focusing its attention on when it first thought about introducing the machines. Last week the machines were put in place. Clara's is the only department where management is not finding itself having to defend its computer decision.

Good leaders have developed managerial skills.

MANAGERIAL SKILLS Effective leaders have managerial skills. There are three in all: technical, human, and conceptual. *Technical skills* are needed for "doing" things. They are extremely important for lower-level managers such as foremen. *Human skills* are needed for dealing with people. They include the ability to communicate, motivate,

Figure 7.3

Skills needed at
different hierarchical
levels.

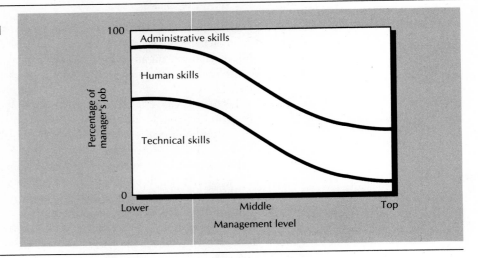

and lead personnel. *Administrative skills* are conceptual in nature. They include the ability to pull together all parts of the organization, determine how each can be integrated into the overall picture, and formulate a long-range plan of action based on the results. Figure 7.3 illustrates these three skills and their role in the management hierarchy.

All three skills require the ability to communicate effectively. At the lowest levels, the leader must be able to tell the subordinates "how to do it." At the middle levels of the hierarchy it is the leader who must translate top management's orders into lower-management action. The individual must be a buffer between the two levels. At the upper levels, the managers must use communication to pass on information related to long-range plans and policy implementation. The next section spells out how these tasks are carried out via effective communication.

**Implications
for
Management**

1. Keep in mind that subordinates look to leaders for guidance and direction. So it is important to maintain the right image and decorum. Avoid losing your temper, saying things for which you might later be sorry, or embarrassing subordinates in front of their peers. These actions are not leaderlike and will damage your effectiveness.

2. Remember that, although you are probably very highly motivated to get things done, not all subordinates share this enthusiasm. Your values may differ from their values. This is where social exchange theory comes in. By rewarding those who do the best job, you will help establish a cause–effect relationship between performance and payoffs. Those who like this arrangement will work harder for you; those

who do not will try to transfer to other departments. In either event, your work group output will go up.

3. Remember that no matter what level of the hierarchy you are at, effective communication is needed for using the requisite managerial skills. For example, when using technical skills, you must be able to communicate "how to do it." When employing human relations skills, you must be able to deal effectively with people. When using conceptual skills, you must be able to translate long-range desires into operational action.

LEADERSHIP STYLES AND COMMUNICATION

There are many different types of leadership styles. One way of presenting them is in terms of leader–subordinate interactions. How does the leader interact with the members of the work group? Figure 7.4 illustrates these four styles. The *authoritarian leader* tells the subordinates what to do. The *paternalistic leader* does the same but also allows the personnel to discuss matters and provide feedback. This leader tends to be very much like a parent, selling the subordinates on his or her ideas with the cliche, "Do it this way; it'll be good for your career" or "Trust me, would I ever lie to you or ask you to do something that wasn't in your own best interests?" The *participative leader* allows the subordinates to communicate back up the line as well as with each other. There is a free flow of ideas in a participative leadership setting. Finally, there is a *laissez-faire leadership* in which the subordinates communicate with each other and do the work while the leader takes a very passive role.

> There are four basic leader–subordinate interactions.

These four types of interactions help describe how leaders behave. However, they do not capture the essence of leadership and communication. They do not explain how the leader uses his or her influence to direct people toward goal attainment. For this we must turn to a discussion of leadership models. We may choose from a host of models, depending on which level of the hierarchy we are examining. The following looks at leadership models and communication at the lower, middle, and upper levels of the hierarchy.

LOWER-LEVEL MANAGEMENT The lower-level manager, often known as the supervisor or foreman, is the first level of management in most organizations. This individual's job is to directly manage and lead those who are producing the goods or services being sold by the enterprise. The leader's primary job is to get the work done. In so doing, the individual places heavy reliance on the path–goal theory of leadership.[4]

The *path–goal theory* is a supervisory leadership theory because its value is greatest at the lower levels of the hierarchy. It is also a contingency theory because it tells the manager what to do under different circumstances. The basic concepts behind the theory can be presented both visually and in writing. Figure 7.5 illustrates the path–goal theory of leadership. The logic behind it can be summarized this way:

Figure 7.4

Leader–subordinate interactions.

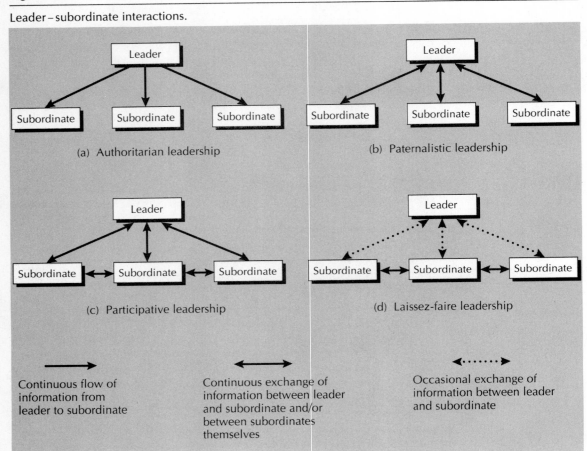

(a) Authoritarian leadership

(b) Paternalistic leadership

(c) Participative leadership

(d) Laissez-faire leadership

Continuous flow of information from leader to subordinate

Continuous exchange of information between leader and subordinate and/or between subordinates themselves

Occasional exchange of information between leader and subordinate

1. Leaders can improve their subordinates' motivation by making rewards for performance more attractive. For example, by giving the personnel raises, promotions, and recognition, the leader can increase the subordinates' desire for goal attainment.

Path–goal theory tenets.

2. If the workers are unsure of what they are supposed to be doing, the leader can increase their motivation by providing them structure. This structure can take such forms as goal clarification, direct supervision, and/or training. By reducing the subordinates' role ambiguity, the leader makes it easier for the subordinates to pursue goal attainment.

3. If the subordinates already know their job, there is no reason to introduce additional structure. Instead the leader should focus on the personal needs of the people by offering attention, praise, and support.

Figure 7.5

The path–goal
theory of leadership.

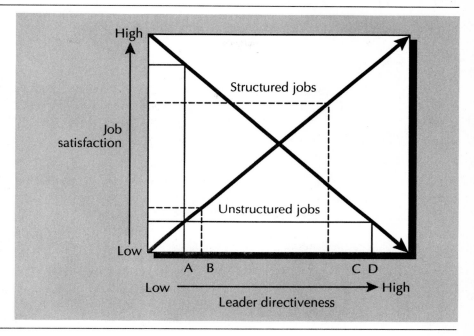

Let us illustrate the practicality of the path–goal theory with some examples. First, with structured jobs, the leader should offer little direction. Otherwise job satisfaction will decline. In Figure 7.5 we have shown two examples of leader directiveness on structured jobs. The first is Point A, in which the leader offered low leader directiveness. Notice that the result was high job satisfaction. The second is Point D in which the leader again offered high directiveness; this time job satisfaction was low.

Second, with unstructured jobs the leader should offer a great deal of direction. This is illustrated in Figure 7.5 at Points B and C. In the first the leader offered low directiveness and the result was low job satisfaction. In the second the individual offered high directiveness and the result was high job satisfaction.

The path–goal theory is still being researched. However, it does offer some very important insights regarding how to communicate and lead lower-level personnel. Notice that the leader's communication efforts fall into two categories: work-oriented and people-oriented. If people need to know more about how to carry out their assignments, the leader focuses on the first of these orientations. If the personnel already know what to do, the leader focuses on the second of these orientations.

Third, the path–goal theory urges the manager to use a contingency approach to leadership. It also recommends that the leader give the workers what they need, that is, use a needs approach in motivating them. If they require assistance in getting the job done, tell them what they need to know; if they want psychological support for having done a good job, give them verbal praise, and so on.

**The path–goal
theory urges a
contingency
approach.**

INTERNATIONAL COMMUNICATION
Made in the U.S.A.

When a company goes overseas, one of the biggest problems for its managers is that of effectively leading the local workforce. Quite often the people are not accustomed to the same leadership style as that used in the home country. The Japanese, in particular, have been finding that their way of leading workers is not very effective with Americans. The Americans like a leader who is basically participative and who delegates authority. They also like to be involved in the decision-making process and want to feel they are important. This is not the way the Japanese manage their own workforces.

The Koreans, on the other hand, have found that there is a simple way to resolve this leadership problem. They send their young people to the United States to be educated. In the process, these people learn the language and the customs, and they understand what American workers are looking for from their bosses. As a result, the Koreans are proving to be very effective leaders.

Korean firms are also promoting American-educated managers into higher-level positions so that these managers are the company's direct interface with high-level American managers. This is particularly helpful when a Korean firm is negotiating a contract with an American company. Since all the top managers are familiar with the American way of doing business, they have little trouble "talking the same language." These managers are also adept at understanding problems that trouble the United States. *Business Week* put it this way:

The new executives understand why their trade surplus is so sensitive in Washington, and they may invest more in the U.S. But they also come equipped with far better knowledge of how to penetrate the U.S. market. "They are going to become better partners," says . . . a Korean expert . . . "but also better competitors." If that's true, the new generation could be even tougher than their predecessors.

They are also going to be more effective international managers because they know how to communicate in their largest world market.

SOURCE: Laxmi Nakarmi and William J. Holstein, "Korea's New Corporate Bosses: Made in America," *Business Week*, February 23, 1987, pp. 58–59.

Fourth, the path–goal theory encourages two-way communication. This becomes obvious when we realize that the supervisor must take care not to be overly directive on structured jobs. How does the individual know when he or she is making this mistake? Feedback from the subordinates should provide it.

MIDDLE-LEVEL MANAGEMENT The middle manager is often known as the individual who is "caught in the middle." This person must keep top management happy by achieving desired results; the middle manager must also keep lower-level managers happy by being reasonable and fair and at the same time convince top management that he or she is working as hard as possible. When top management is unhappy with performance, it lets middle management know about it; when lower-level management is displeased with new work assignments or salaries, it lets middle management know about it. The people in the middle have to communicate both up and down the structure. Of all three groups in the management hierarchy, the middle-level manager has the greatest need for a flexible leadership style. Successful managers at this level can benefit greatly from an understanding and application of the ideas in the *contingency leadership model*.[5]

This model was developed by Fred Fiedler and is based on over 30 years of work. It is useful because it focuses on matching the leader for the purpose of attaining the greatest possible effectiveness. At the heart of the leadership model are two important concepts: the least preferred co-worker scale and the situational variables that characterize the environment in which the leader operates.

The *least preferred co-worker scale* (LPC) uses a questionnaire to determine the individual with whom the leader can work *least* well. A copy of the LPC is provided in Self-Assessment Quiz 7.2. The person filling out the questionnaire is asked to describe the individual with whom he or she can work least well. This person being described can be a current worker or someone with whom the leader has worked in the past. In either event, if the leader were to describe this least preferred co-worker in very mild terms, the individual would end up with a much higher score than if the co-worker were described in very harsh terms. Fiedler found that individuals with very high LPC scores tend to be relationship oriented, obtaining a great deal of satisfaction from close personal relations with other group members. On the other hand, leaders with low LPC scores tend to be task oriented, obtaining a great deal of satisfaction from the successful completion of tasks, even if this came at the expense of poor interpersonal relations with the workers. Figure your LPC score by taking Self-Assessment Quiz 7.2.

In addition to the LPC, Fiedler sought to determine the major situational variables that described group settings. He uncovered three:

- *Leader–member relations* — describes the influence and trust the leader has among the followers. These relations are measured by how well the personnel feel they can rely on the leader's word and can count on the individual to do what is in their best interests.

Major situational variables of groups.

- *Task structure* — describes the degree to which the leader's job is programmed or set out in detail. Highly structured jobs require the leader to handle problem solving in a predetermined manner; highly unstructured jobs give the leader a great deal of flexibility and freedom in deciding what to do.

- *Leader position power* — the authority vested in the leader's position. Higher-level managers have a great deal more position power than do middle-level managers, who in turn have more position power than lower-level managers. Position power increases as one goes up the hierarchy.

SELF-ASSESSMENT QUIZ 7.2

Least Preferred Co-Worker Scale

Regardless of your age, you have undoubtedly worked or interacted with many people on the job, in social settings, at church, and so on. Some of these co-workers were probably very easy to get along with, whereas others proved to be quite difficult. Think of all the people with whom you have ever worked and pick out the one with whom you were able to work *least well*. You may have personally liked the individual, but he or she was most difficult to work with. Describe this person on the scale that follows by placing an "X" in the appropriate space. For example, if you feel the individual was quite untidy, put your "X" in the second space.

Very Neat	____	____	____	____	____	____	X	____	Very Untidy
	8	7	6	5	4	3	2	1	
	Very Neat	Quite Neat	Usually Neat	A Little Neat	A Little Untidy	Usually Untidy	Quite Untidy	Very Untidy	

LEAST PREFERRED CO-WORKER SCALE

Pleasant	____	____	____	____	____	____	____	____	Unpleasant
	8	7	6	5	4	3	2	1	
Untrustworthy	____	____	____	____	____	____	____	____	Trustworthy
	1	2	3	4	5	6	7	8	
Friendly	____	____	____	____	____	____	____	____	Unfriendly
	8	7	6	5	4	3	2	1	
Nasty	____	____	____	____	____	____	____	____	Nice
	1	2	3	4	5	6	7	8	
Supportive	____	____	____	____	____	____	____	____	Hostile
	8	7	6	5	4	3	2	1	
Insincere	____	____	____	____	____	____	____	____	Sincere
	1	2	3	4	5	6	7	8	
Considerate	____	____	____	____	____	____	____	____	Inconsiderate
	8	7	6	5	4	3	2	1	
Backbiting	____	____	____	____	____	____	____	____	Loyal
	1	2	3	4	5	6	7	8	
Kind	____	____	____	____	____	____	____	____	Unkind
	8	7	6	5	4	3	2	1	

Cold	___	___	___	___	___	___	___	___	Warm
	1	2	3	4	5	6	7	8	
Accepting	___	___	___	___	___	___	___	___	Rejecting
	8	7	6	5	4	3	2	1	
Gloomy	___	___	___	___	___	___	___	___	Cheerful
	1	2	3	4	5	6	7	8	
Interesting	___	___	___	___	___	___	___	___	Boring
	8	7	6	5	4	3	2	1	
Distant	___	___	___	___	___	___	___	___	Close
	1	2	3	4	5	6	7	8	
Open	___	___	___	___	___	___	___	___	Guarded
	8	7	6	5	4	3	2	1	
Tense	___	___	___	___	___	___	___	___	Relaxed
	1	2	3	4	5	6	7	8	
Agreeable	___	___	___	___	___	___	___	___	Quarrelsome
	8	7	6	5	4	3	2	1	
Inconsiderate	___	___	___	___	___	___	___	___	Considerate
	1	2	3	4	5	6	7	8	

Total
Score

Follow this logic in filling out the least preferred co-worker (LPC) scale on the next page. When you are finished, total your overall score at the bottom of the page. An interpretation of scores is presented at the back of the book.

Fiedler then brought together the LPC scores, which identified leadership style, with the situational variables. His objective was to determine which leadership worked best in each situation.

Figure 7.6 presents Fiedler's results. Notice at the bottom of the figure that there are eight different combinations of the three situational variables. In situation 1 things are very favorable. Leader–member relations are good, the task is highly structured, and leader position power is strong. As one continues across the figure, things get progressively poorer for the leader. Situation 8 is the worst of all: leader–member relations are poor, the task is highly unstructured, and leader position power is weak. What type of leader will do well in each of these eight situations? This question is answered by the jagged line running across Figure 7.6. When things are going well or poorly, the task-oriented leader is most effective. When things are moderately good or moderately bad, the relationship-oriented leader does best. Fiedler explained it this way:

The contingency model has consistently shown that the task-motivated (low LPC) leaders tend to perform most effectively in situations in which their control and influence are very high and in situations in which it is relatively low. By contrast, relationship-motivated (high LPC) leaders tend to perform best in situations in which their control and influence is moderate.[6]

Fiedler's theory is particularly useful in tying together effective communication with leadership style. The leader's job is to influence people. This requires communication. However, should the leader use a "from the top down" approach, a participative approach, or some combination of the two? Fiedler's model points out the importance of sizing up the situation. This requires consideration of two factors: the environment and the leader. If the environment is one in which a task-oriented style is called for (situations 1–3, 7, and 8 in Figure 7.6), then the leader needs to focus on a work-centered approach. If the environment is one in which a relationship-oriented style is best (situations 4–6), then a participative, two-way style of communication is best.

Effective communication can be tied to leadership style.

Figure 7.6

Fiedler's contingency leadership model.

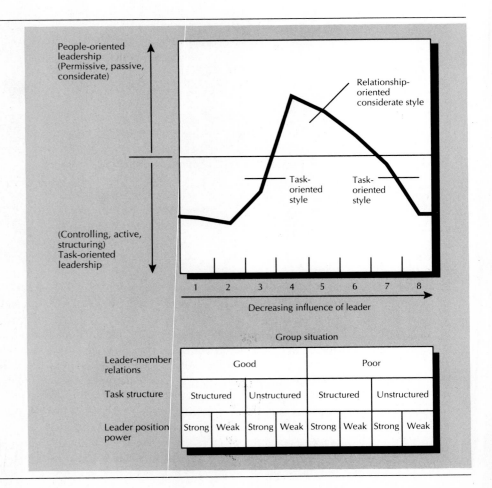

What if the situation calls for the leader to be task oriented, but the individual is a very human relations type of person? What can the leader do? The answer is to change the situational variables so that the combination falls within situations 4–6. For example, if a human relations leader who is accustomed to communicating openly and freely with her people finds herself in situation 8 of Figure 7.6, she needs to determine how she can alter the variables and move back to, say, situation 6. This can be done by structuring the tasks. Notice that the only difference in the variables between situations 8 and 6 is that the task structuring is different. If this is not possible, the leader can try moving from situation 8 to situation 4 by improving leader–member relations. Notice that the only difference in the variables between situations 8 and 4 is leader–member relations.

Fiedler's model is particularly useful in effective communication because it helps leaders adjust the situation to fit their personalities rather than vice versa. Remember that it is much easier to find an environment in which one can work comfortably than it is to change one's personality to adjust to a particular environment. Fiedler recommends changing the environment and matching its characteristics to the style of the leader. The value of this theory to effective communication is that it helps the leader understand the varied environments in which he or she is functioning and encourages the individual to create that environment which is most conducive to his or her own style of communication and management.

TOP-LEVEL MANAGEMENT Top-level managers have to be concerned with both the external and the internal environment. They need to keep abreast of economic, political, social, and technological developments that affect their enterprise. They also need to be aware of what is going on within the organization. One of the most useful leadership models for understanding top-level management is the *managerial grid*.

The managerial grid was developed by Robert Blake and Jane Mouton. The grid is depicted in Figure 7.7.[7] Notice that it has two axes. One measures "concern for production" and the other measures "concern for people." These two dimensions, production (or work) and people, are the two basic ones for all leaders. Every manager uses some combination of a work/people orientation in leading subordinates. On the grid there are nine degrees of each dimension. However, rather than examining all 81 possibilities attention is most usually focused on the five presented in Figure 7.7.

A "1" represents a low concern for the dimension; a "9" represents a high concern for the dimension. In describing a particular leader, the first number *always* relates to the work or production orientation. So a 9,1 leader puts a very strong emphasis on concern for work but a very weak emphasis on concern for people. Conversely, a 1,9 leader has a very low concern for work but a very high concern for people. Let us look at these five basic leadership styles in more depth.

The 1,1 managerial style describes the *impoverished manager*. This person tends to give people work assignments and then leaves them alone. Virtually no checking is done on performance, nor is followup done for the purpose of interaction, praise, and encouragement. The leader has a low concern for both the work and the people.

The 9,1 managerial style describes the *production pusher*. This individual puts a very high emphasis on the work to be done but has a very low concern for the people.

Figure 7.7

The managerial grid®.

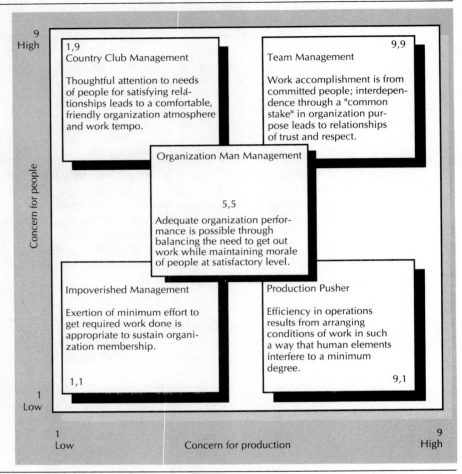

SOURCE: Adapted from Robert R. Blake and Jane S. Mouton, *The Managerial Grid III* (Houston, Tex.: Gulf Publishing Co., 1985).

This leader is interested in getting the work out. If someone cannot keep up, he or she is pushed aside in place of someone who can.

There are five basic leadership styles.

The 1,9 managerial style describes the *country club manager*. This individual has a very high concern for the people doing the work but a very low concern for the work to be done. This leader is interested in obtaining loyalty from the subordinates and tries to motivate them to do their work through the exercise of a genuine concern for their well-being. Pressure is at a minimum. Everyone is encouraged to be happy in their work.

The 5,5 managerial style typifies the *organizational leader*. This leader assumes that there should be a balance between a concern for production and a concern for people. On the other hand, the individual does not believe in maximizing this concern. Hence, he or she ends up in the middle of the managerial grid, exercising a moderate concern for both dimensions.

The 9,9 managerial style is used by the *team leader*. This individual believes that a maximum concern for both production and people will result in the greatest overall efficiency. Many managers regard this as the ideal leadership style. It is certainly the most popular of all. Leaders using the 9,9 style focus attention on their subordinate's higher-level needs, involve the individuals in decision making, and assume that the goals of the personnel and those of the organization are in harmony.

Each leadership style requires a different communication pattern.

The grid is useful in helping understand how top managers should communicate because it allows one to think in terms of work and people orientations. If the manager feels that a "hands-off" approach is best, the 1,1 style should be employed and communication should be kept to a minimum. If a work orientation is required, communication should follow the 9,1 style — directed at defining task assignments, clarifying how things are to be done, and obtaining feedback on performance. If a people orientation is needed, communication should be along 1,9 lines — focused on building morale, esprit de corps, and loyalty. If an intermediate concern for both is best, communication should follow the 5,5 style — a moderate emphasis on work balanced with an accompanying emphasis on people. Finally, if a strong work/people orientation is needed, communication should follow 9,9 lines — directed at subordinate involvement in decision making and a meshing of the goals of the personnel and the organization.

The grid can be used in describing and analyzing leadership at any level of the hierarchy. However, it is of greatest value for top managers who must confront many different challenges, each requiring a different communication pattern. The top manager must keep in mind that in those matters where he or she must become directly involved, the 9,9 has proved to be most useful. More top managers favor the 9,9 style than any other style. Yet it is equally important to remember that no one style will be most efficient or effective every time. The leader must choose the style that provides the best requisite blend, remembering that at the upper levels of the hierarchy, effectiveness tends to be more important than efficiency.

Although all these leadership theories are useful and relevant to various management levels, some new areas of research have been opened into what constitutes effective leadership. These new trends center around the concepts of transformational leadership and empowerment.

NEW TRENDS IN LEADERSHIP STUDIES

Effective leaders empower others.

In recent years, leadership experts have begun to describe effective leaders in very humanistic terms. Tom Peters, co-author of *In Search of Excellence* and *A Passion for Excellence*, says that today's leader is a "cheerleader, enthusiast, nurturer of champions, hero finder, wanderer, dramatist, coach, and facilitator."[8] According to Peters and many who follow his way of thinking, the most important leadership attribute is the ability to encourage others to work enthusiastically, creatively, and with commitment. Similarly, Jay Conger defines leadership as "the art of empowering others."[9]

This idea of empowering others is central to the new thinking about leadership.

Empowerment can simply be defined as "the act of strengthening an individual's belief in his or her sense of effectiveness."[10] Empowered workers are more effective and are satisfied that their work is meaningful and important. Typical tools of empowerment include delegation of responsibility and authority, participative decision making, management by objectives, and quality circles. In the 1990s, however, empowerment will go beyond these now traditional tools. Conger and Kanungo state:

> Empowerment is defined here as a process of enhancing feelings of self-efficacy among organizational members through the identification of conditions that foster powerlessness and through their removal by both formal organizational practices and informal techniques of providing efficacy information.[11]

Thus the empowerment process includes finding out what makes employees feel powerless and removing those root causes. Warren Bennis, a foremost expert in the field of organizational development, tells us that employee empowerment is found in four themes:[12]

1. People feel that what they do has meaning and significance.

Employee empowerment is found in four themes.

2. Learning and competency are held in high regard. Leaders rely on effort and feedback to build mastery.

3. Employees feel they are part of a community. "Ultimately in great leaders and the organizations surrounding them, there is a fusion of work and play."[13]

4. Work is exciting. Leaders energize employees and imbue in them a feeling of camaraderie and fun. Leaders communicate the visions and goals of the organization and provide ample feedback to employees about their individual roles.

This feeling of empowerment and the resulting excitement it produces among workers are characteristic of a leadership style called *transformational leadership.* It is in this area that we expect the most work will be done in the 1990s. According to Robert W. Goddard, director of publications for Liberty Mutual,

> Transformational leadership is encouraging them [employees] to connect emotionally and intellectually to the vision, priorities and people of their work unit. The leaders of transformational organizations are developing and communicating a new vision for their companies and are getting others to see the vision and to commit to it.[14]

Transformational leadership is vital in times of change.

Transformational leadership flourishes in times of change, innovation, and entrepreneurship. Unlike some leadership theories, proponents of transformational leadership insist that it can be learned and implemented, albeit it is surely aided by a charismatic personality. Well-known transformational leaders include Lee Iacocca of Chrysler Corporation, and Jack Welch of General Electric Company.

What characterizes the transformational leader? Tichy and DeVanna, authors of "The Transformational Leader," cite seven characteristics.[15]

1. Transformational leaders take on the mission of dramatically changing the organization to be more effective.

2. They are courageous people and are eager to take a stand.

3. They believe in the necessity to empower employees. One of Jack Welch's most central themes at GE is ownership of your business, coupled with the pushback management philosophy. This means that people further down are to be empowered to make things happen. They are the ones who need to make the decisions and carry them out, and stand up for them as well.

4. Transformational leaders are value-driven. They fiercely believe in and communicate the central values of what the organization stands for.

5. They are lifelong learners. They see failure as learning experiences.

6. They are able to deal with change and uncertainty in a complex environment.

7. They are able to verbalize their visions and get others to share them.

In summary, transformational leaders communicate visions, values, and excitement. They empower employees to share in those visions and in the accomplishment of corporate and work team goals.

Implications for Management

1. Be aware that effective leadership style requires an understanding of communication. Remember that the style you used at the lower levels of the hierarchy may need modification as you move up the chain. Position requirements change, and so must communication patterns.

2. When you assume a new position in the hierarchy, step back and examine the way the previous manager communicated with the personnel. Was the individual an authoritarian manager? A paternalistic leader? A participative individual? A laissez-faire manager? Having identified the previous style, now ask yourself: how effective was this individual? If your predecessor did a very poor job, you should consider different leadership and communication styles. If the previous manager was very effective, you should consider emulating his or her approach.

3. Match your communication objectives with the needs of the position. Lower-level managers have a need to get things done and help out their subordinates. Work to develop communication patterns that will accomplish this objective. At the middle levels of the hierarchy you should be concerned with the behavioral side of the job. Use your human skills in getting things done. At the upper levels of the hierarchy, remember that people look to your for leadership and role modeling. Act the part. Show them that you are as concerned with them as you are with the work they are producing. Communication is necessary in conveying the ideas and images you want your people to know. Use it as a leadership tool in supplementing your own particular style.

4. Learn to embrace the challenge of change and be a transformational leader.

CASE IN POINT

Revisited

Having read the chapter, you should now realize that Fred's biggest problem is that he attempted to exercise directive leadership when none was required. Things were well organized before he got there. His work group had extremely high output, and their performance represented more than the company norm. Fred would have been wise to follow the path–goal theory of leadership. This certainly is what his boss advised. Remember how he told Fred to let the workers do things their way?

Fred should have spent his time trying to clear away roadblocks and ensure that the personnel were able to do their work quickly and efficiently. In his role as supervisor, there was a lot less directive leadership than Fred thought. He does not realize that leadership is an influence process. Fred thinks it means rolling up your sleeves, getting in there, and telling people how to do things.

Fred needs to realize that one of the primary rules of effective leadership is: Don't butt in where you are not needed.

YOU BE THE CONSULTANT

The Chief Executive Officer's Job

Sid Wertz really has his hands full. As the new chief executive officer at Darban, Inc., he is finding himself getting to the office at 8 A.M. and not getting away until late in the evening. Over the last month, he has found his time being spent on a series of critical issues.

One is the new union–management contract. Darban has its own industrial relations department that handles formal negotiations. However, there is a lot that goes on behind the scenes that takes Sid's time. For example, the company negotiators cannot make an offer without first clearing it with top management. Sid has talked to the negotiating team for better than an hour a day during each of the last 15 days. Present at the meeting were the head of the finance department, the company's comptroller, and three members of the negotiating team. Most of the time Sid just listened as the finance people spelled out exactly what the company could afford in the way of salary increases and a benefit package. He then talked to the negotiators about their approach to the entire contract, urging them to be "flexibly firm."

A second issue is newly proposed legislation related to tax investment credits. Darban is planning to purchase $25 million of machinery and equipment this year. If the government revises its current tax credit, this will affect Darban's purchase plans. The company will buy more new equipment if the credit is increased, less if the credit is decreased. Sid has been talking to both the local U.S. representative from the area and one of the U.S. senators. Both have promised him that they will push for an increase in the credit, although they are not sure the administration will go along. The President is trying to hold down the size of deficits, and, unless he is convinced that the tax credit will generate additional tax revenues through increased employment, he will not support the measure. Sid has already spent three evenings over the last month meeting with other corporate presidents in an effort to generate greater political pressure on the congressmen around the state. He is convinced that the tax investment credit is critical to the state of the economy.

A third issue that has taken a lot of Sid's time is the company's strategic plan. This plan is updated every year at this time. Since the firm uses a bottom-up approach to planning, inputs begin at the lowest levels of the hierarchy where supervisors meet with their superiors to discuss objectives and budgets. Working its way up the line, the ultimate result is a series of overall objectives that the business would like to pursue over the next one to five years. These objective are tied to a budget, and the final proposals are reviewed by top management and modified as necessary. This year the company requests are $9 million greater than the budget will allow. Some cutting must be done. This will take place next week when Sid meets with the major department heads. During this meeting there will be give and take on each side. Since the total of all requests is greater than the budget, each department head is going to have to defend his or her requests. This is done by having each manager list the three main objectives to be pursued and show how the three largest budget requests all support these objectives. For example, if one of the production department's objectives is to increase productivity by 4 percent and the largest budget request is for new machinery, the individual must show how these new machines will increase productivity. If a department is unable to defend one of its large requests, this amount is dropped from consideration.

In most cases the department heads have done their homework and can defend the large requests. So it becomes a matter of getting down to smaller items in the proposed budget and seeing if any of these can be cut. Sid seldom spends any time on these matters. He generally makes an across-the-board decision such as cutting $4 million out of marketing's requests, $3 million out of manufacturing's request, and $2 million out of finance's requests. Then he tells them, "Okay, that's the bottom line. Now go back to your respective budgets and pare out these amounts." The executives may not like his final decision, but they know that Sid does not have time to work the budget line by line. It is up to them to straighten things out and get the budget back on target. In addition, by placing the burden on their shoulders, he is saying, "Look it's your department. You decide what goes and what stays. Why should I make this decision? You know best. You do it."

The chairman of the board and Sid had dinner last night. They talked about all the problems and issues confronting Sid. "I don't know how you do it," the chairman told him. "You have a million things to do and have to interact and influence people at every level of the hierarchy as well as outside of the organization." Sid agreed: "It's not easy. I've got to have a very flexible leadership style, depending on the situation. Most of the time I figure out what will work best for me and use it. However, tomorrow I'm having one of our internal consultants work with me for a full day. This individual is going to watch me in action and then offer me some suggestions regarding the type of leader I am and how I can be more effective. The recommendations should prove interesting."

Assume that you are the internal consultant. Based on what you know about Sid's job and his responsibilities, what would you be able to tell him about the topic of leadership and how he can be a more effective leader? Which of the models in the chapter would you use to describe leadership to him? How would you work a discussion of efficiency and effectiveness into your consultation? What specific recommendations would you offer to him? Be as complete as possible in your answers.

Key Points in This Chapter

1. Leadership is the process of influencing people to direct their efforts toward the attainment of particular goal(s). In this process the emphasis is on both efficiency and effectiveness. Efficiency is the ability to do things right and is measured by the equation: output/input. Effectiveness means doing the right things. Lower-level managers are more concerned with efficiency than effectiveness, but this pattern changes as the individual moves up the structure.

2. The communication effectiveness triad consists of the leader, the subordinates, and the environment in which the work is done. The leader needs to establish credibility with the subordinates through the use of drive, dependability, and competence. The individual also needs to develop teamwork among the group members and work to modify the environment so that is supports intragroup and intergroup effort.

3. Although there is no universal list of characteristics for leaders, five are particularly characteristic of successful leaders: superior intelligence, emotional maturity, motivation drive, problem-solving skills, and managerial skills. Each was described in the chapter.

4. Lower-level managers need a work-oriented focus. In this regard, path–goal theory concepts are very useful to them. Middle-level managers are the buffer between upper- and lower-level management. They need to be flexible and to adapt to changing conditions. Fiedler's contingency model is very useful in explaining how they can adjust to these conditions. Upper-level managers need to focus on both external and internal changes. An understanding of the managerial grid can be very helpful to them in both communicating and leading their people.

5. Empowerment and transformational leadership skills will be the cornerstone of effective leadership in the 1990s. They promote teamwork, commitment, and excitement about the job.

Questions for Discussion and Analysis

1. In your own words, what is meant by the term *leadership?*

2. How does efficiency differ from effectiveness? Compare and contrast the two. In which would a lower-level manager be most interested? In which would an upper-level manager be most interested? Explain.

3. What is the communication effectiveness triad? Explain it, being sure to emphasize the role of communication.

4. Effective leaders have similar behaviors. What is meant by this statement? What are some of these behaviors?

5. Do effective leaders have any characteristics in common? Identify and describe three, being sure to include in each a discussion of the importance of communication.

6. How to the communication patterns of the following leaders differ: authoritarian, paternalistic, participative, laissez-faire? Compare and contrast each.

7. How do lower-level managers communicate? In what way does the path–goal theory help them get their job done? Explain.

8. What do middle-level managers do? How does an understanding of Fiedler's leadership model help them carry out their job? Explain.

9. What kinds of challenges do upper-level managers face? How can an understanding of the managerial grid help them do a better job? What role does communication play in this process? Explain.

10. What is empowerment? What are some characteristics of employee empowerment?

11. Describe at least five characteristics of the transformational leader.

Exercises

1. Joan Allen has just been promoted to first-level supervisor by the First State Bank of Central City. Joan will be supervising ten tellers at the Third Street Branch. Randy Harris is a vice president for consumer loans at First State. He and Joan have known each other from high school days. One day while having a cup of coffee, Joan and Randy start debating who has the tougher job. Joan feels it is particularly hard to be a first-level supervisor; Randy thinks his job in upper middle management is much harder. Assume the roles of Joan and Randy and debate the issue.

2. Refer back to Joan and Randy from Exercise 1. What specific types of communications will be very important to each leader? How will the distributions of their communication time differ? What kinds of communication problems is each likely to meet?

3. Using the managerial grid, write a paragraph on the expected communication style of each kind of manager. Then read the following employee comment and decide how each type of leader (1,1; 1,9; 9,9; 5,5; and 9,1) would likely respond. *Employee* (to leader): Harry, I've got a real problem. I know you want this job done today, but I need to leave early to take my daughter to the doctor.

References

1. Richard M. Hodgetts, *Modern Human Relations at Work*, 2nd ed. (Hinsdale, Ill.: Dryden Press, 1984), p. 291.

2. Warren Bennis and Burt Nanus, *Leaders: The Strategies for Taking Charge*, New York: Harper & Row, 1985, p. 4.

3. Jay Hall, "To Achieve or Not: The Manager's Choice," *California Management Review*, Summer 1976, pp. 5–18.

4. Robert J. House, "A Path–Goal Theory of Leader Effectiveness," *Administrative Science Quarterly*," September 1971, pp. 321–338.

5. Fred E. Fiedler, "The Leadership Game: Matching the Man to the Situation," in Jane Whitney Gibson and Richard M. Hodgetts, eds., *Readings and Exercises in Organizational Behavior* (Orlando, Fla.: Academic Press, 1985), pp. 122–130.

6. *Ibid.*, p. 126.

7. Robert R. Blake and Jane S. Mouton, *The Managerial Grid III* (Houston, Tex.: Gulf Publishing Co., 1985).

8. Tom Peters and Nancy Austin, *A Passion for Excellence: The Leadership Difference* (New York: Random House, 1985), p. 265.

9. Jay Conger, "Leadership: The Art of Empowering Others," *The Academy of Management Executive*, February 1989, pp. 17–24.

10. *Ibid.*, p. 18.

11. Jay A. Conger and Rabindra N. Kanungo, "The Empowerment Process: Integrating Theory and Practice," *Academy of Management Review*, July 1988, p. 474.

12. Warren Bennis, "Why Leaders Can't Lead," *Training and Development Journal*, April 1989, pp. 35–39.

13. *Ibid.*, p. 39.

14. Robert W. Goddard, "Viewpoint: Reshaping Today's Organizations for Tomorrow's Needs," *Personnel Journal*, June 1986, p. 12.

15. Noel M. Tichy and Mary Anne DeVanna. "The Transformational Leader," *Training and Development Journal*, July 1986, pp. 27–32.

Annotated Bibliography

Bass, B. M., *Stogdill's Handbook of Leadership* (New York: The Free Press, 1981). This comprehensive compilation of research on the subject of leadership is both readable and informative. Everything you want to know about leadership is in here somewhere.

Blake, Robert R. and Jane S. Mouton, *The Managerial Grid III* (Houston, Tex.: Gulf Publishing Co., 1985).

> The grid theory identifies five general theories about how to lead. It discusses their strengths and weaknesses, their similarities and differences. This book represents Blake and Mouton's thinking after working on the grid for 25 years.

Conger, Jay A., Rabindra N. Kanungo, et al., *Charismatic Leadership: The Elusive Factor in Organizational Effectiveness* (San Francisco: Jossey-Bass, 1988).

> This book looks at another personality variable important to leadership effectiveness—charisma. A variety of articles focus on the nature of charismatic leadership, the sources of charisma, how to develop charisma, and the strategic vision that charismatic leaders often have.

Kotter, John P., *The Leadership Factor* (New York: The Free Press, 1988).

> This book argues that very few firms have sufficient people with leadership skill. The emphasis is on what can and should be done about this problem.

Sayles, Leonard R., *Leadership: Managing in Real Organizations*, 2nd ed. (New York: McGraw-Hill, 1989).

> Sayles believes that society greatly underestimates the need for creative, demanding, and talented leadership work in today's managerial ranks. This book describes the author's formal and informal studies as they relate to middle management and the need for dedicated, competent leadership.

Tichy, Noel M. and Mary Anne DeVanna. *The Transformational Leader* (New York: John Wiley & Sons, 1986).

> At the time of this writing, this is the definitive book discussing transformational leadership. The authors illustrate this charismatic, energizing, and empowering leadership style through case studies showing how transformational leaders create major change in organizations and mobilize the workforce to institutionalize that change.

Part Four

ORGANIZATIONWIDE COMMUNICATIONS

Part Four examines organizationwide communication. This discussion will extend from formal to informal organizational communication and address communication barriers that have not been discussed in earlier chapters.

Chapter 8 focuses on formal organizational communication. Downward, upward, lateral, and diagonal communication flows are discussed in terms of their purposes and ways to improve their use. Particular attention is given to how the perception of employees affects communication.

Chapter 9 looks at informal communications. After the term *grapevine* is defined, the characteristics, advantages, and disadvantages of the grapevine are discussed. Then four basic types of communication network are examined and the way in which information is conveyed in network structures is explained. The latter part of the chapter sets forth the descrip-

tive properties of networks and explains how network analysis can be carried out.

Chapter 10 addresses organizational communication barriers. Deliberate and unintentional types of distortion in upward, downward, and horizontal communication are described, and recommendations are presented regarding how to manage these problems. Attention then is focused on information underload and information overload and ways in which these problems can be addressed.

When you have finished studying all the material in this part of the book, you will understand formal communication flows and how to handle the problems that accompany them. You also will know the characteristics of the grapevine and how to manage information communication. Finally, you will be aware of communication distortion and communication load and know how to deal with them.

CHAPTER 8

Formal Organizational Communication

"The average manager would rather admit to chronic alcoholism than to having communication problems."

Allan D. Frank, "Can Water Flow Uphill?" *Training and Development Journal*, May 1984, p. 118.

Objectives

1. To relate the purposes of downward channels.

2. To identify reasons for problems in downward channels.

3. To discuss methods of downward communication and opportunities for improvement.

4. To relate the purposes of upward communication.

5. To examine employee perceptions of upward communication and causes of upward communication problems.

6. To describe ways of improving upward communication.

7. To relate the purposes of lateral communication.

8. To discuss the most common types of lateral communication and to describe the relative effectiveness of this form of communication.

9. To investigate diagonal communication in the organization.

C A S E   I N   P O I N T

No Time for Bad News

When Lisa Dandright was brought into the firm three months ago, the president breathed a sigh of relief. "At last we've got the executive vice president's position filled," he told the board of directors. "Now maybe we can get back on track and start increasing our overall productivity and profit." Over the previous six months the executive vice president's position had been vacant, and this individual is the one charged with running the company on a day-to-day basis. During these six months the president had filled in as best he could. However, the president's job keeps him on the road four days a week and he does not have time to stay in the office and oversee day-to-day matters.

As soon as Lisa took over, she called a meeting of the other top management staff. After a general introduction during which she asked everyone for his or her support, she spent the rest of the hour explaining the importance of having an upward flow of communication in the company. "If we don't know what's going on in the field and at the lower levels of the organization," she said, "We're sunk. We need to keep our ear to the ground at all times. If there are problems, the sooner we learn about them the faster we can resolve them. That's the way I ran things in the company I was in before and that's the way I'd like to see things done over here." The top managers were delighted to hear these remarks.

At the next weekly top management meeting, however, something happened. One of the executives was reporting on sales activities in his northern region. Sales were 30 percent above projections, and Lisa went out of her way to praise the executive. The next manager reported that sales in one of his regions was 35 percent below projections. Lisa listened quietly and then began to ask questions. As the discussion went along, it became obvious to everyone that Lisa was upset over the news. Throughout the remainder of the meeting, Lisa followed the same basic approach, praising those who had good performance and being critical toward those who did not. Later that week the top managers learned that the executive whose sales group was most off target had received a memo from Lisa telling him that things would have to improve if the man hoped to keep his job.

At the next meeting of the executives, all sales reports were positive, and this pattern continued for the remainder of the meetings up to last week. At that time, the accounting department reported that overall sales for the year were running 18 percent lower than projections. The executives apparently have not been reporting all the sales progress in their regions, just those cases in which sales were ahead of projections. Upon learning the news, Lisa hit the roof. She called the executives together and lambasted them. On the way out the door, one of the managers said to another, "If she thinks anyone is going to give her any bad news after this last performance, she's sadly mistaken. I personally intend to go right on telling her what she wants to hear. Lisa's problem is that she confuses bad news with the messenger who brings it."

What is Lisa doing wrong? What exactly is the problem? What now needs to be done? Write down your analysis of the situation and put it to the side. We will return to it later.

INTRODUCTION

Many types of communication channels are available in organizations. Formal channels are very important to managers and will be examined in this chapter. In particular, this chapter focuses on downward, upward, horizontal, and diagonal channels that are sanctioned by the organization to carry information. Although some problems are associated with each formal channel, there are ways of dealing with them. In this chapter we examine the nature of these channels, the problems, and ways of resolving them. Before beginning our discussion, starting with downward communication, examine your own current knowledge of formal organizational communication by answering the questions in Self-Assessment Quiz 8.1.

SELF-ASSESSMENT QUIZ 8.1

What Do You Know About Formal Organizational Communication?

Directions: Carefully read each of the following statements and place a T (True) or F (False) to the left of each.

_____ 1. Before 1920 downward communication was the only basic system recognized by managers.

_____ 2. Data regarding corporate procedures and policies are best channeled through the upward communication system.

_____ 3. Managers generally rate downward communication as less effective than employees rate them.

_____ 4. Managers and employees alike rate upward communication as more satisfactory than downward communication.

_____ 5. Studies show that employees prefer to get information from their peers rather than their supervisors.

_____ 6. Formal communication is mostly written.

_____ 7. Studies show that the most effective downward communication is oral communication with a written followup.

_____ 8. Feedback on employee attitudes and feelings is best provided by the upward communication system.

_____ 9. Building a corporate atmosphere of trust is the key factor in improving upward employee communication.

_____ 10. Coordination of interdependent units is a primary concern of lateral communication.

Answers are in the Answer section at the back of the book.

DOWNWARD COMMUNICATION

As noted in Chapter 2, downward communication was the only significant type of communication recognized by managers of the classical school. The one important exception was the early recognition of horizontal communication by Henri Fayol. We would logically assume that since formal downward communication channels have been recognized for a long time, they should function fairly smoothly by now. Unfortunately, this is not always the case. Before examining the current state of downward communication, however, it is important to understand the types of messages carried by downward communication channels.

Purposes of Downward Channels

Common purposes of downward communication

The five most important reasons for downward communication are (1) to provide specific instructions about the duties of the job and how to perform them; (2) to provide employees with the rationale for doing a particular job and an understanding about how that job relates to other jobs; (3) to provide necessary data regarding the procedures, policies, and practices of the organization; (4) to provide performance feedback to employees regarding how they are doing; and (5) to provide information that will convey a sense of mission and an understanding of corporate goals.[1]

An examination of each of these reasons shows just how important downward communication is.

JOB INSTRUCTIONS These types of communication provide the employee with the necessary data to do the job. Precisely what is expected of the individual? What authority and responsibility does the person have? What constitutes a good job? Job instructions take many forms including job descriptions, supervisory guidance, training programs, and a variety of orders and directives.

JOB RATIONALE This type of information lets the employee understand his or her role in the organization and how this job relates to that of others. Without such understanding, most employees would question the necessity of many of the job instructions they receive and would become demotivated by the seemingly unnecessary and unimportant tasks they are given.

PROCEDURES, POLICIES, AND PRACTICES These forms of communication are fundamental in socializing the employee regarding the corporate climate. This process begins during the individual's orientation program when general policies and procedures are explained. On-the-job practices are most often communicated by the direct supervisor and the informal group in the department.

PERFORMANCE FEEDBACK This category of information is of critical importance to the career progress of the individual employee. How is he or she measuring up to standards? What are the person's weaknesses? What are his or her career opportunities? What training programs should the person participate in?

MISSION AND GOALS Too often employees have no idea what the mission of the organization is, and corporate goals are guarded as if their public revelation would result in company failure.

Employee Perceptions of Downward Communication

Employees who do not receive sufficient information in the above areas often feel alienated from the organization. For them work can become a series of meaningless tasks to be done in the easiest way possible. Although some managers rationalize their failing communication systems by saying that employees really are not interested in anything broader than their precise job, studies repeatedly have shown that this is not true. One CEO cites personal experience to say that well-informed employees are motivated and committed to organizational goals.

> The question for a CEO, I've come to realize, is not whether you owe it to your employees to keep them abreast of company affairs. That's irrelevant. Forget what you owe your employees. Focus instead on your own interests and those of your company. If my experience is any guide, you'll discover that the more open you are, the more responsibility your people will take on. . . . And the more committed they'll feel to you and your organization.[2]

Informed employees tend to be productive. Informed employees are better able to relate their work group activities to overall corporate goals. This, in turn, eliminates much of the conflict between heretofore competing groups since all now are working toward the same objectives.

Morgan and Schiemann echo these findings. Based on a study conducted by the Opinion Research Corporation (ORC) of 30,000 employees and their satisfaction with organizational communication, they found that not more than 40 percent of the participants, regardless of job level, felt their organizations did a good or very good job of letting them know what was going on in the company. The group that rated downward communication the highest was, as expected, managers. Figure 8.1 shows the relative percentages among job levels.

In terms of sources of employee information, the ORC study showed that employees prefer to get their information from their supervisors and from group meetings with management, and all groups say they are getting less information from these sources than they prefer. This led Morgan and Schiemann to conclude that "ORC's data indicate that top management is, in effect, cutting itself off from its employees. Both the upward and downward flows of information have suffered."[3]

Another study, by the International Association of Business Communications (IABC) and the management consulting firm of Towers, Perrin, Forster and Crosby (TPF&C), surveyed 32,000 employees in 26 U.S. and Canadian organizations. Although downward communication was rated higher than upward communication, the current picture was far from satisfactory. Only 70.9 percent of the participants agreed that their organization tried to keep employees well informed; only 65.3 percent were able to agree that they had been given sufficient information to perform their jobs; and only 51.1 percent responded in the affirmative when asked if their organization's downward communication was candid and accurate.[4] The survey also compiled a list of subjects that were of most interest to the participants. Table 8.1 shows the 17 subjects as ranked in order of interest. Note that these subjects either are totally covered by the downward communication system or *should be*.

Figure 8.1

Percentage of employees who rated downward communication as good or very good.

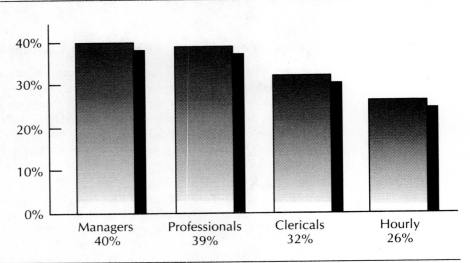

Managers 40%	Professionals 39%	Clericals 32%	Hourly 26%

SOURCE: Adapted from Brian S. Morgan and William A. Schiemann, "Why Internal Communication Is Failing," *Public Relations Journal*, March 1983, p. 16.

Two of the IABC/TPF&C conclusions are especially pertinent to downward communication:

1. Employees want to hear more organization news directly from top executives in their organization.

2. More than any other subject, future organizational plans and productivity improvement are what interests employees.[5]

In a third study by Gibson, 1,062 surveys were collected from 58 firms representing ten industries. The results showed that only 44.4 percent of all respondents felt that downward communication was better than "adequate" in their firms.[6] Two of the main reasons for these problems for employee dissatisfaction with downward communication are:

1. Organizations have grown so large that many managers cannot do an adequate job of keeping employees informed, so they stop trying.

2. Many managers delegate the complete job of keeping employees informed to the manager in charge of the internal house organization. The weekly newsletter thus becomes the only regular conduit of information from managers to the employees.

Methods of Downward Communication

The two basic methods for processing information downward through the organization are oral and written. Both have advantages and disadvantages.

Table 8.1

WHAT SUBJECTS ARE OF MOST AND LEAST INTEREST TO SURVEY RESPONDENTS?

Rank	Subject	Combined Very Interested/ Interested Responses
1	Organizational plans for the future	95.3%
2	Productivity improvement	90.3%
3	Personnel policies and practices	89.8%
4	Job-related information	89.2%
5	Job advancement opportunities	87.9%
6	Effect of external events on my job	87.8%
7	How my job fits into the organization	85.4%
8	Operations outside of my department or division	85.1%
9	How we're doing vs. the competition	83.0%
10	Personnel changes and promotions	81.4%
11	Organizational community involvement	81.3%
12	Organizational stand on current issues	79.5%
13	How the organization uses its profits	78.4%
14	Advertising/promotional plans	77.2%
15	Financial results	76.4%
16	Human interest stories about other employees	70.4%
17	Personal news (birthdays, anniversaries, etc.)	57.0%

SOURCE: Julie Foehrenback and Karn Rosenberg, "How Are We Doing?" *Journal of Communication Management,* Vol. 12, No. 1, 1982, p. 7.

Oral communication offers immediacy.

Oral communication has the advantage of immediacy. Information is provided quickly and in a direct, face-to-face manner. Listeners often feel that if management is taking the time to say this personally, it must be correct. They are also likely to pay more attention to any information received personally. According to at least two experts, "The face-to-face medium, including group discussions, speeches, and videotape presentations, convey the human side of the executive and the cues of personal interest, caring, and trust that are filtered out of a written medium."[7] The major problem with oral communication is that, unless the manager is able to assemble virtually the entire organization to hear the oral message, he or she can count on the message being distorted as it moves from one level to another. This problem of serial distortion will be more closely examined in Chapter 10.

Written communication offers formality.

Written methods of downward communication have more formality and permanence, and, quite often, that is what formal communication is all about. Often, subordinates are urged by their boss to "put it in writing" or "send me a memo." The disadvantage of written downward communication is that dozens of memos are sent every week. So many of them are submitted that many people quickly save them and then file them in the circular file. Many managers complain that their employees do not read the memos they receive. The reason is that impersonality and lack of immediacy between sender and receiver are equated in the mind of the receiver as lack of importance, and they treat the memo accordingly. One of the best ways of assuring effective downward communication is to combine the two methods: first, communicate orally; then follow up in writing.

Written reinforcement serves several purposes. First, it reminds everyone of what was said, and repetition is often the best way of ensuring that a message is understood. Second, it lets everyone know that this topic is important, and research indicates that employees pay most attention to information that they perceive is important to their boss. Third, it helps eliminate the distortion which sole reliance on oral channels inevitably brings. Fourth, it provides a formal record of what was said, a record that can be referred to in the future without relying on the treachery of memory.

Assessing Available Methods

Level and Galle have suggested that seven factors determine the most effective channel for downward communication.[8]

1. *Availability*. As a first step, managers need to examine the communication methods currently available to them. Is there a house organ that is widely disseminated and read by employees? Are there strategically located bulletin boards? Is there a loudspeaker system that connects everyone in the organization? Is there a large meeting room that can accommodate mass information meetings? After inventorying current media, managers can decide what other methods are needed for effective downward communication.

2. *Cost*. The expense associated with each medium should be determined. Cost is not an isolated factor, however, and must be considered in conjunction with the effectiveness of the medium and speed of transmission. It will not be a major factor if the message is considered very important. A long-distance phone call, for example, nearly always costs more than a letter, but it often is chosen because of the need to communicate quickly. If information is routine and the need for speed and interaction is not judged important, less costly channels can be used.

3. *Speed*. When urgency is the foremost criterion, the fastest communication should be selected. A carefully planned communication program can go far to control the times when this criterion becomes foremost.

4. *Impact*. The medium will have an impact on the receiver. If the organizational culture requires that most downward communication be oral, a written medium will carry greater weight if used sparingly. Conversely, if written memos and reports are typical, a visit to a subordinate's office can have greater impact.

5. *Purpose*. The purpose of the communication must be examined. What is the manager trying to accomplish? Whom is the individual trying to inform? Persuade? Motivate? Direct? If he or she is trying to disseminate information, a written report often is the best method; but if the purpose is to persuade or motivate, the personal touch generally is more effective.

Criteria to use in assessing a downward communication channel

6. *Interaction*. The type and degree of interaction must be considered. Will feedback be necessary? Will the employee need to ask questions for clarification? If the manager is instructing employees in a new procedure, a face-to-face approach, at least initially, often is best because it allows the individual to answer questions and provide on-the-spot explanations.

7. *Capabilities*. The communication skills of the receiver(s) must be considered. What is their educational level? What is their work experience? Which media will be most effective in addressing their capabilities?

Table 8.2 lists some of the many written and oral communication media available in most organizations and examines the availability, cost, speed, interaction, and impact of each.

Lengel and Daft have offered another method of choosing between written and oral communication media. Figure 8.2 shows that the critical variables in manager selection of oral versus written media is the routineness of the message. The more routine the message, the more likely the manager is to choose a written medium such as a memo. The more nonroutine or complicated the message, the more likely the manager is to choose an oral medium such as a meeting or person-to-person communication.[9]

Table 8.2

EFFECTIVENESS OF COMMUNICATION MEDIA

	Generally Available	Relatively Low Cost	High Speed	Immediate Interaction	High Impact and Attention
Written					
Letters	x	x			
Memos and reports			x		x
Telegrams			x		x
FAX			x	x	x
Newspapers and magazines	x				
Handbooks and manuals	x	x			
Bulletins and posters	x	x			
Inserts and enclosures	x	x			x
Oral					
Telephone	x	x	x	x	x
Intercom and paging	x		x		x
Closed-circuit TV				x	x
Conferences and meetings	x			x	
Speeches	x			x	

SOURCE: Adapted from Dale A. Level, Jr., and William P. Galle, Jr., *Business Communications: Theory and Practice* (Dallas, Tex.: Business Publications, 1988), pp. 91, 93.

Figure 8.2

Manager selection
for routine versus
nonroutine
messages.

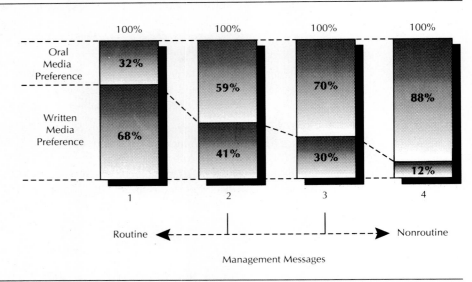

SOURCE: Robert H. Lengel and Richard L. Daft, "The Selection of Communication Media as an Executive Skill," *The Academy of Management EXECUTIVE,* August 1988, p. 228.

Opportunities for Improvement

The manager who assesses the available downward communication methods and chooses the best one is taking a step in the right direction. However, other matters must also be considered. For example, the message content must be accurate, specific, forceful, receiver oriented, easy to understand, and have no hidden meanings.

The important fact to remember is that improved downward communication can be achieved if management wants it. A case in point is the International Paper Company, which employs 50,000 employees scattered in mills and logging camps all over the country. In 1975 the firm surveyed its employees and found that they wanted to know more about what was happening in the company. Most importantly, they wanted to hear it from management! At the time they said they were getting most of their information from the grapevine, the union, and local newspapers. International Paper decided to take a proactive stance and made several changes. First, the Corporate Communications Division was beefed up with bright, articulate managers who were dedicated to good communication. Second, a new department, Employee Communications Development, was formed within the Corporate Communications Division. Third, the company began a program called Operation Breakthrough, which had as its cornerstone plant managers who set up regular meetings with employees followed by reports in the local employee newsletter. The meetings provided a formal setting for employees to hear about plant operations, the overall health of the business, and other matters of general concern. Fourth, a company news wire called Newslink was established. News about the company was sent at 9 A.M. to every one of the International Paper facilities,

Management must
want improved
downward
communication.

and the employees at these locations had the news by 10 A.M. The results were very positive. The company credits the communication program for dramatic safety improvements and for better labor negotiations.[10]

Implications for Management

1. Be aware that employees want to know what is going on and that their preferred source of information is management. Do not be reluctant to communicate with your people.

2. Recognize the advantages and disadvantages of written and verbal communication media. Assess each type as to its availability, cost, speed, impact, purpose, and interaction. Then choose the one that offers the most effective means for communicating your message.

3. When planning your communication, be sure that it is accurate, specific, forceful, receiver-oriented, simple, and without hidden meaning. Think through what you have to convey and then put yourself in the other person's shoes and interpret the message. This will help you get on both sides of the communication channel: sender and receiver.

4. Remember not to use downward communication to the exclusion of all other types. Upward channels are every bit as important to overall organizational communication effectiveness.

Effective downward communication can help improve organizational performance. However, management also needs to focus on ways of improving upward communication.

UPWARD COMMUNICATION

With the advent of the human relations school, management began to turn its attention to the social needs of employees. One result of this attention was the introduction of formal upward communication channels where only downward channels existed before. Upward channels allow for information flow from subordinate to superior, and this two-way system greatly aids the manager in learning what is going on in the organization.

Purposes of Upward Channels

Common purposes of upward communication

For managers who want to listen, upward channels provide a wealth of information. The main benefits include: (1) feedback regarding employee attitudes and feelings; (2) suggestions for improved procedures and techniques as well as for new ideas; (3)

feedback regarding how well the downward communication system is working; (4) information about production and goal attainment; (5) requests from subordinates for supplies, assistance, and/or support; (6) a surfacing of employee grievances before small problems erupt into major ones; and (7) stronger involvement of employees with the organization and with their jobs. A brief examination of each of these seven reasons shows the importance of upward communication.

FEEDBACK ABOUT EMPLOYEE ATTITUDES AND FEELINGS If managers care to listen, upward channels can reveal a great deal about how employees regard their jobs, their supervisors, the mission of the organization, and many other aspects of work life. By using these channels, supervisors can spot morale problems before they become a major issue. They also can become aware of highly motivated individuals with potential for helping the organization and of demotivated employees or departments that can cause problems.

SUGGESTIONS FOR IMPROVED PROCEDURES AND NEW IDEAS Upward channels that encourage employee participation are abundant in many of today's well-run corporations. Suggestion boxes, quality circles, Scanlon plans, and a host of employee participation systems all strive to obtain maximum employee input.

FEEDBACK REGARDING THE EFFECTIVENESS OF THE DOWNWARD COMMUNICATION SYSTEM Feedback is the best way to determine whether downward communication has been received, is accurate, and is being taken seriously and put into action. Feedback from upward channels has the potential of identifying those subjects about which employees need information *before* that information gap becomes a serious problem.

INFORMATION REGARDING PRODUCTION AND GOAL ATTAINMENT Productivity reports should not be an annual event or something that gets discussed only at budget time or during performance appraisals. Effective upward channels provide a conduit by which this information is routinely and regularly funneled to higher management.

REQUESTS FROM SUBORDINATES Open-door policies and managerial willingness to listen have gone far in encouraging subordinates to ask for whatever they need in order to do their jobs better. These requests may take the form of informing management that the XYZ department needs more clerical help or more cooperation from the sales department, which does not seem to appreciate the budgetary limitations of the XYZ staff.

SURFACING OF EMPLOYEE GRIEVANCES Small problems that go unnoticed have a way of mushrooming into major problems. Healthy upward channels can take the steam out of employee problems before this happens.

STRONGER INVOLVEMENT OF EMPLOYEES This is perhaps the foremost purpose of upward communication systems and provides the greatest benefit both to the employee and management. In the most basic sense, upward channels are motivational because they allow the employees who use them to satisfy their psychological needs for belonging and for feeling wanted and needed.

Perceptions of Upward Communication

Despite the obvious value of upward communication as an information source and a form of employee motivation, not all organizations use them to the extent necessary. One reason is that these channels are time consuming. A second is that few managers really know how to get and keep these channels open. A third is that many employees find it difficult to engage in upward communication; they are accustomed to receiving information, not generating it.

As a result, research from industry does not paint a very bright picture regarding the use of upward communication. For example, in a study he conducted among 150 human resources professionals, Frank asked each professional to rate the effectiveness of upward communication in his or her organization.[11] Only 16.7 percent of those polled felt that management always or almost always responded to upward communication, whereas 21.4 percent felt that management sometimes or almost never responded. In addition, 42.7 percent of the professionals felt that management encouraged employees either "little" or "very little" to send messages upward in the organization.[12]

Upward communication channels are not seen as very effective.

Foehrenbach and Rosenberg have reported even more discouraging results about upward communication. "A particularly disappointing finding is the apparent failure of upward communication programs to meet employees' needs. Employees place upward communication programs near the bottom of the list of current sources of information: 53.6 percent of all employees say it is not a source at all for them.[13] Moreover, only slightly more than half the respondents said that communication was a two-way street in their organization and less than half said that management acted on employee ideas.

Gibson also found significantly more satisfaction with downward communication channels than with upward ones (see Table 8.3). Although 44.4 percent of all respondents rated downward communication in their organization as either good or excellent, only 37.5 percent rated upward communication the same way. Conversely, whereas 24.6 percent rated downward communication as fair or poor, 28.9 percent rated upward communication in the same manner.[14] Going farther, Gibson broke down both downward and upward communication responses into managerial and nonmanagerial groups. With regard to downward communication, 52.7 percent of managers thought these channels were good or excellent and 41.7 percent of nonmanagers agreed. However, both groups were dissatisfied with upward communication, although managers were more positive in their comments than nonmanagers; 49 percent of the managers rated upward communication as "excellent" or "good," while only 35.3 percent of the nonmanagers did the same.

Causes of Upward Communication Problems

Reasons for upward communication problems

To some extent this issue will be addressed in Chapter 10 where organizational communication barriers are examined in depth. In addition to problems of distortion and communication load, however, there are other causes for upward communication problems. McClelland has identified three:

Table 8.3

OVERALL COMMUNICATION SATISFACTION (*n* = 1,009)				
Degree of Communication Adequacy	Downward Communication		Upward Communication	
	Relative	Cumulative	Relative	Cumulative
Excellent	12.1%	12.1%	8.0%	8.0%
Good	32.3	44.4	29.3	37.3
Adequate	27.1	71.5	28.6	65.9
Fair	15.0	86.5	17.5	83.4
Poor	9.6	96.1	11.4	94.8
Do not know	4.0	100.1	5.1	99.9

SOURCE: Jane Whitney Gibson, "Satisfaction with Upward and Downward Organizational Communications: Another Perspective," *Proceedings of the Southwest Academy of Management,* March 1985, p. 150.

1. *Fear of reprisal.* In many organizations, rewards go to the people who echo the ideas and support the decisions of their managers. People are afraid to speak out or to be the voice of dissent.

2. *Filters.* Employees often feel that their ideas and concerns are modified as they are transmitted from their direct supervisor upward through the organization. Filtering occurs both deliberately and innocently as will be discussed in Chapter 10.

3. *Time.* Many managers give the impression that they don't have the time to listen to what employees have to say.[15]

When condensed into one overall statement, the major upward communication problem is that in many organizations an atmosphere of distrust separates subordinates and superiors. A corporate climate built on trust will eliminate much of the upward communication distortion discussed above. However, this is easier said than done.

Improving Upward Communication

Fortunately, some steps can be taken to improve upward communication. The most important prerequisite is a commitment by upper management to improve the situation and carefully monitor efforts to that end. Old habits are hard to break, and for a company to change old communication patterns, conscious, consistent efforts must be undertaken. McMaster offers the following hints on clearing the bottom – up communication channels:

1. When management calls meetings, participants should be encouraged to bring nonmanagement specialists with them. This ensures the authority of knowledge

and eliminates the manager having to interpret his or her staff person's input to the rest of the participants. Thus a level of distortion is bypassed.

2. Top managers should get to know their first-line and middle-line managers and have them personally make regular, short presentations. This eliminates filtering and allows the top manager to gain first-hand knowledge of the firm's managerial human resources.

Ways of improving upward communication channels

3. The use of junior executive boards to analyze problems or opportunities and make recommendations to more senior management should be undertaken. "In addition to generating ideas top and middle management have not thought of, junior boards also are valuable in giving top management an entirely different perspective from ideas that are filtered through middle managers and vice-presidents."[16]

4. Every company with a formal suggestion system should have an equally formal system to ensure that suggestions are handled seriously and objectively. For example, the coordinator of the system might report directly to the CEO on suggestions. This approach would bypass other levels of managers who might downplay or ignore valuable suggestions for a myriad of personal reasons.

5. Employee attitude surveys should be used in finding out how employees feel about their jobs. Often managers resist such surveys for fear of what the results might indicate. However, if survey instruments are carefully constructed, anonymity is ensured, and both managers and employees get feedback on the results, surveys can be very helpful. Such feedback can also be a basis for the adoption of employee suggestions, or at least an explanation by management as to why such adoption is not feasible at the present time.

6. Formal progress reports should indicate reasons for deviations from stated objectives. This procedure, which may seem negative at first, makes the supervisor pinpoint where the problem is and provides the manager with a basis for remedial action. McMaster also explains that

> Too often, someone outside a supervisor's jurisdiction is responsible for the supervisor's failure to reach his or her goals. In such cases, supervisors may fail to communicate where remedial action can be ordered for fear they will injure intraorganizational relationships or appear to be tattlers. However, when such reports are required by the CEO, top management can be apprised of difficulties one organizational unit causes another without the reportee being accused of initiating the report on his own.[17]

7. Management audits should serve much the same purpose as the formal reports just described. McMaster recommends that, "For the most complete and objective reports of what has not been accomplished according to standards, or not done at all, the internal audit group should report directly to the CEO. Otherwise, the audit results might be watered down by managers who do not want to pass along unfavorable reflections on themselves."[18]

In addition, McClelland advises that employees be assured access to senior management.

> Employees want to be able to talk to senior executives face to face. This is clearly their first choice for communication. . . . Over the years, the authority and information-sharing

process for managers and supervisors has eroded. When employees ask questions, supervisors do not have answers; when employees offer ideas, supervisors lack authority or knowledge to make changes. Therefore, employees seek an interface with executives who have information and clout.[19]

An atmosphere of trust is a critical element.

As noted earlier, the most important factor in improving upward employee communication is building a corporate atmosphere of trust. If the relationships between superiors and subordinates are good and mutual trust is present, upward communication channels will exist. If that trust does not exist, the chances of getting employees to communicate honestly with their supervisor are extremely remote. In addition, if supervisors do not trust their employees or fear that they might go over their head with negative news, receptivity to upward communication will be restricted. Rogers and Agarwala-Rogers reported a study done in a very large New York bank that started a "Sound Off" program. The program urged all employees to take their problems to their supervisor. The policy, however, was ambiguous and left some people thinking they could bypass their direct superiors and go directly to the personnel department, whereas others wondered if they could continue their complaints up to higher levels of management. Regardless of the fact that the new program was posted on the bulletin board, subsequent research found that only 40 percent of the supervisors and 25 percent of the workers knew about it. Supervisors were overwhelmingly against the system! Ninety percent felt employees should not use it. One supervisor noted that, "There have been several cases of people bypassing me. I don't feel mad about it, just hurt. They should follow the chain of command. I don't take any disciplinary action, but I don't like it." [20]

When employees were polled as to their opinions about "Sound Off," it was found that most were very hesitant to bypass their supervisors. As one put it, "You bypass the supervisor once and get fired. There is nobody to appeal to, buddy. The supervisor . . . he's it. If you go to Personnel, the first thing they do is get the supervisor on the phone and tell him everything. Next, you're in trouble."[21]

Upward feedback should be rewarded.

If upward feedback is so easily thwarted in organizations, what else can be done to facilitate a more open flow? A corporate philosophy of rewarding upward feedback must be superimposed on the trusting climate that obviously is a prerequisite. Employee suggestion boxes can be a valuable tool if employees are convinced that their input is read, valued, and used when possible. A recent visit to a large American Express facility in the southwestern part of the United States by one of the authors revealed an obvious corporate commitment to employee input. By every elevator on every floor were two displays of flyers. One contained questionnaires called "Expressline," which offered confidential answers to work-related questions, concerns, problems, or opinions; the other called "Quality Through Ideas," provided forms for suggestions or ideas.

Another useful approach, offered by Peters and Waterman in their celebrated book *In Search of Excellence*, describes a method of management that they call MBWA (management by wandering around). They suggest that executives of excellent companies learn about their employees, their problems, concerns, and suggestions by spending a lot of time walking around, being visible and available to the average employee.[22]

An increasingly popular avenue for improving upward communication is quality circles, first conceptualized by the Americans and then popularized by the Japanese. These circles provide a routinized vehicle for assuring employee input on matters of quality. In brief, these circles consist of groups of employees headed by a team leader, who meet on company time to discuss suggestions for alleviating departmental problems, increasing quality, facilitating productivity, and so on. Several benefits regularly emerge. First, employees often come up with valuable suggestions for improvement in areas where no one else has the necessary insight or expertise. Second, and almost a byproduct, these circles are motivational to employees who form a closer identity with each other, the job, and the company.

For a look at how upward and downward communication flows are used in other countries, refer to "International Communication in Action: They Are Doing Pretty Well."

Implications for Management

1. Be aware that the most important prerequisite for satisfactory upward communication is a corporate climate of trust. If workers think they are going to be punished or criticized for their feedback, they will not provide it.

2. Reinforce and reward upward communication with both attention and feedback. When upward transmissions of information are ignored, subordinates quickly abandon this channel of communication.

3. Be aware of the morale-building potential of an upward communication system. Also be alert to the fact that such a system can be useful in tapping the full human resource potential of many creative employees, who until now have been reluctant to express their ideas or recommend unique solutions to problems because they felt that management would not be appreciative.

4. Keep in mind that many organizational problems can be avoided if managers tune into the advanced signals provided by upward communication channels. These often tell the alert manager that something is going wrong or needs attention. Failure to heed these messages always results in problems later on.

5. Remember that research studies show that managers and employees alike are more discouraged with upward communication than with downward communication. Just about every enterprise can show improvement in this area if the management sets its mind to doing so.

HORIZONTAL COMMUNICATION

Until relatively recently, *horizontal* or lateral, *communication*, which takes place between people on the same level of the hierarchy, received little attention within the formal structure. Yet the complexity of today's organizations makes this subject vital. Much of what is called lateral communication takes place in the informal system and will be discussed in the next chapter. However, some formal horizontal communication considerations are very important, and these will be discussed here.

INTERNATIONAL COMMUNICATION IN ACTION

They Are Doing Pretty Well

Many U.S. managers are not good two-way communicators. They like to pass on a message and not be bothered with feedback. Are managers in other countries more effective in this process? Research shows that they are not. The table below provides some interesting input regarding the preferences of international managers for one-way and two-way communication.

PREFERENCES REGARDING ONE-WAY AND TWO-WAY COMMUNICATION

	Belgium	Denmark	India	Italy	Norway	U.K.	U.S.	Total
Number of managers	47	30	34	47	88	36	31	313
Number of groups	5	5	6	7	18	4	6	51
Percent preferring as sender[a]								
one-way communication	6.4	10.0	20.6	6.4	3.4	13.9	6.5	8.3
two-way communication	87.2	83.3	79.4	91.5	95.5	86.1	93.5	89.5
Percent preferring as receiver[b]								
one-way communication	2.1	10.0	11.8	0.0	1.1	8.3	0.0	3.8
two-way communication	95.7	90.0	88.2	95.7	97.7	91.7	100.0	94.9

[a] Percentages may not total 100; the remainders represent those expressing no difference in their attitude.
[b] Found significant at the 0.05 level, chi-square analysis.

SOURCE: Adapted from G. V. Barrett and R. H. Frank, *Communication Preference and Performance: A Cross Cultural Comparison*, MRC Technical Report No. 29, August 1969 and reported in Simcha Ronen, *Comparative and Multinational Management* (New York: John Wiley & Sons, 1986), p. 105.

A close look at the table shows that American managers have a higher preference for two-way communication *both* as senders and receivers. Over 93 percent of the U.S. managers surveyed said that when they send messages, they prefer two-way communication. Only the Norwegians had a higher preference for two-way communication than the Americans. This is in sharp contrast to Danish, Indian, and British managers, for example, who were much more supportive of one-way communication.

When receiving messages, all the American managers who were surveyed said that they preferred two-way communication. Again, the Danish, Indian, and British managers were much less supportive of two-way communication channels.

Overall, the data show that American managers, on average, had higher preferences for two-way communication than did any of the other groups. So although U.S. managers may not encourage the use of feedback as much as they should, in contrast to their international counterparts they are doing pretty well.

Purposes of Horizontal Channels

Horizontal communication serves at least five important purposes.

First, it is the primary method of coordinating efforts between interdependent units and departments. Without effective horizontal channels, for example, the sales department will be unable to predict delivery dates accurately. Their lateral channels with the production people keep them coordinated in their efforts and working as a team.

Second, horizontal communication builds the social support system of the organization. The difference between enjoying one's job and merely tolerating the work hours is often the feeling of camaraderie among peers. This is a direct benefit of an effective horizontal communication system that is used to socialize people into the system and give them a sense of belonging.

Common purposes of horizontal communication.

Third, it is a primary method of information sharing. By avoiding the time-consuming vertical channels, horizontal communication allows peers to share information on a regular basis. Healthy horizontal communication also helps avoid the hoarding of information.

Fourth, horizontal communication facilitates problem solving of all sorts. It allows people and units to learn from one another and to avoid "reinventing the wheel" every time a new person encounters an old problem. It also facilitates problem solving between units or departments. Effective solutions usually arise among peers rather than being imposed from above.

Fifth, it prevents interdepartmental conflict resulting from misconceptions, communication distortion, and lack of understanding. Horizontal communication promotes a cooperative spirit across the organization and lessens the "we-they" attitude that is all too likely to develop among interdependent units.

Types of Horizontal Communication

Horizontal communication is usually less formal than vertical communication. The horizontal often involves communication among peers rather than superiors and subordinates. Typical examples are the following:

1. *Telephone conversations.* How would anyone ever get anything done in the office without the phone? Phones often are the primary means of coordinating activities with others, getting necessary input, and avoiding longer, more costly meetings.

Horizontal communication is somewhat informal.

2. *Social events.* Although primarily a setting for informal communication, social activities such as picnics, tennis teams, and the like frequently provide the backdrop for formal small talk.

3. *Meetings.* These are a primary method of horizontal communication and integrating organizational efforts. An entire chapter deals with this subject later in the text.

4. *Task forces.* Task forces or standing committees often are formed to integrate interdependent efforts over a period of time.

5. *Written communication.* Memos and notes flourish in horizontal channels. Often these notes are much less formal than those allowed in the vertical system. A handwritten note, for example, might be totally acceptable in a lateral channel but this is rarely so in the vertical system.

6. *Productivity improvement groups.* Called many things including quality circles, standing groups of voluntary participants often are used to discuss ideas for work improvement. Although these groups often focus only on a particular unit or department, their suggestions can involve the entire company.

Effectiveness of Horizontal Communications

Horizontal channels are seen as being fairly effective.

Horizontal channels frequently are assessed to be more effective than downward and upward channels. Frank's study found that 84.6 percent of 150 human resources development (HRD) professionals rated their organization's formal horizontal communication system as at least somewhat effective. This was a higher rating than found for formal downward channels (82.7 percent) or formal upward channels (64 percent). This led him to conclude that, "These results verify the high level of horizontal communication that I perceived in my interviews. Today's business climate has generated great interest in participatory management, decentralization (to the point of setting up companies within the company), quality circles, and project teams."[23]

One must wonder whether the results would have been favorable, if the employees of these companies had been interviewed instead of the HRD professionals. We would expect a small difference but would likely find fairly satisfied attitudes about horizontal communication since it is more controlled by the employees themselves, who are thus less likely to be critical of their own system.

Of course, some problems can occur within the horizontal system. Horizontal communication can weaken the authority of the vertical structure, and an overproliferation of horizontal communication can occur with no filtering mechanisms. (These problems will be examined further in Chapter 10, our chapter on organizational communication barriers.) So suffice it to say that managers need to recognize the potentials and pitfalls of horizontal media.

DIAGONAL COMMUNICATION

Diagonal communication occurs between people at different levels of the organizational hierarchy and in different departments. For example, a personnel recruiter at a manufacturing company may regularly communicate with the sales manager when he or she is recruiting and screening candidates for open sales positions. Similarly, an accounts receivable clerk might call a regional marketing manager to find out if there is any reason why a customer who normally pays on time has fallen behind in his bills. Less is known about diagonal communication in organizations than the other three channels (downward, upward, and horizontal) because very little research has been done in this area. We do know that in modern, complex organizations, diagonal communication serves a number of important purposes.

Purposes of Diagonal Communication

First, diagonal communication strengthens the philosophy of open communication and participative management. The fact that the accounts receivable clerk mentioned above can pick up the phone and call the regional marketing manager makes the clerk feel she is an important, fully participating member of the team. If the clerk had to take the problem to her supervisor and have that person investigate the problem, she would feel that a hierarchical distinction was complicating the problem by causing more people to become involved. Diagonal communication reinforces the concept of "authority of knowledge" rather than "authority of position."

Benefit of diagonal communication.

Second, like horizontal communication, diagonal communication facilitates the smooth operation of interdepartmental coordination. Both types of channels nurture an organizational culture where cooperation is valued and internal competition is discouraged. For the individual employee, it helps the person see where his or her job fits as part of the total organizational system.

Third, diagonal communication saves the organization time and money. By not sending messages up and down successive layers of the organizational hierarchy, questions are answered, information is shared, and problems are solved at the first possible level.

Problems with Diagonal Communication

The culture must support diagonal communication.

Any time an employee skips organizational levels in communicating, he runs the risk of offending supervisors and others who feel they should have been involved in the communication. How well diagonal communication works depends on how valued it is within the organizational culture. If the culture is conservative and traditional, supervisors and managers may resent anyone who "goes over their heads" to communicate directly with someone at a higher level. However, if the organization has a more human resources philosophy and encourages decision making at the lowest possible levels, diagonal communication will not only be sanctioned but also rewarded. Employees should always, however, keep their supervisors and managers informed so that communication gaps do not occur.

Implications for Management

1. In your efforts to improve upward and downward communication, do not ignore horizontal channels. Left unattended, they can wither and lack of coordination can result.

2. Remember that in order to avoid a "we-they" mentality from developing within your organization, effective formal horizontal channels are necessary. They help develop teamwork and trust among the members.

3. Watch out for the dangers, however, of overproliferation of horizontal channels and the concomitant weakening of the vertical system. Although horizontal communication is important, it is no substitute for effective downward and upward communication channels. Use horizontal channels to complement the other two, not as a replacement for them.

4. Recognize the importance of diagonal communication. It makes people feel more responsible for communication; it helps foster interdepartmental cooperation; and it saves time and money for the organization.

C A S E   I N   P O I N T

Revisited

Having read the chapter, you can see that the problem is quite evident. Lisa does not like to hear bad news. When upward communication reveals that things are not going according to plan, Lisa becomes upset. The problem is that this approach addresses only the effect, not the cause. It is not necessarily the manager's fault that the work in his or her region is not going well. What Lisa needs to do is to join with the manager in finding out what is wrong. She needs to develop a two-way communication dialogue with the managers.

Remember that Lisa's job was open for six months, and during that time managers were fending for themselves. It is quite possible that things began to slip during this period, and the managers need someone like Lisa to help them get back on track. Instead of attacking them, what Lisa needs to do is work with them in identifying the causes of the lower-than-expected sales and then help them formulate solutions. This case reinforces the material in the chapter, which explains that many people in today's organizations are not satisfied with upward communication.

YOU BE THE CONSULTANT

The New Approach

Dunsing, Inc., a large New York-based conglomerate, was founded in 1926 and reached the billion dollar mark in 1976. Part of the firm's growth has been a result of acquisition and mergers. Over the last five years, for example, the conglomerate has purchased seven firms in unrelated industries.

One of the firms that Dunsing acquired is Willow Bros., a moderately successful retail chain in the southwestern part of the United States. Willow was founded in the late 1940s and soon became one of the dominant retail establishments in its geographic region. The chain's greatest growth years were during the late 1950s and 1960s. During the 1970s Willow's sales began to slow up, and it was passed by three major competitors.

When Dunsing looked over Willow's operations, the conglomerate management was convinced that there were great opportunities for profit. The chairman of the board put it this way, "Willow has not been run properly for at least a decade. Its management is old in terms of operating philosophy. If we buy this chain and put our own management in charge, I think we can turn it around. One thing's for sure. We can't do any worse than the Willow family has been doing."

The final arrangements for the sale were completed six months ago, and within three months the conglomerate had installed its own people in the upper ranks of Willow. They brought with them a different style of management. The Willow family had always used very close control. All major decisions, and many minor ones as well, were made by the family. Creativity, imagination, and a willingness to assume responsibility were all discouraged. The Willows let it be known that things would be run their way or the person would not be with the firm very long.

The new management has a different approach. It believes that authority should be delegated down the line and that store managers and department managers should assume greater responsibility for day-to-day operations. Over the last 90 days the conglomerate has tried to make this crystal clear. One way was through the installation of a management-by-objectives program that delegated both authority and responsibility down to the operating levels.

Many of the store managers and personnel admit that they like this new approach. However, they have been working under the Willow approach for so long that they find it hard to change. For example, a suggestion box was installed in each retail store and any employee who offered money-saving ideas was promised 25 percent of the first year's savings. To date only three suggestions per store have been generated. Similarly, the store managers have been urged to call on the senior management staff for assistance and advice, but no one has yet taken up the conglomerate management on this offer. Even at the lower levels of the hierarchy a fear of changing is evident.

None of this has gone unnoticed by the conglomerate management. However, they are not sure how to draw out the people and get them to participate more. For this reason, next week they intend to bring in a consulting team to study the situation and make recommendations regarding what to do.

Assume that you are the head of the management consulting team. Based on your reading of the case, what type of communication problem does the conglomerate face with this new acquisition? What is the reason behind the problem? What would you recommend be done? In your answers be sure to explain your reasoning and offer specific suggestions regarding courses of action.

Key Points in This Chapter

1. The five basic reasons for downward communication are to provide specific job-related instructions; to provide employees with a rationale for doing a particular job and an understanding of how that job relates to others; to provide necessary data regarding organizational procedures, policies, and practices; to provide perform-

ance feedback to employees; and to provide information that will convey a sense of mission and an understanding of corporate goals.

2. Most employees prefer to get their information from group meetings with management. Moreover, most are more satisfied with downward communication than with upward communication, although the downward is far from satisfactory.

3. There are a number of reasons for downward communication problems. Some of these include organizational size and failure of the manager to delegate sufficient authority. Methods of dealing with the problem were offered in the chapter, although the best approach is the one that balances consideration of availability, cost, speed, impact, purpose, and interaction.

4. Some of the major purposes of upward channels include: feedback regarding employee attitudes and feelings; suggestions for improved procedures and techniques as well as for new ideas; feedback regarding how well the downward communication system is working; information about production and goal attainment; requests from subordinates for supplies and/or assistance; surfacing of employee grievances; and stronger involvement of employees with the organization and with their jobs. Each of these was described in the chapter.

5. Organizational personnel are not as satisfied with upward communication channels as they are with their downward counterparts. A number of researchers have found employee dissatisfaction with the upward flow of information. Some of the causes include employees' concealment of their thoughts; the belief that management is not interested in employee problems; a lack of rewards for employee feedback; and a lack of response and/or accessibility of supervisors.

6. Upward communication can be improved in several ways, including personal interaction among personnel, the use of junior executive boards, formal suggestions systems, employee attitude surveys, formal progress reports, management audits, and management by wandering about.

7. Horizontal communication takes place between people on the same level of the hierarchy. Some of the purposes of horizontal communication include coordination of effort between interdependent units and departments; the building of social support systems in the organization; information sharing; and the facilitation of problem solving. Some of the most prevalent types of horizontal communication include telephone conversations, social events, meetings, task forces, written communication, and productivity improvement groups. Researchers have concluded that horizontal communication is more effective than either downward or upward channels. One of the major reasons may well be that these channels are controlled by the employees themselves.

8. Diagonal communication takes place between people at different levels and in different departments. Its benefits include strengthening the philosophy of open communication and participative management, facilitating the smooth operation of interdependent units, and saving the organization time and money. The disadvantage of diagonal communication is that managers and supervisors left out of the line of communication may feel threatened and resentful.

Questions for Discussion and Analysis

1. What are the purposes of downward communication? Identify and describe four of them.

2. How satisfied are organizational personnel with downward communication? Explain.

3. What are some of the most common reasons for downward communication problems? Identify and describe two of them.

4. In downward communication, what are six factors that determine the choice of media? Briefly describe each. How does message routineness impact on media choice?

5. How can downward communication be improved? Offer two suggestions, being sure to explain and defend both.

6. What are the purposes of upward communication? Identify and describe four of them.

7. How well are upward communication channels viewed in comparison to downward channels? Explain.

8. What are some of the causes of upward communication problems? Identify and describe three.

9. How can upward communication be improved? Offer three recommendations.

10. How do horizontal communication channels flow? What are the purposes of these channels? What forms do they take? Explain.

11. How effective are horizontal communication channels in contrast to downward and upward channels? Explain, being sure to cite research evidence in support of your answer.

12. What is the purpose of diagonal communication? Give an example.

Exercises

1. Prepare two sets of instructions by which the other students in your class can draw a house. First, deliver the instructions in the form of one-way, downward communication. Listeners may not ask questions or give you any clues to their understanding while drawing the picture according to specifications. Second, deliver the instructions in a two-way, upward and downward manner. Now, listeners are free to interrupt you, ask questions, and so on. Which of the two resulting drawings was most accurate? Were the students frustrated when they could not ask you questions? Which drawing took the most time? Discuss.

2. Practice giving upward communication of feedback by discussing with your instructor your concerns and/or desires for this course. How is this similar to what happens in organizations? What factors encouraged you or inhibited you from being candid? Explain.

References

1. Daniel Katz and Robert Kahn, *The Social Psychology of Organizations* (New York: John Wiley & Sons, 1966), p. 239.

2. Everett T. Suters, "Show and Tell: The More Your Employees Know About How Your Company Is Doing, the Better Off You'll Be" *Inc.*, April 1987, p. 112.

3. Brian S. Morgan and William A. Schiemann, "Why Internal Communication Is Failing," *Public Relations Journal*, March 1983, p. 16.

4. Julie Foehrenbach and Karn Rosenberg, "How Are We Doing?" *Journal of Communication Management*, Vol. 12, No. 1, 1982, p. 5.

5. *Ibid.*, p. 3.

6. Jane Whitney Gibson, "Satisfaction with Upward and Downward Organizational Communications: Another Perspective," *Proceedings of the Southwest Academy of Management*, March 1985, p. 150.

7. Robert H. Lengel and Richard L. Daft, "The Selection of Communication Media as an Executive Skill," *The Academy of Management EXECUTIVE*, August 1988, p. 230.

8. Dale A. Level, Jr., and William P. Galle, Jr., *Business Communications: Theory and Practice* (Dallas, Tex.: Business Publications, 1988), pp. 88–90.

9. Lengel and Daft, *op. cit.*, p. 228.

10. Gerard Tavernier, "Using Employee Communications to Support Corporate Objectives," *Management Review*, November 1980, pp. 8–13.

11. Allan D. Frank, "Trends in Communication: Who Talks to Whom?" *Personnel*, December 1985, pp. 41–47.

12. *Ibid.*, p. 42.

13. Foehrenbach and Rosenberg, *op. cit.*, p. 5.

14. Gibson, *op. cit.*, p. 151.

15. Valorie A. McClelland, "Upward Communication: Is Anyone Listening?" *Personnel Journal*, June 1988, pp. 127–128.

16. John B. McMaster, "Getting the Word to the Top," *Management Review*, February 1979, p. 63.

17. *Ibid.*, p. 64.

18. *Ibid.*, p. 65.

19. McClelland, *op. cit.*, p. 128.

20. Everett M. Rogers and Rekha Agarwala-Rogers, *Communication in Organizations* (New York: The Free Press, 1976), p. 98.

21. *Ibid.*, pp. 97–98.

22. Thomas J. Peters and Robert H. Waterman, Jr., *In Search of Excellence*, New York: Harper & Row, 1982.

23. Allan D. Frank, "Can Water Flow Uphill?" *Training and Development Journal*, May 1984, p. 118.

Annotated Bibliography

Katz, Daniel, and Robert Kahn, *The Social Psychology of Organizations* (New York: John Wiley & Sons, 1966).

This very important book looks at, among other things, the various communication systems in organizations. This is must reading for students interested in learning about formal and informal organizational systems.

Peters, Thomas J., and Robert H. Waterman, Jr., *In Search of Excellence* (New York: Harper & Row, 1982).

A very popular book, *In Search of Excellence* explores the common characteristics of America's highest performing companies. Management by wandering about (MBWA) is described as a corporate philosophy that reinforces the strong core values and people orientation of these organizations.

CHAPTER 9

Informal Communication

"Though the work itself is important to the workplace community, what is most neglected by those concerned with its problems is the nature of the human relationships: the rituals such as greetings on arrival, coffee breaks, lunch times, smoke breaks, teasing, in-jokes, and endless talk about almost everything are the important ways in which the community maintains itself."

Robert Schrank, *Ten Thousand Working Days* (Cambridge, Mass.: MIT Press, 1978) p. 78.

Objectives

1. To define the term *grapevine*.

2. To describe the characteristics, advantages, and disadvantages of the grapevine.

3. To relate the four basic types of communication networks.

4. To explain how information is conveyed in network structures.

5. To relate the roles played by gatekeepers, liaison people, bridges, isolates, opinion leaders, and boundary spanners.

6. To note the descriptive properties of networks.

7. To explain how network analysis can be carried out.

C A S E   I N   P O I N T

Getting Things Moving

When he first joined Farnsdell Consolidated, Jack Skinner could hardly believe his luck. Farnsdell is one of the fastest growing conglomerates in the country. Each year it hires thousands of people. Only a small number, however, ever get into its prestigious management training program. Scuttlebutt around the firm says those who complete this program have the inside track when it comes to raises and promotions. Both the current president and senior vice president went through the program. In fact, one-third of the top management started with the company as newly hired management trainees.

When Jack got the letter telling him that he had been chosen for the new program, he was overjoyed. During his first six weeks in the program, Jack began to realize why so many of the trainees eventually wound up in top management. It was clear that only the very best had been chosen. Ninety percent were new college graduates; the other 10 percent came from the company's ranks. Every six months when a new management trainee group was formed, managers were allowed to nominate individuals for the program. From all over the country, these people were sent to headquarters for the six-month program.

One of the trainees with whom Jack became friendly was Bill Maway. Bill started with Farnsdell more than three years ago. He was hired right out of junior college. However, since his job required him to be on the road one day a week, it was difficult for him to take all the courses he needed. Bill is scheduled to complete his degree in two more semesters. His job performance has been excellent. Of the 1,100 people in his territory, he has been ranked in the top five. The manager of that territory has ten places "reserved" for those he chooses to send to the program. This is how Bill got in.

During the program the trainees learned how the company operated its various divisions. They also received a lot of first-hand experience in managing. Two days a week they were assigned to a major department, and there, under the watchful eye of a senior manager, they were given assignments. Every

Friday the trainees received feedback on how well they had done that week. Jack's ratings were always above average. Bill's, however, were excellent. When Jack asked him what he did during these assignments, Bill noted, "I spend the first fifteen minutes trying to figure what my boss wants. Anyone can get a job done right. However, if you can please the boss at the same time, you're going to go a lot farther in this firm."

Another of the program features that Jack liked was the visits from top management. At least once a week a senior-level manager would come by and talk to them for half an hour. The favorite of the entire group was the senior vice president. Once he talked to them for over an hour about his early experience with the firm. In concluding, he said, "If there is anything I can do for you, just let me know. Give me a phone call; write me a note. I'll remember who you are. Never worry about that."

The last assignment each trainee was given was to develop a plan for a particular part of the company. Jack and Bill worked as a team to construct a sales plan for Bill's territory. With modifications, the plan could be used in any territory. After the formal graduation exercise, each was given his new assignment. Jack was sent to a large sales group on the East Coast, whereas Bill returned to his group on the West Coast. Before leaving, Bill told his friend, "I'm going to get our plan put into action on the West Coast. You should do the same in your territory." Jack agreed.

Unfortunately, things did not work out as expected. Jack submitted his plan, but his boss did not act on it. "I'm going to have some people look it over and then I'll get back with you," he told Jack. That was six months ago. Yesterday Jack received his evaluation. He was rated above average on everything. He had hoped his proposed plan would get him an excellent overall rating, but apparently the report was sitting on someone's desk. Later that evening, he received a call from Bill. Bill had not only received an outstanding rating, but his plan was going to be implemented within the next three months. When his friend asked him how he managed to get it accepted, Bill said, "Heck, it was easy. I sent a copy to the senior vice president with a note telling him that we had developed this plan during the training program. In turn, he called my boss, said he liked the plan, and wanted to know when he would be implementing it." Jack sat and listened quietly. It had never occurred to him to do that. More importantly, he was unsure of what to do next in terms of getting the plan moving.

What did Jack do wrong? What should he do now? In your answer be sure clearly to identify the errors Jack made and then offer him the most realistic recommendations possible. Help him get out of his dilemma without getting him into trouble with the organization. Write down your recommendations and put them to the side. We will return to this case later.

INTRODUCTION

In addition to a formal communication system, every organization has an informal communication system known as the *grapevine*. (The term grapevine has been with us since the Civil War, when it referred to telegraph lines that were hazardly strung through trees; the resulting "vines" frequently produced distorted messages, not unlike the organizational grapevine of today.[1]) Whatever the name, the grapevine is inevitable. Managers who spend time bemoaning that fact could profit from learning, instead, to understand and then to use it constructively.

Exactly what is the grapevine? What purposes does it serve? From an organizational viewpoint, what are its advantages and disadvantages? How can the manager use this knowledge to further organizational goals? In addition to answering these questions, this chapter will examine organizational networks and the methodology of network analysis that can be extremely helpful to the manager in locating informal power sources in the organization. Before proceeding, however, try your hand at Self-Assessment Quiz 9.1 and see how much you know about the grapevine.

SELF-ASSESSMENT QUIZ 9.1

What Do You Know About the Grapevine?

Directions: Answer the following questions with a T (true) or F (false).

___ 1. The corporate grapevine is composed mostly of rumors and gossip.

___ 2. At least 50 percent of information transmitted by the grapevine is incorrect.

___ 3. Effective management can eliminate the need for an organizational grapevine.

___ 4. Managers should try to ignore the grapevine whenever possible because paying attention to it only gives it legitimacy.   (*Continued next page*)

_____ 5. Healthy, active, formal communication channels will largely eliminate the need for the grapevine.

_____ 6. If employees want a quick answer to something, they will go to the formal organization system.

_____ 7. In times of stress and change, the grapevine becomes less active than under more stable conditions.

_____ 8. Managerial-level employees rarely get involved in informal communication.

_____ 9. The grapevine has been shown to be negatively correlated to job satisfaction.

_____ 10. The corporate grapevine is usually detrimental to organizational health.

Answers are in the Answer section at the back of the book.

THE GRAPEVINE

Grapevine described

The term *grapevine* describes the informal organizational communication system. It refers to any communication taking place outside of the prescribed formal channels.

Characteristics of the Grapevine

Despite its often negative connotations, the grapevine flourishes in every organization and manages to serve some very important employee needs. In general, it has six characteristics.

Characteristics of the grapevine

1. It transmits messages fast.

2. It is predominantly oral.

3. It is geared toward handling out-of-the-ordinary events.

4. It is oriented toward people, rather than things.

5. It is controlled and fed mainly by the workers.

6. It motivates employees.

Table 9.1 summarizes these and additional key comparison points about the formal and informal systems.

Advantages and Disadvantages of the Grapevine

An active grapevine is one indication of organization health. Davis and Newstrom put it this way:

The grapevine is important to morale.

> Since the grapevine arises from social interaction, it is fickle, dynamic, and varied as people are. It is the expression of their natural motivation to communicate. It is the exercise of their

Table 9.1

THE FORMAL AND INFORMAL COMMUNICATION SYSTEMS: A COMPARISON OF CHARACTERISTICS

Formal Communication	Informal Communication
Slow	Rapid
Deliberate, planned	Spontaneous
Largely written	Largely oral
On-the-record	Off-the-record
Oriented toward routine events	Oriented toward out-of-the ordinary events
Oriented toward things	Oriented toward people
Management controlled	Employee controlled
Management motivating	Employee serving

freedom of speech and is a natural, normal activity. In fact, only employees who are totally disinterested in their work do not engage in shoptalk about it.[2]

On a more macro note, grapevine gossip serves to stir up competitiveness and creativity in dynamic industries. Silicon Valley provides a good example.

The key event in the history of the personal computer industry occurred in 1975 when Silicon Valley gossips began spilling details about Intel Corporation's still secret eight-bit microprocessor. The rumors quickly inspired rival companies to copy Intel's new 8080 chip and offer their versions at half Intel's selling price. But instead of devastating Intel, as might have happened in other industries, the knockoffs forced the company to match the lower price — and, as a result, to dominate the market.[3]

Simon sees candidness as the chief advantage of the grapevine. It provides what he calls a "barometer of public opinion in the organization."[4] If the manager is sensitive to this, he or she can gather a great deal of information about the attitudes and interests of the employees.

The grapevine has several other positive benefits. First, it acts as a sounding board, a place for employees to let off steam and air their anxieties and frustrations. This psychological safety valve can be very important to the long-term, smooth operation of the organization. Second, the informal system greatly influences the social environment and the quality of work life. A healthy grapevine promotes social compatibility and a cooperative, team-oriented work group. The informal system really establishes the behavioral norms and quickly socializes newcomers as to what is, and what is not, acceptable behavior. Finally, informal channels take up slack by processing information not handled by formal channels.

The grapevine helps to get the work done. If employees were restricted to formal channels, in many firms work output would cease when the manager left. Let's illustrate with a typical example. (Use Figure 9.1 to follow the flow of communication.) Randy is applying for a job as assistant manager in production with the XYZ Company. She knows there are many other applicants but feels she is very well qualified. Her cousin,

Figure 9.1

An informal system in action.

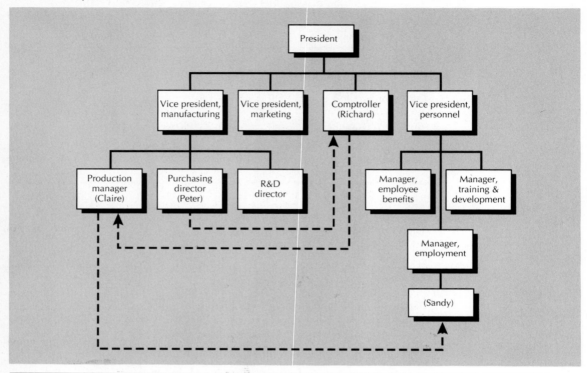

Peter, is director of purchasing for the firm, and she calls and asks him for help in getting the job. In turn, he calls his friend Richard, who is the corporate comptroller. He, then, calls his friend Claire, who is the production manager. Finally, Claire calls Sandy in personnel and asks her to send down Randy's file right away. The conversation goes something like this:

Claire: I've heard really good things about one of the applicants for the job as my assistant manager. Her name is Randy Smithfield.

Sandy: Yes, I have her application right here. But to tell the truth, we've got others who are more qualified than she.

Claire: Well, qualifications don't tell the whole story, Sandy. It takes a lot more than formal education to get along in our department. I've heard Randy has what it takes. I'd like you to get her in to see me as quickly as possible.

Sandy: I really wanted to set up appointments with you for four or five others as well.

Claire: Listen, Sandy, my schedule is jammed. Get Randy in here first. If I need to see anyone else, I'll let you know.

Randy comes in for the appointment the next day and is formally on the job by Monday morning. Is this a realistic scenario? Very! Often, the hiring of a new employee is a result of the informal communication system.

The informal organization also has disadvantages. The four primary ones are as follows:

1. Some degree of error is carried in the grapevine, although studies have shown this error is not as great as many people think. For example, Davis has found that 75 to 95 percent of grapevine information is accurate.[5]

2. Employees sometimes feed the grapevine with self-serving information. They create "facts" rather than simply report them.

But it has its disadvantages.

3. Information processed by the grapevine is not protected by limited responsibility. When someone puts a message into the formal system, he or she takes responsibility for it. If there are questions or comments about it, people know where to find the source. This is not true, however, with the informal communication system, and this lack of focused responsibility can cause confusion. There is no locus for feedback.

4. Although the formal system is mainly explicit, the informal system often relies on ambiguous implicit communication where messages are not delivered in a straightforward manner. See International Communication in Action: When in Rome for more on this subject.

Managing the Grapevine

Management must pay heed to the grapevine and actively get involved in using it to supplement the organization's formal chain of communication. To ignore the grapevine is to cut off a valuable communication resource. Studies show, for example, that five out of every six messages processed by an organization are carried via informal channels. As Lewis has so aptly noted, ". . . managers need to learn to adapt to, manage, and control the grapevine. One approach is to open up all organizational communication channels, fight rumors with positive presentation of facts, prevent employee idleness and boredom through better job design, and develop long-term credibility of managerial communication."[6]

Some managers deliberately use informal channels to get the word out quickly. Says one expert,

> Management may even deliberately use what is sometimes termed the gossip chain to informally get out the word. A West Coast businessman cites the example of a huge corporation headquartered in San Francisco: top executives there, he claims, relay messages downward by filling the ears of select, certified-reliable gossips, called pass-on-ers. At other companies, trial balloons may be floated on these hot winds.[7]

This approach, of course, requires the creation of a trust relationship between management and the employees. If it can be accomplished, it will go far in eliminating the negative consequences of the grapevine while nurturing its benefits. Such a relationship will also help squelch rumors that tend to flourish when employees feel insecure and have limited access to information. In addition, it helps management deal with the three major principles of rumor behavior.

INTERNATIONAL COMMUNICATION IN ACTION

When in Rome

Many American managers find it difficult to work through informal channels. They like the rules and regulations of the formal organization. They feel that the informal approach to getting things done consists of too many tenuous and vague agreements which, if the other person does not follow through and do what has been promised, cannot be formally enforced.

These managers would like it even less if they were working in Japan, for the Japanese make very heavy use of implicit communication. They do not say things outright; they are intentionally ambiguous. However, their subordinates understand what is being implied, and they act accordingly. The accompanying figure illustrates the differences in the use of explicit and implicit communication by a host of different countries and geographic regions.

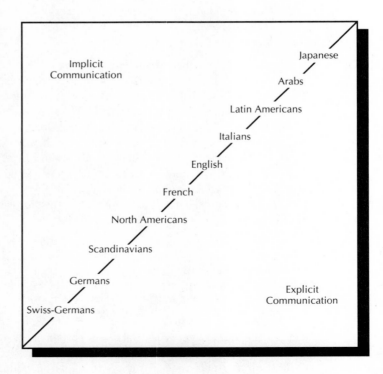

SOURCE: Adapted from Martin Rosch, "Communications: Focal Point of Culture," *Management International Review*, Volume 27, Number 4, 1987, p. 60.

Implicit communication is particularly disturbing to managers from other countries who are trying to do business in Japan. Whom do they talk to when they want to sell their goods to a Japanese firm? Does this individual have the authority to bind the company to a contract? Who else will be involved in the final decision-making process? These questions often go unanswered or the seller arrives at the wrong answer. In describing this dilemma, one researcher has put it this way:

> Americans expect others to behave just as we do. Many are the unhappy and frustrated American businessmen or lawyers returning from Japan with the complaint that, "If only they would tell me who is really in charge, we could make some progress." The complaint displays a lack of understanding that, in Japan, no one individual carries responsibility for a particular turf. Rather, a group or team of employees assumes joint responsibility for a set of tasks. While we wonder at their comfortableness in not knowing who is responsible for what, they know quite clearly that each of them is completely responsible for all tasks, and they share that responsibility jointly. Obviously, this approach sometimes lets things "fall through the cracks" because everyone may think that someone else has a task under control. When working well, however, this approach leads to a naturally participative decision making and problem solving process.[1]

Doing business in Japanese, Arab, and Latin American countries can be frustrating for those who are used to explicit communication. American managers have to understand that managers in these countries tend to be much more implicit in their communication. As one international expert put it, "When you are in Rome, you have to do it the way the Romans do."

[1] William G. Ouchi, *Theory Z* (New York: Avon Books, 1981), pp. 41–42.

Major principles of rumor behavior

1. **The principle of external control.** Rumors arise when important events are beyond the control of those involved in them.

2. **The principle of cognitive unclarity.** Rumors originate when situations are unstructured and unpredictable.

3. **The principle of integrative explanation.** Details tend to be distorted to conform to the dominant theme of a rumor.[8]

The best way to control rumors is to provide substantial and accurate information. If rumors do occur, the effective manager can then pick up on them and stop them by providing correct information. In turn, the rumor will have provided management with insights regarding where employees lack information and have concerns. Management's role in influencing this information organization is to (1) accept and understand the informal organization; (2) consider possible effects on informal systems when taking any action; (3) integrate, as far as possible, the interests of informal groups with those of the formal organization; and (4) keep formal activities from unnecessarily threatening the informal organization in general.[9]

COMMUNICATION NETWORKS

A network is a pattern of communication interactions.

A *network* is a pattern of communication interactions. Every large organization has multitudes of these networks. They exist between organizational members who frequently interact. When examined in terms of organizational communication, three different levels of network become evident. First, the entire organizational communication system is a network. Second, people can use individual or personal networks in getting things done in the organization. Third, there are group networks as in the case of groups, departments, and so forth. We will focus on this third level in the remainder of this chapter. However, you should also be aware that there are formal networks.

Formal Networks

Greenbaum has identified four different types of formal networks: the regulative network, the innovative network, the informative-instructive network, and the integrative network.[10]

The *regulative network* is predominantly found in the formal communication system and consists of the channels used to disseminate regulations, company policies, practices, and procedures. It is the network, for example, that lets employees know that sick days may not be taken to extend vacation time or that vacation days may not be carried over from one year to the next.

The *innovative network* has as its sole purpose the task of making the organization flexible and adaptive to the changing demands and environments which all organizations today must confront. This network, developed by the formal communication system, is a direct result of the participative management theory, which believes that many creative ideas can come from the employees. The recent growth of quality circles in this country is a good example of the type of program that emanates from the innovative network. Suggestion systems are another example.

The *informative – instructive network* provides the training function deemed necessary by the formal organization. As with the other three networks, the informative – instructive network furthers the organizational needs of adaptiveness, morale, conformity, and institutionalization. All of these, in turn, add up to increased productivity.

The *integrative network* focuses on employee morale. The reward system functions here, whether it be a raise in pay or an informal pat on the back. The grapevine is also operative here. This network most closely approximates the informal communication network with which the rest of this chapter will now deal.

Informal Networks

An interesting aspect of network analysis, and one we will be discussing at greater length, is how the informal networks compare and contrast with the formal organization chart. Figure 9.2 illustrates that the formal and informal systems always overlap to some degree. The charting of this overlap can give the manager a significant amount of insight into how the organization *really* operates.

Before examining network analysis, let us take a look at how networks are formed. What decides who relates with whom in an organization? Here we are not discussing

Figure 9.2

The informal and formal communication systems.

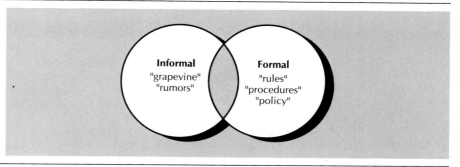

the obviously imposed relationships of superior and subordinate but the spontaneously formed networks of informal communication. Baird tells us three main factors influence the development of these networks.

Factors influencing network development

1. Networks seem to develop along friendship lines. What starts out as friendship pairs or trios in an organization can quickly expand by the addition of friends to the developing network.

2. The more success a person has with a particular communication channel, the more likely he or she is to use that channel again.

3. People who use a channel for one purpose and find it satisfactory are likely to use it for other purposes as well.[11]

A fourth contributing factor to network development is *propinquity* or nearness. People working closely together are more likely to establish regular informal communication lines or networks. If an individual is moved from one location to another, the person's former network will begin to contract and eliminate the individual as a member, whereas the new network will slowly absorb the person. At this point the individual is in a unique position to serve as a bridge between one network or clique and another. More will be said about this topic later.

Network Structures

As with all other organizational structures, some forms of networks seem to handle communication more efficiently and effectively than others. Although many different forms of networks are possible, four main types are generally identified: the wheel, the circle, the chain, and the all-channel systems. Figure 9.3 depicts each of these structures. The lines and arrows indicate open communication flows. In each case six people are used as an example.

The wheel has one central person.

THE WHEEL   The wheel is characterized by one central figure who speaks to the other members of the clique and to whom everyone else communicates directly. This may seem unrealistic, but consider the regional sales manager who operates out of his office

Figure 9.3

Network structural forms.

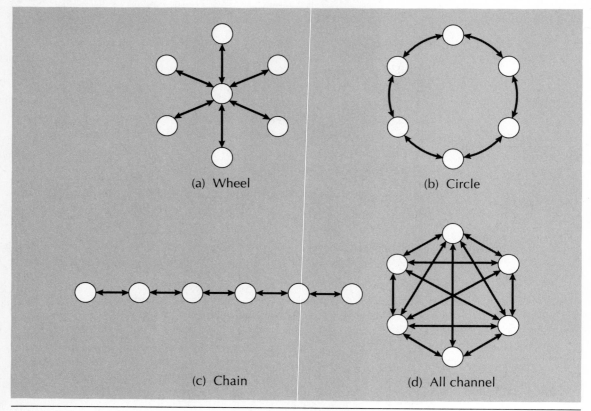

(a) Wheel

(b) Circle

(c) Chain

(d) All channel

in Orlando. All his local sales representatives may be working in different territories throughout the state. So although they all talk to the regional manager on a daily basis, they hardly ever get a chance to communicate directly with each other. If the manager is faced with a problem such as making a recommendation on the marketability of a new product based on test sales in the different territories, he will ask each of the representatives for their input. After talking to them, the manager will process the data and come up with a recommendation. Very likely, he will tell each of the reps what his conclusion was and why. The critical point to note, however, is that the manager does all of this alone. There is no participation by the reps. The wheel results in a very autocratic style of decision making.

THE CIRCLE   The circle is a more complicated network than the wheel. There is no clearcut leader in the circle: each member is an equal participant. Diagram (b) in Figure 9.3 shows that each person in the circle communicates with two and only two other

In the circle each member is an equal.

persons. The circle has to communicate information full cycle in order to be effective, for only then can the input of all members be processed.

The most positive attribute of the circle is that participation and equality are guaranteed; member interrelationships are usually good, and morale tends to be high. In addition, the quality of resulting decisions tends to be higher than that in the wheel format.

On the negative side, the circle network is slow and cumbersome in processing information. Since each person talks only to two people, it takes quite a few interactions to get any single idea communicated to everyone. Moreover, the rate of distortion is high because messages are repeatedly encoded, decoded, and then recoded as they are passed on to the next link.

THE CHAIN The chain as shown in Figure 9.3, diagram (c), is found in informal networks where members are peers in terms of organizational level. Those on either end of the chain are usually quiet, perhaps introverted, employees who choose to communicate with only one other person in the chain. The central positions of the chain are occupied by people who communicate with two other people. A leader may or may not emerge in this process; if one does emerge, he or she will not reside at the terminal points of the chain.

> Members of a chain are organizational peers.

In contrast to the circle, the chain has two major advantages. First, it is faster. Second, it tends to be more accurate than the circle because the distortion caused by multiple transmissions is not as likely to occur.

On the negative side, the group never sits down and mutually hashes out problems, and member satisfaction is usually not very high.

THE ALL-CHANNEL The all-channel network provides the optimum in member participation. In this format, everyone talks to everyone else. The leader, if there is one, tends to use a highly participatory style. The all-channel network typically processes large amounts of data.

> The all-channel provides for optimum member participation.

This network possesses two positive aspects. First, it tends consistently to produce the best decisions. This is because everyone has a chance to speak his or her mind and to receive the benefit of feedback from everyone else. Second, member satisfaction is extremely high.

The biggest problem with the all-channel network is that it often becomes bogged down in its participatory processes and is typically the slowest network in reaching decisions. In addition, distortion can be high because of the large number of communication channels available for use. Table 9.2 summarizes the key attributes of these four network forms.

The question may arise as to why one type of network may develop in contrast to another. Wofford and associates have shed some light on this subject by suggesting that five factors determine the appropriate network form or predict which form will emerge.[12]

> Factors determining network form

1. *Task and functional determinants.* These factors center around the information an individual needs to satisfy task requirements and personal needs. The latter is very important because an employee may communicate not only to acquire data needed to do his/her job, but to satisfy social needs as well.

Table 9.2

RELATIVE MERITS OF THE WHEEL, CIRCLE, CHAIN, AND ALL-CHANNEL NETWORKS

Attribute/Network Form	Wheel	Circle	Chain	All-Channel
Speed	Fast	Slow	Fast	Slow
Accuracy	High	Low	Moderate	Moderate
Distortion	Low	High	Moderate	High
Quality of decisions	Low	Moderate	Moderate	High
Member satisfaction	Low	High	Moderate	High
Type of leadership	Autocratic	None	Emerging	Participatory

2. *Conventions and normative determinants.* When entering a new network, these constraints are particularly important. The norms and conventions of the network largely dictate what type of communication activity will take place. On a larger scale, the norms and conventions of the organization impact on the type of networks that will form. If the organization's climate is open and participatory, for example, it is highly likely that all-channel networks will form.

3. *Environmental determinants.* This category largely looks at the effect of proxemics on the development of networks. Location of work spaces and seating arrangements are two factors to be considered here. A classic example is found in the King Arthur legends. The round table was a symbol of equality and still serves to foster an all-channel network.

4. *Personal attributes.* The characteristics of the individuals making up the network cannot be overlooked. Their skills in interpersonal relations as well as their perceptions, codes of past experience, motivations, and attitudes all play a role in shaping the communication network.

5. *Group process variables.* As with personal attributes, group attributes cannot be overlooked. Factors to be considered here include group cohesiveness, group identity, status, roles, and goals.

To assess your understanding of the various network forms, take Self-Assessment Quiz 9.2.

Communication Roles in Networks

A useful approach to studying network communication is to identify various members as holding the roles of gatekeeper, liaison, bridge, isolate, opinion leader or star, and boundary spanner. Not every network member assumes one of these roles, but identification of those who do can be very helpful to the manager in understanding and using the informal communication system. The following is a brief description of each role.

SELF-ASSESSMENT QUIZ 9.2

How Well Do You Understand Network Forms?

Directions: Answer each question below by indicating W for Wheel, C for Circle, Ch for Chain, and AC for All-Channel.

———— 1. Which network will solve a problem most quickly?

———— 2. Which network provides the greatest member satisfaction?

———— 3. Which network will provide the highest quality answer to a problem?

———— 4. Which network will be the slowest to solve problems?

———— 5. Which network provides for the greatest member participation?

———— 6. Which network provides members with the fewest communication opportunities?

———— 7. Which network most clearly indicates autocratic leadership?

———— 8. Which network most clearly indicates participative leadership?

———— 9. Which network most closely approximates the organizational hierarchy?

Answers are in the Answer section at the back of the book.

Gatekeepers regulate information flow.

1. *Gatekeeper.* The gatekeeper regulates the flow of information to other members of the clique. In an organization, the classic example of a gatekeeper is an executive secretary who controls the phone calls, appointments, and messages that reach the executive. Similarly, people in networks who choose to pass along or not pass along information to others in the group are also gatekeepers.

Liaison people perform a linking function.

2. *The liaison.* The liaison performs a linking function between cliques while not actually belonging to any one clique. Figure 9.4 shows the relative position of a liaison.

Bridges also help link cliques.

3. *The bridge.* Like the liaison, the bridge performs a linking function through which various networks or cliques communicate. Unlike the liaison, however, the bridge does belong to one of the networks. Figure 9.5 shows the bridge position.

Isolates play little role.

4. *Isolate.* The communication role of isolate is perhaps a misnomer because this person does little, if any, regular communicating. The isolate is basically removed from the regular daily flow of communication. A semi-isolate, though showing some communication activity, exhibits fewer than average communication transactions.

Opinion leaders are centers of activity.

5. *Opinion leader.* The opinion leader or star is the center of a disproportionate amount of network communication activity. This person is the receiver of the most transaction arrows. The individual can be an important asset to the manager since he or she wields a great deal of power in most organizations.

Figure 9.4

Liaisons tie
together cliques.

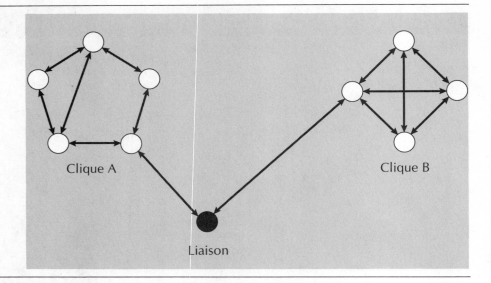

Clique A

Clique B

Liaison

**Boundary spanners
link the network
with the outside
environment.**

6. *Boundary spanner.* The boundary spanner, also called a cosmopolite, links the network with the external environment, that is, outside of the organization. Although liaisons and bridges perform a linking service, boundary spanners keep the network alive and alert by collecting and reporting data from outside sources.

Figure 9.5

Bridges tie
together cliques.

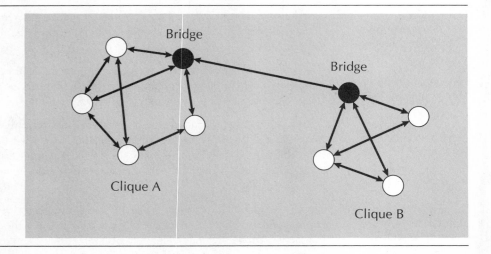

Bridge

Bridge

Clique A

Clique B

Descriptive Properties of Networks

A number of methods have been developed for quantifying and qualifying clique/networks as a whole as well as for diagnosing the individual members. Rogers and Rogers have identified four measurements that look at clique structure as a whole: clique connectedness, clique dominance, clique-openness, and clique integration with the rest of the organizational system.[13]

Clique connectedness measures the actual number of communication transactions in a clique as compared to the total possible number of transactions. The resulting ratio may vary up to 100 percent; the higher the ratio, the more connected or cohesive is the group. In a group of five people, for example, if everybody indicated they spoke to everyone else, there would be 20 possible transactions. If, however, only 10 transactions actually take place, the clique connectedness ratio is 10/20 or 50 percent, which indicates a low connectedness rate within a clique. If 18 transactions had taken place, the connectedness rate would have been 18/20 or 90 percent, indicating a significantly more cohesive group. Figure 9.6 illustrates these two examples.

Clique dominance refers to the degree of communication dominance by one or two individuals in the group. Clique dominance tends to correlate negatively with clique connectedness. In the wheel form depicted in Figure 9.3(a), for example, the hub of the wheel completely dominates the communication of the group. In turn, the connectedness rate of the group is extremely low.

Clique openness and *clique integration* refer to the ways in which the clique interrelates with its external environment. As with any system, a clique must be relatively open if it is to survive and grow. This openness allows it to exchange information with others who are not members of the clique. Clique integration looks at structural links with other cliques in the overall system. Bridges and liaisons are particularly important in this analysis.

O'Reilly and Roberts also have studied group connectedness and intergroup links and have suggested quantifiable clique attributes. Three of them are (1) two-way communication, (2) vertical differentiation, and (3) horizontal differentiation.[14]

Two-way communication examines the number of two-way or reciprocal communication links within a clique. For example, in Figure 9.6 showing connectedness ratios, the number of reciprocal links is 3 in the low-connected clique and 8 in the high-connected clique. The two-way communication rate tends to correlate positively with the connectedness ratio.

Vertical differentiation looks at the number of hierarchical levels represented in the group. The numerical value is attained by counting the number of levels and dividing it by the total number of people in the group. In a group of 8, for example, we might find 7 employees of a peer level and one foreman. The vertical differentiation rate therefore would be 2/8 or 0.25.

Horizontal differentiation refers to the number of different job categories (at relatively equal levels) that exist in the group compared to total group size. In our last example, the foreman would be one job type. If he also had 5 assemblers and 2 welders in the group, we would then have a horizontal differentiation factor of 3/8 or 0.375.

In research reported by O'Reilly and Roberts, vertical differentiation, two-way interaction, and clique connectedness were found to be positively related to accuracy of

---

Sidenotes:

Clique connectedness measures communication transactions.

Clique dominance is often exercised by one or two people.

Openness and integration deal with interrelationships with the external environment.

Figure 9.6

Connectedness ratios.

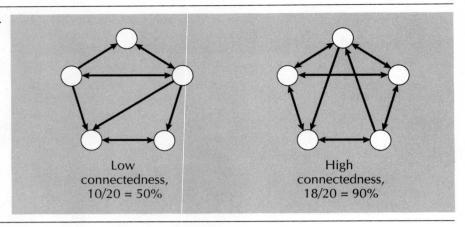

Low
connectedness,
10/20 = 50%

High
connectedness,
18/20 = 90%

communication. Connectedness and horizontal differentiation were found to be positively related to openness of communication. In summary, both accuracy and openness were correlated to effectiveness, the ultimate goal.[15]

Network Analysis

Network analysis is a method of studying organizational communication by plotting the patterns of informal cliques. It is grounded in the techniques of sociometry and relies largely on researcher observation and/or employee-answered questionnaires. Network analysis provides us with a reservoir of information, although, like a snapshot, it is truly accurate only for the instant of time in which it was constructed. As a micro tool for learning more about the macro organization, network analysis has a fairly recent history. Its two main branches have been laboratory research on small groups and sociometric studies of communication interactions within organizational systems.

Network analysis can be used to study communication patterns.

Perhaps the earliest roots of small group research came from the Hawthorne Studies. We saw in Chapter 2 how important these studies were in demonstrating the critical nature of both informal communication and social relationships within organizations.

Jacob Moreno is credited with having developed the sociometric approach to gathering data about small groups. Quantitative data are obtained by gathering responses to specific questions such as "With whom do you communicate most frequently?" "To whom do you go with a work-related problem?" and "With whom do you socialize most often?" The resulting relationships are plotted using sociograms with directional indicators. One-way choices, as well as mutual choices, are plotted and communication roles such as isolates, opinion leaders, bridges, and liaisons are determined. Figure 9.7 shows a basic sociogram for a department of ten in response to the question, "To whom do you go with a work-related problem?"

It was still a long step, however, from these early beginnings to the network analysis

Figure 9.7

A sociogram.

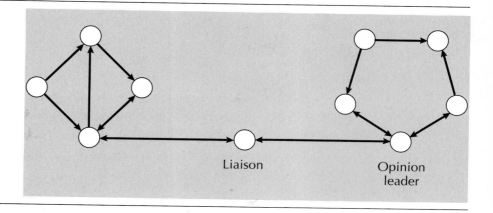

Liaison

Opinion
leader

research of today. Although the early studies focused on somewhat contrived laboratory experiments, network analysis is conducted in an on-going organization and studies actual social structure. The first network analysis was done by Jacobson, Seashore, and Weiss working out of the Institute for Social Research at the University of Michigan. Together, they studied communication links within the U.S. Office of Naval Research by asking each member to relate how frequently he communicated with every other member in the organization.

> This technique arranged all of the organization's members down one side of a matrix (the "who" or "seeker" dimension), and all of the same individuals on the other side (the "whom" or "sought" dimension). This who-to-whom matrix of interpersonal communication patterns was then rearranged so that individuals who interacted more frequently with each other were placed closer together on the dimensions of the matrix. The subgroupings or cliques that gradually emerged within the matrix were considered the building blocks of the informal structure. The "cement" that held these blocks together was the liaisons and bridges, who provided interpersonal connections among the subsystems. This focus on liaisons led to the realization, only very gradually in future years, that the integration of the informal subsystems within an organization was an important function of communication in organizations.[16]

The Jacobson, Seashore, Weiss work was largely unnoticed in the 1950s. Little, if any, further attention was given to network analysis until the late 1960s when network studies began to be the focus of research by faculty and students at the Department of Communication at Michigan State University. By the early 1970s at least five kinds of network analysis had been recognized:

1. *Residential analysis.* In this type of analysis, the researcher moves into the organization to perform live observation of the group being studied.

2. *Participant analysis.* More widely used than the first method, this type of network analysis relies heavily on the participants answering questions or filling out questionnaires about their communication.

Five kinds of
network analysis
have been
recognized.

3. *Duty study*. This method relies heavily on the observation of the researcher, who stations himself or herself at a set spot in the system and charts all communication activity that is directly observed.

4. *Cross-section analysis*. This method takes a one-episode snapshot of communication by plotting all communication taking place in a particular situation.

5. *ECCO analysis*. ECCO, which stands for Episode Communication Channels in Organizations, traces a specific piece of information as it is communicated through the system. This method is probably the most widely used, but in a majority of cases combinations of the above are found.[17]

ECCO analysis is clearly linked to earlier "small world studies," which centered around the occasional phenomenon we all have shared: the experience of finding a stranger who knows our best friend and of concluding "Isn't it a small world?"

NETWORK ANALYSIS METHODS   How then is this effective tool for measuring organizational communication flows actually used? What steps are typically taken in carrying out network analysis? There are five.

1. Identify the unit of study. A formal department is often a good place to start. Although numbers over 20–25 are difficult to analyze by hand, computer programs can process much larger numbers of employees.

2. Gather sociometric data about the identified group. This can be done through questionnaires, interviews, observation, or a combination of the three. For the beginner, questionnaires are the simplest. Questions should be carefully designed to elicit the most useful information. We recommend the following four questions for students making their first attempt at network analysis:
   a. With whom do you communicate most frequently?
   b. With whom do you socialize most frequently?
   c. To whom do you go with a work-related problem?
   d. Whom do you consider to be in your work team? (If you are drawing sociograms by hand, it is usually wise to limit choices to a maximum of five on each of these questions.)

There are five steps
in carrying out
network analysis.

A modified version of the matrix questionnaire so useful for beginners is provided in Table 9.3. The names of all the people in the department are listed in the left-hand column, and questions are listed across the top. All the respondent has to do is check off 0–5 responses for each question. Notice that the respondent's name is circled; in this case Tom Samuels is the respondent. If we could not identify the respondent, it would be impossible to draw the sociogram.

3. Be sure that virtually everyone returns the questionnaire. Without a high response rate, the resulting sociograms will be incomplete and misleading.

4. Carefully analyze the returned instruments and begin grouping mutual choices. Slowly, cliques will begin to emerge. Drawing the first sociogram may be frustrating but with a little practice, it will become progressively easier.

Table 9.3

SAMPLE NETWORK ANALYSIS QUESTIONNAIRE

Directions: Please check off a maximum of 5 answers for each question. The questions are as follows:
1. With whom do you communicate most frequently?
2. With whom do you socialize most frequently?
3. To whom do you go with a work-related problem?
4. Whom do you consider to be in your immediate work team?

Employees	Question One	Question Two	Question Three	Question Four
Sandy Anderson	—	—	—	—
Ralph Edwards	—	—	—	—
Linda Evanston	—	—	—	—
Frank Gerlick	—	—	—	—
Jeannette Johnson	—	—	—	—
Mark Kaplan	—	—	—	—
Marion Manfred	—	—	—	—
Robert Olson	—	—	—	—
Roberta Peterson	—	—	—	—
Leslie Roberts	—	—	—	—
(Tom Samuels)	—	—	—	—
Craig Thompson	—	—	—	—
Joan Wilson	—	—	—	—
Lynn Yaeger	—	—	—	—

5. Do not begin your analysis until after the sociograms (one for each question) are completed. Up to this point the steps have been purely data gathering and display. This final step is the one that provides the benefits of network analysis. What then should you look for?

Begin by labeling the cliques and the communication roles. Who are the opinion leaders, the liaisons, the bridges? What are the connectedness ratios of the cliques? Are there any isolates? Do the cliques and roles change with the various questions? The "social" opinion leader, for example, may not be the same as the "work-related" opinion leader.

Next, compare these configurations with the formal organization chart. Which of the informal channels are sanctioned by the hierarchy? Which are outside the proscribed channels? Is there a close match or is much important communication activity taking place through strictly informal channels? At this point, it is appropriate to interpret these findings according to your knowledge of the organization. How do you explain the patterns found? What are the implications for the firm? Are the patterns functional?

By now, you should have concluded that network analysis is a rich tool for taking a snapshot of the current organization and of analyzing the communication dynamics of that organization.

Implications for Management

1. Do not fight the grapevine. Recognize it as an inevitable but manageable part of the organization. Accept the challenge to understand the grapevine and add it to your personal list of organization resources.

2. Know where the power is in the informal system. Whom do people most respect and go to for advice? Make sure that this person has accurate data to pass along to the others.

3. Try to create an open communication environment. Avoid information ownership and make sure employees have the information they need or want. This will greatly lessen the rumors and distortion carried in the grapevine.

4. Do a network analysis of your department at least once a year. This will give you a wealth of important information. It can also help you understand those changes that have occurred in the informal communication system. This is especially important in times of accelerated change or anxiety such as before or after company layoffs.

C A S E   I N   P O I N T

Revisited

What did Jack do wrong? Perhaps the question is better phrased: What should Jack have done that he did not do? The answer is evident after reading the chapter. He failed to take advantage of the informal power structure. Remember from the case that Bill always did better than Jack during the "hands on" part of training program. Why? Because Bill had experience with the firm (Jack had just graduated from college) and knew how to get things done. He understood the value of the informal organization. In contrast, notice how Jack took his plan and sent it through channels where it became bogged down. Jack is not "street wise" in the ways of the company.

Can Jack straighten out the situation and get his plan accepted? This is not an easy question to answer. We know that Bill told the senior vice president that

he and Jack had formulated the plan. So, to some degree at least, Jack should be getting credit with the firm. In terms of springing his own plan loose, he should first talk with Bill and see what Bill recommends. Bill certainly seems to know how to get things done. Second, he could drop the senior vice president a note and say that he has recommended a plan to his own boss and is sending the vice president a copy to review. This might lead to a call from the vice president to Jack's boss. Barring these two eventualities, the best approach is to sit tight, wait and see what happens with the plan in the formal structure, and use this as a lesson of what *not* to do in the future. If Jack had known what you know from having read this chapter, he would not have made the mistakes he did.

YOU BE THE CONSULTANT

Fighting Rumor

"Computers. They're the wave of the future," noted the president of Paulsen Manufacturing. "We use them down on the line, in the office, and just about everywhere else. Why, just yesterday I signed a requisition for 25 portable personal computers. These machines are going to be given to our executives who are on the road so often that they just don't have time to keep up with all of their memo and report writing duties. Once they learn how to use these machines, I expect that they will be able to generate more work than ever before. Yes, I tell you, computers are beginning to touch all of our lives." With that the president concluded his brief Monday morning talk to the top management and sat down. The meeting wound up a few minutes later and everyone left for their respective offices.

On the way out, Tim Flynn bumped into one of the other plant managers, Paula Gillespie. "What did you think of the old man's remarks?" he asked his associate. "Ah, same old nonsense. If he's not yelling about computers he's talking about some other newfangled development. The only thing that worries me is that someday we'll have to use those machines to make on-the-spot decisions. Then we'll find out who really doesn't know what's going on in his department and it's bye-bye for that person. Otherwise, what's to worry about? Every time we put in additional computerized machinery down on the line, we create more jobs for more people. Hell, if we computerize any more, we'll drive national unemployment down to 5 percent." Tim laughed and walked on.

Back in his department he looked over the morning mail and made a couple of calls. He then began reading through the office correspondence. There was a one-page summary of the minutes of a meeting that had been held the previous Thursday. The meeting was between the head of manufacturing and the head of finance. The agenda item was computerization of manufacturing facilities. Although the firm has computerized approximately 15 percent of its work, the minutes of the meeting pointed out that for $17 million in additional investment, another 23 percent of production operations could be computerized. The heads of both manufacturing and finance, according to the minutes, seem to think this is a good idea. Tim did not pay much attention to the memo after reading it. He had it filed with a bunch of other papers that had been sent to him to read. This was two weeks ago.

A week ago Tim had a brief visit from one of his supervisors. The individual was upset over some rumors she was hearing around the department. They related to a management plan to computerize all production operations and throw the workers out of jobs. Tim listened quietly and then reassured her that the rumor had no truth at all. "I've read the minutes of the meeting to which you're referring," he told her. "The management is proposing adding more computerized operations but that will not result in any unemployment. Look at what has happened so far. We have computerized part of our operation and the number of people working in this department has gone up. The rumor just doesn't make sense. Don't let it trouble you. There are always wild tales floating around. Forget it and it'll go away."

Unfortunately, the rumor has not gone away. Over the last three days Tim has had visits from the shop steward, the president of the local union, and a group of troubled employees. All have heard that the management is going to replace the production workforce with computerized machinery. Moreover, the union's lawyer has read the collective bargaining agreement very carefully and has concluded that the management is at liberty to do this just as long as it gives each worker one week's severance pay for every year of employment with the firm. This interpretation of the contract has added fuel to the union's fire.

Tim has talked to all these groups and has assured each that they are dealing with rumor. He has had no success. Earlier today he called the vice president of production and told him the situation. The vice president echoed Tim's arguments and asked if he would have the various groups drop by and see him. The meeting was held during the late morning. The executive was no more successful than Tim in convincing them that they were wrong. In fact, the vice president is somewhat concerned because on the way out of the room the president of the union made a comment regarding a strike. Before taking the matter up to the president, the vice president would like Tim to join him in a final meeting with the group. If this does not work, he is determined to turn the matter over to the president and the company lawyers. "I want you to set up a meeting with these people in your office for 3:00 P.M. this afternoon. In the interim, I am going to call in one of our consultants. This person is excellent at handling these types of communication breakdown problems. I'll have the individual here for lunch. I want you to join me in the executive dining room. We'll talk to the consultant, get an evaluation of the situation, and then use all of the ammunition the individual gives us during our 3:00 P.M. meeting."

Assume that you are the vice president's consultant. Based on your reading of the case, what is the problem being faced by the managers? Why did it arise? Could it have been prevented? What needs to be done now? Be as realistic as you can while incorporating into your recommendations the ideas contained in this chapter.

Key Points in This Chapter

1. The grapevine is a term used to describe the informal organizational communication system. It refers to any communication that takes place outside of the prescribed formal channels.

2. The six characteristics of the grapevine are: (a) rapid transmission, (b) predominantly oral, (c) geared toward handling out-of-ordinary items, (d) oriented toward people, (e) controlled mainly by the workers, and (f) employee motivating.

3. Some of the main advantages of the grapevine include: (a) it is a gauge of the organization's esprit de corps; (b) it is a barometer of public opinion in the organization; (c) it allows people a place to let off steam; and (d) it influences the social

environment and quality of work life. On the negative side, the grapevine: (a) sometimes carries erroneous information; (b) can be self-serving; and (c) is not protected by limited responsibility.

4. In the organization at large, the four formal types of networks are the regulative, the innovative, the informative–instructive, and the integrative networks.

5. There are four network structural forms: the wheel, the circle, the chain, and the all-channel. Each can be compared along such lines as speech, accuracy, distortion, quality of decision, member satisfaction, and type of leadership. Of the four, the all-channel offers the best mix of the six characteristics noted here.

6. There are many different types of communication roles in networks. One way of looking at network roles is to identify the various members in terms of their functions such as gatekeeper, liaison, bridge, isolate, opinion leader, or boundary spanner.

7. One way of quantifying and/or qualifying clique/networks as a whole is by looking at measures such as clique connectedness, clique dominance, clique openness, and clique integration. For practical application, however, it is necessary to chart and study the interactions that actually occur between the group members. This process is called network analysis, and the last part of the chapter explained how it can be carried out.

Questions for Discussion and Analysis

1. In your own words, what is the grapevine? In your answer, be sure to describe its characteristics.

2. How does the formal communication system differ from the informal one? Compare and contrast the two.

3. What are the advantages and disadvantages of the grapevine? Explain.

4. What are the three major principles of rumor behavior, and what relevance do they have for the effective practice of management?

5. What is the purpose of each of the following formal networks: regulative, innovative, informative–instructive, and integrative? Be complete in your answer.

6. How is communication managed in each of the following network structures: wheel, circle, chain, all-channel? In your answer be sure to describe each.

7. Why does one network develop in contrast to another? What are some of the major causal factors that are involved? Cite and describe at least three.

8. What do individuals in each of the following roles do: gatekeeper, liaison, bridge, isolate, opinion leader, boundary spanner? Describe each.

9. What are four measurements that look at clique structure as a whole? Describe them.

10. How can a manager use network analysis? Offer guidelines regarding how to gather information on measuring organizational communication flows.

Exercises

1. Interview five managers from different organizations. Ask them: What is the corporate grapevine? What are its benefits? What are its negative aspects? Analyze your results. Did all interpret the word "grapevine" the same way? Were they noticeably negative in their attitudes about the grapevine? Based on your reading of this chapter, how accurate were their perceptions?

2. Form groups of five or six. Have each person answer the following questions, choosing only other members of the group.
   a. With whom do you communicate most frequently?
   b. To whom do you go with a class-related problem? As a group, draw the resulting sociograms. *Hint:* Start out with a diagram of five or six circles, one for each member. Put each person's name within the respective circle. Example:

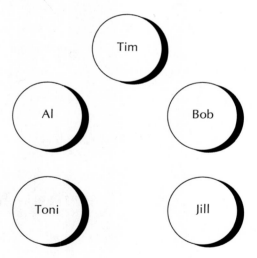

3. Following the instructions given in the chapter, do a network analysis on your department, club, or class.

References

1. Keith Davis, "The Care and Cultivation of the Corporate Grapevine," *Duns's,* July 1973, pp. 44.

2. Keith Davis and John W. Newstrom, *Human Behavior at Work*, 8th ed., New York, McGraw-Hill, 1989, p. 371.

3. John S. Tompkins, "Gossip: Silicon Valley's Secret Weapon," *Science Digest*, August, 1986, p. 58.

4. Herbert A. Simon, *Administrative Behavior*, 3rd ed. (New York: The Free Press, 1976), p. 148.

5. Davis and Newstrom, *op. cit.*, p. 371.

6. Philip V. Lewis, *Organizational Communication* (Columbus, Ohio: Grid, 1980).

7. Walter Kiechel III, "In Praise of Office Gossip," *Fortune*, August 19, 1985, p. 253.

8. L. Festinger, D. Cartwright, K. Barber, J. Fleischl, J. Gottsdanker, A. Keysen, and G. Leavitt, "A Study of Rumor and Its Origin and Spread," *Human Relations*, August 1948, pp. 464–486.

9. Davis and Newstrom, *op. cit.*, p. 380.

10. Howard H. Greenbaum, "The Audit of Organizational Communication," *Academy of Management Journal*, December 1974, p. 742.

11. John E. Baird, *The Dynamics of Organizational Communication* (New York: Harper & Row, 1977), pp. 273–274.

12. Jerry C. Wofford, Edwin A. Gerloff, and Robert C. Cummins, *Organizational Communications* (New York: McGraw-Hill, 1977), pp. 280–283.

13. Everett M. Rogers and Rakha Agarwala-Rogers, *Communication in Organizations* (New York: The Free Press, 1976), pp. 142–143.

14. Charles A. O'Reilly, III, and Karlen H. Roberts, "Task Group Structure, Communication and Effectiveness in Three Organizations," *Journal of Applied Psychology*, December 1977, p. 676.

15. *Ibid.*, p. 679.

16. Rogers and Agarwala-Rogers, *op. cit.*, p. 124.

17. Robert K. Allen, *Organizational Management Through Communications* (New York: Harper & Row, 1977), pp. 68–69.

Annotated Bibliography

Davis, Keith, and John W. Newstrom, *Human Behavior at Work*, 8th ed. (New York: McGraw-Hill, 1989).

> Davis is the best known researcher in the area of the corporate grapevine. This text is popular and reader-friendly. It covers a wide range of topics, but Chapter 15 is devoted to informal communications.

Rogers, Everett M., and Rekha Agarwala-Rogers, *Communication in Organizations* (New York: The Free Press, 1976).

> This book has several excellent chapters on systems theory as it applies to organizations and on networks and network analysis. As a whole, it provides outstanding ancillary reading to this chapter.

Schrank, Robert, *Ten Thousand Working Days* (Cambridge, Mass.: MIT Press, 1978).

> This fascinating autobiography traces Schrank's progress through more than a dozen blue collar and white collar careers. Throughout the book he draws conclusions about the nature of work and employee satisfaction and focuses on the informal organizations he continually encountered.

Simon, Herbert A., *Administrative Behavior*, 3rd ed. (New York: The Free Press, 1976).

> This edition expands slightly on Simon's classic work and shows how his theories can lead to more effective decision making. The chapter on communication firmly establishes informal communication as an important determinant of overall organizational effectiveness.

CHAPTER 10

Organizational Communication Barriers

"A common mistake made quite frequently in business organizations is to assume that more data is the same as more, and *better,* communication."

Reed Sanderlin, "Information Is Communication." *Business Horizons*, March/April 1982, p. 40.

Objectives

1. To describe the deliberate and unintentional types of distortion that occur in upward communication.

2. To explain how distortion in upward communication can be reduced.

3. To relate some of the most effective ways of dealing with distortion in downward communication.

4. To explain deliberate and unintentional types of distortion in horizontal communication and how they can be handled.

5. To describe how both information underload and information overload can lead to communication problems.

6. To relate some of the ways of dealing with communication underload and communication overload.

C A S E   I N   P O I N T

Sheryl's Workload

When Sheryl Cantutti got home from work, she immediately took a nap. By 6:00 she was feeling much better. After a light supper, she went into her study and opened her attache case. Inside were three reports. She took the first and began to read it. As she went along, Sheryl put comments in the margin and wrote to herself on a separate pad of paper. It was well after 10:00 P.M. by the time she finished the second report. She stopped at that point and got ready for bed.

By 6 A.M. the next morning she was already up and showering. As the commuter train pulled to a stop in downtown Manhattan, Sheryl had read half of the third report. The rest would have to wait until that evening.

Most of Sheryl's workday consisted of meetings, phone calls, and discussions about work-related problems. Approximately 40 percent of this work was unscheduled. For example, on two occasions her boss came by and asked, "Do you have a minute?" He then entered the office and began to talk about some particular problem that was brewing and what he wanted her to do about it. "Sometimes," Sheryl thought, "I wish my office wasn't next to his. This would prevent him from dropping by so often to give me additional assignments."

By the end of the day, Sheryl's desk was cluttered with papers and reports. Most of the work she had hoped to get to would have to wait until tomorrow. The number of interruptions and crisis situations that diverted her attention seemed to be growing on a daily basis. Most of the paperwork on her desk had been there from the day before. The only real work progress she had made in the last couple of days was the reports she had taken home with her at night. "Perhaps," she pondered, "that's the only way to really get work done around here. Take it with you and bring it back when you're finished."

As she began packing her attache case for the trip home, she paused to read a couple of memos that had arrived the previous week. One of them was stamped "For Your Immediate Attention." The message asked her to respond to a query before the monthly planning meeting. "Your input is required," read part of the memo. The planning meeting took place yesterday. A few other memos were even older. One was located down at the bottom of some reports and, based on the stamp Sheryl's secretary puts on all incoming material, must have been on the desk for at least two weeks. Sheryl threw some of these memos in her attache case. She also put back the report she had been reading on the commuter train. Realizing that there was still a little more room in the attache case, she added two more thick reports which she knew had to be taken care of within the next three days. "Might as well get to them as soon as I can," she told herself. On her way to the elevator, Sheryl bumped into her boss. He, too, was going home, Sheryl noticed that he was not taking any work with him. As they left the building he bid her good night and said, "Don't work too hard."

Based on your understanding of the case, what problems does Sheryl face on her job? Give some examples. What needs to be done about these problems? Offer some recommended solutions. Then put your analysis to the side. We will return to it later.

INTRODUCTION

Earlier in this book, you were introduced to interpersonal communication barriers. These barriers are found in organizational as well as interpersonal settings. In addition, a variety of organizational communication barriers exist in all organizations. These barriers can be classified under two headings: communication distortion and communication load. In this chapter, we will examine each. Before doing so, however, take Self-Assessment Quiz 10.1 and check your knowledge about organizational communication barriers.

SELF-ASSESSMENT QUIZ 10.1

What Do You Know About Organizational Communication Barriers?

Directions: Answer the following questions with a T (true) or F (false).

_____ 1. In most organizations, much of what is communicated through numerous levels eventually becomes distorted.

_____ 2. An "open-door" communication policy is the best way to avoid distorted communication.

_____ 3. Physical distance between employees often leads to more effective communication.

_____ 4. Horizontal communication, contrary to popular belief, can never be overused.

_____ 5. The less information people receive in organizations, the less communication distortion will occur.

_____ 6. Upward organizational communication channels tend to be self-serving to the employees who use them.

_____ 7. "Information ownership" refers to the policy of making decisions on the basis of expertise.

_____ 8. Bypassing levels in the organization hierarchy always leads to problems of one type or another.

_____ 9. The amount of trust employees have in their supervisors has very little to do with the accuracy of upward communication.

_____ 10. Employees with high aspirations are usually more accurate in their communication than those with low aspirations.

_____ 11. Studies show that most employees do not want more downward communication.

_____ 12. The more times a message is repeated the more likely it is that the employee will hear and understand it.

_____ 13. Although information overload is an obvious problem, information underload is a condition rarely found in today's organizations.

_____ 14. Routine, self-contained jobs are less likely to suffer from information overload than dynamic, highly integrated jobs.

Answers are in the Answer section at the back of the book.

COMMUNICATION DISTORTION

In every organization, much of what is communicated, especially when done orally, becomes distorted. Listeners filter messages as they repeat them to others. Gordon Lippitt has suggested the following list of filters in vertical communication:

Downward filters

- Sheer mass of communication.

- Boss is not available.

- Overresponse to secrecy/sensitivity of information.

- Lack of confidence and/or trust in subordinates.

- Originator overresponds to trivia by those above him or her.

- Deliberate generalizations when management is unsure what is wanted by those above.

- Boss adds his or her embellishments.

- Boss wants only an assured, predictable response — selects carefully what is communicated.

- Background differences: format, semantics, idiosyncrasies.

- Oversimplification of the problem expressed in the message.

- Communication does not make clear the action desired or who is responsible for such action.

- Multichannel distortions (i.e., several top people disseminate different versions of the message).

Upward filters

- Lack of two-way communication.

- Inappropriate timing of message.

- Overformalization (e.g., everybody in the act; everyone must sign off the message).

- Supervisors' insensitivity to problems and issues (e.g., trivia reported).

- Conscious, deliberate distortion, or omission.

- Overassessment by originator of his or her ability and of what he or she has a right to communicate.

- Personal relationships get in the way.

- Poor "packaging" of information (e.g., need to follow required organizational format).

- Complexity of data, especially that presented by professionals.

- "All is well" is only thing reported.

- Defensive of top echelon.

- Unstable upper management (e.g., many and frequent changes of personnel).[1]

This distortion can be deliberate or unintentional depending on whether the distorter is aware that the communication meaning is being altered. It can occur in upward, downward, and horizontal communication. Table 10.1 shows some of the most common types of distortion. Each is discussed in the sections that follow.

Upward Communication

Upward communication is used to obtain feedback on problems and job performance. Lack of adequate employee feedback can lead to devastating results.

If President Reagan and Oliver North are to be believed, the Contra scandal and embarrassment were a function of inadequate subordinate–superior communication. If reports of the

Table 10.1

TYPES OF DISTORTION IN ORGANIZATIONAL COMMUNICATION		
Level	Deliberate Distortion	Unintentional Distortion
Upward communication	Desire to look good Avoiding responsibility for failure Reluctance to give the boss bad news Bypassing levels	Subordinate's trust in superior Subordinate's aspiration needs Insecurity of employees Physical distance Formal organization structure
Downward communication	Inadequate feedback Uncomfortable with bad news	Managerial anxiety Multiple transmissions
Horizontal communication	Gossip and rumors Work specialization	Used as a substitute for downward and upward communication Overproliferation of horizontal communication
Diagonal communication	Bypassing levels	Communication gaps
All levels	Information ownership	Uncertainty absorption

48 hours preceding the tragic launch of the Challenger are accurate, the problem was an inefficient method of conveying information from subordinate to superior.[2]

Many deliberate and unintentional communication distortions can occur in upward communication. The following examines each.

DELIBERATE DISTORTION   A great deal of deliberate distortion takes place in upward communication. Everyone likes to look good to other people; thus they sometimes bend the truth to put themselves in a better light.

> There is a great deal of distortion in upward communication.

Another reason for deliberate distortion is that employees and managers like to tell their superiors what will make them happy and avoid passing on bad news. For example, a sales manager will not hesitate to tell his boss that his team made 120 percent of quota this month. If the figures show, however, that the team has made only 75 percent of quota, the boss will probably have to ask before getting this less happy information. No one likes to be the bearer of bad tidings if only because many superiors have trouble dealing with the situation. This is particularly true for those who cannot stand criticism.

> Distortion is used to avoid reporting failure.

A third intentional distorter of upward communication comes from bypassing levels in the hierarchy. Employees tend to do this when they perceive their immediate supervisors as unsympathetic, powerless, or the actual cause of their problem. Skipping links in the chain of command, for whatever reason, usually causes misconception, distortion, and communication gaps. For example, Ralph is having a problem with his immediate supervisor, Sam. Instead of confronting Sam with the issue, he walks into the general manager's office and blows the whole problem out of proportion. After all, Ralph reasons, he needs to make it sound worthy of the general manager's attention. Sam, upon later finding out what Ralph has done, becomes angry and resentful that Ralph has "gone over his head." Their problem, whatever it is, will undoubtedly become worse as a result of Ralph's action. When do people jump levels? Lewis reports ten of the most common times as

> Bypassing can cause distortion.

1. When it is necessary to get things done faster.

2. When it is easier to instruct the operator than to train a supervisor.

3. When there is an emergency.

4. When the supervisor tries to corral more responsibility.

5. When an employee has excessive ambition to get ahead, by fair means or foul.

6. When supervisors are so hard to deal with that they invite being bypassed by superiors or subordinates.

7. When the supervisor has differences with another supervisor on the same level and bypasses him or her to avoid personal contact.

8. When misunderstanding exists between supervisor and subordinate, and the subordinate goes to the supervisor's boss to tell the story.

9. When the channel jumper wants to punish or discipline the person jumped.

10. When the subordinates feel that they are being held back by their supervisor or that their ability is being overlooked.[3]

UNINTENTIONAL DISTORTION Much unintentional distortion also occurs in upward communication, but because of its lack of deliberateness, it is more difficult to identify. Four of the most frequent types of unintentional distortion are (1) the trust employees have in their superior, (2) the aspiration needs of the employees, (3) the security level of the employees, and (4) the physical limitations imposed by the organization structure.

The employee must trust the supervisor.

The impact of trust on honest, upward communication is easy to understand. If an employee intuitively feels he or she can trust the supervisor, without fear of reprisal or becoming the subject of gossip, then upward communication is more likely. This trust is built up over a period of time and is mostly subconscious.

Employee aspirations distort communication flow.

The aspirations of the employees also play a supporting role in communication. Supervisors often fail to note the differing aspirations of their employees. Joan may be very career oriented with firm intentions of "moving up the ladder as quickly as possible." Margaret, on the other hand, may merely want to put in her time and collect her paycheck with the minimum effort possible while waiting for her big break as a model to come along. Both Joan and Margaret have aspirations; in Joan's case they are directed toward the company, but in Margaret's case they are not. When a chance arises for these employees to report some personally favorable information to the manager, Joan will seize the opportunity immediately; Margaret will not bother. She does not care about pats on the back from her manager. However, if the need arises to tell the supervisor something less positive — for example, that she has just lost an important account — the two women will react differently. Joan will be reluctant for the manager to receive this news. If there is no way she can avoid the situation, she will find excuses for the loss; in other words, it wasn't her fault! The resulting distortion is obvious. Margaret, on the other hand, will be less threatened by this loss. Since she is not looking for upward mobility, Margaret is more likely to give an accurate interpretation of what happened.

Security needs distort communication.

Closely related to the factors of trust and aspirations is the security level of employees. The more secure an employee is, the more likely the individual is to be open and honest. Relate this idea for a moment to Maslow's famous need hierarchy. People with a heavy security need want to avoid "rocking the boat." These individuals will stay on the same job for 40 years because it has a good pension plan. Their primary motive is job tenure and financial security for themselves and their families. They do not want to attract a lot of attention; they tend to maintain a low profile. Their communication style is deliberately unprovocative. They often choose to ignore bad news rather than communicate it. Very secure people also have high aspirations. They, too, want to stay with the company in order to feel secure. At the same time, however, they desire upward mobility. These individuals operate at the upper levels of the need hierarchy, seeking challenge, increased responsibility, and the opportunity to achieve.

Physical distance promotes distortion.

Finally, physical distance imposed by organizational structure can impede and distort upward communication. The majority of organizational communication is done between those whose offices are in close proximity. You are much more likely to share your latest findings with the person in the office next door than you are with an individual whose office is two floors up and on the other side of the building. To get to a person far away, you have to call the person on the phone, make an appointment, or walk all the way over to that office. You often save yourself all this time-consuming trouble until you have something really important to say. Since most of your communiques will not be major, you will share them only with those in close proximity.

An effective manager has many means available to reduce distortion in upward communication. The first is to be fully aware that such distortion exists and to be cognizant of the sources of that distortion. Second, the manager should look at ways in which he or she can directly manipulate these distortion patterns. Distortion caused by physical distance is a prime candidate. An open-door policy, though attractive, is not necessarily the answer — unless employees use it. For the manager to get the message across that he or she wants to know what is going on, the individual has to get out of the office and regularly visit the employees. Going to lunch with them, sharing coffee breaks, and attending meetings are all helpful ways of plugging into the day-to-day communication activities of the department. A third important guideline is to be slow to chastise subordinates reporting poor personal performance: instead use "mutual" problem solving such as, "What can *we* do to prevent this in the future?"

A fourth method is to use an employee intermediary when communication is touchy.

> One method for providing subordinate–superior communication without incurring the wrath or damaging the ego of an upper-level manager is to employ intermediaries whose job is to solicit such messages and analyze them for consumption by upper management. The problem with this intervention strategy is that information may be distorted to make it attractive to superiors. Top management, however, can make an effort to discourage altering the essence of the information.[4]

A slow, deliberate attempt by the manager to improve upward communication will result in an equally slow but important increase in trust and security levels. It will also reduce the bypassing of levels because employees will now be more willing to go directly to the manager. "In short, effective employee communication will not occur on its own or by virtue of organizational processes that may be in place. It will occur only if the supervisor takes steps to make it happen."[5]

Downward Communication

Downward communication in organizations is used to carry rules, policies, procedures, and task instructions.

> The most effective way for any member of a work organization to stimulate incoming communication is to make every effort to ensure that outgoing communication is occurring. This certainly applies to the supervisor who wishes to inspire increased upward communication from the work group. In the process of actively supplying the employees with the means by which to communicate upward, the supervisor is actually communicating downward in a way that increases the likelihood of employees communicating upward.[6]

As with upward communication, however, downward communication is often subverted by the intrusion of deliberate and/or unintentional disorders.

DELIBERATE DISTORTION Downward communication often contains elements of deliberate communication distortion. The two main reasons are inadequate feedback and managerial discomfort in delivering unpleasant news.

Inadequate feedback from supervisors to employees can cripple an organization's productivity. The vast majority of employees thrive on feedback, especially positive information. All too often, however, supervisors give feedback only when it is negative. Most managers say that they do not have the time to systematically provide feedback and reinforce employee behavior on a continuing basis. Yet feedback is critical to employee success. It helps workers clarify their roles and responsibilities, and it provides them a measure of their performance and a knowledge of where they stand. High achievers particularly are frustrated with inadequate feedback.

Many managers resist giving feedback.

Managers who are uncomfortable handling bad news cause another communication barrier. Many managers are reluctant to deliver unpleasant messages and often delay such news until the last minute. Glossing over employee performance appraisals is a good example of this type of reluctance.

Many managers are uncomfortable delivering bad news.

UNINTENTIONAL DISTORTION Two primary sources of unconscious distortion in downward communication are managerial anxiety and multiple transmissions. (Multiple transmissions can also take place in upward communication.)

Managerial anxiety causes internal conflict and can result in distorted information entering the downward communication system. This anxiety can be caused by status anxiety and/or competition anxiety. *Status anxiety* refers to the conflict between the dictates of being boss and the desire to be liked by one's employees and co-workers. Depending on which imperative is the stronger, the manager can act quite differently in terms of communication content. *Competition anxiety* refers to the conflict produced in those failing to come to grips with the competitive nature of managerial work. The world of the manager is a political one, whether the individual is working in the public or private sector, and the political realities of the job explain much of the resultant distortion in communication.

Managerial anxiety can cause distortion.

Multiple transmission distortion is quite common. As shown in Table 10-2, every time a message is repeated, it can stray farther and farther from its original content. Many of us have played the parlor game in which something is whispered into our ear and we in turn pass it on to the next individual. By the time it gets to the last person and that individual repeats it out loud to the group, the results are often hilarious. In the workplace, the results can be disastrous. To help you realize just how serious this problem is, consider the research findings of Nichols, who, you will remember from Chapter 3, did much of the early research on listening. In examining message transmission through the organizational hierarchy, he found the following loss of information at each level.[7]

LEVEL	LOSS OF INFORMATION RECEIVED
Board	0%
Vice president	37%
General supervisors	44%
Plant manager	56%
General foremen	70%
Workers	80%

Notice that with the very first transmission of the information, there was a 37 percent loss!

Table 10.2

THE NUMBER OF LINKS CAN BE A COMMUNICATON BARRIER

Unit workers to foreman	The new incentive payment plan doesn't look too bad. A couple of the guys are going to try it out. However, the salary offer is a good 2 percent too low, and the fringe benefit package and new work rule proposals are lousy. We're telling the shop steward that if the company can't improve these, we should walk out.
Foreman to supervisor	Some of the workers are going to support the new incentive payment plan, but the fringe benefit package and new work rules are going to be fought by the union. The proposed across-the-board salary increases are also a little low, and we're going to get static on them, too.
Supervisor to plant manager	The workers seem fairly positive about our proposed incentive plan, but they don't like the fringe benefit package and they are somewhat opposed to the new work rules.
Plant manager to senior vice president	The workers really like the new incentive plan, but I don't think the union will agree to our fringe benefit package.
Senior vice president to chief executive officer	The new incentive plan is being well received. We're getting a lot of positive feedback on it. I wouldn't be surprised if we had a new union contract signed by the end of next week.

SOURCE: Richard M. Hodgetts and Donald F. Kuratko, *Management,* 2nd ed., (San Diego: Harcourt Brace Jovanovich, 1988), p. 273.

Sharpening emphasizes part of the message.

What causes this distortion? Two reasons are sharpening and leveling.

Sharpening, as defined by Hawkins and Preston, "involves the selective perception and retention of actual facts in a situation. Details picked up by one listener and repeated to another listener are said to be sharpened."[8] It is difficult to say just what part of the message will stick in the listener's mind. Often it is something that appeals to a personal need or value. Other times it is an emotion-laden word that "strikes a nerve" in the listener.

Leveling refers to the tendency of each listener to condense a story, internally summarizing and then repeating those points he or she thinks are most critical. Details of the original transmission eventually become clouded or lost altogether.

Multiple transmission distortion can be avoided as described in the following eight methods:

1. Cut back on the number of levels a message must pass through. The problem inherent in skipping levels, however, is the anxiety it creates in those who are passed over.

2. Repeat the important parts of your message. Preview and review the critical points of the message to be sure the receiver hears the key points.

3. Do not overload the message. Keep it simple and free of extraneous, sometimes confusing, information.

4. Plan the message and deliver it in a logical, organized manner.

Ways of avoiding multiple transmission distortion
5. Position the important points at the beginning and end of the message, thereby improving the chances that it will be heard and understood.

6. Be clear as to whether facts or opinions are being stated.

7. Solicit feedback to see that the message has been understood.

8. Word the message to suit the audience, being careful to use shared vocabulary, experiences, jargon, and the like. The more the sender knows about the receiver(s), the easier it is to get the message understood.[9]

Horizontal Communication

As discussed in Chapter 8, the purpose of horizontal communication is to avoid the time-consuming process of working information up the chain of command and back down. Because of its directness, this type of communication should contain much less distortion than either upward or downward communication. Although this is partially true, distortion still exists in horizontal communication.

DELIBERATE DISTORTION The types of intentional distorters found in horizontal communication result mainly from the transfer of gossip and rumors and from the specialized nature of the work itself.

Gossip and rumors are typically spread via horizontal communication. Once this communication channel is established, it requires continual information. If no factual data are put into the channel, rumors and idle chit-chat will fill the gap. This is especially true when downward and upward communication is fairly restricted.

The specialized nature of work is another cause of deliberate distortion. Employees have a lot of information about their own jobs but very little about related functions. At the same time, however, the need for "boundary-spanning" activity is accentuated, and the parochial nature of individual focuses and interests makes this communication difficult. Why, reasons the sales manager, should she even try to make the production manager speed up an order? He will never understand the critical nature of the account. Instead she goes up the hierarchy to the general manager and pleads her case for assistance. Vested interests and narrow points of view thus result from specialized functions, and these in turn impede successful lateral communication.

UNINTENTIONAL DISTORTION In Table 10.1 we noted that the overuse of horizontal communication to the detriment of upward or downward communication can become a problem. As Baird tells us:

> . . . lateral communication may serve as a substitute for upward or downward communication. Rather than struggle to overcome the barriers that obstruct vertical communication,

workers often find it more comfortable to communicate with their peers, using that transaction as an outlet for their problems, frustrations, and fears . . . lateral communication has another unfortunate tendency: occasionally it shows uncontrolled proliferation.[10]

The problem with such proliferation is that it is uncontrolled. This haphazard nature of horizontal communication provides no routine check or feedback system for monitoring distortion. Moreover, it encourages people to bypass the vertical communication systems, further distorting upward and downward communication.

Management pays less attention to horizontal communication than to either upward or downward communication. A concerted effort to bring order to this system, however, can yield positive results. In particular, managers should

Horizontal communication should be encouraged and nurtured.

1. Attempt to improve interdepartmental knowledge and rapport, with particular emphasis on mutual and related goals, by facilitating regular meetings of peers.

2. Make use of professional integrators, that is, people chosen and placed for their boundary-spanning abilities and on whose job description liaison duties will be clearly specified.

3. Implement and maintain a healthy, open hierarchical communication system. This in itself will eliminate many of the negative consequences of horizontal communications.

Diagonal Communication

Diagonal paths are used to communicate between people at different levels and in different departments or organizational units. Two major sources of distortion in diagonal communication are bypassing levels and communication gaps.

DELIBERATE DISTORTION   As detailed in the section on upward communication, bypassing levels in the hierarchy is always a potential source of trouble. In diagonal communication, levels are always bypassed. Many times this direct line to another department is sanctioned by the immediate supervisor; in other cases it is not.

Bypassing one's supervisor may cause distortion.

Our discussion of upward communication noted that bypassing levels usually occurs when supervisors are perceived as unsympathetic or difficult. In diagonal communication, this is not the case. Diagonal communication lines occur to expedite business as in the case cited in Chapter 9 where an accounts receivable clerk calls a regional marketing manager to find out why a customer who normally pays on time has fallen behind in his bills. In this instance, the clerk saves time by going directly to the person with the information, that is, the marketing manager. The clerk does not ask her supervisor to check into the matter but goes after the information directly. On the other hand, the accounting clerk's supervisor may be embarrassed at a later date when the marketing manager comments about how unusual it is for this particular customer to be late in paying the bill. The supervisor finds herself in the uncomfortable position of having to admit she knows nothing about the situation.

UNINTENTIONAL DISTORTION   As a direct result of skipping levels of formal communication in the hierarchy, a communication gap results. Information is shared between departments but not necessarily within the department. Outsiders to the

Diagonal communication often results in intradepartmental communication gaps.

department usually assume that everybody in the department is informed. For example, when the marketing manager mentioned above finds out that the accounts receivable supervisor does not know the story about this special customer, the manager may resent having to repeat the whole story again. The manager may also wonder why the accounts receivable people do not talk to one another and share information. To eliminate these communication gaps, it is important to nurture an atmosphere of sharing within the department. This is especially important when a lot of diagonal or even horizontal communication takes place between employees of different departments.

All Levels

In addition to distorters that tend to work predominantly with one direction of organizational communication, there are two that operate equally in *all* directions. The deliberate distorter is information ownership; the unintentional distorter is uncertainty absorption.

INFORMATION OWNERSHIP Employees at all levels sometimes hoard information. They feel it gives them a competitive edge over those who do not have the same information.

> Information has great value. Those who possess it have something others do not have and, presumably, need or want. And whether a person possesses information or not also indicates his status and role. When something has high value, people try to acquire it. Many of them use extraordinary means to do so. Once acquired, it is used to influence others. It may even be hoarded. Those with access to inside information have both prestige and power. They know what others do not. When we whisper, it is not so much to convey information as to ensure that the "wrong" persons do not gain it without our permission. People who are not in the know are nonequals. Small wonder that we get so uptight about communications. Small wonder that we give our own needs high priority and so often neglect the needs of others.[11]

Implications for Management

1. Establish a healthy organizational climate where people are encouraged to share bad news as well as good news. Be careful how you yourself react to receiving bad news. If you fly into a rage when things do not go as planned, your employees will quickly learn to censor their reports to you.

2. Build feedback systems into your communication channels. Be aware that multiple transmissions cause grave distortion. Check to see that important messages have gotten through.

3. Watch out for signs of information ownership. Structure your organizational reward systems to support cooperative effort rather than heroic one-person shows.

UNCERTAINTY ABSORPTION The concept of uncertainty absorption, first introduced by March and Simon, refers to how people fill in the gaps and add personal interpretations to a story before transmitting it.

Uncertainty absorption takes place when inferences are drawn from a body of evidence and the inferences, instead of the evidence itself, are then communicated. The successive editing steps that transform data obtained from a set of questionnaires into printed statistical tables provide a simple example of uncertainty absorption.[12]

In order to deal with uncertainty absorption,

1. Set an example for the organization by being careful to share accurate, complete information with others.

Some ways to avoid uncertainty absorption

2. Do not personally hoard information; this not only tends to create an information ownership barrier but also leads to increased uncertainty absorption.

3. Take time to check your sources when information is passed to you.

4. Watch out for people who tend to riddle their messages with unannounced inferences. Ask these persons if what they are saying is an opinion or a known fact. Encourage the persons systematically to be aware of this penchant for using inferences.

COMMUNICATION LOAD

The second major barrier to organizational communication is communication load. Load is actually another reason for distortion, but it is such a pervasive issue that we treat it as a separate barrier.

Communication load refers to the amount and the complexity of messages received by a unit of analysis, that is, an individual, a work unit, a department, or the organization as a whole. In this discussion, we will focus on the individual, but all points are equally applicable to larger units. The two basic foci are the *amount* of communication messages involved and the *complexity* of those messages. The majority of research conducted on communication load centers with good reason on the problem of quantity.

Amount of information determines load.

The amount of information a peasant might require in the Middle Ages was limited, but the information needed today is boundless. . . . We are bombarded with messages from morning until night. And we bombard others. This results in a frightful cacophony. That the Adam-and-Eve model of the human receiving set — which is all we are — might not be equal to the new demands should surprise no one.[13]

The amount of information received, regardless of communication media, will vary directly with the number of channels to which the person under study is privy. A sales manager, for example, has many more channels within the organization than the average sales representative who works mainly in the field.

Complexity of information is central to load.

In addition to the amount needed to be processed, one must consider the complexity of that information. Relatively simple to understand, routine messages can be handled in much greater abundance than unpredictable and complex messages.

A large amount of information can be successfully handled if the complexity of those data is relatively low. Alternatively, a small number of very complex messages can

Figure 10.4

Communication load:
A working model.

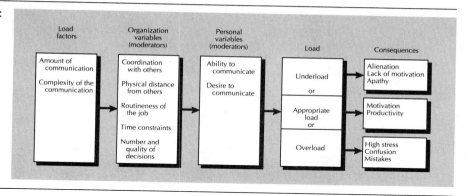

Overload problems
can perpetuate
themselves.

decisions and a need to ask questions. This leads to even more input data. The "A" loop in Figure 10.3 is completed. At the same time, Loop B is activated because the manager has not taken action or passed along information to other people. These people generate more questions and requests for information, again closing the circle.

The organizational factors illustrated in Figure 10.2 also contribute to overload. A high need for coordination with others tends to increase the overload potential of a manager's job. Relatively short physical distances also increase overload in that it leads to regular formal and informal communication channels. There is also a positive correlation with nonroutineness of the job; the greater the number of changes occurring in the job, the more information the manager is going to need, ultimately resulting in information overload.

The personal factors depicted in Figure 10.2 also are related to overload. People who have a high ability to communicate generally use those skills more often than those with a low ability, thereby encouraging additional communication input. When the person's desire/need to communicate is high, the same phenomenon will be observed. Figure 10.4 provides a working model of communication load incorporating all factors discussed to this point. Take Self-Assessment Quiz 10.2 to see if you are a victim of communication overload.

There are numerous
effects of overload.

The effects of information overload can be examined in terms of the organization as well as the individual. For the organization, information overload results in inefficient, ineffective information processing, a decrease in the quality of decisions, and a plethora of lost opportunities. In addition, it can produce four serious organizational consequences: decreased job satisfaction, decreased overall productivity, increased absenteeism, and increased turnover.

For the individual, overload usually is accompanied by stress-related symptoms. Ivancevich and colleagues report that "The greatest stress is one that keeps an individual feeling impatient, constantly hurrying, and giving him the feeling that he has not done everything he feels he should have done in a single work day."[16] The personal consequences of overload-produced stress can be divided into physical, psychological, and behavioral categories. The physical consequences of stress are probably the most dan-

SELF-ASSESSMENT QUIZ 10.2

Are You a Victim of Communication Overload?

Directions: Answer "yes" or "no" to the following questions:

_____ 1. Do you find yourself unable to ever completely clear your in-basket?

_____ 2. Are you frequently interrupted by phone calls and visitors who really cannot wait?

_____ 3. Are you receiving more reports on a monthly basis than you can possibly read, no less digest?

_____ 4. Do you have an active, functioning open-door policy of which your employees regularly take advantage?

_____ 5. Are you spending more than one hour a day on a regular basis in meetings?

_____ 6. Even when you attempt to be highly organized, do you often find it impossible to take the time to go out for lunch?

_____ 7. Do you often find it difficult to gather all the information you need to make a quality decision?

_____ 8. Do you often feel impatient and hurried, with the feeling that you cannot possibly accomplish everything you need to do in a single day?

_____ 9. Do you sometimes completely ignore seemingly low-priority communication because there simply is not time to deal with everything?

_____ 10. Are you unable to find the time to train others to do some of the parts of your job which could be delegated, if only your employees knew how to do it?

Answers are in the Answer section at the back of the book.

gerous. Primary among these are cardiovascular diseases and nervous disorders. The psychological consequences include mental fatigue, lack of confidence, and lowered self-esteem. The behavioral consequences range from temper tantrums to alcohol and drug abuse.

Some ways of dealing with overload   A number of approaches can be used to reduce information overload. First, the art of delegation should be taught and followed. For many managers this is not an easily learned skill. Quite often they are reluctant to give up decision-making authority in anything but the smallest matters. They need to be taught to operate by the _exception principle_, which holds that managers should concern themselves with exceptional cases, not routine results. Under this principle, significant deviations, such as very good or very bad profit performance, merit the manager's time far more than average or expected results.[17]

Another useful guideline in handling communication flow is the *horizon principle*, which holds that the information a person needs is directly related to his or her horizon of company problems. Often called the need-to-know approach, this principle can be very helpful in reducing, and sometimes preventing, communication overload.

A third useful approach is training employees in effective time management. Many cries of "overload" vanish when disorganized work habits are replaced with effective time-management principles that set priorities, delegate work, and group together similar activities in order to save time and effort.

Finally, communication technology such as electronic mail and fax machines are helpful in preventing information overload. Managers are able to process information quickly using these techniques. See "Communication Technology. Going Cellular" for a discussion of cellular phones and their use in organizational communication.

Implications for Management

1. Remind yourself at all times that more information is not necessarily better; nor does it ensure that communication, that is, the transfer of meaning, has taken place.

2. Be aware that employees differ in their abilities to handle large amounts of information effectively. Be on the alert for symptoms of overload. Early attention to the potential burnout victim can save your company a valuable human asset. Likewise be alert to the communication isolate. Employees who feel completely left out of the information flow are likely to become cynical and demotivated.

3. Periodically examine your management information system. Is it giving your employees the data they need when they need it? Ask report preparers what value their reports have to the company. Does anyone really need that information? If not, dump it. Manage your information system; do not let it manage you.

4. Provide training in time management for those most likely to be affected by overload problems. Teach them to work smarter, not harder.

C A S E   I N   P O I N T

Revisited

This case deals with communication overload. Sheryl has too much work to do. She is unable to get ahead even when she takes work home with her at night. Consider the fact that she brought home three reports and was able to get only two of them done by 10:00 P.M. She also took a nap as soon as she came in, indicating that she was quite tired. The case data give us no indication that Sheryl works until the early hours of the morning. On the contrary, she probably went to bed around 11:00 P.M., so she is getting seven hours of sleep a night. The fact that she needs a nap upon getting home is an indication that she is physically fatigued from the day's activities. In addition, the case tells us that she is having trouble getting to all the correspondence being sent to her. Simply stated, she is overworked.

COMMUNICATION TECHNOLOGY

Going Cellular

Businesspeople these days are facing communication overload in a number of different ways. One way is the backlog of messages that pile up when they are away from the office. Many managers find that when they return from a trip, it takes them a full day to catch up on their phone calls. To avoid this problem, many traveling managers call back to their offices and check on things. For example, businesspeople traveling in commercial jets make use of air-to-surface calls. Some industry experts predict that by the turn of the century, telephones will be available in every airplane seat and passengers will routinely use them. A second good example is found in airports where managers rush from their planes to find a phone and begin placing business-related calls. The waiting time for telephones is often 15 minutes or more, and some locales place a time limit on how long a person can use a phone in order to give others an opportunity to make their own calls. This is an inconvenience, of course, but at least the individual can get to a phone. If the person were in his or her car, this would be impossible — unless the manager had a mobile phone, and this is exactly what many of them are having installed.

The latest research reveals a boom in mobile phone demand. In the 48 months between January 1985 and December 1988 the number of cellular phone customers increased by a factor of 20. So many people want these phones that the telephone companies are having to scramble to keep up. The fastest growing demand is in major metropolitan areas such as New York, Boston, Washington, Chicago, and Los Angeles where annual demand is increasing by 67 percent. If the present trend continues, industry experts predict that there will be more than 10 million cellular phone users in the United States by 1993.

The cost of cellular phone use is fairly high, but for those managers who are constantly on the road, the cellular phone is becoming indispensable. Moreover, the costs are more than offset by the convenience and the amount of extra revenue they can generate by allowing managers to stay in touch with their office and customers. Some industry experts predict that in the future the telephones will be small enough to fit into a person's pocket and everyone will have one. If necessity is the mother of invention, then certainly managers will have a model of this phone before the end of this decade and some executives will be wondering how they ever got along without them.

SOURCE: Calvin Sims, "Meeting Mobile Phone Demand," *New York Times*, July 19, 1989, pp. 25, 30.

Many different solutions to her problem are possible. One is that her boss should sit down with her and discuss her work habits. A second is to get her more assistance. Keep in mind that her boss did not take any work home with him. Is this because he is a more efficient person than she? Or does he simply delegate most of his work so that he can finish everything before leaving the office. Using the material in the chapter, you should have been able to construct a recommended plan of action. Remember that, since you do not know what is actually causing the problem, you should have made recommendations that are both personal (to help Sheryl deal with the problem) and organizational (to help the company direct resources to deal with the problem).

YOU BE THE CONSULTANT

The Strategic Plan

Every six months the board of directors at Wilshire Industries reviews the company's strategic plan. This plan is formulated and approved every October, implementation begins in January, and progress is monitored in June. During each of the last three years the board has found that by June the Plan is usually off course and by the end of the year things have gotten even worse. Last year's desired return on investment was 18 percent and market share was projected at 9 percent. By June the return was running at an annual rate of 16 percent and by December it had dropped to 12 percent. Market share figures for both of these periods was 8 percent and 7.1 percent respectively. The new chairman of the board is very upset over these results. This was his first year on the board, and he went out of his way to make a good showing. Now he wants to know why things did not work out as expected.

One of the individuals with whom he has talked is the president, Charles Chetnik. Chuck has urged the chairman not to get upset over the results. "Bob," he told him, "we are doing the best we can with the figures we're getting from our people. We have at least 15 different reports that are coming in from the field telling us how well we are doing. Additionally, we are getting monthly sales figures from the computer. On the basis of these data, we put together actual and projected return on investment and market share progress. Each year we start off just fine, but as the months go along we seem to fall farther and farther off the mark. Sometimes I'm glad the year has only 12 months. I shudder to think what would happen to these figures if the year lasted 24 months."

Bob understands what Chuck is saying. Nevertheless, he feels that if the company is not doing very well by March or April, this situation should be reported back to management and reflected in the revised strategic plan. Why is there always a big difference between expected and actual performance? In his mind the answer rests in the data being communicated from the field to the home office personnel and/or from the personnel to the top management. Somewhere along the line there is a problem.

Bob has decided to get at the problem by having Chuck send one of his people down the chain of command to find out why sales estimates being fed into the strategic plan are always out of line with reality. Chuck assigned the job to Mary Ender. She spent three weeks checking the flow of information from the field all the way up the line. She has talked to salespeople, sales managers, marketing forecast people, strategic planners, and top managers. Her report, which was submitted to Chuck earlier this week, identified a number of problems with communication flows affecting the strategic plan. Some of her primary conclusions were the following:

1. Most salespeople are given quotas that are too high. As a result, they have very little chance of meeting them. Nevertheless, since they are told that the top management expects them to meet these projections, the salespeople continue to write rosy reports about future market developments. For example, if a salesman is expected to sell $1 million worth of goods this year and by the end of the second quarter he has sold only $250,000, the individual indicates that the other $750,000 will be sold in the latter part of the year.

2. Proceeding from this erroneous input, the sales managers pass this information up the line to their own bosses. No one questions the optimistic, and continually erroneous, sales projections because everyone is afraid of being called on the carpet.

3. The strategic planning people accept whatever information they are given from the sales department. There is no independent audit of the data despite the fact that over the last five years the information has *never* been more than 70 percent correct.

4. The salespeople believe that top management does not want to know what is going on in the field. The big brass is interested only in performance. As a result, no one is willing to blow the whistle on this nonsense and admit that the current sales projection input to the strategic plan is worthless.

The president read the report carefully. When he was finished, he spent 15 minutes talking to Mary about her findings. The next day the chairman asked Chuck when he expected Mary to be finished with the report. Chuck said that the finishing touches were being put on it that very day. "I'm having my assistant look it over and condense it down to five pages. It's currently about 25 pages and that's a little too long for the average board member."

Earlier today the report was presented to the chairman. In essence it said that because of unexpected economic fluctuations in the market arena, past strategic plans had been based on erroneous information. Now that the economy is straightening out, the projected and actual strategic plan results should be in line with each other. There was no mention of Mary's four points. After reading over the report, Bob has concluded that there is still something wrong. "I can't believe this," he told his assistant. "I want an outside consultant to come in here and look things over. Something is very wrong."

Assume that you are the consultant who has been brought into the organization. Based on the information in this case, what is the problem? Why does it exist? What is being done to perpetuate it? What would you recommend be done now? Be complete and realistic in your response.

Key Points in This Chapter

1. Upward communication is used to obtain feedback on problems and job performance. A number of forms of communication distortion occur in the upward flow of information. Some of the deliberate forms include the omission of qualifying data, reluctance to deliver bad news, and bypassing hierarchical levels. Some of the deliberate unintentional forms include employee trust in the boss, aspiration needs of the workers, security level of the employees, and physical limitations imposed by the organizational structure. Ways of dealing with these problems were discussed in the chapter.

2. Downward communication is used to carry rules, policies, procedures, and task instructions. Two of the most common deliberate distorters are inadequate feedback and managerial discomfort in delivering unpleasant news. Two primary unintentional distorters are managerial anxiety and multiple transmissions. Steps for handling these problems were explained in the chapter.

3. Horizontal communication is used to convey information to, and receive information from, individuals on the same hierarchical level. Some of the most prevalent forms of deliberate distortion include gossip, rumors, and problems resulting from the specialized nature of the work itself. Some of the unintentional distorters include using horizontal communication as a substitute for downward and upward communication and the overproliferation of lateral communication.

4. Diagonal communication occurs between people at different levels in different departments. Bypassing formal hierarchical channels can be a deliberate distorter, especially if the employee's supervisor is not aware of the diagonal channel. The unintentional distorter is the resulting communication gap within each department if information obtained from diagonal channels is not shared.

5. At an overall level, the most frequent deliberate distorter is information ownership and the most frequent unintentional distorter is uncertainty absorption. Steps for dealing with each were set forth in the chapter.

6. Communication overload refers to the amount and complexity of messages received by a unit of analysis. Underload occurs when an employee is cut off from the mainstream of the organization's communication network. Overload takes place when a person is unable to process the amount of information being received. Steps for dealing with underload and overload problems were offered in the chapter.

Questions for Discussion and Analysis

1. What are some of the reasons for deliberate distortion in upward communication? Identify and describe three.

2. What are the four common types of unintentional distortion in upward communication? Identify and describe each.

3. What kinds of deliberate distorters exist in downward communication? Describe two.

4. In what way are status anxiety and competition anxiety unintentional downward communication distorters? Explain.

5. What is meant by the terms *sharpening* and *leveling?* What relevance do they have to communication distortion?

6. How can a manager deal with multiple transmission distortion problems? Explain.

7. There are both deliberate and unintentional distorters in horizontal communication. What does this statement mean? Explain.

8. How can distortion occur because of diagonal communication?

9. In what way is information ownership a communication problem? Explain.

10. How does communication overload differ from communication underload? Compare and contrast the two.

11. What are some of the organizational and personal variables that influence underload and overload? Identify two organizational and two personal factors that play a role here.

12. In what way can communication overload become a circular response? Use Figure 10.3 to explain your answer.

13. What can managers do to reduce information overload problems? Be specific in your answer.

Exercises

1. Study the model presented in Figure 10.3, which describes the circular nature of overload. In small groups, consider the following questions.
   a. What factors contribute to *underload?*
   b. Is underload also circular in nature?
   The group should develop a model depicting how underload works. Each should then share its model with the rest of the class.

2. (For working students) Analyze your current load situation using the variables presented in Figure 10.2. How do you stand in regard to these variables? Consider each as a continuum and rate yourself as follows.

   a. Coordination with others required to do the job

Small		Moderate		Great
1 2 3	4	5 6	7	8 9 10

b. Physical distance from others

Great				Moderate					Small
1	2	3	4	5	6	7	8	9	10

c. Routineness of the job

High				Moderate					Low
1	2	3	4	5	6	7	8	9	10

d. Time constraints

Low				Moderate					High
1	2	3	4	5	6	7	8	9	10

e. Number and quality of decisions to be made

Low				Moderate					High
1	2	3	4	5	6	7	8	9	10

f. Your ability to communicate

Low				Moderate					High
1	2	3	4	5	6	7	8	9	10

g. Your desire to communicate

Low				Moderate					High
1	2	3	4	5	6	7	8	9	10

Scoring:

7 or above = You are problably now in an overloaded state.
3–6 = Your load is probably an appropriate one for you at this time.
1–2 = You are probably underloaded and relatively unmotivated.

3. (For nonworking students or all students) Study the variables presented in Figure 10.2. In small groups, draw up a job profile of an imaginary employee operating at the far left and one of someone at the far right. Be sure to answer the following questions.
   a. What job titles are these people likely to have?
   b. What is a "typical" day like for each individual?

4. The instructor will give one student a short message. The first student orally passes it to the second student who orally passes it to the third and so on until the last student. The last student will write it on the board, and it will then be compared to the original message. As a class, consider the following questions:
   a. What part(s) of the message got through clearly? What part(s) were garbled or dropped?
   b. Where did sharpening take place? Leveling?

References

1. Gordon L. Lippitt, *Organization Renewal* (Englewood Cliffs, N.J.: Prentice-Hall, 1983), p. 99.

2. Alan Zaremba, "Communication: The Upward Network," *Personnel Journal*, March 1989, p. 39.

3. Philip V. Lewis, *Organizational Communication: The Essence of Effective Management* (Columbus, Ohio: Grid, 1980), p. 132.

4. Zaremba, *op. cit.*, p. 39.

5. Charles R. McConnell, "Making Upward Communication Work for Your Employees: Processes and People, with Emphasis on People (Part 3 of 3)," *Health Care Supervision*, January 1987, p. 72.

6. *Ibid.*, p. 71.

7. Ralph G. Nichols, "Listening IS Good Business," *Management of Personnel Quarterly*, Winter 1962, p. 4.

8. Brian L. Hawkins and Paul Preston, *Managerial Communication* (Santa Monica, Calif.: Goodyear, 1981), p. 81.

9. *Ibid.*, pp. 85–91.

10. John E. Baird, Jr., *The Dynamics of Organizational Communication* (New York: Harper & Row, 1977), p. 272.

11. David S. Brown, "Barriers to Successful Communication, Part 1: Macrobarriers," *Management Review*, December 1975, p. 26.

12. James G. March and Herbert A. Simon, *Organizations* (New York: John Wiley & Sons, 1958), p. 165.

13. Brown, *op. cit.*, p. 26.

14. "Upward/Downward Communication: Critical Information Channels," *Small Business Report*, October 1985, p. 85.

15. Hawkins and Preston, *op. cit.*, p. 94.

16. John M. Ivancevich, James H. Donnelly, Jr., and James G. Gibson, *Managing For Performance* (Plano, Tex.: Business Publications, 1983), p. 589.

17. Richard M. Hodgetts, *Management: Theory Process and Practice*, 4th ed. (Orlando, Fla.: Academic Press, 1986), p. 74.

Annotated Bibliography

Brief, Arthur B., Randall S. Schuler, and Mary Van Sell, *Managing Job Stress* (Boston: Little, Brown & Co., 1981).

> As we have noted in this chapter, both overload and underload can produce stress. This book comprehensively examines these and other causes of job-related stress and offers various methods for dealing with them.

Lakein, Alan, *How to Get Control of Your Time and Your Life* (New York: New American Library, 1973).

If you are a victim of overload, this is the book for you! If you follow it carefully, you cannot help but be more organized and less harassed. Lakein's highly readable treatise deals with all aspects of life, not just the job, and focuses on the necessity of conscientiously and continually formulating goals and priorities.

Mackenzie, R. Alec, *The Time Trap: How to Get More Done in Less Time* (New York: McGraw-Hill, 1972).

This book provides excellent guidelines for dealing with the overload problem. It deals with such critical areas as planning, organizing, and delegating — all of which, when properly done, can reduce information overload.

Part Five

APPLICATIONS FOR MANAGEMENT

Part Five studies applications-oriented concepts that will help you be a better communicator. This includes such critical communication-oriented areas as power, persuasion, negotiation, the management of change and conflict, the management of meetings.

Chapter 11 deals with power, persuasion, and negotiation. These three concepts are central to an understanding and application of many of the ideas discussed in this book. The first part of the chapter examines the nature of power and explains how one can improve persuasion and negotiation skills. The latter part of the chapter addresses negotiating styles that are useful in helping achieve a "win–win" situation in which both parties get what they are after.

Chapter 12 examines the management of change and conflict. After defining the term *change,* attention is focused on why there is resistance to change, the form such resistance tends to take, and the most useful strategies to use in managing the situation. Then the

term *conflict* is defined and some of the major causes of conflict are set forth. The chapter concludes by presenting specific steps for handling conflict resolutions.

Chapter 13 examines the interviewing process. In addition to identifying and describing the basic elements in the process, a comparison of directive and nondirective interviewing is presented. Then the three basic types of interviewing are discussed: employment interviews, performance interviews, and discipline interviews. In each case, the nature of the type of interview is described, and suggestions and guidelines designed to improve the manager's effectiveness are offered.

Chapter 14 focuses on the management of meetings. In addition to identifying and describing the ten characteristics of meetings, some of the most popular myths about meetings are set forth and debunked. Then attention is devoted to the major advantages and disadvantages of committees. Committees also are analyzed in terms of four basic criteria: objectives, size, session, and orientations. The latter part of the chapter concentrates on answering the eight key questions used in effectively planning a meeting, the five major steps that must be followed in conducting a meeting, and the reason why post-meeting followup is crucial to the overall effectiveness of a meeting.

When you have finished study-ing all the material in this part of the book you will know how to apply many of the ideas you have studied in this text. You also will have a solid understanding of how change and conflict work and what can be done to manage them effectively. Finally, you will know how to interview people and how to manage meet-ings.

CHAPTER 11

Power, Persuasion, and Negotiation

"Never get angry. Never make a threat. Reason with people."

Don Corleone, *The Godfather*, by Mario Puzo

Objectives

1. To define the term *power*.

2. To contrast and describe the following types of power: reward, coercive, legitimate, referent, and expert.

3. To describe the relationship between different types of power and organization performance.

4. To explain how to gain power in persuasion and negotiation processes.

5. To relate the importance of time in persuasion and negotiation efforts.

6. To describe how information can be used to give the manager the upper hand in persuasion and negotiation efforts.

7. To compare and contrast the win – lose negotiation style with the win – win negotiation style.

C A S E   I N   P O I N T

The Contract Negotiation

Geoffrey Babbell is the owner–manager of a small print shop. When he opened the firm a year ago, Jeff realized the industry was very competitive, and in his state the union was quite strong. He hired 27 people, most of whom belong to the union. Within 30 days of the time operations began, Jeff and the union had negotiated a one-year contract. As the year was coming to a close, both Jeff and the union representative expressed an interest in sitting down and negotiating a new arrangement. Jeff's initial offer was a 5 percent raise in both salary and fringe benefits. This offer was in line with what large printing firms in the area were offering their people. However, the union representative pointed out that Jeff's business had a much higher profit than the average print shop and a fairer offer would be a 5 percent salary raise and an 8 percent increase in benefits. After talking to his accountant, Jeff countered with an offer of 5 and 5½ percent, respectively, for salaries and benefits. The union representative told Jeff that he would have to get back to the workers. He also wanted to talk to some people at the union's regional and national headquarters. It took the representative almost ten days before he responded to Jeff's offer. At this time there were only six working days left until the contract expired. The representative told Jeff that the union counteroffer was 5 and 7¾ percent, respectively. Again Jeff huddled with his accountant to go over the numbers. Jeff felt that the maximum offer he should be making was 5 and 5¾ percent. With two days left on the contract, he called the representative and gave him the offer. The latter told him, "Let me get back with you as soon as possible." The morning on which the contract expired, Jeff got a call from the man. "Can we meet at two o'clock this afternoon?" he asked. Jeff agreed. The crux of the discussion was as follows:

Representative: I've talked to my people and we'll go for 5 and 7¾ percent, respectively. I don't think I can get my people to drop down any lower than this.

Jeff: Well, I'm willing to try to meet you guys part way and go to 5 and 6 percent, but I don't have the dollars to go higher than that.

Representative: Look, I can go back and tell my people that I can get 5 and 7¾ percent on salaries and benefits. But if I come in any lower than this, I'll get booted out of my union position. If we can't agree on these numbers, I'm afraid we'll have to call a strike effective the end of the work day this afternoon.

Jeff: You're kidding. I was hoping that we could wrap this up amicably by four o'clock this afternoon.

Representative: Me, too. However, I'm in a bind. I can't agree with your numbers. Well, I've got to go. If you change your mind, please call me at union headquarters. I'll be there until five. If we go out on strike, there is a mess of paperwork that I'm going to have to fill out over there.

With this the meeting broke up. Jeff was shocked. He did not know what to do. He talked to his accountant and to his business partner. Finally, at 4:45 P.M. he called his lawyer and told him the final arrangements. His lawyer was aghast. "You've got to be kidding. You're not really going to settle on that type of a contract are you?" he asked. "You're being had. You call the union back and tell them to drop dead! I'll be right over. You aren't going to sign anything formal until I'm with you. Those guys must think we're of bunch of morons. Sit tight. I'll be there in ten minutes.

What did Jeff do wrong? What did the union do right? What is Jeff's lawyer likely to tell him about skillful negotiating? In what way did Jeff play into the union's hands? Write down your answers. We will be coming back to them later.

INTRODUCTION

Power, persuasion, and negotiation are closely related concepts. In discussing one it is impossible to avoid talking about the others. Effective persuasion and/or negotiation depends on the presence of power. This power may be *real* in that the individual wielding it can back up his or her persuasive efforts with rewards or punishments, "If you don't do what I am asking you to do, I'll see that you're fired." On the other hand, it is possible to have power without possessing the ability to reward or punish just as long as the other party *thinks* you have this power.

POWER

Power involves influence.

Power is the ability to influence, persuade or move another person to one's own point of view. Figure 11.1 shows the five types of power bases that are available to managers.[1] Three of these, reward, coercive, and legitimate, are based on one's position in the organization. Two others, referent and expert, are based on personal characteristics. Most managers use more than one of these power bases, and communication with employees depends on the power base being used. Before examining each of these power bases, take Self-Assessment Quiz 11.1.

Reward Power

Reward power is an extrinsic satisfier.

Reward power is held by those who can give extrinsic satisfiers to others who do what they want them to do. These include pay, promotion, and better working conditions. Such rewards are within the purview of the manager who can either give them or withhold them.

Most people are satisfied or motivated by external rewards. Thus these rewards remain one of the most powerful tools for persuasion and negotiation. The big question

Figure 11.1

Types of power bases.

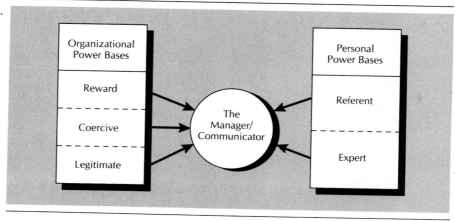

SELF-ASSESSMENT QUIZ 11.1

Power and You

There are many types of power. Depending on the situation, the manager's use of each will vary. The following situations are each followed by five alternatives. Read every situation carefully and choose the alternative that you would most prefer. Put a "1" next to this choice. Then place a "2" next to your second favorite choice on down to a "5" next to your least favorite choice. There can be no ties; it is a forced-choice selection. When you are finished, transfer all your responses to the scoring key at the end of the quiz.

Situation 1: You have just been informed that one of your people must be transferred to another department. You believe the best choice is Robert and have called him in to your office. He appears somewhat upset with your decision. You believe it is time to use your power to persuade him to take the transfer. What would you do?

_____ **a.** Explain to him that this new position is a good career move and offers greater promise than his current job.

_____ **b.** Tell him that if he does not take the transfer his promotional status will be greatly endangered.

_____ **c.** Remind him that you are the boss and in that capacity have made the decision for him; his job is to go along with it.

_____ **d.** Point out to him that you have always looked out for his best interests and would never do anything that was not going to advance his career in the firm.

_____ **e.** Show him how carefully you went about selecting the best person for the transfer and why he fits the bill perfectly.

Situation 2: Mary has been late for the third day in a row. You have not said anything until now but believe that it is important that you now have a talk with her. How would you handle the situation?

_____ **a.** Remind her that rewards are directly tied to performance and if she keeps coming in late she is going to jeopardize her chances for a good raise to say nothing about eventual promotion opportunities.

_____ **b.** Tell her that tardiness is not condoned, remind her of the starting time, and make it clear if she is late again you will see that her pay is docked.

_____ **c.** Tell her that as the boss your job is to enforce the rules and that means insisting that she show up on time from now on.

_____ **d.** Remind her that you got where you are by being on time and if she wants to move up the hierarchy she will have to start coming in on time.

_____ **e.** Explain to her that her workload is tied directly to the workday and if she does not come in on time she is going to have great difficulty getting everything done by quitting time.

Situation 3: George has been running a football pool. This has been called to your attention by some of your people and, since the practice is in violation of company rules, you have called George in for a talk. How would you handle the situation?

———————— **a.** Tell George that violation of the rules could endanger his status with the firm and result in his not getting promoted as fast as he would like.

———————— **b.** Tell George that you will not tolerate violation of the rules and will fire him if he does not stop the practice immediately.

———————— **c.** Explain to George that rules are rules and as manager you are required to enforce them, so he must end the football pool practice.

———————— **d.** Remind George that you got where you are by following the letter and spirit of the company's rules and regulations and urge him for his own good to do the same.

———————— **e.** Tell George that your experience with the firm is that these practices always end up causing trouble for the individual and urge him to stop running the pool.

Answers: Transfer your answers to the scoring key below by placing your five numbers for each situation (a–e) across the page in the same order in which they appear above. Then add each of the five columns to give a total for a–e, respectively.

Situation 1 ————— a ————— b ————— c ————— d ————— e

Situation 2 ————— a ————— b ————— c ————— d ————— e

Situation 3 ————— a ————— b ————— c ————— d ————— e

Totals ═════ ═════ ═════ ═════ ═════

For an interpretation of your answers, finish reading this section on power and then check your answers at the back of the book.

for the manager is "What *specific* rewards will motivate my people to work harder?" Some may want more money, others may prefer better benefits, and still others may want improved working conditions. To the extent that the manager helps meet these needs through the dispensing of appropriate rewards, the personnel will be persuaded to do what the individual wants.

Reward power is not, however, limited to extrinsic rewards alone. "At a given time, for instance, some people may be primarily motivated by a desire for recognition and acceptance. To the extent that a manager's praise and acknowledgement satisfy those needs, the manager has an additional form of reward power." [2] In this example, managers can use their communication skills to reward employees through praise and recognition.

Coercive Power

Coercive power is held by those who can fire, demote, or dock the pay of those who do not comply with their directives. It is the ability to administer various sanctions or punishments.

Coercive power is the opposite side of the coin from reward power. However, the way in which this power is used will vary by leader and organization. For example, in many white collar firms, sanctions take the form of reward denial. Instead of firing someone (coercive), the individual is simply not given a raise (lack of reward). Thus there can be a linkage between reward and coercive power. In blue collar occupations coercive power may be more punishing in nature. Workers who report late or turn out shoddy output can be sent home without pay or be fired.

Coercive power can punish people.

The coercive leader constantly communicates to employees what will happen if things do not go the way the leader wants. Coercive powerholders typically say things like, "If you know what's good for you, you'll get this job done fast," or "If you value your job here, you'll start coming to work on time." Coercive communication therefore relies on threats. Coercive power is out of step with today's values of equality and participation. Coercive power may work in the short run, but it fosters resentment and long-term problems. So, why is this power base still present in today's organizations?

The use of such power is heavily dictated by, among other things, the personality of the leader and his or her beliefs regarding how to manage the personnel. This point was explained in Chapter 2 when we discussed Theory X, Theory Y, and their relevance to leadership behavior.

Legitimate Power

Legitimate power is vested in the manager's position. Those farther up the hierarchy have more legitimate power than those farther down the structure. This type of power is often referred to as "delegated authority." It is the minimum amount of power that a manager has. At the upper levels of the hierarchy, it is often enough to ensure that things get done. At the lower levels, however, managers often find that they need to supplement this power with some of the other types discussed here. This becomes particularly evident in organizations characterized by a great deal of power grabbing and by upper-level managers intent on building empires of their own. Lower-level managers are often left with very little authority; it is all centralized with the manager of the division or department, and to enforce a rule or reward a person it is necessary to get an okay from higher up. For this reason, most managers seek supplemental sources of power.

Legitimate power is hierarchical.

Legitimate power is strengthened in an atmosphere of trust, respect, and honor. Table 11.1 shows communication behaviors that help a leader strengthen his or her legitimate power base.

Referent Power

Referent power is based on the follower's identification with the leader. If the subordinates like the leader, they are likely to do what the individual requests. They obey based on *who* gives the order rather than on *what* order is given. Referent power can be increased in a number of different ways. One of the most common is by developing a reputation for fairness. Another is by cultivating a winning personality. A third is by developing credibility with the work group. To the extent that subordinates enjoy their association with the leader, the leader's referent power increases.

Referent power rests on leader identification.

In many organizations the leader develops referent power by building high espirit de

Table 11.1

COMMUNICATION BEHAVIORS FOR INCREASING LEGITIMATE POWER

1. Persuasion
2. Patience
3. Gentleness
4. Willingness to learn
5. Acceptance of others
6. Kindness
7. Openness
8. Compassionate confrontations
9. Consistency
10. Integrity

SOURCE: Blaine N. Lee, *Executive Excellence,* Vol 5, No. 8, August 1988, pp. 12–14.

corps among the members of the work group. People begin to like working for the leader, and when he or she embarks on a particular project, they roll up their sleeves and pitch in. They let the individual speak for them, count on him or her to get the best possible salary raises and promotions for them, and feel a sense of pride from their association with the leader. Referent powerholders communicate their liking for new employees and in so doing increase the loyalty and camaraderie of the work team.

Expert Power

Expertise is another power source.

Expert power is a result of the leader's knowledge, skill, and/or experience. The expert leader communicates in such a way that employees will listen to the person because they are sure of his or her competence and skill. Thus expert power is based on information. People go to the expert with questions about the job. Of course, expert power might be fleeting because there is always the chance that someone with more expertise may come along. Expert power is also based on trust. Followers believe that the expert will have the right answer and will use that information in the right way. Like other forms of power, it is possible to lose expert power. The following excerpt about Henry Kissinger, former secretary of state, gives an example.

> . . . expert power is highly selective and besides credibility, the agent must also have trustworthiness and relevance. By trustworthiness is meant that the person seeking expert power must have the reputation of being honest and straightforward. In the case of Kissinger, events such as the scandal of Nixon's corrupt administration and Kissinger's role in getting the Shah of Iran into this country undoubtedly eroded his expert power in the eyes of the American public. He still has unquestionable knowledge about foreign affairs, but he has lost expert power because he may no longer be trustworthy.[3]

Power and Performance

When it comes to persuading and negotiating with people, are some types of power more effective than other? The answer is yes. Bachman and his associates, though acknowledging that any use of power must be dictated by the circumstances, have reported the following conclusions:

Power and performance findings

1. Expert power is more strongly and consistently related to satisfaction and performance than is any other type of power.

2. Legitimate power, along with expert power, is rated as the most important basis for complying with leadership wishes, but it is an inconsistent factor in determining organizational effectiveness.

3. Referent power is of intermediate importance as a reason for complying with leader directives but it is positively correlated with organizational effectiveness.

4. Reward power is of intermediate importance for complying with leader directives and has an inconsistent correlation with performance.

5. Coercive power is the least valuable in bringing about compliance to leader directives and is negatively related to organizational effectiveness.[4]

Power is an important part of the persuasion and negotiation processes. Without it, the manager will find it very difficult to sway people to his or her point of view.

Implications for Management

1. Remember that power is a two-sided sword. If you use it properly, you can motivate your people to do what you want done. If your use it improperly, you can end up with major problems on your hands.

2. Whenever possible, use reward power as opposed to coercive power. Tell your people what you want done and ensure that they understand your instructions. Do not berate them or make them look foolish in front of their peers. When they do things right, reward them. When they do them wrong, discuss their problems in the confines of your office and encourage them to improve. If things do not go well, then demote or fire as necessary, but once this has been done get on with the job. Do not linger on old memories by continuing to tell them, "Remember the time you messed up on the rush order?" This only serves to create problems. You may not forget, but as an effective manager you must learn to forgive.

3. Keep in mind that the most lasting sources of power are those that you yourself control or influence. Referent power and expert power are your two most important sources. No matter how much authority or reward power the organization gives you (or does not give you), you both build and "own" referent and expert power. In the final analysis, they are basic foundations of your ability to influence and persuade others to your point of view.

PERSUASION AND NEGOTIATION

Persuasion and negotiation are similar processes. *Persuasion* is the process of getting someone to do something by means of argument, reasoning, or entreaty. *Negotiation* is the process of arranging or settling something through such means as discussion or conference. In communication, managers often persuade people to their point of view through a negotiation process. Consider the following:

Boss: Tim, it's your turn to work late tonight.

Tim: Oh, boss, I've got a heavy date. I'll tell you what. If you get someone else to work late tonight, I'll stay tomorrow.

Boss: Okay, I'll arrange for Jack to cover tonight and you can take his turn tomorrow.

Notice that in our example both persuasion and negotiation were occurring simultaneously. In carrying out these processes, three critical variables are present: power, time, and information.

Power

In persuasion and negotiation, it is important that those who are being persuaded have a genuine perception of choice.[5] In our above example, the boss had someone else fill in for Tim, so there was an option for solving the problem. The two could negotiate a settlement. When no options exist, the person without an option usually ends up doing something he or she does not want to do. For example, in contract negotiations, the side with the strongest position usually makes a counteroffer just before the old contract runs out, that is, Company A's management tells the union, "There's only three hours until the old agreement expires. Here's our latest offer. If it's not good enough we'll have to close the plant." What options are available to the union? If it has a large strike fund and can afford to walk out, it will examine the offer and counter with its own series of demands. If the company does close its doors, the union will tap its strike fund. On the other hand, if the union is weak and has no strike fund, it will take the offer. After all, what options does it have?

It is important to have options.

The concept of options in persuasion and negotiation is not the only source of power. The presence of competition, legitimacy of rules and regulations as guidelines, the ability to walk away from negotiation, the amount of investment already committed, and the capability of the negotiator to appear relaxed all enhance the negotiator's power.

Competition helps.

COMPETITION When trying to persuade people to one's point of view, the leader's position is enhanced if he or she can show that others will consider the proposal under discussion. Consider the manager who says, "If you don't think this is a good idea, I'll go talk to Joe about it and see if he wants to implement it." Will the listener say, "Great idea. Why don't you do that?" or will the listener likely say, "Wait a minute. I didn't say it was a bad idea. Let me think about it." The latter is the more likely response. Whenever competition enters the picture, the manager gains power for his or her persuasive efforts. Major sports provide a good example of how power and persuasion are important in a competitive environment and also pose the question of the ethics of persuasion. See "Ethics in Communication: Is Persuasion Motivation or Manipulation?".

Is Persuasion Motivation or Manipulation?

Napoleon, in commenting on warfare, once said, "Morale is 90 percent of the game." Many baseball managers feel they are engaged in a form of warfare when their team takes to the field. This is particularly true for those teams that finished first and last in the previous season. Those that win the World Series one year almost never seem to win the next. Therefore these managers are more determined than ever to get their people motivated for maximum performance. Those that finish in the cellar are always concerned that they will fall back there again and history will repeat itself. This can result in a reverse Pygmalion effect in which losers come to regard themselves as losers, and so they are unable to win. How do managers who are on top stay there? How do managers who finished last get their teams motivated to win? A number of methods may be used, but they all have one thing in common: They create the right mental image in the players' minds. Here are some examples.

Jim Lefebvre, Seattle Mariners. Lefebvre puts the primary focus on winning. Every day before the game, he talks to his team about what they have to do to win. The group reviews those basics that have to be implemented in order to beat this day's opponent. Then, armed with a positive plan of action, the team takes the field.

Frank Robinson, Baltimore Orioles. A few years ago, Robinson's Orioles opened the season with 21 straight losses, a major league record. The next year the team was leading its division halfway through the season. How did Robinson do it? By not talking about the past year's losses but focusing instead on the current year's plan of action. Fortunately, he also had a large number of new players who had not been part of the previous disastrous season, so this made it easier to proceed on a positive note.

Sparky Anderson, Detroit Tigers. Sparky spends a lot of time getting to know his players and figuring out how he can get the best out of them. He assumes the responsibility of understanding them and learning what they can and cannot do. Armed with this information, he then works to hone them into a well-coordinated team. For example, Sparky likes to find out a player's early background, where he went to school, what he likes to do in the off-season, and what is important to him. Sparky then uses this information to help him communicate with the player and show the individual what he wants done. Once Sparky knows how to link up with the player, effective communication soon follows.

Of course, not everyone tries to win over their players by developing a congenial mental set. Some like to use fear. When the late Billy Martin was manager of the New York Yankees, the players used to like to win just to keep him off their backs. On the other hand, most of the managers who have used this approach are no longer coaching. Baseball owners have come to realize that positive persuasion is a lot more effective than the threat of punishment or the use of fear.

SOURCE: Murray Chass, "Managers Work on Keeping Players in Good Mental Shape," *New York Times,* April 2, 1989, p. 23.

Consider another case. A company would like to borrow $7 million from a local bank. How should it go about persuading the bank to make the loan? If it goes in and says, "Please lend me the money. I really need it," the bank is likely to turn it down. After all, a good risk should not have to beg and plead. On the other hand, consider the advice offered by Herb Cohen, one of the world's leading authorities on the subject of negotiation.

> Here's the approach to use. If you're a man, put on a gray, three-piece bank-loan suit. If you're a woman, put on a conservative-looking dress suit. Wear an expensive gold watch and a Phi Beta Kappa key if you can borrow one. Have three of your friends — your entourage — outfit themselves the same way. Walk through the bank, exuding vibrations that say, "Hi there! I'm a top executive striding through the bank. Keep away from me with your lousy money . . . I don't need it. I'm on my way to mail a letter!" Do that, and the lending officer will follow you out of the bank and breathlessly trail you halfway home.[6]

LEGITIMACY People are accustomed to obeying rules and regulations. When the rules are regarded as legitimate, they are very useful in helping the manager persuade and negotiate. For example, one of the authors was an acting chairperson responsible for hiring faculty for the department. One of the individuals who was being recruited was determined to come into the job with tenure. He stated clearly that without it he would not come. The author's response was, "I know what you mean. However, at this university absolutely no one has ever been hired with tenure. It's just not done. Why even I didn't come on board with tenure." Realizing that this was university policy, the individual dropped his demand and agreed to join the faculty. The author was able to legitimize the no tenure decision by pointing it out as a nonnegotiable point. When it is in the manager's best interest, he or she should use legitimacy or past precedent as a reason for urging people to do (or not do) certain things.

Past precedent helps.

Know when
to say no.

WALKING AWAY In persuading people to do something, it is important to know when to walk away and not concede any further points. Consider the following case:

Husband: Honey, I'm calling to tell you that the company has asked me if I would accept a transfer to Rochester. I know it means picking up our roots here, but they tell me they'll give me a salary raise of between $3,000 and 8,000 depending on what they can swing out of the budget.

Wife: That's wonderful. Mom and Dad live only 25 miles away, and you know I've always wanted to move back to that region. Let me know how things turn out. I'm packing already.

If you were the husband's boss, how much would you offer him for a salary raise? If you were aware of the conversation, you would probably stay around $3,000 if you wanted to save the company money. The husband is going to feel pressure to take the transfer regardless of money. After all, his wife is so happy over the arrangement she can hardly wait to move. Will he turn down the transfer? Not very likely.

Investment and
power are related.

INVESTMENT The power to persuade and/or negotiate is heavily influenced by the amount each side has to win or lose if an agreement is not reached. For example, Company X wants to borrow $10 million for 24 months. After examining all its financial statements, the bank decides to make the loan. The terms of repayment are $2.5 million every six months with the outstanding balance carried at two points over the prime rate. In addition, because the loan is so large, the bank is simply going to act as an intermediary for one of the larger financial institutions in the city. It will receive a finder's fee of $200,000 upon signing of the note. Does Company X have any room for negotiation? It certainly does. If the loan falls flat, the bank will lose its out-of-pocket expenses for setting up the loan, say, $15,000, as well as its $200,000 fee. The bank does not want the deal to fall apart. So now consider a new wrinkle in the case. The president of Company X calls the bank president and says, "We've looked over the terms of the loan. The interest rate is fine, but we can't pay back $2.5 million every six months. The best we can do is $2.5 million at the end of the first year and the remainder at the end of the second year." Will the company get these terms? Maybe not, but the bank is certainly going to work to accommodate the firm. Whenever one side is faced with an all-or-nothing situation, it will work hard to negotiate the terms necessary to ensure the success of the deal.

The value of
relaxing.

RELAX If a manager is too upset or concerned about persuading someone to do something, this will influence the individual's ability. It is difficult to convey an aura of power and control when it is obvious to all in the room that the negotiation means so much. In our example of the $10 million loan, how much stress or tension is the company president under? Some but not a great deal — at least right now. The bank president, however, is under a lot of stress because if the deal falls through the bank loses a lot.

Time

The more time people have invested in an undertaking, the greater their desire to bring matters to a fruitful close. The salesperson who spends 15 hours showing a potential customer a new house would like the individual to say, "I'll take it." Otherwise the seller's time has been wasted. On the other hand, not all people who use their time in an activity like selling will be anxious to close a sale. Consider the salesperson at Sears. Whether or not the customer buys a washing machine, the individual will still get a salary. Commissions are a very small part of the overall compensation package. So time is a useful tool only if the other party has to produce results. When this is the case, the negotiator should understand the role of open agendas, extended effort, repetition, persistence, and deadline refusal.

AGENDA Everyone has an agenda or a list of things to do, regardless of whether or not they actually write it down. For many people this list is more psychological than anything else; that is, even though Charles does not have to finish the control report today, he goes out of his way to do so. When people have an agenda, the person attempting to persuade or negotiate with them has them at a disadvantage. They have certain things they have to do; the other person does not. By figuring out their agenda, he or she can use it to advantage. For example, the director of purchasing of a large corporation calls the local auto dealership and tells the salesperson, "I'm entitled to a new company car this year, and I'd like to get one as soon as possible. Can I stop by after work this afternoon and see what you've got?" Does the salesperson know the manager's agenda? Absolutely. How much leeway will the manager have in terms of bargaining? Very little. Besides, it's a company car. The director of purchasing is not paying. So why argue over price? The salesperson will now work on picking out a couple of cars that are likely to fall within the director's budget — nothing too fancy, nothing too cheap. By revealing the agenda, the director has put himself at a negotiating disadvantage by giving the salesperson time to prepare.

Agendas dictate action.

EFFORT The more personally involved people get in something, the more likely it is that they will expend effort. Of course, there is also time being spent, but it is the effort that really tells the story. Someone doing something they like may spend an hour without realizing it. Someone working hard wonders why the clock is moving so slowly. The more one party can get the other to expend effort, the more likely it is that the other will be ready to negotiate. Let us return to our example above.

Director: I sure appreciate you making these four cars available for me to look at. I think I like the third one best.

Salesperson: Fine, I can have the paperwork all wrapped up by 9 A.M. tomorrow.

Director: Well, before you do that, I better schedule my four assistants to come over and look at these cars. You know, we're only entitled to one car and all five of us have to share it. I'll see if I can have one of them drop by tomorrow. By the way, how much are you asking for the car?

Notice that the manager has now introduced additional people into the negotiation. The salesperson will have to sell five people. When will a final decision be made? Maybe not for days or weeks. Moreover, with five people involved, there is always the chance that they will start shopping around. After all, there are a handful of them and they can easily cover five to ten dealerships in a morning. The salesperson may find a lot of his time being eaten up for just one sale. Every time he sees another one of the

Invested effort dictates action.

company people coming back he'll think, "Oh brother. Another half hour shot. And all of this for the commission on just one car." The time will come when he will be prepared to give them the best deal they will get in town. It is all a matter of when he feels he has expended enough effort and does not want to go any further.

REPETITION   A third time-related factor is repetition. The more someone has to repeat something, the less likely he or she is going to enjoy it. The talk or presentation loses its novelty. The individual begins just to go through the paces. Consider the case of outside consultants brought in to make a proposal to management. Assume that the firm has asked for proposals related to strategic planning, that is, how can your consulting firm help us do a better job of strategic planning? Many consulting firms would like to bid on this type of job. In almost all cases the price will be extremely high but will be accompanied by a very polished presentation. Management would like to get beneath this veneer and also get the firm to lower its price. One way in which this often is done is to have the firm come in and make a presentation to the top management. When this slick, Hollywood skit is over the following conversation then ensues.

Chairman: Very interesting. What you have to say makes a great deal of sense. However, there are a number of top-level line managers who should be included in this decision because they are actively involved in strategic planning.

Vice Chairman: Right, J.B. We can't leave them out. When could you schedule another presentation for another group of our top people?

Consultant: Uh, well. How about the day after tomorrow?

Chairman: Terrific. My secretary will make all the arrangements. Coordinate with her and be sure to give them the same presentation that you gave us. I know they'll be impressed.

Repetition has advantages.

It sounds as if the consulting firm is going to get the contract. However, what the chairman is doing is forcing the consultants to give their talk a second time, and it is going to get difficult to do so without losing some of the gloss. By the time the consultants come to the fifth group of managers who need to learn about the consultants' presentation, the consultants are going to be asking themselves, "How many more times do we have to do this? When are we going to get the okay to move on with the consulting?" This is when the company will ask about the fee. Whatever amount is stated, the firm will balk and suggest something lower. In addition, since no two presentations are ever the same, all the managers will have questions regarding what is (and is not) to be done by the consultants. When they finally come to an agreement on what is to be done and how much it is to cost, the company will be dictating the terms. Why? Because it has used time to its own advantage. In repetition, it has used effort and agenda (it knows what it wants, while the consultants still do not know how well they are doing) to its advantage.

PERSISTENCE   In order to persuade or negotiate successfully, persistence is needed. Simply stated, it means "don't give up." As with the other ideas mentioned in this section, persistence is a time variable. It requires that the manager stick to his or her guns

Persistence often pays off. for however long it takes to achieve the desired objective. However, this does not mean that the individual gets *everything* for which he or she is negotiating. Persistence should be selectively employed. Consider the following true case. A large corporation decided to build a new headquarters. The 30-story building had a price tag of $110 million. During the construction the firm asked for some changes in the plans, and the contractor complied. When everything was complete the additional charges came to $17 million. However, the company architect and chief financial officers noted that there were overcharges and bills for work that had not been done. The final bill, by their count, was $121 million. The contractor disagreed but the company was persistent. The chief financial officer told the contractor, "We're not paying. Get a lawyer and sue us if you like, but we'll countersue. We'll tie you up in court for 10 years. Or you can settle out with us for a net price of $122 million." After six months of haggling the contractor settled for a total of $122.5 million. The company's persistence had paid off.

Persistence is particularly important when negotiating or trying to bring people to your point of view. Look at how President Carter got Anwar Sadat and Menachem Begin to come to an agreement. He tucked both of them away at Camp David.

> Knowing this, and realizing that he wanted to achieve "acceptable minimum results," Carter cleverly saw to it that there were only two bicycles for fourteen people and a total lack of other recreational facilities. Evenings, to relax, those present for the extended stay had a choice of watching one of three insipid motion pictures. By the sixth day, everyone had seen the films twice and they were bored out of their minds.
>
> But every day at 8:00 A.M. Sadat and Begin heard the usual knock on their cabin door followed by the same familiar monotone, "Hi, it's Jimmy Carter, ready for another ten boring hours of the same dull stuff." By the thirteenth day of this, if you were Sadat and Begin, you would have signed *anything* to get out of there. The Camp David peace agreement was a classic, attributable to the patience and persistence of Jimmy Carter.[7]

DEADLINE REFUSAL How can the manager prevent the other side from using time as a weapon? The best way is by ignoring deadlines or by keeping them in proper perspective. This can be done by answering the question: what will happen if this deadline is not met? Deadlines are usually established for the purpose of ensuring work progress. However, many jobs are not completed on time, and the company still continues to operate profitably. The deadline was not as critical as those working on the project thought it was.

Consider a common example faced by every taxpayer: April 15 tax filing. What happens if you mail your tax forms in on April 16? If you owe the government $80 and enclose a check, are you going to be penalized for one day's interest? Hardly. If the Internal Revenue Service (IRS) owes you money, can it refuse to pay? No. So April 15 is *not* a hard and fast rule. Millions of people are a few days late with their return and nothing happens to them. However, the IRS has most people so nervous about the filing deadline, that these taxpayers will actually drive around town to find an all-night post office so they can get their envelope stamped before midnight on that day. The very worst that can happen to the average honest citizen is that he or she files a couple of weeks late, owes the government a few hundred dollars, and gets a bill for interest on the money. The interest is tax deductible next year. The lesson is clear. File on time. If you cannot, do it as soon as possible (or get an extension, which is easy enough) and pay the interest. However, do not get rushed into filing a return by April 15 if you are not ready. Whenever possible, avoid having to meet deadlines set by others. Cohen offers other useful deadline refusal guidelines.

1. Since most concession behavior and settlements will occur at or even beyond the deadline, be patient. True strength often calls for the ability to sustain the tension without flight or fight. Learn to keep your automatic defense responses under control. Remain calm but keep alert for the favorable moment to act. As a general rule, *patience pays*. It may be that the thing to do when you do not know what to do, is to do nothing.

Useful guidelines for controlling time

2. In an adversary negotiation your best strategy is not to reveal your real deadline to the other side. Always keep in mind that since deadlines are the product of a negotiation they are more flexible than most people realize. Never blindly follow a deadline, but evaluate the benefits and detriments that will ensue as you approach, or go beyond, the brink.

3. The "other side," cool and serene as it may appear, always has a deadline. Most often, the tranquility it displays outwardly masks a great deal of stress and pressure within.

4. Precipitous action should be taken only when it is guaranteed to be to your advantage. Generally speaking, you cannot achieve the best outcome quickly; you can achieve it only slowly and perseveringly. Very often as you approach the deadline a shift of power will occur, presenting a creative solution or even a turnaround by the other side. The people may not change, but with the passage of time, circumstances do.[8]

Information

Information is knowledge. When related to persuasion or negotiation efforts, information often gives a person the upper hand. There a number of ways of getting information or of making the other party believe you have it.

EXPERTISE When a person is an expert in some area, the individual has power over those who lack such information. For example, when you go to the post office and ask the clerk the fastest way to ship something to London and the individual tells you to use air mail, you do it. You defer to the other person's judgment because you feel he or she has more expertise or information on the subject than you do. The same is true in persuading and negotiating. If you can convince members of the other party that you have more information than they have, your power over them increases.

When dealing with individuals who do have expertise, the first step is to learn as much about the situation as possible. If the matter is complicated or technical, it is usually possible to learn only some facets of the situation. Yet sometimes this can be enough. For example, during top management meetings the executives will frequently hear a number of reports related to work progress. After a while all the numbers run together, and it is difficult to know whether the managers making these reports are providing accurate information. Most top executives assume they are being given the

Expertise is based on information.

facts. However, some executives will often "persuade" their people to "tell it like it is" by thoroughly preparing themselves on some particular issue and checking to see whether the reports are in line with this information. The manager will often become a minor expert in relation to either the first report to be presented (thereby saying to everyone else who will be presenting, "I know what's going on so your data better be right") or the one that is most crucial to operations (thereby saying to everyone else, "I'm well aware of performance in the most crucial areas of operations; you can't fool me with incomplete or inaccurate data"). In either event, the executive convinces those presenting reports that they had better have their facts straight. Consider the following:

Executive: Before you continue with your report, you still haven't told us how many widgets were produced last month or how that compares with a year ago. How much of an increase have we attained in productivity?

Manager: Oh, well, let's see (looking at his notes); last month we produced 17,000 widgets and last year that figure was 16,000. Our cost per unit has fallen from $6.88 to $6.02.

Executive: That's not right. Last week we turned out 17,311 widgets as against 15,877 last year. Our cost per unit is down from $7.10 to $5.88. Where are you getting all of your statistics from? Did you prepare these data yourself or what?

Manager: Uh, well they were worked up by the boys in production and sent over to me yesterday.

Executive: All of them? Or did you do some calculating of your own?

Manager: I did some of them. Maybe I worked a little too fast. Can I send you correct numbers tomorrow?

Executive: Before I answer that, let's hear the rest of your report.

Notice that the executive is not an expert on the data. However, the individual has worked up some numbers to show some degree of expertise. Now the manager, who should be in charge, is in a position of having to negotiate with the executive. Depending on which side of the table one is on in terms of expertise, it is possible to turn things around by getting the upper hand.

PAST PRECEDENT By past precedent we mean how things have been done in the past. For example, if a company car is involved in a traffic accident the insurance company may take 15 working days to settle the claim. This is because with so many claims to be processed it cannot get to the company's case in less time. Another reason may be that the insurance firm has found that most claimants will wait 15 days after the accident, and this allows the firm to earn more interest on its bank deposits.

When negotiating with others, if the manager knows how they have done business in the past, he or she has an advantage over them. For example, in some industries goods are sold on terms of "two ten, net thirty." This means that if the buyer pays within 10 days, there is a 2 percent discount on the bill; otherwise the full invoice is payable in 30 days. These terms are not always binding. In certain industries everyone ignores them and takes the 2 percent discount regardless of when they pay. If the seller complains,

The past often dictates current behavior.

they point to everyone else and say, "Heck, it's industry practice. What are you talking about?"

Another example is provided by firms that give educational discounts. If a teacher buys from these companies, a 10 to 20 percent discount is typical. (Even IBM, so well known for its refusal to discount, gives a price reduction to faculty who buy personal computers from them.) Business firms with training departments can also get these discounts by pointing out that they are in the education business, that is, educating managers to be more effective in their jobs. In fact, discounts are so common that just about everything a firm buys retail can be reduced if it shops around to find the lowest priced seller. All the company has to know is, who has given discounts in the past?

CURRENT CUES   A third way of getting information is in the form of cues. The three basic types of cues are unintentional, verbal, and behavioral. *Unintentional cues* are those that transmit inadvertent messages. A classic example is the Freudian slip. A number of years ago a famous politician was running for president and campaigning in the farm belt. His standing with the farmers was poor; most felt he was opposed to assisting them. During his speech, he said, "If elected I will get rid of the farmers . . . I mean the farm surpluses." Many newspapers the next day wondered aloud if the Freudian slip was a slip at all. In any event, he failed to carry the farm belt.

Cues can provide much information.

Verbal cues take the form of voice intonation and emphasis. A manager who says, "I will not go along with her on *this* issue" is saying one thing; a manager who says, "I will not go along with *her* on this issue" is saying something else. The first relates to the issue; the second relates to the person.

Behavioral cues take the form of posture, eye movement, facial expression, hand gestures, and other types of body language. The manager who keeps his hands in his pockets and stares at the floor while talking to subordinates is unlikely to convey a positive image. Few of the personnel are going to believe that this person is an outstanding leader. The behavioral cues all point in the opposite direction.

The three types of cues discussed here are not isolated or independent. A communicator will often provide all three to the receiver. The question is: what do they mean? When brought together, what is the individual *really* saying? The answer tells the receiver how to respond. Sometimes, if the listener does a good job, little response is required. The speaker does just about everything. Consider the following:

Insurance agent: I know your company has suffered a loss due to the negligence of my client. Let's not argue that point. I've seen your bills for the accident and we'd like to settle out of court as soon as possible. I'm empowered to offer you 35 percent of the total bill. And remember that your client was partially to blame, so I doubt whether any court in the land will give you full settlement.

Corporate attorney: That's ridiculous. Two of our people were injured as a result of your client. We could sue for more than just the medical and property damage and you know it.

Agent: All right, we'll go 50 percent of the bill.

Attorney: Fifty percent, huh?

Agent (nervously): Okay, 70 percent but that's it.

Attorney: You say you're offering 70 percent of our submitted bills, is that right?

Agent (quickly): Well, I might be able to go to 80 percent, but that's really pushing it.

Attorney: You're going to give us 80 percent of medically justified bills. Is that what you're telling me?

Agent: Okay, we'll pay them all. But I'll need a letter saying that this will settle everything and there will be no additional fees of any type.

Attorney: Okay. Send me a letter saying you approve the bills I submitted and I'll send you the letter you want.

Agent: Great. I knew we'd be able to reach an agreement if we just talked about it.

Notice in our example that the attorney got one set of verbal cues ("I'm empowered to go to 50 percent of the total submitted bill") and then another (the agent started raising the percentage). The agent also gave the attorney behavioral cues (notice the references to nervousness and quick responses). Based on these pieces of information, the attorney was able to negotiate with the agent effectively.

REMAIN ALERT Managers need to follow a number of important guidelines in gathering information for purposes of persuasion and negotiation. One is to assume the posture of information seeker. Rather than firing out and telling the other individual, "Here's what I want you to do and why you ought to do it," the manager should let the other person talk first. This provides the manager an opportunity to clarify exactly what the issues are and how the other party feels they ought to be addressed. Also remember that when someone wants something, he or she often has very good reasons for it. Trying to defeat such individuals point by point is usually fruitless. At some juncture they will turn the argument around or be able to present a rebuttal that the manager cannot match. It is wisest to let the person first put all his or her cards on the table.

Knowing what the other person wants, the manager is then in a position to process this information. Sometimes this can be done in a matter of seconds; other times it takes a couple of days to think things through. When more time is needed, the manager should say, "I'll get back with you as soon as I can. I want to check on some things and talk to a couple of people." Never feel that you have to respond immediately; remember what we said about agendas.

Finally, having thought through the matter, the manager can then call the individual in and see if they can reach an agreement. Notice in our discussion here that we have assumed that the subordinate is asking the manager to do something. If the reverse is the case, the manager should have already investigated the matter. It may then be necessary to give the subordinate time to think about whether he or she wants to comply with the request. The most important aspect of persuasion and negotiation is that the process should never be carried out in a situation where if one party gets what it wants, the other will suffer as a result. This win–lose approach is very dangerous. Whenever possible a win–win approach should be used. The following section examines these two negotiating styles. Before reading further about negotiating styles, take Self-Assessment Quiz 11.2.

SELF-ASSESSMENT QUIZ 11.2

Your Approach to Persuasion and Negotiation

You have just developed a new marketing plan for a product that is scheduled to hit the market in three months. Your plan needs the approval of your boss. You know that he will not approve the plan immediately: he always likes to think things over. Three other people have also worked up similar plans. The boss can choose the one he thinks is best. You want to persuade him to accept yours and to do it as quickly as possible. Below are a number of different approaches that can be used in accomplishing your objective. Read the entire list one time to familiarize yourself with the options. Then go back and place a "1" next to your favorite choice and keep going until you have rank-ordered all nine of them.

_____ **a.** Get others involved in the decision by asking the boss if it is all right also to explain your plan to some of his top people. Use the argument, "You're going to want to consult them on this anyway. How about if I save you some time by making a presentation to them and bringing them up to date on my proposal? This way they will be prepared for any questions or suggestions you might have."

_____ **b.** Remind the boss that new marketing plans are always approved before the vice president's meeting, which will be in ten days. Work to get the boss to see the importance of "doing things by the book."

_____ **c.** Get the boss involved in reading and commenting on the plan. The more time he puts in on it, the more likely it is that he will opt for your plan rather than one of the others.

_____ **d.** Talk the boss into reviewing and giving you feedback on your plan before he does the same for those who have drawn up similar plans. For example, ask him, "Can we meet on this a week from today so I can get your feedback and incorporate it into a final plan for action?"

_____ **e.** Deliberately leave a section of the report unfinished and tell the boss. "This part requires your expertise. In fact the whole plan rests around what you put in here. It won't take very long but it is crucial to the entire proposal." By getting the boss to expend some of his personal effort on the plan, you help ensure that he will favor your proposal over the others. After all, to some degree, it will be his proposal too.

_____ **f.** Be persistent. Schedule meetings with the boss on a daily basis if possible. Keep banging his door down. Count on his saying, "Oh, not that person again. I better approve that plan or I'll never get rid of him (or her)."

_____ **g.** Get as much information as possible regarding how to sell the boss on your plan. Focus more on persuading him than on writing the best possible plan. Sell yourself! Then count on the individual saying, "Heck, that person really knows what's going on. This plan must be great. Forget the others and implement this one."

_____ **h.** Find out how plans of this kind have been approved in the past. What should they contain? How did the boss go about giving his approval last time? Did he put it into a committee or make the decision personally? What past precedents are likely to dictate how the current situation is handled?

_____ i. Go in and visit the boss. Ask a lot of questions for cues regarding what he would like to see in the report (as well as what he would like to see left out). Be particularly receptive to verbal cues and body language. Based on this feedback, alter the report if necessary and then work on selling the boss "his own" report.

Take your answers and transfer to the scoring key below. Then add up the numbers in each column.

Column I.	Column II.	Column III.
_____ a	_____ d	_____ g
_____ b	_____ e	_____ h
_____ c	_____ f	_____ i
Total _____	_____	_____

An interpretation can be found in the Answer Section at the back of the book.

Implications for Management

1. Remember that effective persuasion and/or negotiation is based on the proper use of power, time, and information. In fashioning an effective strategy, examine these three areas and determine the critical factors in each. Then work on how you can bring these together into an overall game plan.

2. In both persuading and negotiating, keep in mind that these are two-way processes. For example, you may be trying to get a subordinate to agree to something before he goes home at 5 P.M. This time objective is useful in that it establishes a parameter within which your goal is to be accomplished. On the other hand, by setting such an objective you saddle yourself with an agenda. This gives power to the subordinate. The same factors that you can use to work for you can be used by the other party to work against you.

3. Never get too personally involved in persuading or negotiating. The greater your commitment, the more you have to lose and the more likely it is that you will not be as objective as you should. Step back and try to approach things from a less involved standpoint. Always ask yourself, "If this does not turn out the way I'd like, will it be the end of the world? Or the end of my career?" Since the answer is undoubtedly no, slow up and do not take things too seriously.

NEGOTIATING STYLES

The many ways of negotiating or persuading someone to your point of view can be broken down into two basic styles: win–lose and win–win. The first is important because it helps describe how *not* to negotiate, at least if you want to maintain the ongoing trust, confidence, and reliance of the other party. The second is important because it is the style that ensures the best long-run payoffs to *both* sides.

Win – Lose

In a win – lose style there is a winner and a loser. Each side negotiates so as to outwit or fool the other. This approach is often referred to as Soviet-style negotiating. If you think for a moment about how the Russians conduct foreign policy, the logic behind this statement becomes clear. Consider the case of the Korean Air Lines passenger plane that was shot down in 1983. How did the Russians handle the matter? First, they denied shooting it down. Then, they said it was a spy plane for the United States. Next, they said that they used every means possible to signal it to land but it refused, thus they were left with no alternative. Finally, they ignored world opinion and counted on time to make people forget. This type of approach is typical for the Soviets, although many negotiators use it from Moscow to Miami. Before moving on, let us make our point more clearly lest you think we are unfairly picking on the Soviet Union. Let us take the case of the 1980 Olympics, which were held in Russia. Quite obviously, the three major American television networks were anxious to secure the broadcasting rights. How much should the winner have paid? In the past the final prices had been:

1960	$500,000
1964	$3,000,000
1968	$5,000,000
1972	$13,000,000
1976	$22,000,000

How much should the 1980 winner have paid:? Based on the above numbers, a figure of around $40 million would be ballpark. However, the Soviets got NBC to pay $87 million. How did they accomplish this? By getting the networks (ABC, CBS, and NBC) to bid against each other. When they had reached the low 70s, the three were then told that they had won the right to participate in the final bidding process. Realizing that they were being lied to, the three broke off negotiations and returned to the United States. The Soviets then announced that the rights to the Olympics had been given to a small American firm named SATRA. Only after they coaxed NBC into raising the ante to $87 million did the Soviets squeeze SATRA out of the picture.

The lesson is clear. If someone is determined to win at all costs, one party is almost always going to be a loser. This is especially the case if the winner maintains an extreme position and refuses to budge until the other person meets all demands. Yet this is not the only way to recognize win – lose negotiators and persuaders. Another is to know when those who are doing the negotiating have limited authority.

LIMITED AUTHORITY   Whenever two sides negotiate, each assumes that the other has the authority to make a decision or, at worst, has significant input regarding the decision. In win – lose situations, however, the side intent on winning sends someone to the bargaining table who either does not have the authority to completely negotiate anything or must check back on every minor development. A good example is provided by auto dealerships. No matter how skillfully the buyer negotiates with the salesperson, the final decision is always up to the manager. The salesperson must get the contract cleared with the boss. This puts the dealer in the best position because if you strike a poor deal with the salesperson, the manager can approve it as is. If you strike an excellent deal, the manager can adjust the figures by telling the salesperson that the dealer cannot sell that low. Either way the dealer wins and the buyer loses. The key to success here is the limited authority given to the salesperson.

Some negotiators have no power.

GUILT When made to feel that they have done something wrong, most people will try to rectify the situation. In win–lose bargaining it is common to find one side trying to make the other feel guilty. The way in which this is done will vary, but the outcome is always the same. The use of emotional tactics is a typical ploy. It usually takes the form of one party yelling at the other. "A *million* dollars for this? You must be kidding! You *know* it's not worth anything close to that." What is the person *really* saying? "You should be ashamed of yourself for doing this. I really thought you were an honest person." The objective, of course, is to get the other party to reduce its asking price. Another popular approach is silence. By just staring at the other person and saying nothing, the individual hopes to embarrass or make the person nervous. Hopefully, this is followed by a comment like, "Okay, then what would you say to a price of . . .?" A third ploy is laughter. It, too, is designed to evoke guilt on the part of the person making the offer. However these tactics are used, they are all designed to make the other party revise its bargaining position and move closer to that of the first person.

Some negotiators use guilt.

MINIMUM CONCESSIONS In win–lose negotiations it is common to find minimum concessions being made. In fact, a generous concession by Party A is regarded as a sign of weakness by Party B. It also puts Party B in an advantageous position because the final solution is likely to be closer to its position than to that of the other party. For example, consider the following price bargaining:

Still others are stingy.

Mr. A: I'll give you $12,700 for the car.

Mr. B: I think $15,300 would be a fairer price.

Mr. A: I'll go $13,000.

Mr. B: $14,500.

Mr. A: $13,300.

Mr. B: $14,000.

Br. A: $13,500.

Mr. B: $13,750.

Mr. A: Let's split the difference at $13,625.

Mr. B: Okay, you've got a deal.

Which of the two people was more effective in using a win–lose strategy: It was the buyer, Mr. A. Notice that they started out $2,600 apart with A offering $12,700. They ended up with A paying $925 more than his initial price. In the process B gave up $1,675 in concessions. Notice also that on the first round A gave up $300 and B reduced his price by $800. In situations where win–lose is inevitable, auto purchasing being an excellent example, it is important to use some of the win–lose strategies we have discussed here. Another, which is part of this win–lose package and which was discussed earlier in the chapter, is that of not having an agenda. Rather than telling the dealer, I'll get back with you by Friday. Please don't sell the car," the astute buyer says, "If you can shave $1,000 off the price I think we might be able to talk. Here's my telephone number." Then on the piece of paper, the individual writes the price he would consider, that is, $12,800. Put the time problem on the other person by implying, "If I don't hear from you by Friday, I'll buy from someone else." Before closing our discussion of win–lose, there is one final point that merits discussion. If the other party has at least as much information as you, your ability to best them in a win–lose strategy is nonexistent. When buying a new car, all the new car dealers in the area who sell that model know what their prices are and know how low the other person will go. This means that your chance of pitting one against the other is a pipe dream. If the lowest offer you have is $13,200, telling a dealer that you have an offer of $13,000 will not work. The individual knows you do not and will say, "If you can show me that offer in writing, I'll see what I can do." The individual does not want to embarrass you because he'd like to sell you a car. However, he knows you are lying to him.

Successful managers know that in the long run, win–lose strategies are self-defeating. Whenever possible, a win–win approach should be used. We now turn to a discussion of this topic.

Win–Win

With a win–win strategy, the manager negotiates with mutual satisfaction in mind. This is done by first determining the needs of the other party and then deciding how to bring about an arrangement that is agreeable to both sides. A win–win strategy is "one where both parties' needs are met. Obviously, not all problems can be resolved in this way. Nevertheless, the integrative approach seems to offer a better alternative to the more common adversarial one practiced by most managers."[9] The following discusses how this can be done.

First gain trust. **TRUST** The first step in a win–win negotiating strategy is to gain the trust of the other party. Let us use an example. George has been told that he is scheduled to go into the field for two years as a sales manager. George has been with the firm for five years, and during this time he has done a very good job. However, all his experience has been at the home office. His boss, Henry, feels that this may be the time for George to make the move into the field. Here is how their conversation goes:

Henry: George, I wanted you to come by and talk to me because I really think you are top management timber. However, in order to move up in this department, you have to have some field experience. You have done an excellent job in the home office but you are not really seasoned yet. This requires field experience.

George: I knew that sooner or later I'd be called on to go into the field. However, I have to admit that I have some reservations about the matter. In particular, it will mean a lot of traveling, and I'll be away from my family quite a bit.

Henry: This might sound trite, but every successful manager in the company has had field experience. Without it, it's just about impossible to move up. Now I know you have a family, and this will mean giving up quite a bit of time with them over the next two years. However, you and I have been together for a long time. Have I ever steered you wrong?

George: No, you haven't. You've always been on my side. And I trust you. However, I've still got to go home and talk it over with Sandy.

Henry: We want you to feel comfortable with the decision. Remember, there's nothing more important to you than your family. You can get another job; you can't get another family. Talk it over with Sandy and the kids. Then let's sit down again. How about late next week? Would that be okay?

George: That would be fine.

Notice in our example that Henry worked to establish trust with George. He asked George to trust him; he pointed out the importance of the family and urged George to do what was in his own best interest. Who could ask for more? Is George likely to go along with Henry's suggestion about going into the field for two years? Probably. But even if he does not, George knows that Henry is not out to take advantage of him or give him bad advice. Henry wants George to make a decision that will be good for himself *and* for the company. No win – win negotiation can proceed without building trust between the two parties.

Then build confidence.   **CONFIDENCE** In persuasion and negotiation, trust and confidence are not the same thing. We may trust someone not to lie to us, but that does not mean we have confidence in the individual's judgment. If one of your best friends tells you that when she had a cold last week she took Medicine A and got better in one day, you may believe her. However, that does not mean you will have confidence that Medicine A will work for you. So after building trust, a manager who is determined to pursue a win – win strategy has to gain the confidence of the other party. Remember from the above dialogue that Henry suggested that George talk things over with his wife. This is one way of securing a person's confidence. It says "Don't take my word for this. Check it out yourself. Be confident that what I am telling you is in your own best interests."

Another thing that Henry will want to do is to set up a meeting between George and the individual with whom he will be working in the field. This allows George to ask questions, get feedback, and develop a sense of what it will be like out there. As George begins to get support from his wife and realizes that the sales manager in the field and he are going to get along well, his confidence in agreeing with Henry's recommendation will increase.

OPPOSITION Despite all attempts to promote a mutually satisfying solution to the situation, the manager occasionally will find strong opposition. When this happens, the manager has three options.

Tell the truth.   **Facts** First, the individual should get the facts. For example, what if George says, "I don't want to go into the field. No one has ever returned to the home office. That's a deadend job." Is that true? What are the facts? The best way of dealing with this situation is to find out if George is right. In our dialogue Henry said that every successful manager had field experience. Where did Henry learn this? He had better back up and be sure of his facts before pushing on. If he is wrong, Henry needs to admit his error but stick to his guns if he thinks field experience is necessary for George. However, in win–win negotiations it is extremely important to follow the rule: *tell the truth at all times*. Table 11.2 presents 12 guidelines for getting support for an idea rather than opposition.

Compromise Regardless of whether he was right or wrong, Henry is asking George to make a decision that will be painful for his family. This is obvious from a close reading of the dialogue. In dealing with the opposition that may arise because of this situation, Henry should consider compromise approaches. Perhaps George cannot go into the field for two years in a row. How about this year and the year after next? Is this possible? Remember that if George's wife or family give him a hard time about the matter, compromise may be the only way to solve the situation on a win–win basis.

Compromise if necessary.

Balance Theory Finally, the manager needs to be aware of *balance theory*. This theory is particularly useful to managers who are attempting to bring about change. Balance theory comprises three critical elements: the manager, the employee, and the proposed change. A balance among all three is needed. Let us start with a simple example of our current situation: Henry wants George to go into the field. Henry thinks it is a good move for George, and (for the sake of a starting position) George thinks it is a good idea. In this case we have a balanced triad as depicted in Figure 11.2. The triad will remain balanced as long as there are all positives or two negatives and one positive.

Balance theory is extremely useful.

Table 11.2

KEY STEPS FOR BOOSTING YOUR PERSUASIVE POWER

1. Specify the exact goal.
2. Develop fallback positions.
3. Present the idea as a question or speculation to allow you to assess the opposition.
4. Be willing to give away the credit and ownership of the idea.
5. Describe it in terms of their own interests.
6. Ask for more than is needed to allow room for concessions.
7. Begin the negotiation on a point with which the others can agree.
8. Let the audience say no about something minor early on.
9. Anchor the idea in writing.
10. Counter any objections with benefits.
11. Seek a higher authority if necessary.
12. Show gratitude by writing a thank you note.

SOURCE: Jimmy Calano and Jeff Salzman, "Persuasiveness: Make It Your Power Booster," *Working Woman*, Vol. 13, No. 10, October 1988. pp. 124–125.

Figure 11.2

A balanced triad.

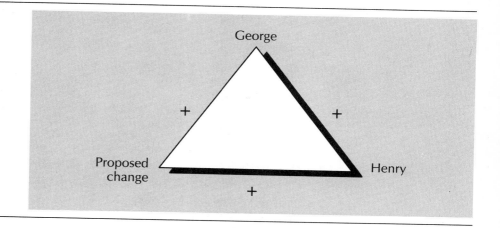

Let us illustrate this last example by altering Figure 11.2 so that it shows Henry and George being negative toward the change. This is illustrated in Figure 11.3. We again have a balanced triad because the individuals involved are in balance. Both like each other and agree that the move to the field would be a bad idea for George.

Any combination of pluses and minuses, other than those illustrated in Figures 11.2 and 11.3 will result in an unbalanced triad and problems for the manager. For example, if Henry thinks the move to the field is a good one for George but George disagrees, there is a negotiating problem. We cannot have a win–win situation unless one of them changes his mind about the value of the move to the field for George. In putting together a mutually satisfying arrangement, it is sometimes necessary for the manager to change the attitudes or beliefs of the other party. Balance theory can be particularly useful in this process.

Figure 11.3

Another balanced triad.

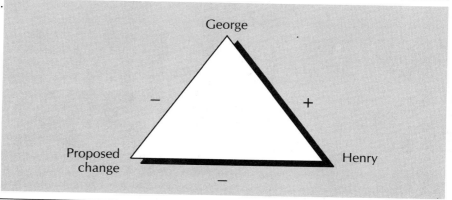

Implications for Management

1. Remember that if you are negotiating with people in your organization, tomorrow is another day and you will have to work with them again. Using a win – lose strategy for personal advantage can be self-defeating. Very few people make it to the top by continually besting their peers. As you approach the vice presidential level there is great emphasis on teamwork. Win – lose strategies go out the window. Everyone has to pitch in and help out. Failure to realize this can mean the end of your career as your colleagues gang up to prevent your further advancement.

2. In dealing with subordinates, always try to use a win – win strategy. This approach is very helpful in creating and increasing your referent power. It points you out as a person who can be trusted and relied on. This type of reputation can be invaluable as you begin your climb up the organizational ladder.

3. When persuading or negotiating with subordinates, remember that it is important to balance a concern for the needs of the organization with a similar concern for the needs of the people. Both have to be given attention. If you always favor the organization, you will be unable to build trust among the personnel. You will be identified as a company person who has no loyalty to the workers at all. If you always favor the subordinates, you will have trouble getting promoted because management will realize you are not interested in representing it to the workers; you are only interested in seeing what you can do for your people. Both extremes are dangerous. Use persuasion and negotiation tactics so as to achieve the best balance between the needs of both sides.

C A S E   I N   P O I N T

Revisited

Having read the chapter, you should now be able to see what Jeff did wrong. Basically, he let the union know his agenda while he failed to find out their agenda. They knew he wanted to settle, and they threatened him with a strike if he did not. What Jeff failed to realize is that by sticking to his agenda he was reducing his options. What he should have done was put the burden back on the union by sticking to his guns and forcing them to come to him. Remember that he was engaged in a win – lose situation. The union is his adversary in these proceedings. If he is too open or honest with them, they are going to look

on this as a sign of weakness and attempt to exploit it. His lawyer is going to tell him to refuse to sign the verbal contract, demand that the union take less money or walk, and then wait them out. Remember that Jeff can always sign later on. However, he should stay with a get-tough approach until he is sure that it is not working. Notice from the case that Jeff never did find out how strong the union was. He is not sure they will actually walk out. All he has is a verbal statement from the union representative, hardly the most authoritative source. Jeff needs to learn the fundamentals of win – lose negotiating strategies.

YOU BE THE CONSULTANT

The Licensing Agreement

Sam Simeon spent the first three years of his working career in the personnel department. He was well liked because of his personable, friendly manner. That was why his boss, Rita Charlton, picked him to be on her international management team. This team, formed three months ago, is charged with helping the firm go international. The company intends to be flexible in its approach but basically would like to license overseas companies to produce industrial machinery. The president of the firm believes that it will be a much more lucrative venture if the company licenses foreign firms than if it sets up its own operations. He told the board of directors, "It can cost a bundle to build a plant overseas. And then there's the political risk factor to be considered. If we license overseas firms, we get a piece of the action without any of the risk." The board agreed and Rita's team was formed.

A number of companies in both Europe and the Orient (specifically Japan) have expressed an interest in entering into a license agreement with the firm. Rita's team chose six. One of them is in Great Britain with headquarters in London. Since her team is quite small (nine people), Rita and the president agreed that they would send only one person to a country. In getting each prepared, the engineering and production people spent weeks explaining how the various products are made and why the approach used by the firm must be followed to the letter. Each committee member was also briefed by the finance people regarding desirable contract terms. The president talked to the group about negotiations. He said, "Look, make the best deal for us that you can. You're going to be our representative on site, and we will be relying on you to get us the best possible terms. All of you have been chosen because of your ability to work with people. Rely on those behavioral skills during your negotiations. We estimate that it will take you about two weeks to cut a deal with the companies to which we're sending you. Get out there and bring home the bacon."

Everyone was excited about their assignment. Sam was sent to Great Britain. His job was to meet with the management of a large industrial firm that wanted to produce engines for the Common Market. Sam's firm was convinced that this contract would be more lucrative than any other; that is why they were sending him. Sam was to be met by a representative of this company and would be a guest of the firm during his entire stay.

When Sam landed in London, he immediately claimed his luggage and prepared to clear customs. The lines were quite long and he joined the end of one. He then heard himself being paged over the speaker system. Responding to the page, Sam was greeted by a representative from the British firm who quickly ushered him through customs and into a waiting limousine. On their way into London, the two exchanged small talk. Sam was to be the guest of honor at a company luncheon. He would then be taken to the firm's estate on the outskirts of the city where a suite had been prepared for him. Dinner that evening would be with the board of directors and other top managers. Sam was very impressed.

The next day the representative came by for him at 9 A.M. "I thought you might like to see London while you're here," he said, "so I've arranged for a very private tour. You, I, and the tour guide are going to see London the way it ought to be seen." What a day! Sam was delighted. The next day the man came by and together they had a long enjoyable lunch with the president and three of the directors. They then went to a play and gathered at the estate for dinner. The next day the firm took Sam and a small entourage to Scotland where they spent two days touring and playing golf. At the end of the first week Sam asked the president when he would like to sit down and talk about the licensing agreement. "Plenty of time for that, young man," said the president. "The important thing is that you are over here for only a short time and we want to give you a taste of British hospitality. By the way, when is your scheduled departure?" Sam told him that he was taking the night flight to New York on the following Friday. "Fine, fine. I'll arrange everything with that in mind and have my secretary confirm your reservations." Sam expressed his thanks to the gentleman for the assistance.

On Monday and Tuesday of the next week Sam toured the company's facilities and talked to some of the managers. Each day at about 3 P.M. the representative came to take him away for some free time, a movie, a casual dinner, and the like. Same was beginning to think that he would like to live like this forever. On Wednesday there was a one-hour meeting between Sam and the management regarding the specific terms of the licensing agreement. Sam presented his company's desires to the board members. On Thursday there was another one-hour meeting during which the members asked questions about the agreement. On Friday there was a farewell dinner for Sam. Then he, the president, the chairman of the board, and the chauffeur got into the limousine and headed for the airport. Once they were underway, the president reviewed Sam's terms on the licensing agreement, explained some modifications that his firm would like to see made in the contract, and gave the reasons behind these changes. Sam was in agreement. "Well, then," said the president, "I'd say we have a deal." Sam was very happy. "When do you think we might have this put into writing and signed?" he asked. The president smiled and withdrew a sheaf of papers from his attache case. "We' have already signed ours. All you have to do is put your name on the bottom line next to mine and we're in business." Sam did so. "Wow!" he exclaimed. "For a while there I thought I'd have to go home without a completed deal." the chairman smiled. "I thought that was the case. That's why I insisted that Archie, here, bring the contracts to the airport with us."

When Sam got back to the office he dropped off the contracts at the president's office. The next day he attended a meeting of Rita's committee. All of those who had gone to other countries had come back with signed agreements. In summing up the events of their two-week visits, the president said, "All of you have done very good work. I'm quite happy because I think from this we are all going to learn some important lessons about what *not* to do the next time we go out. Take Sam's contract. I think it's an excellent example in support of those who believe that the British have still not forgiven us for the Revolutionary War." Everyone laughed. "Seriously, now," said the Chief Executive Officer, "most of these contracts are less than what they should have been. That's because we didn't prepare you people for effective negotiating. You invaded a foreign country and they won. Next week I am bringing in a negotiating expert to discuss how to conduct business deals in foreign nations. I think you'll all find out that there is more to it than just a pleasing personality and a desire to do business." With that the meeting broke up and the president went around the table to personally thank everyone for their efforts.

Assume you are the negotiating expert that has been brought in by the president. In analyzing Sam's situation, what did he do wrong? What did the British do right? Which of the three critical variables in persuasion and negotiation did the British use effectively? What would you tell Sam and his colleagues regarding how to negotiate more effectively? Be as complete as possible in your answers.

Key Points in This Chapter

1. Power is the ability to influence, persuade, or move another to one's own point of view. The five types of power are reward, coercive, legitimate, referent, and expert. Reward power is held by those who can give extrinsic satisfiers to others who do what they want. Coercive power is held by those who can fire, demote, or dock the pay of those who do not comply with their directives. Legitimate power is vested in the manager's position. Referent power is based on the followers' identification with the leader. Expert power is the result of a leader's knowledge, skills, and/or experience.

2. Power and performance are related in that some types of power are more likely to bring about high performance than are others. Expert power is more strongly and consistently related to satisfaction and performance than is any other type of power. Coercive power is the least valuable in bringing about compliance to leader directives and has been found to be negatively related to organizational effectiveness.

3. Persuasion is the process of getting someone to do something by means of argument, reasoning, or entreaty. Negotiation is the process of arranging or settling something through such means as discussion or conference. In persuading and negotiating, three critical variables are present: power, time, and information.

4. Power can be obtained in a number of different ways. Some of the most common are (a) have options available, (b) be able to show that others will consider the proposal under discussion, (c) make use of rules and regulations to establish the legitimacy of one's position, (d) be prepared to walk away if things do not shape up as desired, and (e) realize that the more someone has invested in a project the less likely he or she is to give up on it.

5. Time is important and can be used to one's benefit if the following are remembered: (a) most people have an agenda and want to stick with it; (b) the more effort people put into a project, the more they will work to see things through; (c) repetition can be used to slow the pace of negotiations and give one a chance to look things over carefully; and (d) persistence can be a virtue.

6. Information is very useful in persuasion and negotiation. Some of the ways of getting it include: (a) develop expertise, (b) be aware of past precedent, and (c) be tuned in to current cues.

7. The two basic types of negotiating styles are win–lose and win–win. With the win–lose style the other side gives its negotiators limited authority, trying to use guilt as a weapon, and makes minimum concessions. The win–win style is characterized by mutual trust and the establishment of confidence. If there is opposition, the manager will work to get the facts, compromise where necessary, and use balance theory.

Questions for Discussion and Analysis

1. In your own words, what is meant by the term *power?* Describe it.

2. How does reward power differ from coercive power? Compare and contrast the two.

3. What is meant by the following types of power: legitimate, referent, expert? Identify and describe each.

4. When it comes to persuading and negotiating with people, are any types of power more effective than others? Explain your answer.

5. What is meant by the term *persuasion. Negotiation?* How are the two terms similar? How do they differ?

6. In persuasion and negotiation, power is often held by the individual who has options. What does this statement mean?

7. When trying to gain power during negotiations, investment and legitimacy can be two important areas of consideration. What does this statement mean?

8. If you know someone else's agenda but they do not know yours, how can this help you persuade them to do something?

9. What role do effort, repetition, and persistence play in helping the manager persuade someone to his or her point of view?

10. How is expertise useful in persuading someone to your point of view? Explain.

11. In what way are unintentional cues of value in the negotiating process? Verbal cues? Behavioral cues? Explain.

12. How does a win–lose strategy work? What are some of the characteristics of such a strategy?

13. How does a win–win strategy work? What are some of the characteristics of such a strategy?

Exercises

1. John Harris has just become assistant manager of the Fielding Art Supply Manufacturers. After only six weeks on the job, he has become concerned because his

employees seem to go to Linda Reynolds whenever they have a problem and not to him. Linda is the resident artistic consultant and has been on the job for ten years. While having no direct authority over other employees, she knows a lot about the organization and is always willing to help out. What kind of power does John have? Linda? Discuss John's "problem" in terms of power bases. What, if anything, should John do?

2. Role play the following situation. In each case, assume that the supervisor is recognized as having one of the following power bases: legitimate, expert, coercive, referent, and reward. "Supervisors" should role play appropriately. After each role play, ask the following questions:
   a. How did the employee feel?
   b. Is permanent change likely to occur?
   c. How did this conversation affect the relationship of supervisor to employee?

After all power bases have been role played, ask which was more effective in solving the problem. *Situation:* Mark Reading is the supervisor of the purchasing department. He has ten buyers working for him. One of these, Janice Walters, has been with the department for six months. She is punctual, hard working, and always meets deadlines, but she is sometimes abrasive on the phone to suppliers. This morning, Mr. Whiting from Whiting Electrical Works has called you to complain about Janice. He feels she was extremely rude to him this morning and is so incensed that he told you to take your business elsewhere or "get rid of that creep." You've spoken to Janice about this problem before but realize that you've got to get this straightened out once and for all. You call Janice into your office and close the door.

3. In small groups of three to five, analyze your current jobs or a job you have at one time held. What type of power did you have? What type of power did your supervisor have? How did you feel about your supervisor? Can the group, through personal experiences, come to any conclusions as to what kind of power "works best"?

References

1. John R.P. French, Jr., and Bertram Raven, "The Bases of Social Power," *Studies in Social Power*, Downin Cartwright, ed. (Ann Arbor, Mich.: Institute for Social Research, 1959), pp. 155–164.

2. Gregory Moorhead and Ricky W. Griffin, *Organizational Behavior* (Boston: Houghton Mifflin Co., 1989), p. 259.

3. Fred Luthans, *Organizational Behavior*, 4th ed. (New York: McGraw-Hill, 1985), p. 394.

4. Jerald G. Bachman, David G. Bowers, and Philip M. Maracus, "Bases of Supervisory Power: A Comparative Study in Five Organizational Settings," in *Control in Organizations*, Arnold S. Ranenbaum, ed. (New York: McGraw-Hill, 1968), p. 236.

5. Alan Zaremba, "Beyond Reason: Strategies for Effective Persuasion", *Industrial Management*, Vol. 30, No. 2, March/April 1988, pp. 29–31.

6. Herb Cohen, *You Can Negotiate Anything* (New York: Bantam Books, 1980), pp. 56–58.

7. *Ibid.*, pp. 83–84.

8. *Ibid.*, pp. 98–99.

9. Philip I. Morgan, "Resolving Conflict Through "Win–Win" Negotiating," *Management Solutions*, August 1987, p. 6.

Annotated Bibliography

Cohen, Herb, *You Can Negotiate Anything* (New York: Bantam Books, 1980).
  This book uses a very down-to-earth, practical approach to negotiating. Cohen not only provides copious examples but also stresses the importance of win–win persuasion styles. A must for anyone seriously studying the process of persuasion.

Deal, Terence E., and Allan A. Kennedy, *Corporate Cultures: The Rites and Rituals of Corporate Life* (Reading, Mass.: Addison-Wesley, 1982).
  This book describes the ways in which people in organizations behave and relates them to the enterprise's culture. In terms of understanding why people do what they do, and how you can employ many of the ideas in this chapter in persuading them and negotiating with them, this book contains a wealth of information.

Jay, Antony, *Management and Machiavelli* (New York: Bantam Books, 1967).
  Jay gives an excellent insight into the use of power for the purpose of accomplishing one's ends. This book is not confined to Machiavelli per se, and it makes an excellent supplement to the material in this chapter.

Korda, Michael, *Power! How to Get It, How to Use It* (New York: Random House, 1976).
  Another name for this book is "everything you ever wanted to know about power but were afraid to ask." It is jam-packed with useful ideas for both getting and using power. From games and symbols of power to living with power, it is all here.

The Traditional View

Until recently, managers, like society as a whole, have been taught that conflict is dysfunctional and should be avoided at all costs. The effective manager, it was believed, could spot brewing conflict and would jump in before things got "out of hand." If conflict did erupt, the manager would quickly intervene and both help settle the dispute and look for ways to avoid future disagreements. This attitude, that conflict signaled something wrong in the organization and was to be quickly eliminated, is easy to understand given society's traditional values toward conflict. Before proceeding, assess your own attitudes on conflict by taking Self-Assessment Quiz 12.1.

SELF-ASSESSMENT QUIZ 12.1

What Is Your Attitude Toward Conflict?

For each of the following paired statements, indicate which of the two most closely reflects your personal belief by placing a check mark ( ) at the end of the statement you choose.

T	C	T	C
1. Conflict is almost always nonproductive. _____	Conflict is usually productive. _____	6. It is important to suppress individual desires for the common good. _____	It is important to look out for number one! _____
2. One should avoid conflict whenever possible. _____	One should encourage conflict in order to get the air cleared. _____	7. The boss is the boss — that is all there is to it. _____	You should challenge authority if you do not agree with the order being given. _____
3. It is important to follow the rule: hold your tongue! _____	It is important to follow the rule: speak your mind! _____	8. Conflict destroys morale. _____	Conflict builds morale. _____
4. Conflict is unhealthy. _____	Conflict is healthy. _____	9. Conflict stifles creativity. _____	Conflict breeds creativity. _____
5. Organizational conflict can be eliminated. _____	Organizational conflict cannot be eliminated. _____	10. Conflict is unmanageable. _____	Conflict is manageable. _____

An interpretation of your answers can be found in the Answer section at the back of the book.

As small children, we were all taught the merits of getting along with our peers and of not answering back to our elders. Childhood arguments and fights were punished, and we often received long lectures about how nice children acted. Although conflict has undeniably been a part of our lives, we have all been urged to control our anger and other unsocial impulses. Religion has taught us to "turn the other cheek"; schools have taught us to be quiet and obey the rules; and our families have taught us to be "seen and not heard." When we join the workforce, we learn the rule of "hear no evil, see no evil, speak no evil." Good employees, above all else, have been urged to be cooperative in much the same way that we were taught as Boy Scouts and Campfire Girls. Managers often see conflict as an aberration, a symptom of unhealthiness, and/or a breach of decorum by whoever is embroiled in the conflict. After all, the conflicting parties are expending time and energy on nonproductive activities when they were enmeshed in conflict. All of this is the traditional view.

The Current View

Today traditional attitudes toward conflict are changing, for two main reasons.

Today conflict is seen as healthy.

First, as noted in the section on change, society as a whole and organizations in particular have been undergoing a traumatic rate of change. Such change automatically brings more conflict into daily life: conflict between our values and what we find happening around us; conflict by the tremendous increase of information and people to whom we are exposed; conflict because of the complexity of our organizations and the resulting strain on our ability to mesh personal goals with organizational necessities. Modern managers have been forced to admit that conflict *does* exist and will continue to do so. As a result, it has become obvious that rather than suppress conflict, it is more beneficial to accept its existence and work to manage it.

Second, personal values have changed over the last two decades. Few would deny that we are in the midst of a massive allegiance to the philosophy of "I am," the importance of individual self-fulfillment over all else. Christopher Lasch in his *Culture of Narcissism* has pessimistically characterized modern American society as "the culture of competitive individualism, which in its decadence has carried the logic of individualism to the extreme of a war of all against all, the pursuit of happiness to the end of a narcissistic preoccupation with the self."[14]

The implications for conflict of this "me first" value are clear. Whereas in earlier days, people were willing to suppress their desires and beliefs for the "common good," there now is little reward for that type of behavior. Challenging authority has become a way of life — almost a cliche, but a cliche that brings with it a great deal more open, interpersonal conflict than ever before as people "look out for number one."

The result is that managers now realize that conflict is a normal part of organizational life. It can be a creative force if organizational members learn to interact positively with each other in conflict situations.[15]

The absence of conflict now is seen as symptomatic of employee apathy and a withering organizational culture. "People in organizations should admit to having conflict, even welcome it. The presence of conflict suggests that there may also be constructive controversy. And out of controversy, new ideas are born and improved."[16]

Conditions Related to Conflict

Organizations are excellent breeding grounds for a wide variety of conflicts. Alan Filley, an often-quoted expert in the field of conflict resolution, has identified nine conditions related to conflict.[17]

1. *Unclear jurisdictions.* When the extent of individual responsibility is unclear, conflict often occurs. In organizations job descriptions and organization charts are designed to reduce such ambiguity, but even these fail to resolve all jurisdictional questions.

2. *Conflict of interest.* In a world of scarce resources and the resulting competition, conflict of interest is a frequent organizational concern. University department heads regularly argue over the relative merits of their respective budgets. Whose department, for example, should get the additional staff member? Similar situations occur in all other enterprises.

3. *Barriers to communication.* There are numerous reasons for communication barriers, both at the interpersonal and organizational level. These range from perception, language, and inference to status, power, and ineffective listening.

4. *Dependency.* When people or groups are dependent on one another to accomplish organizational goals, the chances for conflict increase. Most complex organizations require a considerable degree of integrated activity, and interdependency is a considerable source of conflict.

5. *Increasing differentiation.* Complex organizations are increasingly differentiated, and the resulting levels of authority and specialization can create a multitude of conflict sources. Some of these include jurisdictional disputes, information ownership, conflict of interests, and difficult interdependent relationships.

6. *Increased interaction.* Despite the obvious merits of participative management and shared authority, the more people interact, the more likely they are to come into conflict with one another. This, of course, is one of the worries that keep some managers from instituting group decision-making processes. A better strategy is to train people in conflict management techniques so that they can better capitalize on the advantages of group decision making.

7. *Need for agreement.* Whenever group consensus is required, conflict can result. It is sometimes possible to eliminate it by allowing decisions to be made by simple majority rule. Unless mature individuals are involved, however, this may only cause "win–lose" conflicts to occur.

8. *Regulations for behavior.* Although behavioral standards such as getting to work at the specified time are helpful in promoting uniformity, they act to impose control over employees. Controls, in turn, are often resisted, especially by people with strong individualistic values. Worse yet, if the same standards are not applied to everyone, conflict will undoubtedly increase.

9. *Presence of unresolved conflict.* Unresolved previous conflicts have a way of staying

Some conditions related to conflict

in the back of one's mind until the next "bone of contention" comes along. At that time, it is again raised, serving to add fuel to the fire.

The nine characteristics described here are not causes of conflict but rather conditions that are likely to be present when organizational conflict ensues. The actual reasons for the conflict are many and varied. Before looking at them, however, it is important to realize that conflict occurs at various levels in the organization.

Levels of Conflict

Organizational conflict can occur at the intrapersonal, interpersonal, group, and inter-organizational level. The following examines each.

INTRAPERSONAL CONFLICT Intrapersonal conflict usually involves goal conflict. The three main types of goal conflict are approach–approach, avoidance–avoidance, and approach–avoidance. Approach–approach conflict occurs when an individual desires two mutually exclusive goals. On the personal level, an example would be deciding whether to buy a new car or go to Europe for the summer. Both goals are attractive, but the individual cannot afford to do both. Another example is deciding what to eat for lunch. Should you have french fries with your burger or eat light and have dessert? In the organization, approach–approach conflict is common. The busy manager experiences it when she tries to decide whether to get started on a new interesting project or call the staff meeting she has been meaning to have. An employee experiences it when he tries to decide whether to sign up for the next company training program or give himself the extra time to relax at home with his family. In each case, all goals are agreeable, and the choice of which one to pick is often difficult.

Intrapersonal conflict involves goal conflict.

Avoidance–avoidance conflict occurs when a person must choose between two unattractive and mutually exclusive goals. It is a matter of choosing the "lesser of two evils." A manager must decide whether to write that performance appraisal report he has been dreading or take another stab at understanding that statistical report that was sent over yesterday for his comments. Another manager must decide whether to meet Sharon and tell her she's fired or first see Ralph and tell him he is not getting the promotion he was counting on.

Approach–avoidance conflict occurs when a person experiences conflict over the *same* goal. In the beginning, the goal is viewed as very desirable and effort is expanded in working toward it. Then as the person nears the goal, he or she begins to have second thoughts. Is this really a desirable objective? What are the negative consequences? Should we take that promotion we have worked for? It would provide extra income and prestige (approach), but it also would mean more time out of town and that is sure to cause problems at home (avoidance).

INTERPERSONAL CONFLICT Interpersonal conflict occurs quite often. Two people competing for scarce resources or disagreeing over an issue are examples of interpersonal conflict. In this type of conflict personality clashes, value differences, and generation gaps often present themselves. It is also the time when people test their individual power relative to that of others. Interpersonal conflicts are often called "power moments" because they test who has the greatest power at that time. This

Interpersonal conflict often involves personality clashes.

conflict can be competitive or disruptive depending on the circumstances. Filley has suggested four types of reactions depending on similarity of interests and availability of resources (see Table 12.2).

When resources are scarce and interests are similar, people find themselves in competition with one another. For example, when two employees are striving for the one available promotion, competitive conflict results.

If resources are scarce and interests are dissimilar, fights and disruption may result. Consider, for example, two managers arguing over budgetary needs. Money is tight and each feels his proposed project is better than the other's. Each is likely to fight for his position.

When resources are available and interests are similar, a process of mutual problem solving can take place. In this process, each party talks through the situation to see how it can mutually benefit from cooperation.

When resources are abundant but interests are dissimilar, disagreement or debate may result. In the case of the two feuding managers noted above, the level of conflict is substantially different because each now realizes that it is possible for both to get what they want.

Group conflict involves a "we-they" mentality.

GROUP CONFLICT Earlier in the book the importance of group behavior in an organizational setting was discussed. Group conflict refers to conflict between groups, to the "we-they" mentality that breeds dysfunctional competition. There are two primary kinds of intergroup conflict: functional and line versus staff.[18]

Functional conflict is based on the differing perspectives of departments. Production often sees R&D as a bunch of "eggheads" who are wasting money; R&D typically views production as a bunch of dullards who are not interested in anything but how many widgets can be produced in a day.

Line and staff conflict exists in most organizations. Line people are those who produce the goods or services being sold; staff people act in an advisory capacity and support the work of the line. A typical example of line–staff conflict is the manufacturing division versus the personnel department. Manufacturing wants to hire the most experienced foremen it can find; personnel is concerned with doing so within the

Table 12.2

INTERPERSONAL CONFLICT TYPES

Interests	Resources	
	Scarce	Abundant
Similar	Competition	Mutual problem solving
Dissimilar	Fights and disruptions	Disagreement or debate

SOURCE: Adapted from Alan C. Filley, *Interpersonal Conflict Resolution* (Glenview, ILL.: Scott, Foresman, 1975), p. 3.

affirmative action goals of the organization. As with functional conflict, line and staff conflict can degenerate into stereotyped views of each other. Manufacturing ends up seeing personnel as a bunch of pencil pushers who do not earn their keep; personnel sees manufacturing as nothing more than neo-neanderthals who do not understand the importance of personnel procedures and practices.

INTERORGANIZATIONAL CONFLICT Just as individuals and groups can become engaged in conflict, organizations sometimes have conflicts with other organizations. Examples include friction between Company A and its supplier, Company B, because Company B is delaying shipment until a previous bill is paid. At the same time, Company A is in conflict with the local Occupational Safety and Health Administration (OSHA) office, which says its fire hazards have not been removed. In addition, a fired employee has filed a suit with the Equal Employment Opportunity Commission (EEOC), and the firm is facing an EEOC audit. The company is also spending a lot of time negotiating with the local union, which represents 67 percent of its employees. The list could go on and on, for most firms face a host of interorganizational conflicts.

Interorganizational conflict involves outside organizations.

Common Causes of Conflict

Although there are four basic levels of conflict, all share some common causes. The following examines nine of these causes.[19]

1. *Competition for rewards.* Organizational members are constantly competing for promotions, recognition, praise, status, a better office, a better assignment, more responsibility, more money, and so on. Organizations compete for rewards such as a larger market share, greater customer loyalty, and a higher return on investment.

2. *Interlevel incompatibilities.* Perspectives differ along with location in the organizational structure. Most top managers have a longer range orientation than do line foremen, who are immersed in day-to-day work.

3. *Functional conflict.* As mentioned before, various functional departments, especially those that interact on a continuous basis, are breeding grounds for conflict. This is easily seen when we consider the basic philosophy of various departments. That is, marketing tends to be optimistic and willing to expand; finance is conservative and typically urges caution. Production usually operates between these two extremes.

4. *Specialists versus generalists.* Over the past 20 years, we have become a nation of educated specialists. Yet managers, as typified by the MBA holder, have become increasingly generalists. The result is that managers often supervise people who have more technical expertise than they do. This can create conflict for both groups and lead to professional rather than hierarchical loyalties. The latter occurs, for example, when an R&D employee identifies himself as an engineer rather than a member of the R&D lab at the XYZ Corporation. These professional loyalties are bolstered by membership in, and resulting acquired status from, professional associations. Unions serve much the same function for other employees.

5. *Work flow problems.* Work flow is supposedly regulated by such factors as the

organizational hierarchy, job descriptions, and procedures. Yet, as Bradley and Baird have pointed out, work flow may directly produce conflict under three conditions.

Here are some common causes of conflict.

First, when communication flows in only one direction, usually downward, stress and conflict typically result. . . . Second, people may become hostile and engage in conflict when changes in work flow occur unexpectedly and unpredictably. Most of us seek an environment that is stable and predictable. . . . Third, conflicts seem most likely when inadequate interaction occurs between individuals who must work cooperatively from time to time.[20]

6. *Informal versus formal system conflict.* This type of conflict develops when norms of the informal network contradict those of the formal system. For example, work groups often limit their production through the use of informal standards that are unrelated to formal requirements. When managers or individual employees try to break through these informal norms, conflict is certain to develop.

7. *Status conflict.* Status is the relative ranking of an individual in the organization. Status is very important to most personnel. During a recent department move at one of our universities, it was surprising to see the degree of faculty concern over who was given offices with windows. Although many professors held the same faculty rank, additional status was ascribed to having an office with a window! Status conflict is also exemplified by new employees being given jobs at a higher level than those held by long-time employees. Another example is younger employees supervising older, more experienced ones.

8. *Political conflicts.* Organizations are political entities, and political conflicts are easy to spot. Whenever employees try to "make points" with the boss by calling attention to their own merits or by showing an interest in the boss's opinions, political conflict can result because other employees invariably resent this type of behavior. Even worse is the conflict that results when employees are vying for the same promotion and each is trying to discredit the other in the process.

9. *Interpersonal clashes.* Some organizational conflicts must be attributed to personality clashes. The people involved simply do not like each other.

A growing source of conflict in multinational organizations is overseas assignments where employees are forced to choose between staying at home with family and friends versus advancing their careers. The conflict inherent in an international assignment depends at least in part on the location of that assignment. For more information on this subject, see "International Communication in Action: Keeping Them Satisfied."

CONFLICT RESOLUTION

Lose–lose strategies are most defeating.

The three basic strategies for dealing with conflict are lose–lose strategies, win–lose strategies, and win–win strategies. Lose–lose methods are the most defeating. Nobody accomplishes what they want. Some examples of lose–lose methods include: (1) compromise where neither side is satisfied; (2) side payments where one side compensates or

INTERNATIONAL COMMUNICATION IN ACTION

Keeping Them Satisfied

Conflict and change are inevitable in organizational life. This condition is particularly evident in multinational firms that staff their overseas operations with local personnel. Of course, not everyone ends up going overseas, but many people are happy to accept these assignments. First, such an assignment helps further their career by increasing promotion potential. Second, it provides an opportunity to live in a new geographic locale and to give one's children a chance to travel and to expand their educational horizons. Third, it presents the opportunity to do a job for which a person is highly qualified, and an opportunity that is not available stateside. Fourth, the individual feels that overseas experience is required of all managers who hope to remain and grow with the organization.

Does an overseas assignment ever result in personal conflict? It can if the individual is assigned to a hardship site like Beijing or Moscow. (Some managers rank Tokyo in this group as well, because of the major cultural differences between Japan and the United States.) On the other hand, many managers end up getting very good assignments. What are the favorite countries? The figure on the opposite page shows the preferences reported by Swedish managers. As can be seen, these managers preferred countries that had the same general living standard or level of industrial development as their own. Similar language and religion were also important factors. Americans, meanwhile, seem to prefer Anglo countries and more industrialized nations. Few seem to care for hardship posts, even though most companies give these managers extra monthly supplements as a form of motivation.

Most importantly, research shows that when managers are not satisfied with their assignment, they tend to return home before their tour (usually 12 to 24 months) is over. Thus it is very important to match the individual and the country. Low satisfaction or general conflict with the assignment can cost the company thousands of dollars in personnel costs associated with bringing people back and sending over replacements. In the presence of strong opposition to the assignment, it is often best to reassign the person to another country or return the individual to the earlier post in the states. To do otherwise typically creates more problems than it solves.

SOURCE: Much of the information in this section can be found in Richard M. Hodgetts and Fred Luthans, *International Management* (New York: McGraw-Hill, 1991), Ch. 7, in press.

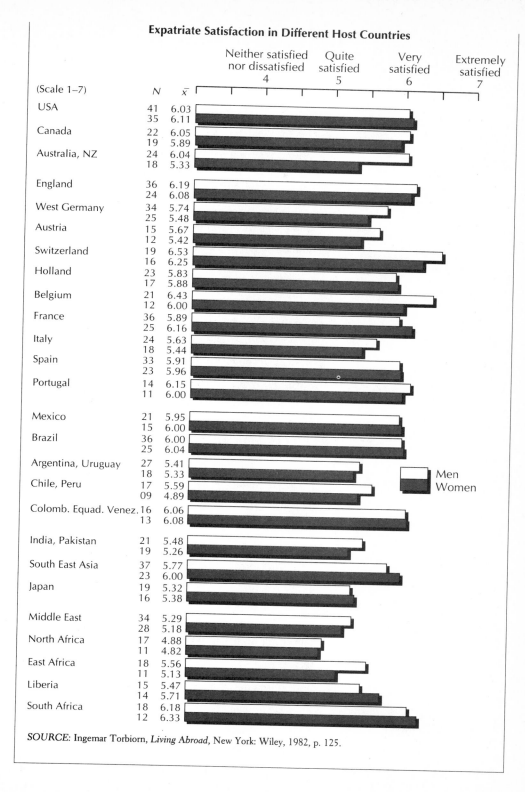

Expatriate Satisfaction in Different Host Countries

(Scale 1–7)	N	$\bar{x}$
USA	41	6.03
	35	6.11
Canada	22	6.05
	19	5.89
Australia, NZ	24	6.04
	18	5.33
England	36	6.19
	24	6.08
West Germany	34	5.74
	25	5.48
Austria	15	5.67
	12	5.42
Switzerland	19	6.53
	16	6.25
Holland	23	5.83
	17	5.88
Belgium	21	6.43
	12	6.00
France	36	5.89
	25	6.16
Italy	24	5.63
	18	5.44
Spain	33	5.91
	23	5.96
Portugal	14	6.15
	11	6.00
Mexico	21	5.95
	15	6.00
Brazil	36	6.00
	25	6.04
Argentina, Uruguay	27	5.41
	18	5.33
Chile, Peru	17	5.59
	09	4.89
Colomb. Equad. Venez.	16	6.06
	13	6.08
India, Pakistan	21	5.48
	19	5.26
South East Asia	37	5.77
	23	6.00
Japan	19	5.32
	16	5.38
Middle East	34	5.29
	28	5.18
North Africa	17	4.88
	11	4.82
East Africa	18	5.56
	11	5.13
Liberia	15	5.47
	14	5.71
South Africa	18	6.18
	12	6.33

Scale labels: Neither satisfied nor dissatisfied (4), Quite satisfied (5), Very satisfied (6), Extremely satisfied (7)

Legend: Men, Women

SOURCE: Ingemar Torbiorn, *Living Abroad,* New York: Wiley, 1982, p. 125.

bribes the other side to give in on the issue; (3) use of an arbitrator to settle the issue, which usually results in a middle-ground compromise acceptable to none; and (4) resort to ad hoc or established rules to solve the question.

Win–lose strategies are most frequently used. They are rooted in our value of competition. The Likerts describe them this way,

Bargaining, negotiating . . . and similar approaches to the handling of conflict are essentially forms of win–lose confrontation. They all start with a relatively clear solution which each party to the conflict prefers and wishes to attain. Each party strives to attain its preferred solution by forcing it on the other party, by outsmarting the opponent. If unable to achieve complete success, each party seeks to attain as much of its preferred solution as possible. A *polarized, adversary* orientation is maintained at all times.[21]

Win–win strategies are by far the most effective. They focus on both problem solving and confrontation, and they tend to avoid the continuation of suppressed conflict which is so typical in the other two methods. Solutions are satisfactory to all; everyone is a winner.

> **Win–lose strategies are the most common.**

> **Win–win strategies are the most effective.**

Conflict Management Communication Strategies

Five communication styles for conflict management have emerged out of the work of Blake and Mouton, well known for their development of the managerial grid.[22] Figure 12.2 is based on Rahim's interpretation of these styles: avoiding, obliging, dominating, compromising, and integrating.[23]

The two dimensions of the model are (1) concern for self, or the degree to which a person tries to protect his or her own interests in a conflict situation; and (2) concern for others, or the degree to which a person wants to satisfy the view of others. The five styles result from these two dimensions.

AVOIDING The "avoiding" strategy is a decision to do nothing. The manager assumes that if he or she ignores the situation, the conflict will go away without requiring any personal involvement. This attempt to maintain neutrality often aggravates both parties to the conflict. This strategy is often used by weak, uninvolved leaders. However, a wise manager dealing with highly professional, independent employees may choose at least initially to get involved in the conflict. Managers may also avoid the conflict situation while they take time to gather the facts.

OBLIGING The "obliging" conflict style shows a higher concern for the needs of others and a low concern for self. This manager tries hard to accommodate the other party, often repressing his or her own needs or point of view. The obliging style may make the other person feel good for a while, but it does little to resolve the conflict. Thus it is almost always a win–lose strategy. However, if maintaining good relationships really is of prime importance, this may be a reasonable style. A salesperson may decide to give a customer an undeserved refund for obviously used merchandise in order to maintain a good future relationship.

DOMINATING The "dominating" style is characterized by power tactics and domination. It is a win–lose strategy where the manager in question shows much concern for

Figure 12.2

Conflict
management styles.

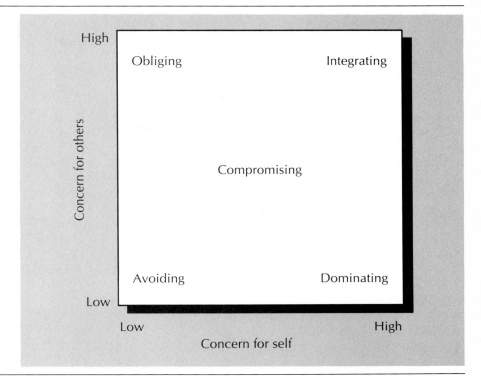

There are five basic
conflict-
management
communication
strategies.

his or her needs and almost no concern for the needs of others. Dominating can be an appropriate style when an immediate solution is required such as in a safety situation, but as a general style for managing conflict, it tends to create bad feelings among the parties involved.

COMPROMISING The manager who "compromises" regularly is often seen as a wishy-washy, unprincipled person who seeks expediency rather than resolution. Yet compromise is often used as a conflict management tactic. It may even be appropriate in a situation where "a conflict is not important enough to either party to warrant the time and psychological investment in one of the more assertive modes of conflict management. In addition, compromise may be the only practical way of handling a conflict situation in which two equally strong and persuasive parties attempt to work out a solution."[24]

INTEGRATING With the "integrating" strategy the manager combines a high concern for the interests of others with a high concern for self. This approach relies on confrontation and collaboration, opening up a disagreement directly and in a problem-solving manner so that the conflict may be worked through.

Confrontation may be the best way to handle conflict, but it is not always easy. It is often uncomfortable for the manager to have to deal directly with a problem, especially when emotions are involved. Confrontation should never be resorted to in anger or in haste. Successful confrontation requires patience, diplomacy, and a knowledge of the confrontation process.

There are six major steps to confrontation.

At least six major steps may be taken in confronting a conflict situation. Figure 12.3 shows these steps. Step 1, awareness that a conflict exists, is a critical first step. Step 2, the decision to confront, has consciously to occur next. Step 3, the confrontation, occurs when Person A decides to confront Person B. Person B may be willing to face the problem or unwilling to proceed further. If there is agreement to continue, step 4 determines the locus of the problem or conflict. This is the tricky part. The people involved in the confrontation should voice their opinions and feelings about the issue in question. The confrontation will not succeed unless the people involved can come to an agreement as to the causes of the problem. It is therefore important that each person hear the others out completely.

Step 5 requires the parties involved to agree on specific measures that should be taken to eliminate the conflict. Step 6 is an agreement to revisit the problem at some specific time in the future to see that resolution has been achieved.

Whatever the basic style of conflict management, Hawkins and Preston have suggested nine useful strategies.

1. *Focus on felt and relational dimensions.* The effective manager must realize the importance of focusing on feelings, because without this recognition of hidden

Figure 12.3

Steps to confront conflict.

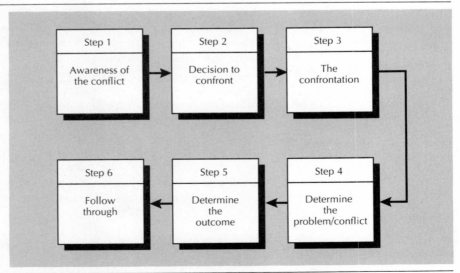

SOURCE: Peter Muniz and Robert Chasnoff, ''Assessing the Causes of Conflicts — and Confronting the Real Issues,'' *Supervisory Management*, March 1986, pp. 37–38.

agendas and mindsets, the immediate conflict will never be fully resolved. It may seem to go away for the moment, but it will come back with renewed force at the very next point of disagreement.

2. *Delay committing yourself.* The manager should try to keep his or her options open by listening fully to all sides involved and by trying to get the participants to work through the problem. Eventually, the manager may have to make a decision, and admittedly the timing may be tricky. However, delaying too long may lead people to criticize the individual for being indecisive.

3. *Focus on the problem, not on specific solutions.* Managers in conflict situations must resist the impulse to jump right to the decision. They must be prepared to struggle to find the root of the problem, for only then can lasting conflict resolution occur.

4. *Don't try to place blame.* When listening to participants explain a particular conflict situation, managers often find themselves mentally sifting through the data, trying to pinpoint the blame. Placing blame does no good except to polarize the participants further.

Other effective strategies for managing conflict

5. *Minimize status differences.* Organizational status and rank often interfere with effective conflict management, particularly when the participants are at different organizational levels. For effective resolution, status differences should be minimized.

6. *Be cautious of your sources of information.* Managers should always check their sources to be sure they have the whole picture. Have their information sources been biased in some way? Do they have a vested interest in the conflict at hand? As seen in the chapter on organizational communication barriers, this information is often self-serving and can be further altered by serial distortion and information overload.

7. *Avoid always going by the book.* Often the manager hopes that an employee's problem will go away as he or she goes through the paces of following procedures. This tactic usually backfires, however, and the employee, after jumping through all the hoops, is back on the manager's doorstep more firmly entrenched than ever! The lesson here is that, although procedures can be very useful, they should not be used as an excuse to ignore a conflict situation.

8. *Resolve the conflict at the lowest possible level.* This involves trying to get the conflicting parties involved, as nobody else can really solve their problem for them. Win–win strategies always follow this approach.

9. *Examine your own biases and predispositions.* Each party in a conflict needs to recognize his or her own attitudes, values, biases, and hostilities. The manager who is facilitating the conflict resolution needs to do the same. In this way, distortion can be eliminated and more effective resolution can be achieved.

Implications for Management

1. Remember that change is inevitable, so there will always be some degree of organizational conflict. The best strategy is not to eliminate conflict but to effectively manage it.

2. Be aware that there are many sources of conflict. At the intrapersonal, interpersonal, and group levels, these sources often have one common thread: the status quo is being affected. Personnel are having their authority challenged, responsibility increased, position threatened, and so on, and they are fighting back. The effective manager must work to resolve this conflict by turning this personnel effort into productive output.

3. Whenever possible employ a win–win conflict resolution strategy. It is the best long-range strategy because it takes everyone's point of view into consideration.

4. In managing conflict, remember that it is as important to understand yourself as it is to know the causes of the conflict. A highly rational approach does not always work with people engaged in conflict. Sometimes you have to appeal to their emotions or personal feelings. In doing so you have to adjust your style to meet the situation, and this means knowing how your approach will affect their behavior.

C A S E   I N   P O I N T

Revisited

What went wrong? Obviously, Adrienne's decision to move Charles was unacceptable to him and he decided to make a move of his own. The big question is why Charles has decided to move. The answer is not completely clear from the case. However, it does seem that Charles is reluctant to go into the field. The fact that he has taken an office job with his new employer indicates that he may have serious reservations about the wisdom of needing field experience before moving up. However, it is also possible that Charles simply does not want any change in his career work. He has always been in the office and may intend to stay there.

A second facet of this case relates to Adrienne's decision. She is proceeding with the idea that Charles wants to move up the hierarchy at Harley. Does he? From what he tells her in the case, he does. However, the fact that his actions tell another story leads us to

believe that Charles is either unsure of what decision to make or is hoping against hope that he will not have to go into the field. In either event, Charles is out of step with the rest of the firm and has made no plans to bring himself into step with it.

Did Adrienne make a mistake? Not really. She failed to tell Charles, but that obviously was not because of bad intentions on her part. She called his mother, and as soon as he returned she met with him. If anything, Adrienne seems to be very interested in helping Charles get ahead at the firm.

Of course, you may read a different interpretation into the case. You may feel that Charles is leaving because Adrienne has forced a change on him. In either event, notice how change affects people. Why? A brief review of the reasons discussed in the chapter indicates that change in the status quo may well be the primary cause.

YOU BE THE CONSULTANT

Jim's Decision

In the manufacturing business, production is proving to be the name of the game, especially among firms that do a lot of subcontracting work. When subcontractors (subs) receive formal requests for bids, they decide whether or not to bid on the contract. If they choose to proceed, they write up a proposal that details how they intend to produce the desired output and what they will charge for the work. The two criteria of major importance in subcontracting work are cost and reputation.

Typically, those subs making the lowest bids are considered for the job. From this group, one is then chosen. The final choice depends on both the cost and the reputation of the sub. Those who previously have done similar work have an edge over those who have not. In the industry word gets around regarding whom to use as subs on different types of jobs.

The Gardine Company had been a manufacturing sub for 37 years. Most of its work has been on large federal contracts, and, overall, the firm is well thought of by the large major contractors. However, in recent years there has been increased pressure among both primary contractors and subs to keep down costs; quality output often is proving to be a secondary consideration. As a result, many subs have turned to computers to help them run their operations and control expenses. Subs are finding that these machines can help reduce inventory levels and improve quality control. Desktop microcomputers (micros) are also being used for making on-the-spot decisions regarding how to allocate materials, assign personnel, and so forth.

Gardine has not yet adopted computers in any of its operations except paperwork functions, basically recordkeeping and checkwriting. The firm's high efficiency has always allowed it ample profit, and the company sees no reason to computerize. As other subs have become more price competitive, however, Gardine has been paying more attention to the value of these machines.

Last month a computer consulting firm was called in to look over the company's operations and make recommendations regarding where and how computers could be used. The consultants spent a week at the company. Two weeks later they presented their report to the management. In the main, the consultants believe the firm can cut costs by 25 percent and not have to lay off anyone. The report is detailed and focuses on four main points.

1. Computers should be used for handling correspondence and other word processing functions. At the present time most of this work is done via electromechanical machines; computers would speed up the entire process.

2. Inventory can be balanced and carrying costs reduced by 33 percent if inventory recordkeeping were tied directly to the computer.

3. Purchasing could be simplified and quality control could be improved if these functions were computerized.

4. If managers would learn how to use computers, desktop micros could be installed for the purpose of providing up-to-the-minute information for both analysis and decision making.

Overall, the consultants estimate that with the use of computers Gardine could increase its overall profit by 13 percent, making it one of the most efficient subs in the country. If the firm were to follow the recommendations in this report, it would be able to bid on more contracts and become one of the five largest subs in the northeastern section of the country.

Jim Gardine believes that computerization will have to be implemented. For their part, the company personnel are aware that the matter is under discussion and there is a great deal of concern. So far this week, Jim has heard from three specific groups. One is the unionized people who are afraid that computerization is going to mean a reduction in jobs. A second is the managers who are concerned that with desktop micros they are going to be called on to make snap decisions that will prove to be wrong. A third is the secretarial staff and others who basically do filing and paperwork jobs. They have told Jim that they hope the company does turn to computerization because they are interested in learning how they can do their jobs faster.

The biggest issue, which is quite evident to Jim, is that computerization will bring problems. Many of the personnel are concerned about the changes that will be introduced and the effect these will have on them. On the other hand, Jim knows that with computerization he will score a big gain on the competition. In his view, the use of these machines is inevitable; it is all a matter of properly introducing the change. In order to take this step with the least amount of problems, he has decided to bring in a consulting firm that specializes in helping firms both introduce and implement major changes.

Assume you are a member of the consulting team that is being brought into Jim's firm. Based on your reading of the case and understanding of the chapter material, how would you recommend the firm proceed? What major problems will they face? What should be done about them? Be as complete as you can in your recommendations.

Key Points in This Chapter

1. Change is a part of our very existence. Yet change often scares people and they tend to resist it. Among the many reasons for such resistance are a vested interest in the status quo, fear of the unknown, habit, tradition, fear of increased responsibility, a low propensity for risk, and economic losses. This fear often manifests itself in absenteeism, turnover, reduced work output, and hostility and conflict.

2. Resistance to change can be managed in several ways. They all call for the manager to give the resistor a chance to explain the reason for resistance and work with the employee in trying to overcome these fears. Some of the most effective strategies include surfacing, honoring, exploring, and rechecking.

3. Conflict is incompatible behavior between parties whose interests differ. The traditional view of conflict is that it is bad and should be discouraged. The current view of

conflict is that it is a healthy sign and should be used in getting things done. In this way conflict becomes a positive rather than a negative force.

4. There are many conditions relating to conflict: unclear jurisdictions, conflicts of interest, barriers to communication, increased interaction, need for agreement, regulations for behavior, and the presence of unresolved conflict. This conflict can occur at any level in the hierarchy; intrapersonal, interpersonal, group, or interorganizational. Some of the major causes for conflict include competition for rewards, functional conflict, specialists versus generalists, work flow problems, informal versus system conflict, status conflict, political conflicts, and interpersonal clashes.

5. Conflict resolution can take many different forms. In general terms these can be condensed to three: lose–lose strategies, win–lose strategies, and win–win strategies. Of them, the win–win is best. The last part of the chapter discussed some of the most useful ways of implementing a win–win strategy.

Questions for Discussion and Analysis

1. Why is there resistance to change? What are some of the most frequent reasons? Identify and discuss five of them.

2. Four of the most useful strategies for dealing with resistance to change are surfacing, honoring, exploring, and rechecking. What takes place in each strategy? How are the four linked together? Explain.

3. In your own words, what is meant by the term *conflict?* How does the traditional view of conflict differ from the current view of conflict? Be complete in your answer.

4. What are some of the major causes of conflict? Identify and discuss five.

5. Conflict can occur at the intrapersonal, interpersonal, group, and interorganizational level. What is meant by this statement? In your answer be sure to provide an example of each of the four types of conflict.

6. In conflict resolution there are lose–lose, win–lose, and win–win strategies. How do each of these differ? Which is most beneficial to all involved?

7. What types of communication strategies are useful to the effective management of organizational conflict? Cite and explain at least four of these strategies.

Exercises

1. Role play the following situation: Herb Meadows has just been appointed manager of human resources. One of his top priorities is instituting an MBO system among top and middle managers. He has full authority and executive support for this

program. As he explains the system to individual managers, he encounters various forms of resistance. What should he say in each instance? (Refer to Karp's typology of resistance.)

   a. Betty Johnson: "I'd love to get involved in this, but I just don't have the time."

   b. Ralph Jones: "I really think you should start this program with first line supervisors."

   c. Marcia Jimenez: "The Board will never go for this!"

   d. Rita Simpson: "I can't believe that on top of everything else you expect me to get involved in MBO."

   e. Sam Donaldson: "I've been here 20 years and our current goal setting system has never let us down."

2. In teams of three to five people, debate the following issue. "Is organizational conflict healthy?" One side should present the positive view and the opposing team the negative, more traditional view.

References

1. Alvin Toffler, *Future Shock* (New York: Bantam Books, 1970), p. 2.

2. Donald F. Harvey and Donald R. Brown, *An Experimental Approach to Organizational Development*, 3rd ed. (Englewood Cliffs, N.J.: Prentice-Hall, 1988), p. 34.

3. Keith Davis and John W. Newstrom, *Human Behavior at Work: Organizational Behavior*, 8th ed., New York: McGraw-Hill, 1989), p. 292.

4. Dale D. McConkey, *Plan for Change: Mastering Proactive Management,"* Credit Union Executive, Vol. 28, no. 3, Fall 1988, pp. 18–23.

5. Dennis J. Gillen, "Harnessing the Energy from Change Anxiety," *Supervisory Management*, March 1986, p. 42.

6. David K. Lindo, "And Another Good Idea Bites the Dust," *Supervision*, Vol. 50, no. 1, January 1988, pp. 17–19.

7. H. B. Karp, "Working with Resistance," *Training and Development Journal*, March 1984, p. 69.

8. Karp, *op. cit.* p. 73.

9. Joseph Stanislao and Bettie C. Stanislao, "Dealing with Resistance to Change," *Business Horizons*, July–August 1983, pp. 74–78.

10. L. David Brown, *Managing Conflict at Organizational Interfaces* (Reading, Mass.: Addison-Wesley, 1983), p. 4.

11. Joyce Hocker Wilmot and William W. Wilmot, *Interpersonal Conflict* (Dubuque, Iowa: William C. Brown, 1978), p. 9.

12. Philip V. Lewis, *Organizational Communication: The Essence of Effective Management* (Columbus, Ohio: Grid, 1980), p. 385.

13. Gerald R. Miller, "Epilogue," in Gerald R. Miller and Herbert W. Simon, eds., *Perspectives on Communication in Social Conflict* (Englewood Cliffs, N.J.: Prentice-Hall, 1974), pp. 206–219. As cited in Brian L. Hawkins and Paul Preston, *Managerial Communication* (Santa Monica, Calif.: Goodyear, 1981), p. 277.

14. Christopher Lasch, *The Culture of Narcissism: American Life in an Age of Diminishing Expectations* (New York: Warner Books, 1979), p. 21.

15. Deborah M. Kolb and Priscilla A. Glidden, "Getting to Know Your Conflict Options," *Personnel Administrator*, Vol. 31, no. 6, June 1986, pp. 77–90.

16. Peter Muniz and Robert Chasnoff, "Assessing the Causes of Conflicts — and Confronting the Real Issues," *Supervisory Management*, March 1989, p. 35.

17. Alan C. Filley, *Interpersonal Conflict Resolution* (Glenview, Ill.: Scott, Foresman, 1975).

18. Patricia Hayes Bradley and John E. Baird, Jr., *Communication for Business and the Professions* (Dubuque, Iowa: William C. Brown, 1983), p. 269.

19. *Ibid.*, pp. 270–274.

20. *Ibid.*, p. 271.

21. Rensis Likert and Jane Gibson Likert, *New Ways of Managing Conflict* (New York: McGraw-Hill, 1976), p. 68. (Emphasis added.)

22. Robert R. Blake and Jane S. Mouton, "The Fifth Achievement," *Journal of Applied Behavioral Science*, October/November/December 1970, pp. 413–426.

23. M. Afzalur Rahim, "A Measure of Styles of Handling Interpersonal Conflict," *Academy of Management Journal*, June 1983, pp. 368–376.

24. Gordon L. Lippitt, "Managing Conflict in Today's Organizations," *Training and Development Journal*, July 1982, p. 70.

25. Hawkins and Preston, *op. cit.*, pp. 296–302.

Annotated Bibliography

Filley, Alan C., *Interpersonal Conflict Resolution* (Glenview, Ill.: Scott, Foresman, 1975).

Filley's often-quoted work first analyzes the conflict process and then explains the effects of language, behavior, attitudes, and organization on interpersonal conflict. Emphasis is on problem-solving methods of conflict resolution.

Likert, Rensis, and Jane Gibson Likert, *New Ways of Managing Conflict* (New York: McGraw-Hill, 1976).

The Likerts apply major research findings concerned with organization and their effective management of conflict. They relate conflict to social values and organization theory and propose a reorganization of organizational structure based on their System 4T model.

Naisbitt, John, and Patricia Aburdene, *Megatrends 2000: Ten New Directions for the 1990s.* (New York: Morrow, 1990).

    Megatrends 2000 is an easy-to-read, fascinating account of changes that will be occurring during the 1990s. These ranges from global economic boom to global lifestyle and cultural nationalism to the triumph of the individual. A must for the student of change and conflict!

Wilmot, Joyce Hocker, and William W. Wilmot, *Interpersonal Conflict* (Dubuque, Iowa: William C. Brown, 1978).

    Wilmot and Wilmot explore the subject of interpersonal conflict thoroughly and offer a myriad of strategies and tactics for successfully handling conflict. They also apply transactional analysis theory to understanding the nature of conflict.

CHAPTER 13

Conducting Effective Interviews

"Managerial interviewing is unquestionably a key to good human relationships in organizations — perhaps the best one presently available."

Phillip V. Lewis, *Organizational Communication: The Essence of Effective Management*, (Columbus, Ohio: Grid, 1980), p. 337.

Objectives

1. To identify and describe the basic elements in the interviewing process.

2. To compare and contrast directive and nondirective interviewing and relate the role played by open and closed questions, leading questions, and hidden assumptions in the structuring of an interview.

3. To describe the nature of employment interviews and offer suggestions and guidelines for improving the managerial effectiveness of this process.

4. To explain how a performance appraisal interview works and how the manager can effectively conduct such an interview.

5. To relate the nature of the counseling interview and offer suggestions and guidelines for conducting one.

6. To explain the nature of the discipline interview and how managers can more effectively conduct such an interview.

C A S E   I N   P O I N T

Letting the Conversation Flow

Every year the Schmidt Company, a medium-sized accounting firm, sends one of its people to the local university to recruit one or two people. Schmidt has found that the quality of the accounting graduates is very high. Of the 25 people at Schmidt, 7 are graduates of this university.

One of the students who recently signed up at the University Placement Service is Tim Marland. Tim is a nephew of the company president, Pete Schmidt. He was one of six people interviewed yesterday by the Schmidt representative, Adam Weeks. After a brief general introduction during which the two men talked about class work and when Tim would be graduating, Adam began directing the interview to the job at hand. Here is how part of the interview went.

A: I'm happy that you decided to interview with us. Schmidt is a very well-known local accounting firm, and there are a great number of opportunities that we can offer a young person. Have you had any accounting experience?

T: Well, nothing formal.

A: No matter. If you come with us, we'll give you more than you can handle — not that we overwork our people — and we pay better than anyone in the area. The fringe benefit package is good also. You are familiar with our benefits are you not?

T: Well, no.

A: I'll see that you get a copy of them. Now tell me, exactly why would you like to work for Schmidt?

T: Well, I heard you're thinking about merging with two other companies, and this means that you'll be one of the largest accounting firms in this five-state area.

A: Right. And we'll not only be handling local clients but we'll have a group of auditors who are out on the road most of time. You know auditing, don't you? And you're not averse to traveling, are you? It would be a very important part of the job.

T: No, not at all. But tell me, what will this type of assignment be like? Will it require a lot of time away from home?

A: If you get the job, you'll learn more about it. However, I'd like to turn to another matter, namely, why you decided on accounting as a profession.

When the interview was over, Adam thanked Tim for coming by and promised to get back to him within the next two weeks. To his surprise, Adam was the one who got early feedback on the interview. The next day his boss called him in and asked, "How many people did you interview yesterday?" Pete told him he had talked to six graduating students. Then his boss asked, "Have you ever had any formal training in interviewing? How do you know how to handle yourself during the session?" Pete explained that he simply let the conversation flow, although he did have five specific questions written down which he got interviewees to answer. His boss smiled. "Look," he said, "Mary Redford usually does our interviewing, but she was out yesterday. That's why I sent you. Why don't you sit in with her the next time she goes back to the university to interview. I think there are some things that you need to find out about effective interviewing. It's a lot more than simply letting the conversation flow."

What was wrong with the way Adam handled the interview? What did he do wrong? Identify his mistakes and then discuss how he can avoid making them in the future. Then put your analysis to the side. We will return to it later.

INTRODUCTION

Many people think of interviewing as a rather simple process. Two people sit down at the table across from each other and begin talking. Each has a set agenda, determined to learn something from the other party. In the case of the employment interview, for example, the interviewer tries to find out if the other person is interested in the job, is able to do it, and would make a positive contribution to the organization. The interviewee is interested in finding out exactly what the requirements of the job are, the potential for promotion, and what the salary and benefit package will be. Quite often the interviewer will take notes, and it is not uncommon also to find the interviewee writing down things that are said. When both parties have had all their questions answered, the interview ends. Sometimes it is a successful meeting; other times it is not. Why? The answer rests in the interviewing process itself. Quite often the interviewer does not know how to conduct an effective interview. The individual has picked up some skills through interviewing experience, but lacks a solid understanding of how to conduct an interview.

The same is true in the case of other types of interviews such as performance appraisal interviews, counseling interviews, and discipline interviews. In this chapter we are going to examine these interviews, discussing things that the manager must know in order to conduct them effectively. We begin by considering the nature of the interview process.

THE INTERVIEWING PROCESS

Some people confuse interviewing with conversation. The two are actually quite different. A conversation is a general chat often with no stated purpose, whereas an interview has a purpose. Conversation is easy and enjoyable, whereas an interview can be difficult, requiring the ability to think, analyze, synthesize, and evaluate. Conversation is often random, whereas an interview has specific goals. An interview can be defined as a deliberate, face-to-face communication session between an interviewer and an interviewee which is focused around specific content and designed to achieve predetermined goals. Let us take a closer look at the five basic elements of an interview: deliberateness, face-to-face communication, interviewer and interviewee, specific content, and predetermined goals.

Deliberateness

Interviews do not just happen.

Interviews, unlike many other kinds of communication activities, do not just happen. One of the two parties involved, usually the interviewer, must decide to initiate the process. In so doing, the individual faces the problem of location and time. Where and when should the interview take place? Effective interviews are not random; they are planned with deliberateness.

Face-to-Face

Most interviews are
face to face.

Interviews, with the possible exception of telephone interviews used mainly in research, take place face to face. This approach encourages the sharing of information and provides the skilled interviewer the chance to observe nonverbal clues to attitudes and feelings. This personal approach is also extremely effective in getting one's point across. So despite their time-consuming nature, face-to-face interviews offer many advantages.

Interviewer and Interviewee

In every interview situation there are two parties: the interviewer and the interviewee. Typically, it involves only two people.

> Each interview is a unique transaction which cannot be understood by looking at either participant in isolation. Once any two people interact, either verbally or nonverbally, a transaction or interdependent relationship is formed. As one person speaks, the other responds and affects the first instantaneously and simultaneously. . . . Although interview relationships can change, each interview situation is unique.[1]

**Two parties are
involved in an
interview.**

An interview does not always involve just two individuals. For example when a personnel manager interviews a panel of union representatives about a grievance case, one interviewer and a host of interviewees are present. Conversely, when a group of faculty collectively interview a job candidate, we have a host of interviewers and one interviewee. Regardless of the number of people in each role, however, two distinct parties are involved.

The major responsibility for the success of the process rests with the interviewer. It is this person's job to see that the objectives of the meeting are accomplished. So whether the individual closely directs the interview or allows it to take its own course, this person carries the burden for success or failure. This is why it is so important for the interviewer to be an effective message encoder and decoder. The person must know how to send messages and how to interpret verbal and nonverbal feedback.

Specific Content

**The interview
should be planned.**

Interviews should be planned, if only in general terms. There is nothing random about an effective interview. The interviewer should know the purpose of the meeting and have prepared a written or mental agenda to be followed. If multiple interviews are to be conducted, as in the case of a personnel manager who will be interviewing ten applicants for the same job, the interviewer should prepare a list of questions so as to ensure consistency and coverage of the most important points. Table 13.1 contrasts the topics discussed in an interview and a general conversation. The S in the table stands for specific, focused content relevant to the purpose of the conversation; the N stands for nonrelevant interchanges. As can be seen from the table, an average conversation will often stray from the subject, whereas an interview will focus almost entirely on content. The only Ns in the interview are in the beginning and end, indicating nonspecific welcoming and closing remarks.

Table 13.1

CONVERSATIONS AND INTERVIEWS: A COMPARISON OF CONTENT

	Conversations		Interviews	
	Party A	Party B	Party A	Party B
	N	N	N	N
	N	S	S	S
	S	S	S	S
	N	N	S	S
	N	N	S	S
	S	N	S	S
	S	S	S	S
	N	N	N	N

N = nonrelevant interchange of information
S = specific, focused content

Predetermined Goals

Objectives should be established.

In an effective interview the specific content mentioned above is all planned to achieve predetermined goals. These goals will vary depending on the nature of the interview, but they are crucial to the overall success of the process. For example, in an employment interview the interviewer will seek information related to the other party's experience, training, and desire for the job. In a performance evaluation interview, the superior will seek to explain where the subordinate did well, where the individual did poorly, and how future performance can be improved.

STRUCTURING THE INTERVIEW

Regardless of the purpose of the interview, there are two basic approaches to interviewing: directive and nondirective.

In the *directive approach* the interviewer asks specific questions designed to keep the interviewee focused on providing the desired type of information. This requires a great deal of planning on the part of the interviewer. In the *nondirective approach*, the interviewer does very little talking; instead the individual encourages the interviewee to express his or her own feelings and thoughts in whatever direction they go. This approach calls for a great deal of understanding on the part of the interviewer. Of the two approaches, nondirective interviewing is usually harder because it requires the interviewer to restrain the natural tendency to participate, if not actually control, the exchange.

Regardless of the type of interview, the exchange can be structured along several dimensions. The following examines these dimensions.

Open and Closed Questions

Interviewer questions fall into two categories: open and closed. *Open questions* allow the responder to frame his or her own answers. For example, during a performance appraisal interview, a supervisor may ask the following questions:

- "What would you like to be doing on the job that you're not currently doing?"
- "How are things going in your department?"
- "What things do you think you're best at?"

Questions like these permit the employee to bring up a wide range of responses that otherwise might never be heard. For example, the second question might result in the supervisor learning about a recurring stock problem of which he had been unaware.

When used appropriately, open questions have distinct advantages. Some of these include:

1. The interviewee is usually more at ease with open questions because he or she knows there is no one right answer and has the time to explain his or her point of view.

2. The interviewee is given the forum to present whatever he or she thinks is important.

3. The questions tend to be motivating for the interviewee because they show that the interviewer is interested in knowing what the other party is thinking or feeling; the questions make the interviewee feel important as well as provide the opportunity to get things off one's chest.

Advantages to open questions
4. The interviewer is often given a comprehensive picture of how the interviewee thinks and feels about certain subjects.

5. The interviewer is able to determine how much an interviewee really knows about a subject.

6. The interviewer is given an opportunity to assess the interviewee's interpersonal skills.

7. Open questions reveal how articulate the interviewee is in terms of personal expression.

The manager must also be aware of certain disadvantages to open questions. The following are five of the most important.

1. They are time consuming. If the interviewer starts asking open questions only to cut off the interviewee because of a lack of time, the open question effort will seem phony.

Disadvantages to open questions

2. With open questions, one risks hearing information that is either irrelevant or unpleasant, the first of which wastes interviewer time and the second puts the individual in a position of having to cope with the surfaced data.

3. The interviewer must be skilled in gleaning the important points from what the interviewee is saying and in noting these points before they have been forgotten.

4. Interviewees may tend to look for "easy" answers and give only generalized responses to open questions.

5. When conducting a series of interviews, it is hard to ensure consistency, that is, covering the same ground with two or more interviewees.

Closed questions permit the interviewer to focus the exchange more narrowly, often ensuring that the desired data are obtained. By their very nature, such questions restrict the information that can be given or received. During a performance appraisal they might include the following:

- "Are you familiar with the new salary schedule?"

- "Did you take that training course we talked about last year?"

- "Have you learned how to operate the new word processor?"

Interviewees are forced into a short, simplified response. Like open questions, closed queries provide various advantages.

1. Some interviewees prefer closed questions because they do not have to explain their answers.

Advantages to closed questions

2. Closed questions give the interviewer clearer control over the progress of the exchange; the needed data can be solicited without having to listen to a lot of extraneous information.

3. The answers are easy to summarize and record.

4. When conducting a number of interviews, answers are easy to compile and compare.

5. Closed questions are generally easier for the interviewer to formulate and to interpret.

6. Interviews conducted primarily with closed questions proceed much more quickly than those based on open questions.

Closed questions also have a number of disadvantages including:

1. They do not allow the interviewee to qualify answers.

2. They may force the interviewee into an either-or answer when, in fact, neither response may be accurate.

Disadvantages to closed questions

3. They often result in interviewees answering yes or no to things they know little about, for example, "Do you think our new pension plan is fair?"

4. They do not reveal the full extent of information that the interviewee has about the subject in question.

5. Their success depends almost solely on the skill of the interviewer in asking the right questions.

6. Interviewees may feel that the interviewer has no real interest in them.

Now that we have examined the relative merits of open and closed questions, it should be stressed that many of the most effective interviews are a combination of the two. The following excerpt from an employment interview is an example.

Interviewer: Did you finish your MBA? (closed)

Interviewee: Yes, and I think it will be very helpful if I get this job.

Interviewer: How do you feel what you studied will help you on the job? (open)

Interviewee: Well, I learned a lot of quantitative skills, but I think I profited most from the courses that taught me how to deal with people.

Interviewer: Do you think you have good interpersonal skills? (closed)

Interviewee: Yes, I seem to get along very well with people.

Forming the Questions

Regardless of whether the interviewer is using open or closed questions, or a combination of the two, certain pitfalls must be avoided. These include leading questions, hidden assumptions, and confusing language.

LEADING QUESTIONS Inexperienced interviewers often introduce bias into the interview by using leading rather than neutral questions. Can you see the critical difference between the pairs of questions below?

LEADING QUESTIONS	NEUTRAL QUESTIONS
1. What do you think of our super new benefit plan?	1. What is your opinion on the new benefit plan?
2. You like your new job, don't you?	2. How do you like your new job?
3. Don't you think Jack's a great guy?	3. How well do you get along with Jack?
4. You don't mind working overtime this week, do you?	4. Do you mind working overtime this week?

Leading questions reveal bias.

Each leading question shows the interviewer's opinion on the subject. The interviewee knows exactly what response will be acceptable. In Question 1, it will be very hard for the employee to answer, "I think it stinks." In Question 3, the interviewer shows pleasure with Jack and makes it hard for the interviewee to disagree. Such bias can prevent the interviewee from giving an honest answer and from the interviewer getting accurate information. Can you recognize leading questions? Take Self-Assessment Quiz 13-1.

SELF-ASSESSMENT QUIZ 13.1

Can You Recognize a Leading Question?

Directions: For each of the following, mark an L for a leading question or an N for a neutral question. In each case, assume there have been no introductory questions.

———— 1. "You do find time for worthy social causes, don't you?"

———— 2. "You can use a computer, can't you?"

———— 3. "Why do you want to work here?"

———— 4. "Where did you go to school?"

———— 5. "How did you like that ridiculous ad campaign?"

———— 6. "Did you take any training courses this year?"

———— 7. "Did you join the company insurance plan?"

———— 8. "Do you know anything about our Credit Union?"

———— 9. "How much do you know about this pain-in-the-neck union we have?"

———— 10. "You don't misuse our sick policy, do you?"

Answers are in the Answer section at the back of the book.

HIDDEN ASSUMPTIONS Another problem in forming questions is the use of hidden assumptions, which show that the interviewer assumes something to be true before even asking. For example, when you ask someone, "who is your favorite rock star?" you have formed a hidden assumption that the individual not only listens to rock music but has a favorite star. The following are additional examples. Can you explain the hidden assumptions in each?

INCORRECT	CORRECT
1. How many new accounts did you get this month?	1. Did you get any new accounts this month? (If yes) How many?
2. Which is your favorite personal computer?	2. Are you knowledgeable about personal computers? (If yes) If you have a favorite, what is it?
3. With your MBA, you know all about finance, right?	3. Did you study finance in your MBA program? (If yes) Do you feel it gave you skills you can use on the job?
4. When did you decide to stop discussing your problems with your supervisor?	4. Do you discuss your problems with your supervisor? (If not) Why?

Each incorrect question shows that the interviewer has made certain assumptions about the interviewee before the conversation even begins.

Another dangerous type of assumption is that the interviewee possesses more information about something than he or she really does. Experiments have shown that rather than admit ignorance, most people simply reply as if they do possess the expertise. Emory reports a survey in which the interviewees were asked, "Which of the following statements most closely coincides with your opinion of the Metallic Metals Act?"[2] The answers are as follows:

1. It would be a good move on the part of the United States.	15%
2. It would be a good thing but should be left to the individual states.	41
3. It is all right for foreign countries but should not be required here.	11
4. It is of no value at all.	3
5. Have no opinion.	30

In reality, there is no such act!

A simple way to avoid this problem is to use a lead-in question asking the person what he or she knows about the subject. This gives the interviewer a chance to assess the interviewee's knowledge of the matter.

Remember that experts have found that

> In situations where the interviewer has more status than an interviewee, such as in a selection, performance, counseling, or diagnostic interview, respondents will very often distort or omit information because they are afraid to say, "I don't know," "I don't remember," or "I'm not sure." They don't want to appear unintelligent or uncooperative.[3]

CONFUSING LANGUAGE Questioning is a precise art. A single word can considerably alter the intended meaning of a question. For example, notice the different meanings among the following sentences.

1. What changes *should* be made in our pension plan?

2. What changes *could* be made in our pension plan?

3. What changes *will* be made in our pension plan?

4. What changes *have been* made in our pension plan?

Each example asks a qualitatively different question. Number 1 requests the interviewee's advice about future changes; number 2 asks the interviewer to generate possible alternatives; number 3 seeks the interviewee's opinion about what is likely to happen in the future; and number 4 taps the interviewee's understanding of past changes.

SPECIFIC TYPES OF INTERVIEWS

Four of the most common types of interviews are the employment, performance appraisal, counseling, and discipline interviews.

Implications for Management

1. When conducting an interview, use both open and closed questions. Even if you are determined to keep the interview highly structured, allow the other party an opportunity for some self-expression.

2. Be aware of leading questions. They add bias to the responses you are going to get from the interviewee. Work hard to develop neutral questions that will cover the topics you want to discuss. In this way you will get feedback from the interviewee that is accurate and reflects this individual's point of view rather than yours.

3. If you are not accustomed to conducting interviews, write down the questions you want to ask and try them out on some of your peers. They should be able to help you spot hidden assumptions, confusing language, and other problems. After you have had some experiences, you will find yourself better able to phrase clear, unbiased questions. Stick with it; it takes some time to get it right!

The Employment Interview

Employment interviews are a part of a larger category of interviews called selection interviews. Employment interviews often take three different paths. The interview to select a person for a specific job is the most usual. The recruitment interview is the second most common. It occurs when a company knows whom it wants to hire and attempts through the interview to sell the person on the job. The third is the information interview. Here, the interviewee may be investigating potential job opportunities in the company or even gathering background data on a specific opening, but the actual application has not been made.[4]

Most employment interviews take place when applications for a job opening have been received. In these interviews employers learn a great deal about prospective job candidates and the candidates form lasting first impressions about the organization. Unfortunately, both sides can make costly mistakes in an employment interview. Employers can fail to motivate the outstanding applicant and end up choosing someone who will not fit well in the organization. Applicants can fail to sell themselves or ask the wrong questions, thus forming an erroneous impression.

What then should the effective employment interview hope to accomplish? There are several major benefits. First, the personal interview allows the employer the opportunity to assess interpersonal skills, the ability to think on one's feet, and the overall communication skills of the applicant. Second, the selection interview allows the employer to ask about incomplete data on the resume and to request more information when needed. Third, the interview allows the interviewee to find out more about the job and the company, at which point both parties are better able to judge if a "match" is possible.

Benefits of selection interviews

Downs and colleagues have suggested four standard purposes of the employment interview.[5]

1. *To initiate personal contact with the applicant.* A critical part of any interview,

especially if it is being done by the supervisor for whom the individual will work, is to see how the employee gets along with the applicant.

Purpose of
employment
interviews

2. *To give an orientation to the specific job and company.* Applicants often know relatively little about the job for which they are applying and the interview provides the first opportunity to provide these data.

3. *To maintain an adequate workforce.* Depending on the level of the job and the quantity of applicants available, an interview may be a sure first step to ensuring an adequate organizational personnel force.

4. *To gather information about the candidate that will enable the interviewer to predict successful performance.* This is, of course, the main purpose of the interview and requires considerable forecasting abilities on the part of the interviewer. Fortunately as with many other things, selection interviewing becomes easier with practice.

CARRYING OUT THE INTERVIEW   Interviewers must plan the interview, conduct it, and evaluate the results. The following examines each phase.

PLANNING   Planning the interview requires that the manager (1) identify and define the skills and knowledge required to do the job well, (2) develop questions that will assess the candidate's ability to perform the job successfully, and (3) develop a list of things to look for when people respond to those key questions.[6]

Long gone are the days of hiring on the basis of a "gut feeling." Today interviewers must know what they are looking for. Three of the most general criteria are

- *Appropriate education.* Does the applicant have the formal training for the position?

Common selection
criteria

- *Appropriate experience.* Has the applicant had related on-the-job experience that should serve to make him or her successful in this position?

- *Personality.* Although harder to measure, does the interviewee have the poise and ability to successfully carry out the demands of the position?

Once the criteria are defined, the interviewer should become prepared in two ways. First, he or she should have sufficient knowledge about the job vacancy. This knowledge will be useful in evaluating the candidate and allow the interviewer more fully to answer applicant questions.

Second, the interviewer should carefully review the applicant's file. Familiarity with these documents prior to meeting the individual allows the interviewer to ask relevant questions and make better use of the interview time.

INTERVIEWING   Five distinct steps are observable in the interview process. Each is described below.

1. *Establish rapport.* The initial introductions are usually followed by a short period of small talk to put the applicant at ease. Questions such as "Would you like some coffee?" or "Did you have any trouble finding us?" are typical ones.

2. *Employ general questioning.* The rapport phase is usually followed by broad questions such as "How did you find out about our company?" or "Tell me about yourself." Note the use of open-ended questions. During this phase too many interviewers end up doing the majority of the talking instead of vice versa. An effective interviewer focuses the conversation on particular areas to be covered and allows the interviewee to address them in his or her own way. Areas that are commonly covered include:

Common interview areas

   a. Education and training
   b. Past experience
   c. Current and future personal goals
   d. Expectations about the current job
   e. Knowledge of the company
   f. Knowledge of the field
   g. Ability to communicate
   h. Ability to work with others
   i. Interest in the job

The importance of careful questioning has increased in recent years as more and more employment questions have been banned as prejudicial and/or illegal. Although it is not our intention here to go into all the legislation covering employment practices, readers should be warned that any questions that can be construed as discriminatory are strictly forbidden. For a quick assessment of how much you know about what can and cannot be asked, take Self-Assessment Quiz 13.2.

Legislation and public concern have also limited the use of the polygraph in employment interviews. See "Ethics in Communication: But How Will We Know If the Person Is Lying?"

3. *Ask specific questions.* Questions generally proceed from the general to the specific, allowing the interviewer to probe more deeply into areas of interest. Examples include, "Tell me about your favorite work experience to date" and "What would you say are your main strengths and weaknesses on the job?"

4. *Invite questions from the applicant.* At this point, the interviewer should invite questions from the applicant. Too often this phase is rushed because the interviewer has already had his or her say. However, effective interviewers try to answer applicant questions as completely and honestly as possible. They realize that the interviewee's assessment of a potential match is just as important as theirs.

5. *Take time to recap and close.* During the summing up period, the interviewer should tell the applicant what to expect next. For example, when can the applicant expect to hear from the company? The interviewer should also find out if the applicant is still interested in being considered for the job.

EVALUATING As soon as possible after the meeting, the interviewer should write down his or her evaluation of the applicant. A checklist is commonly prepared in advance, and the applicant is rated against these previously determined criteria. In addition, comments should be written regarding the interviewer's overall impression of the individual.

SELF-ASSESSMENT QUIZ 13.2

Are These Legal Questions?

Directions: Indicate an I (illegal) or an L (legal) for each of the following questions when used in an employment interview.

_____ 1. Are you pregnant?

_____ 2. Are you planning on getting married soon?

_____ 3. What was your major in college?

_____ 4. Have you ever been convicted of a crime?

_____ 5. How old are you?

_____ 6. Would you mind traveling one week a month?

_____ 7. Who takes care of your children while you work?

_____ 8. Why don't we discuss this over a drink? I'm sure we could have a nice time.

_____ 9. To what religion do you subscribe?

_____ 10. Which religious holidays do you expect to have off?

Answers are in the Answer section at the back of the book.

Part of this impression is derived not from what is said but from the applicant's nonverbal behavior. A study by Gifford, Ng, and Wilkinson found that interviewers judged the "social skill" of applicants by their dress, the length of time they talked, and the rate and type of gestures they used.[7]

Written evaluations are particularly important when interviewing more than three or four people. The strongest impressions grow hazy after talking to many people about the same topics.

The Performance Appraisal Interview

At one time or another, most managers are obliged to conduct a performance appraisal of their subordinates. In some organizations this evaluation is done annually or semiannually; in others, it is conducted only after the manager realizes no formal evaluations have taken place in a long time. The latter often occurs in conjunction with a crisis such as a supervisor trying to build a case to terminate someone, only to find out that no past incidents have been documented.

Performance appraisal skills are a fundamental part of the effective manager's repertoire. Routine, conscientious performance evaluations can provide the following benefits to the company.

But How Will We Know If the Person Is Lying?

Interviewing can be a tough job. There are a lot of questions the interviewer would like to ask but cannot because federal law prohibits it. In the past, some companies were not too upset about these limitations because they used to supplement their interview procedures with a mandatory polygraph (lie detector) test. This test would be used to screen out those individuals who were judged to be untrustworthy. For example, banks would use the test to determine whether the job applicant was prone to stealing. One of the favorite questions of the polygrapher was, "If you thought you would not be caught, would you steal $1 million from this bank." Most people would answer no, and they would be lying. This did not upset the operator because the reason for the question was to get a reading regarding how the individual acts when he or she is lying. Overall, the polygraph machine was used to construct a profile of the person's honesty.

In recent years, however, the polygraph has been outlawed except in specific cases. The major reason for this action is that critics have been able to prove that the machine (or the polygraph operator) is not able to discern between those who are telling the truth and those who are lying. So what does the machine really measure? Critics claim it measures how nervous an individual is, and, at best, it scares people into giving honest replies.

Recent federal legislation now bans the use of polygraph tests by private employers in screening job applicants in most industries. (Security and pharmaceuticals are still allowed to use them as are law enforcement groups and some other governmental agencies.) The law also prohibits an employee from being dismissed, disciplined, discriminated against, or denied employment or promotion solely on the basis of the test. However, some employers are allowed to use them in cases of theft or loss when they have a reasonable suspicion regarding an employee. Banks are a good example. If money has been stolen and the bank believes it was taken by one of four people, it can require them to take a polygraph or lose their job and become robbery suspects.

Overall, however, use of the polygraph is declining sharply. Over the next five years it is estimated that the number of polygraph tests will shrink dramatically, and many polygraphers are now turning to alternative sources of employment: background checks, pen-and-pencil honesty tests, and preemployment interviewing. Many personnel experts see this as a positive move because these forms of testing have been found to be more reliable than the polygraph.

SOURCE: Some of the information in this story can be found in Jane Wooldridge, "Polygraphers Find Little to Celebrate," *Miami Herald*, August 19, 1988, p. 2C.

Benefits of appraisal interviews

1. A unique communication setting promoting open exchanges between supervisor and employee.

2. A historical record of both good and bad employee performance.

3. A formal checkpoint at which time goal attainment can be evaluated, old goals assessed, and new goals formulated.

4. Feedback to subordinates regarding how they are doing and what they can reasonably expect from the company in the future.

5. A setting for discussing problems that are not broached in the normal daily course of events.

6. An opportunity for management to determine the training needs and interests of employees, thus promoting maximum employee development.

7. A basis for current and future decisions regarding salary, promotion, transfers, and terminations.

Despite these benefits, a number of recurrent complaints about performance appraisal arise. Most of these are the result of ineffective interviewing, not the appraisal procedure per se. Some frequent objections follow.

Implications for Management

1. Take interviews seriously! Employment interviews can result in costly mistakes if not handled properly. Investing the proper amount of time and effort now can save you countless problems in the future.

2. Plan the interview carefully. Understand the job thoroughly and know the criteria necessary for doing the job effectively.

3. Don't do all the talking. Start with broadly based questions. Then move to specific, but open, questions to get the applicant talking about himself or herself. Then use your active listening skills and pay attention!

4. Be aware of the legal constraints of the interviewing process. Ignorance of the law is no defense.

5. Immediately after the interview, record your impressions. This will give you a basis for making your comparison and deciding on a course of action.

Complaints about appraisal interviews

1. The evaluation procedure is too subjective and not anchored to any concrete data.

2. Evaluations generate defensiveness among employees and aggressiveness among interviewers.

3. Managers tend to take the easy way out and lump everyone together as being "good" and do not really discriminate among employees as to effectiveness.

The last of these is very typical. Downs and associates have offered the following example:

A manager recently complained to us that he was required by his own company to distribute the ratings of his subordinates according to a bell-shaped curve with 50 percent being rated less than average. The evaluation system did not take into account that the company ought to be choosing capable people through its selection procedures and, therefore, the normal bell-shaped curve should not apply.[8]

Certain communication blunders also make the appraisal interview much less effective than it would otherwise be. Olson has suggested 30 communication "traps" that can be seen at performance appraisal interviews. Here are five examples.[9]

1. *"Off-the-cuff delivery."* Example: "I know there's an appraisal form around here someplace. I saw it on my desk a couple of weeks ago. Well now, we'll just have to proceed without it." (This approach almost guarantees that important areas will be forgotten, and it makes the employee think that the interview is not very important.)

2. *"The surprise party."* Example: "Adams, I've been keeping book on you for the last six months. I have a list here a mile long I want to go over with you. Do you remember back in June when . . . " (This method of dumping on employees immediately puts them on the defensive.)

3. *"The Deaf Ear."* Example: "Sure, sure, whatever you think. Excuse me, I've gotta take this important call." (The employee in this case will know that he or she is not very important to you.)

4. *"The Inquisition."* Example: "Why's your scrappage up $\frac{1}{10}$ of 1 percent? Why did you let that grievance get out of hand? Why aren't you motivating your employees? How come your absenteeism rate is the highest in the division? " (No employee can possibly answer all these accusations.)

5. *"Name-Calling."* Example: "Elizabeth, why are you so unlikeable? " (Like "the surprise party," this puts the employee on the defensive.)

CONDUCTING THE INTERVIEW Three methods of communicating the employee appraisal are (1) tell and sell, (2) tell and listen, and (3) mutual problem solving.

Tell and Sell In this interview, the manager does all the talking. He or she begins by telling the employee about the latest performance evaluation and then proceeds to sell him or her on the necessary course of action to continue progress and/or correct deficiencies. The interviewer must use considerable powers of persuasion if this technique is to be effective. Maier describes the objectives of this technique as: (1) let the employee know how he or she is doing; (2) gain the employee's acceptance of the evaluation; and (3) get the employee to follow the plan outlined for his or her improvement.[10]

Sometimes the manager does all of the talking.

Throughout the interview the employee has little opportunity to respond. The individual must grin and bear it, thereby reassuring the supervisor that he or she both understands what is being said and is able to do it. The benefits of this interview approach are necessarily limited by the employee's lack of participation and the supervisor's narrowness of perspective.

Tell and Listen   This type of interview has two distinct segments. First, the manager tells the employee about his or her evaluation without allowing questions or pausing for comments. Then the manager sits back and listens to the reactions of the individual. The subordinate is encouraged to express his or her feelings about the process. The objective of the listening segment is to provide a cathartic release from the tension of the interview. Employees ideally leave this type of meeting feeling good about themselves and their supervisors, and the manager hopefully makes use of newfound knowledge about the employee's needs and goals.

Other times the manager talks and then lets the subordinate talk.

Mutual Problem-Solving Approach   In this method, the interviewer completely shares power and authority in regard to diagnosing problems and planning for the interviewee's future. This is an ideal approach when employee development is the primary purpose of the interview. Like the tell and listen method, the mutual problem-solving approach offers the interviewer an opportunity to learn, since it stimulates upward communication. The interview also creates a climate for high-quality decision.

In mutual problem solving, both parties share information.

Regardless of the approach used, the interviewer should follow certain guidelines for communicating the performance appraisal. Seven of these are:

- Review what you are going to say at the interview and be sure to include good points and bad points relative to the employee's performance.

- Praise the employee wherever it is deserved. This is a powerful motivator to most employees.

- Express empathy whenever you can. Trying to see the employee's problems and point of view fosters understanding between supervisor and subordinate.

- When you are criticizing performance, try to find the reason for the problem.

- Strive to be objective and concentrate on job performance and not personality.

- End the interview with specific plans for improving future performance or correcting deficiencies.

- Throughout the process, be sure that the employee clearly understands his or her job and responsibilities.[11]

The Counseling Interview

Many managers find themselves unexpectedly required to assume the role of counselor, usually for their direct employees. Often the manager initiates the counseling session because of a problem that needs attention. Other times, an employee will simply walk into the manager's office to discuss a problem. The uncomfortable aspect of counseling interviews is that they usually involve highly personal, and often emotional, matters. Family problems, health, drinking, and drugs are typical topics during such meetings.

**Implications
for
Management**

1. Do not procrastinate. Conduct appraisal interviews regularly and conscientiously. The time and effort they take will be well repaid.

2. Whenever possible use the mutual problem-solving approach in order to maximize employee motivation as well as problem-solving potential.

3. Employ active listening skills and neutral probing when engaging in the performance appraisals. Be open to the wealth of information on attitudes and feelings that this approach can provide.

NATURE OF COUNSELING Counseling has been described as a helping relationship. It uses a positive approach. The positive underlying assumptions of counseling have been defined by Downs and associates as follows.[12]

1. People can grow; they can improve. Without this belief all counseling would be worthless. Interviewers must believe in the worth of the individual and in that person's ability to do better.

2. Counseling is an investment in the individual. This tells the interviewee that the interviewer thinks he or she is worth the time and effort being invested. The interviewer, on the other hand, sees this energy output as an investment with a future payoff for both parties.

Positive
assumptions
underlying
counseling

3. Counseling is a learning process. This basic belief underlies the qualitative difference between imposed change and change brought about by the interviewee because of an inner understanding that certain behaviors are antiproductive and should be corrected. This type of change is much more lasting than mandated change.

4. Counseling can involve confrontation. As part of the growing process, problems, complaints and/or concerns must be brought out in the open. Because counseling involves change and change inevitably leads to stress, some confrontation is bound to occur and is, in fact, healthy.

5. Acceptance of an individual as he or she is provides a good beginning for counseling. Effective counseling involves accepting the interviewee as a worthy human being at a particular stage of development. This can be more of a problem for the interviewee if he or she has a low self-image caused by the problem he or she is confronting.

6. Counseling is a continuous process that is likely to take more than one session. Managers often become frustrated over the slow progress made in a counseling interview. One session is rarely enough to solve any problem, although it might provide some initial insight.

7. The effectiveness of counseling varies with goals, but it generally is determined by some kind of change taking place.[13]

Of course, the big question is, how effective has the interview been? Mahler has suggested several outcomes that point toward counseling effectiveness. First, the subordinate must recognize that a behavioral change is needed. Next, both the executive and the subordinate should share in a deliberate effort to get a behavior change. Third, the deliberate effort should result in a resolution of the problem. The resolution may be a behavior change, or it may be resolved by the subordinate leaving his or her position. Finally, the subordinate should respect the supervisor for imposing standards and for endeavoring to be helpful.[14]

CONDUCTING AN EFFECTIVE SESSION An effective counseling session has five stages (see Table 13.2).

Stage one consists of the first critical minutes of the meeting during which interviewer and interviewee size up each other, establish a climate of trust, and develop a rapport.

Says one expert,

> The point to be made in the opening is that the climate will be informal, permissive, accepting, and nonevaluative. You want to give the interviewee the impression that you can be trusted, are approachable, and can maintain confidentiality . . . Your clothing should be as similar as possible to the respondent's. More important, however, is the way in which you interact and behave. You must be empathetic, neutral, objective, and conversational.[15]

If the proper climate is not established, the rest of the session is likely to be nonproductive. Think of your initial reactions when you have gone to a doctor, a teacher, or a friend for help. If the "feeling" was not right, you probably never brought up your problem. This first stage then is largely affective, although some cognitive logistical consideration may be considered such as time available for the meeting.

Stage two involves actual confrontation of the problem. Here the interviewee gives an overall explanation of the problem. It may be generalized and tentative, as the interviewee has not yet seen how the interviewer will react to the actual problem. This is

There are five stages to effective counseling.

Table 13.2

STAGES OF THE COUNSELING INTERVIEW

Activity	Focus
1. Establishing rapport	Affective
2. Confronting the problem	Cognitive
3. Investigating the problem	Cognitive and affective
4. Problem solving	Cognitive
5. Developing a plan of action	Cognitive

mainly a cognitive stage as the interviewee has yet to go deeply into the problem and confront the emotional issues.

This is done in stage three, which is both a cognitive and an affective discussion of the whole problem. The danger is that many counseling sessions never get to this stage because the manager/interviewer hears the abbreviated version in stage two and fails to encourage the interviewee to take a deeper look. The interviewer decides, instead, to deal with the problem as originally stated — often leaving the interviewee frustrated. Stage three is the critical point at which the interviewer uses his or her best listening and neutral probing skills to get the interviewee to completely investigate the problem. This often uncovers deep emotions about the problem and engenders insights on the part of both parties.

> Unlike other interview types where the ratio of interviewee to interviewer talk is approximately 70/30, in a counseling interview you should be attending to the client from 90 to 95 percent of the time and only talking 5 to 10 percent of the time. One key to being a good listener is to practice good attending behaviors.[16]

When this has been accomplished, stage four commences. Stage four is the problem-solving stage. Since the problem has been fully explored, alternative actions can now be considered. This is a predominantly cognitive stage with the interviewee taking the lead in looking for answers. The interviewer guides the client through a careful consideration of each alternative, weighing the probable pros and cons until a tentative solution has been reached.

Interviewers should be cautious not to be directive and give the interviewee the answer wanted. Advice given by the interviewer to solve the problem may mean that the solution is not "owned" by the interviewee and will not be as effective as if the interviewee had generated his or her own solution.[17]

Finally, in the fifth stage, the solution is made operational by the interviewer helping the interviewee establish a plan of action. The interviewee must realize that one cannot attain anything without first planning out the necessary activities and then accomplishing them one by one. In closing, the interviewer should again reassure the interviewer of his or her continuing interest. A followup meeting may then be scheduled.

One word of caution. Do not be surprised if the five stages mentioned above do not occur in one meeting. This will only be possible for the simplest problems. More complex issues often require multiple meetings before the fifth stage can be reached.

The Discipline Interview

Communication texts are noticeably silent on the subject of discipline. Yet part of every manager's job is that of maintaining control by monitoring policies and procedures and correcting deviations, especially if the deviations are detrimental to the goals of the organization.

Discipline is any corrective action taken by a manager because personnel actions or behaviors have not been in keeping with organizational norms. These actions can further be broken down into disciplinary problems and disciplinary actions.

A disciplinary problem is brought about by an employee who is not behaving or performing up to standard. Although we often refer to specific people as "disciplinary

Implications for Management

1. Keep in mind the importance of effective employee counseling and be willing to commit the necessary time and energy demanded by such counseling.

2. Effective, empathic counseling of employees can greatly increase the employee's feeling of worth to the organization and, therefore, their commitment to the organization. Use counseling for the benefit of both groups.

3. Counsel carefully. Practice active listening and neutral probes. Help the employee solve his or her own problem. Don't "give" them the answers.

4. Remember that a feeling of rapport and trust is central to the counseling relationship. It can make or break your efforts.

5. When counseling, be sure to complete all five stages: building rapport, confronting the problem, investigating the problem, problem solving, and developing a plan of action. Each is important.

---

problems," that is a gross inaccuracy. The specific behavior should not be equated with the employee as a person. This equation adds up to a negative mindset by the manager and a very slim chance that the "disciplinary action" will work. The disciplinary action, which can vary widely, involves the steps taken to correct the problem. This can range from a mere talk with the supervisor to suspension or termination from the job.

TYPES OF DISCIPLINE PROBLEMS Although many types of discipline problems may develop, the following five are among the most common categories.

1. *Insubordination.* In this case the employee is rude to the supervisor or just refuses to do as he or she is told. (The manager must be careful not to equate inability to do something with unwillingness to do it.)

2. *Tardiness.* Some employees do not get to work on time no matter how hard they seem to try. When other employees start commenting about it, it is past time for the manager to act. Hopefully, the manager has been setting a good example by personally being on time.

Here are some common discipline problems.

3. *Excessive absenteeism.* Legitimate absenteeism is to be expected. Absenteeism as a disciplinary problem results when unexcused absences are involved.

4. *Failure to follow procedures or regulations.* This category of disciplinary problems is the most common. It includes everything from taking excessively long lunch hours to ignoring safety regulations. If these incidents are overlooked at first, they can become habitual behavior. When the manager finally speaks up, the employee is often indignant because he or she has been doing it for so long that it seems to be acceptable behavior.

5. *Other unacceptable behaviors.* This catch-all category includes such difficult problems as the alcoholic employee or the male employee who sexually harasses females. These problems are not strictly work related, but they do have serious consequences for the organization.

REASONS FOR DISCIPLINE PROBLEMS Although disciplinary problems may stem from many sources, three broad categories should be recognized: (1) poor organizational communication, (2) employees who do not feel they are an important part of the organization, and (3) general personality/psychological problems. The third is often well beyond the ability of the average manager, but the first two warrant discussion.

Poor organizational communication is responsible for many of the disciplinary problems surrounding failure to follow procedures or regulations. In some cases, employees honestly do not understand the essence of the policy or for some reason do not think it relates to them. Either condition indicates a failure of the organization to communicate its policies and procedures effectively. Merely handing a new employee a procedures manual is not enough. The average manual is voluminous, poorly written, confusing, and boring. Few employees consult it unless they have a specific problem. They certainly do not sit down and study it from cover to cover. The lack of effective communication also convinces the employee that regulations and procedures are not all that important; after all, "rules are made to be broken."

The second category, employees who do not feel they are a valuable part of the organization, manifests itself through negative comments about the enterprise or management and a general "we-they" approach. When employees do not feel appreciated, they have weakened loyalty to the organization. Sometimes they delight in taking advantage of the system, never doing anything more than what is absolutely necessary, occasionally reaching the point of outright stealing or sabotage.

PREVENTING DISCIPLINE PROBLEMS Clearly the best policy in handling discipline problems is to prevent them from occurring. Preston has suggested the following concrete steps for preventive discipline:

- Every employee should be given a well-structured job, with clear responsibilities.

- Employees should be given continuous feedback about their progress and should be told *in advance* about any changes in their jobs that will directly affect them.

- Each individual employee should be encouraged to "get involved" with his or her fellow employees and be given opportunities for participation in programs of professional training and personal growth.

- Bosses should set a good example, as much employee behavior (and mischief) is a reflection of the superior's example.

These are some steps for preventing discipline problems.

- Superiors should establish and maintain a "helping" relationship with employees who are facing problems.

- Superiors should avoid becoming overworked and preoccupied with administrative tasks. This causes them to miss out on their best communication tool: simple observation. Much information can be gained about individual employees by observing their work habits and their interactions with other employees. Such observations can be the first clue to potential problems. The faster these can be spotted, the sooner steps can be taken to prevent possible disruptions and discipline problems.

■ Managers should hold periodic conferences with all employees to be sure they are mastering their jobs and to determine whether they feel satisfied with their work environment. If the manager has created a proper helping relationship, employees will be more likely to express their true feelings about their jobs. Managers also have an obligation to give their employees prompt feedback about their performance, both satisfactory and unsatisfactory.[18]

CONDUCTING THE DISCIPLINE INTERVIEW If preventive measures do not work, disciplinary steps are in order. Some of the most useful guidelines in conducting a discipline interview are the following:

1. Make instructions simple and understandable.

2. Know the rules.

3. Move in promptly on violations.

4. Get all the facts.

5. Permit the employee an opportunity to explain.

6. Decide what action to take.

7. Implement disciplinary action.

8. Keep a record of what has happened.

In implementing these steps, the interviewer should keep these guidelines in mind:

1. Be certain to have all the relevant facts and documentation. Be certain you are not operating on assumptions or jumping to conclusions.

2. Be sure to hold the discipline interview in private. Nobody likes to be chastised in public!

3. Be sure you are in an appropriate frame of mine. Be sure you are not allowing personal feelings of liking or disliking to influence how you appraise the need for discipline.

Here are useful discipline guidelines.

4. Plan to listen to what the employee has to say, but be firm and carry through with whatever action is warranted. "Reprimands, criticism, punishment, and dismissal hurt both you and the employee, but neglecting this duty will only cause problems for both of you in the future."[19]

5. Be calm! Discipline interviews are emotional incidents for both parties. If you lose your temper, hope for an effective remedy fades quickly. Don't be surprised,

however, if the employee reacts emotionally. Remember that any one party to an argument can stop it by simply deciding not to argue!

6. Be future oriented. Mutually discuss how this problem can be avoided in the future.

WHAT ABOUT TERMINATION? In serious cases such as stealing from the company or repeated disciplinary problems, it may become necessary to terminate the employee. These interviews are always unpleasant and emotional because it is a direct attack on the employee's ego. The following steps are suggested for the termination interview. First, be sure you have all the facts and that termination is inevitable. Then, come straight to the point. There is no easy way to say "you're fired." A lengthy discussion of old data does little good if the decision has been made. Third, go over housekeeping details. When will the final paycheck be available? Do you want the employee to leave immediately? (This is highly recommended.) How long will the employee's insurance coverage, and so on, be in effect? Finally, if possible, offer what help you can. If it will be possible for you to write honest letters of recommendation, for example, explain this to the employee.

Implications for Management

1. Gather your facts. Be sure you know what you're talking about.

2. Chastise in private and hear the employee out.

3. Be future oriented and try to solve the problem jointly with the employee.

4. Remain calm and professional during discipline interviews and terminations.

5. Remember to set a good example. Employees look to their supervisors as role models. Don't expect them to be in at 8 A.M. every day if you wander in at 8:15 A.M.

6. When terminating an employee, make it short and clean. Arrange for the person to leave immediately.

7. Keep careful records of all discipline interviews in case of a future grievance.

A word of caution is in order here. Frequently, terminated employees sue the company for being fired unjustly. Employers have a responsibility to act in good faith with employees and to terminate someone only "for just cause." The notion of "just cause" implies all the following.

1. The reason for termination is job related.

2. The employee is aware that the behavior displayed can lead to termination.

3. The investigation that ensued was fair and impartial.

4. Evidence is substantial and clear that the employee both knew the rules and failed to abide by them.

5. Similar problems with other employees have led to termination or would lead to termination if they occurred.[20]

C A S E   I N   P O I N T

Revisited

Having read the chapter, you should now realize that Adam made a number of mistakes. Although you may not have them in this order, you should have noted the following: using leading questions (notice how he asked Tim certain things in the form of a question such as, "You know auditing, don't you?" and "You don't mind traveling, do you?") In addition, notice how the interview just seemed to move from point to point as Adam attempted to direct it. In truth, he is being too directive. Look again at Tim's answers and notice how he has trouble getting in a word. Finally, notice how Adam used either closed questions or open questions followed by an immediate response to Tim's comment. In short, Tim has little opportunity to say much during the interview. Look over the conversation again and note the amount of control Adam exercises. No wonder the company manager has decided to send back the regular interviewer. Quite obviously, effective interviewing involves more than just letting conversation flow.

YOU BE THE CONSULTANT

Be Prepared

Performance appraisals at Whitcomb, Inc. used to be times of anxiety and nervousness. About five years ago all of that started to change. Average performance appraisals began improving. Individuals who were accustomed to receiving "average" ratings began to get "good" scores; those who were receiving "good" scores found themselves getting "excellent" ratings. The trend continued until approximately six months ago. At this point one of the employees was given an unsatisfactory evaluation by his supervisor. The supervisor explained that although she was new in the firm, she had ten years of experience in the business and knew unsatisfactory work when she saw it. The employee countered by pointing out that for the last two years he had received good or excellent reviews from the previous supervisor. Nevertheless, the supervisor recommended that this employee be terminated, and the company agreed. The individual countered by demanding that an impartial judge hear the grievance. A referee, as called for in the union contract, heard both sides and ruled that Whitcomb was wrong in letting the man go. The company was forced to reinstate him with back pay. The result so angered the president that he ordered a complete review of the company's performance evaluation procedures.

It turns out that 95 percent of all evaluations made by the supervisors at Whitcomb over the last two years have fallen into the "good" or "excellent" category. Upon learning of this, the president remarked, "We cannot have a 95 percent rate of good/excellent employees. Most of our people are hard working average personnel. This performance evaluation inflation has to stop. From now on we are going back to bell-shaped performance. I expect to find most people being rated average, while a much smaller percentage fall into the good or superior range and an approximately equal percentage fall into the poor or unsatisfactory range. I also want to see the best workers get the rewards to which they are entitled while the poorest are let go and we don't have to worry about lawsuits as a result of our decisions."

The president's decision was implemented within a week. The firm opted for the paired comparison method, thereby ensuring that only one person in each unit could receive the highest rating. In order to ensure that there were no foul-ups, each supervisor was encouraged to keep a close watch on productivity and personnel actions. If someone did something that was extremely good or bad, this was noted so that it could be reflected on the performance appraisal. If someone was late for work or tardy, this too was noted. At the end of 90 days the company was ready to conduct its first performance appraisal using the new system. Many of the supervisors were concerned that things would not go well. They worried that most workers would feel they were being poorly treated. As one of the supervisors put it, "It's going to be tough for many of these guys. They are accustomed to receiving excellent or good evaluations. Now only a small number are going to get these. Most are going to have to settle for average. And I shudder to think about those who will receive poor or unsatisfactory ratings. They are probably going to scream the loudest."

Nevertheless, management had made the decision and intended to stick to it. However, it also realized that many supervisors would feel nervous or embarrassed about having to tell their personnel that they were not going to be getting the high ratings to which they had become accustomed. In order to help with this, management has decided to bring in a group of consultants both to advise the supervisors and to sit in on their performance evaluation sessions, listen to what they have to say, and suggest ways in which the managers could more effectively conduct their performance evaluation interviews.

Assume that you are one of the consultants who has been assigned to help the supervisors. What advice would you give them regarding how to conduct a performance appraisal interview? Pinpoint specific things you would recommend the supervisor do and/or refrain from doing. Be as helpful as possible in your recommendations.

Key Points in This Chapter

1. An interview is a deliberate, face-to-face communication session between an interviewer and an interviewee, which is focused on specific content and designed to achieve predetermined goals. The five key elements in an interview are deliberate-

ness, face-to-face interaction, an interviewer and an interviewee, specific content, and predetermined goals.

2. In structuring the interview, two alternatives are possible: directive and nondirective. In the directive approach the interviewer asks specific questions designed to keep the interviewee focused on providing the desired information. In the nondirective interview the interviewer does very little talking, allowing the interviewee to express his or her own feelings and thoughts in whatever direction they go.

3. Interviewer questions fall into two categories: open and closed. Open questions allow the responder to frame his or her own answer. Closed questions permit the interviewer to focus the exchange more narrowly, often ensuring that the desired data are obtained. In so doing the interviewer must be aware of such problems as leading questions, hidden assumptions, and confusing language.

4. Several different types of interviews may be conducted. One is the employment interview, used when selecting a person for a job. This interview offers a number of important benefits. However, the interview must be conducted properly, with time given to planning the interview, carrying it out, and then evaluating the results.

5. The performance appraisal interview is used to provide subordinates feedback on their performance and to offer suggestions for improvement and development. In conducting the actual interview, the three basic methods are tell and sell, tell and listen, and mutual problem solving.

6. The counseling interview is used to help subordinates deal with personal and/or emotional problems. The focus is on assisting the interviewee to cope with the particular difficulty under discussion. Attention was directed to the need to use natural probes in this process.

7. The discipline interview is used to address the need for corrective actions or behaviors. This process must be carefully handled. Suggestions were provided in the chapter, as were recommendations regarding what to do if termination of the employee is required.

Questions for Discussion and Analysis

1. There are five basic elements in the interview process. What does this statement mean? Explain, being sure to incorporate a description of all the elements into your answer.

2. How does a directive interview differ from a nondirective interview?

3. In an interview, what role can be played by open and closed questions? Explain.

4. In what way do leading questions and hidden assumptions detract from the value of interview information? Explain.

5. What is the purpose of an employment interview? What do managers need to know about conducting such an interview?

6. When would a manager use a performance appraisal interview? What are its benefits? What does the individual need to know regarding how to conduct one? Be specific in your answers.

7. When is a counseling interview in order? What does a manager need to know about conducting an effective counseling session? Explain.

8. When is a discipline interview in order? What does a manager need to know about conducting an effective discipline interview? Explain.

Exercises

1. In groups of three, role play the following situations with first one person doing a direct interview and then another doing a nondirect interview on the same subject. A third person should observe the two methods and provide commentary on the relative pros and cons of each as used in each scenario.
   Situations:
   a. Judy Meadows has just stepped into your office and asked to see you. You remember that you need to talk to her about her excessive absences.
   b. Rudy Sarton has applied for a transfer to your department. You know Rudy has an excellent reputation as an electronic technician in the production department. You are not sure why he wants the current job of research specialist in the R & D lab except that it would mean more money. Rudy arrives to see you about the job.
   c. Jean Newsome stops you in the hall to tell you how much difficulty she is having with her new clerk, Sandra Mitchell. It seems Sandra cannot get along with the other clerks and what was formerly a happy work environment has deteriorated greatly.
   d. Rick James has just taken a seat in your office. You called him in to discuss his declining sales record over the last six months.

2. Observe your favorite interviewer on television. This may be a TV talk show host or a newsperson. Carefully analyze a specific interview this person conducts. Does he or she use direct or nondirect interviewing? Open or closed questions? Leading or neutral questions? What techniques make this person effective?

3. In groups of three, have one person assume the role of interviewer and one of interviewee while the third person acts as an observer. Pick a topic of current interest such as a news item. The interviewer should use open questions to gather the opinions of the interviewes on the subject. Next, roles are switched and the new interviewer uses closed questions to achieve the same purpose. Discuss how much information was transmitted in each case and what kind of information it was. Which technique worked best? Why?

References

1. William C. Donaghy, *The Interview: Skills and Applications* (Dallas, Tex.: Scott, Foresman, 1984), p. 5.

2. Sam Gill, "How Do You Stand on Sin? " *Tide*, March 14, 1947, p. 72. As reported in C. William Emory, *Business Research Methods* (Homewood, Ill.: Richard D. Irwin, 1980), p. 225.

3. Donaghy, *op. cit.*, p. 110.

4. Michael E. Stano and N. L. Reinsch, Jr., *Communication in Interviews* (Englewood Cliffs, N.J.: Prentice-Hall, 1982), p. 121.

5. Cal W. Downs, G. Paul Smeyak, and Ernest Martin, *Professional Interviewing* (New York: Harper & Row, 1980), pp. 112–113.

6. Barry M. Farrell, "The Art and Science of Employment Interviews," *Personnel Journal*, Vol. 65, No. 5, May 1986, pp. 91–94.

7. Robert Gifford, Cheuk Fan Ng, and Margaret Wilkinson, "Nonverbal Cues in the Employment Interview: Links Between Applicant Qualities and Interviewer Judgments," *Journal of Applied Psychology*, Vol. 70, No. 4, November 1985, pp. 729–736.

8. Downs, et al., *op. cit.* p. 161

9. Richard Fischer Olson, *Performance Appraisal: A Guide to Greater Productivity* (New York: John Wiley & Sons, 1981), p. 129.

10. Norman R. F. Maier, *The Appraisal Interview: Objectives, Methods and Skills* (New York: John Wiley & Sons, 1958), p. 4.

11. D. Keith Denton, "How to Conduct Effective Appraisal Interviews," *Administrative Management*, Vol. 48, No. 2, February 1987, pp. 15–17.

12. Downs et al., *op. cit.* pp. 190–192.

13. *Ibid.*

14. Walter R. Mahler, *How Effective Executives Interview* (Homewood, Ill.: Richard D. Irwin, 1976), p. 4.

15. Donaghy, *op. cit.*, p. 291.

16. *Ibid.*, p. 294.

17. Philip C. Wright, "Counseling and Coaching: Twin Avenues for On-the-Job Employee Development," *Canadian Manager*, Vol. 11, No. 4, December 1986, pp. 8–10.

18. Paul Preston, *Communication for Managers*, Englewood Cliffs, N.J.: Prentice-Hall, 1979, pp. 231–232.

When meetings are being planned, it is important to have a ballpark figure as to what they will cost.

All meetings have ten common characteristics.

- **Time frame.** Although the time allotted for meetings often varies, most have predetermined time frames, for example, 9–11 A.M. These should be clearly delineated in the preliminary planning stages.

- **Advance preparation.** Most meetings require some advance preparation. The room has to be reserved, refreshments must be ordered, equipment requested, and so on. This takes time, but a well-prepared meeting is often a productive one.

- **Program and agenda.** All meetings have some type of plan, although some are more formal than others. A program of events or agenda, shared in advance of the meeting, can help focus the program.

- **Start, middle, finish.** All meetings have three phases. The content part of the meeting, or the middle, is usually planned in advance. Unfortunately, little thought is often given to the start or the conclusion. However, when these two phases are properly orchestrated, participant satisfaction and meeting productivity can be greatly increased.

- **Followup.** Most meetings require some followup whether it be in the form of minutes, plans for another meeting, decisions to be implemented, or actions to be taken. If the followup is not apparent, participants tend to feel their time has been wasted.[2]

Myths About Meetings

The popular myths about meetings need to be debunked because of the negative effect they can have on the way meetings are conducted.[3]

Myth 1: The Leader is Totally Responsible for the Success of the Meeting   It is undeniable that good leadership is an important part of a successful meeting. However, if total responsibility is left to the leader, he or she might as well make the decision or take the required action without benefit of the group. In actuality, both the leader and the participants should share responsibility for the success of the meeting.

Myth 2: The Leader Needs to Have Tight Control   Tight control helps keep the meeting focused on agenda items. However, it often impedes a free-flowing exchange of ideas and spontaneity of conversation: Typically, a very controlling leader will ask each member to give his or her report on the subject and not allow any one else to interrupt. The result has been described this way:

> A bizarre kind of human interaction results: People don't talk to each other directly — they talk to each other through the leader. Watching this go on is like watching a quarterback throw a pass to the split end while keeping his eyes fixed on the coach. The ball is often heaved the wrong way, even into the arms of an opponent. An often unnoticed side-effect is that all conversation is filtered through the biases and fears of the leader as, smiling brightly, he blunts or expands upon, modifies or blocks each input. "Well, I'm sure we'll all agree, John, that your point of view is highly unlikely." We will never know whether we agree,

because John's perspective will never be checked with the group. After effectively blocking John's idea, the leader, still smiling brightly, moves on: "Now, then. Who's next?"[4]

Myth 3: Group Participation is Appropriate in All Circumstances In many cases the myth of overcontrol has been replaced with its antithesis: overparticipation. In this case the manager assumes that every group member wants to participate in every decision. Even the most routine matters are subjected to prolonged discussions that result in little significant action. More can be done in less time if the manager makes routine decisions and saves the unusual cases for group discussion.

Myth 4: If Everybody is Courteous Enough, the Meeting is Bound to Succeed This is not true. Participants quickly come to know when they are expected to mask their true feelings in the guise of getting along with each other. Issues become buried, ignored, or left to fester until they evolve into even larger problems.

Myth 5: Touching Base With Everyone is Good Management In lieu of risking offending someone, many managers invite everyone to meetings. The result is a ponderous, boring setting in which no one can meaningfully participate and very little gets accomplished. The goal of touching base with others is a worthy one but does not have to be done through mass meetings.

These myths need to be debunked.

Meetings: Pros and Cons

Meetings have both advantages and disadvantages. Effective managers try to draw on the positive aspects and sidestep or prevent the negative ones.

ACCENTUATE THE POSITIVE Meetings have many benefits.

1. They facilitate information flow. With the increasing complexity of organization and resultant specialization, meetings help assure that necessary information is shared without the intrusion of a host of communication filters.

2. They help heighten a feeling of camaraderie. The best organizations are social systems in which employees pull together and identify with the corporate goals and philosophy. Meetings help foster this team spirit and socialize individuals into the organizational system.

Advantages of meetings

3. They encourage two-way communication. When supervisors and subordinates alike have a chance to ask questions, request clarification, and state their points of view, group effectiveness increases.

4. They often improve the quality of decisions. Following the adage "two heads are better than one," a group of five to eight people typically can make a more effective decision than a manager working alone.

5. They are a source of teamwork. A carefully formulated set of objectives and a detailed agenda can pull together the group members into a well-disciplined, highly motivated team. This is especially important at a time when the depersonalization of the workplace due to technology demands new team motivation techniques. See "Communication Technology: Eliminating the Physical Distance."

COMMUNICATION TECHNOLOGY

Eliminating the Physical Distance

Meetings can be quite costly. A group of 10 managers, each making an average of $20 an hour and meeting two hours a week, will cost the company $20,800 ($400 × 52) annually. This can be a very expensive way of bringing everyone together. However, the price is quite reasonable when contrasted with committees whose members have to travel to the meeting site. For example, if these same 10 managers were to meet once a week at headquarters and spend $200 for air travel and another $20 for food, the cost would go up by $2,200 per meeting $114,400 ($2,200 × 52) annually.

Because it is so expensive to bring together people who are geographically dispersed, many firms are looking for ways of eliminating the physical distance while still allowing the members to meet. For them, teleconferencing is proving to be a very important technological tool. Teleconferencing is a form of electronically aided two-way communication that can save the firm thousands of dollars annually.

When most people think of teleconferencing, they picture a group of individuals who are interacting with each other through some form of closed-circuit television. This is known as video teleconferencing and is one of the most popular forms. Over the last five years the cost per hour for video teleconferencing has dropped from around $1,000 to about $200 and the cost is still going down. So it is likely to remain popular. However, it is not the only type available.

A second popular form is audio conferencing. Under this arrangement, all of the people in the group can hear each other and talk to each other via a telephone network system. Most managers admit that they like video teleconferencing better, but if costs are a key consideration, audio conferencing often gives the company more value for its money.

Finally, there is computer conferencing which allows committee members to send messages to each other and receive messages from them. This is done through the use of computer terminals that link the participants. Large organizations with geographically dispersed operations are finding that this approach is very efficient and often outweighs the benefits of video or audio conferencing.

During the 1990s more and more firms are going to rely on meetings for helping them manage operations. At the same time they are going to be looking for ways of controlling the expenses associated with these get-to-gethers. For many, teleconferencing will prove to be an important technological breakthrough because of its ability to eliminate the physical distance barrier and allow the participants to communicate directly with each other.

SOURCE: Jane W. Gibson and Richard M. Hodgetts, *Business Communication* (New York: Harper & Row, 1990), p. 50.

6. They aid in the implementation of change. When employees are involved in the process leading up to change, they are more likely to support that change.

BEWARE OF THE NEGATIVE Meetings also have drawbacks of which the manager should be aware.

1. Meetings are often called unnecessarily when a more cost effective alternative would be equally or more effective. These alternatives include one-on-one visits, memos, and telephone calls.[5]

2. They act as a substitute for action. Some managers are known for avoiding decisions of any kind. Meetings become a delaying tactic. If group participants come to suspect that they are being asked to give up time and go to a meeting where no decisions are likely to be made, they will quickly become disinterested in the meeting and resentful of their time being wasted.

3. They are dominated by one or more members who take over. When one or two domineering members of the group use the meeting to ramrod through their preconceived decision, general dissatisfaction will occur among members. Moreover, if one or more members use the meeting time to cultivate their personal agenda rather than to further organizational objectives, other participants will feel bored, angry, and/or resentful. It is a mark of good meeting leadership that such activity is not allowed to get out of hand.

Drawbacks to meetings

4. They can cost a lot more money than they are worth. "For example, consider the cost of several highly paid executives spending a few hours at the conference table. This figure involves only the direct cost of a single meeting, and most managers attend more than one meeting each day. To clearly determine the cost-inefficiencies, consider the number of company meetings held each week."[6]

   Andrew Grove, president of Intel Corporation, estimates that the dollar cost of a manager's time including overhead is about $100 per hour. Thus a meeting of ten people which lasts two hours costs the company $2,000, a far from insignificant sum. Grove points out that a $2,000 expense item would have to be approved by senior management, but almost anyone can schedule a $2,000 meeting.[7]

5. They can result in low-quality decisions. Although meetings may well lead to pooled expertise and better decisions, the chance does exist that decisions will in fact be of lower quality when made in a group. The reasons are twofold. First, the groupthink syndrome discussed in Chapter 6 may become the dynamic force and impede the decision-making process. Second, group members may not actually have the expertise necessary to make a quality decision, but pride prevents them from admitting this and they feel obliged to make a decision.

6. Unprepared participants prevent success. Employees sometimes develop sloppy habits such as neglecting to prepare for a meeting and arriving without necessary facts and figures. This postpones agenda items and causes needless repetition and discussion.

7. Bad logistics cause negative impressions to form about meetings. Calling meetings at noon or late Friday afternoon, for example, is sure to cause employee resistance.

The same is true for regularly scheduled meetings that are held "just because it is Monday," or "one hour" meetings that drag on for two to three hours. Inconvenient or uncomfortable locations also distract staff from the importance of the meeting and cause unnecessary resentment.

Implications for Management

1. Remember that meetings can be very useful in getting things done. Before calling one, however, be sure that you know the objective and purpose of the meeting. What do you want done and how will you know if your objective(s) has been attained? Also, be sure to weigh the costs of the meeting against the benefits. Meetings are an expensive way of getting things done.

2. Don't fall prey to the popular myths about meetings. Although you are responsible for getting the meeting off the ground, you have a right to expect those on the committee to carry their own weight. Use the amount of control and group participation that works best for you and all involved. Be flexible without sacrificing the efficiency of the group.

3. Stay alert to the benefits and drawbacks of committees. You will want to obtain the benefits and avoid the drawbacks. This is usually not possible unless you stay on your toes. Quite often a committee's progress will be good, and then things will start to go wrong. Remember that committee progress must be assessed during and after every meeting. Sometimes things look as if they are going very smoothly and then suddenly problems develop. Carefully monitor your group's progress and stay alert for signs of problems.

TYPES OF MEETINGS

For purposes of analysis, meetings can be analyzed in terms of four basic criteria: objectives, size, sessions, and orientations.

Objectives

Some meetings are held by committees that convene on a regular basis. Others are held by those interested in attaining a specific objective after which the group is disbanded. When examined from this standpoint, there are three basic categories, best described in terms of the type of committee.

STANDING COMMITTEES Standing committees, commonplace in many organizations, are permanent groups that have regularly scheduled membership, meeting times, and purposes. Monthly university faculty meetings are a typical example, as are the biweekly sales staff meetings in a business enterprise. These committees often concern themselves with a wide range of administrative questions that can benefit from collective judgment.

SPECIAL COMMITTEES Special committees deal with particularly complex or controversial one-time issues. Membership tends to include many points of view; there is a predetermined time frame for the group's existence; and specific goals dictate the agenda and nature of the meetings. Examples of special committees include a group to conduct a personnel search to fill an important position, a task force to deal with employee resistance to an impending merger, and a committee to draw up a disciplinary policy or grievance procedure.

There are three
basic types of
committees.

AD HOC COMMITTEES Ad hoc committees deal with unique, one-time matters, but, in contrast to special committees, the subject typically is mundane and noncontroversial. Members are usually selected based on their interest in the subject rather than on their ability to represent a particular point of view. The task, though specific and having a time frame, is usually less complex than that of the special committee. The group may, for example, prepare an exhibit for a particular meeting or do a one-time assessment of office equipment needs.

Size

Another way to categorize meetings is by size. When using this approach, there are three categories: assembly, council, and committee. The *assembly* is a large group of 100 or more people who gather predominantly to listen to a speaker. The sheer size of the group makes any purposeful action rather difficult. The *council* is a medium-sized group of 40 to 50 who are present mainly to listen to a speaker. With this size group, it is possible to field some questions and to support some interaction. The *committee* is a group composed of up to 10 to 12 people. These individuals interact on an equal basis under the leadership of a chairperson.[8] It is this group that we are most often discussing in this chapter.

Committees can be
categorized by size.

Sessions

A third way to categorize meetings is in terms of sessions. The daily meeting is mainly an informal gathering of co-workers or team members who discuss progress toward common objectives. Weekly or monthly meetings are regularly scheduled forums where people who work on different objectives and projects interact. The chairperson has an important role here, as is not the case in the daily meetings. The irregular or special occasion meeting occurs at unplanned intervals and is composed of people whose work is not interrelated and who have little or no other contact with each other. They are a group only to the extent that the specific agenda unites them for that period of time.[9]

They can also be
classified by
sessions.

Orientations

A fourth way to categorize meetings is in terms of orientations: process and mission. *Process-oriented meetings* are routine. They are information-sharing forums that facilitate the process of work being done. *Mission-oriented meetings* are designed to solve specific problems. These meetings are called only when the occasion merits it.[10]

As well as by
orientations

Before deciding which type of meeting to call, the manager should determine whether a meeting is necessary at all. Soden has suggested that as an alternative to a meeting, a memorandum that denotes the problem and processes a solution may suffice. This memorandum should be circulated to all concerned parties for suggestions, amendments, and/or agreements. "The overall result is the avoidance of meetings that attendees would have had to justify somehow, perhaps by suggesting poorly conceived alternatives. The dividend to the corporation is a streamlined decision-making process with efficient use of time toward greater productivity.[11]

Even the memorandum strategy, however, may lead to the generation of alternative solutions that ultimately require a meeting. If one is necessary, careful planning is the key ingredient for success.

PLANNING FOR THE MEETING

Too little time goes into planning some meetings. The result is a great deal of time spent at the meeting with very few results. Planning is the key element to the success of a meeting. When carrying out this process, planners need to consider eight key questions.

1. What Is the Purpose of the Meeting?

The convening manager should know and communicate the real purpose of the meeting. Of course, the meeting usually has a stated purpose, but sometimes it is not the actual purpose. For example, a manager calling a weekly staff meeting for coordination of effort may know full well that this is unnecessary, but may feel that the routine meeting is demanded by corporate ritual or is motivational to attending employees. In either case, the real purpose is buried in the stated purpose, and the stated purpose is recognized as nonsensical by the meeting participants. In other cases, the real purpose is a meaningful one, but it can be determined only after careful analysis of the general topic. Table 14.1 shows some examples.

By expanding general topics into actual purposes with their implied goals, the manager is now in a much better position to judge his or her meeting needs. The labor grievance topic, for example, may be solvable by one meeting, but the training topic may necessitate several, each one treating a specific purpose.

Topics should be expanded into purposes.

Finally, when defining the purpose of the meeting, especially if it is a problem-solving meeting, the manager must be sure he or she has identified the real problem and not just a symptom. "Defining a problem or selecting a topic usually requires careful analysis. Certainly a *symptom* of a problem should not be designated as the problem. It is true that production has slowed down, but installing faster punch presses will not solve the problem. The slowdown is only a symptom of the real problem, which may be low morale among people in the production department. That is the issue with which the conference should deal — not the possible acquisition of newer and faster punch presses.[12]

It also is important for the manager to realize that a problem-solving meeting requires a much greater amount of planning than does an information meeting.

Table 14.1

EXAMPLES OF MEETING PURPOSES

General Topic	Purposes
Training needs	Identify primary training needs for each department. Discuss which training can be done in house. Establish training priorities. Develop a strategy for training.
Labor grievance	Familiarize the group with the specifics of this grievance. Review similar cases from the past. Brainstorm alternative solutions to this case. Develop a corporate strategy for this grievance.
Departmental budget	Review current status on this year's budget. Identify major deviations between projections and actual expenditures. Discover ways to reduce expenses for the balance of the fiscal year. Revise the budget for the rest of the year.

---

2. What Are the Objectives of the Meeting?

The purpose of a meeting often is stated in general terms. However, specific objectives can be determined from the purpose. For example, the "labor grievance" topic above, identifies four purposes. The first is to familiarize the group with the specifics of this grievance. From this purpose specific objectives can be formulated, such as:

An example of meeting objectives

- To inform everyone that a grievance has been lodged and what the specific nature of that grievance is.

- To inform everyone of the corporate grievance procedure.

- To build group consensus surrounding corporate attitude toward this grievance.

- To elicit a spirit of confidentiality from the group regarding the planned handling of this grievance.

Each of the other labor grievance purposes, in turn, will have objectives of their own. It is only by carefully thinking through these objectives that the true purpose of the meeting can be assured.

3. What Type of Meeting Is Required?

Once the purpose has been identified and the objectives have been set, the manager in charge must decide what type of meeting will best suit its goals. There are four basic types: informational, problem solving, brainstorming, and training.

Informational meetings are called to disseminate information to a group of people at the same time. Everyone present simultaneously hears the same message. Questions are usually then invited. A meeting called to explain a new health benefit program is an example of an informational meeting.

Problem-solving meetings are convened to involve people in solving a particular problem or jointly make a decision. This is the most common type of organizational meeting, and examples abound including setting quarterly objectives, cutting the budget, and deciding on the appropriate advertising campaign for a new product.

Brainstorming sessions are sometimes a prelude to problem-solving meetings but differ from them in that they are not expected to yield specific answers. Instead they are held to generate alternatives. A meeting called to come up with new ideas for an advertising campaign is an example of a brainstorming session.

Training meetings take place when specific skills or concepts are to be taught. The actual format can vary from straight lecture to totally experiential. A meeting convened to teach supervisors how to fill out the new monthly cost control report is an example of a training meeting.[13]

There are four basic types of meetings.

4. Who Should Attend the Meeting?

This is not an easy question to answer. Should the manager invite everyone and take the risk of boring people or having nonproductive participants? Or should the manager invite only those whose expertise is needed and risk others feeling resentment at being left out? The answer will vary from organization to organization, based on the dictates of corporate culture. Generally speaking, however, the following four types of people should be invited to meetings.[14]

Four types of people should attend.

1. Those who have considerable knowledge of the subject and can therefore make a contribution.

2. Those who have the power to make a decision.

3. Those who will be responsible for implementing any decision that is made.

4. Those who represent employees who will be affected by whatever decision is made.

As the manager notes the names of those to invite, he or she should remember that small meetings usually are more effective and satisfying than larger gatherings. Many managers, in an effort to keep meetings small but not hurt the feelings of those left out, keep those not attending informed by sending them copies of the minutes. Other innovative approaches are

1. Have people attend only part of the meeting. Participants often sit through hours of boredom while waiting for their agenda item to surface. It can be far more efficient to have such people attend only their parts.

2. Use subcommittees to pare down topics. Subcommittees are a good way to save the total group from long discussion on items that are not of sufficiently high interest to everyone. Subcommittees usually are made up of volunteers with an expressed interest in the subject at hand. They come to tentative conclusions or recommendations and then bring them back to the larger group either in person or in written format.

5. When Should the Meeting Be Held?

The timing of meetings is an important consideration because poorly timed ones can create resentment before they even start. Some people dislike noon meetings because they interfere with their lunch. A meeting scheduled for noon can partially overcome this problem by providing lunch for the participants in compensation for the inconvenience. Many people prefer midmorning meetings, such as 9:30 to 10:30 A.M. This gives participants time to gather their thoughts, take care of leftover work, and get their secretaries and/or departments started on the current day's assignments. Some managers like to hold meetings later in the day. They feel that the subtle pressure of quitting time will force people to come to closure. Which of these three times is best? There is no right answer. The manager must consider the time availability of the personnel and the necessity of getting the meeting objectives accomplished and then make a decision.

Meeting times should be carefully determined.

As for day of the week to schedule meetings. Mondays and Fridays usually are bad. Mondays typically are busy days when everyone is gearing up for the week. Fridays are days when people are trying to bring closure to the week. Tuesday, Wednesday, and Thursday usually are the best days.

Finally, one should consider the length of the meeting. Meetings that last more than 90 minutes tend to have diminished effectiveness. If the manager must have a longer meeting, it is important to schedule a break after 90 minutes so people can stretch, call their offices, get a cup of coffee, and so on. Remember that it is usually better to have several short meetings than one overly long, tedious meeting.[15]

6. Where Should the Meeting Be Held?

Logistics are important to many people. If the organization has large facilities, the manager should give serious thought to room location. If people are coming from different floors, buildings, or addresses, the committee planner will want to locate the meeting in a place most easily accessible for the greatest number of people.

Logistics are crucial.

When considering place, joint consideration should be given to the time of day and number of people. Few things destroy the effectiveness of a meeting as does 20 people, half of them smoking, jammed into a room suited for 10. The first group sits around the conference table and the others take chairs against the wall. This causes an immediate split in the group, who are already uncomfortable because of the close quarters. Items such as air conditioning and heating should also be considered. People should be comfortable or they will be concentrating on physical distractions rather than the issues at hand. Finally, the surrounding facilities should be examined to ensure they are appropriate for the meeting. Are rest room facilities convenient? How about a water fountain? A telephone? These facilities will not ensure a meeting's success, but they can cause its failure.

Creativity in finding a meeting space can sometimes pay big dividends. Having a meeting away from the office, for example, may guard against interruptions and emphasize the specialness of the meeting.[16]

7. How Should the Meeting Room Be Arranged?

From the chapter on nonverbal communication, particularly the information on proxemics, we know that the way meeting space is organized sets the stage for the group dynamics that follow. Obviously, there must be sufficient seating space for the number of participants, but how should these seats be arranged? Figure 14.1 shows a number of possible seating arrangements suggested by Dellinger and Deane. Each encourages a different pattern of interaction.

The theater-style seating arrangement is appropriate for large informational meetings. The leader is cast in the role of lecturer, although the relative informality of the semicircle design allows for some group interaction and ease of question-and-answer sessions.

The schoolroom style also shows who is in charge. The format is mainly lecture, and

Figure 14.1

Meeting room and conference table seating arrangements.

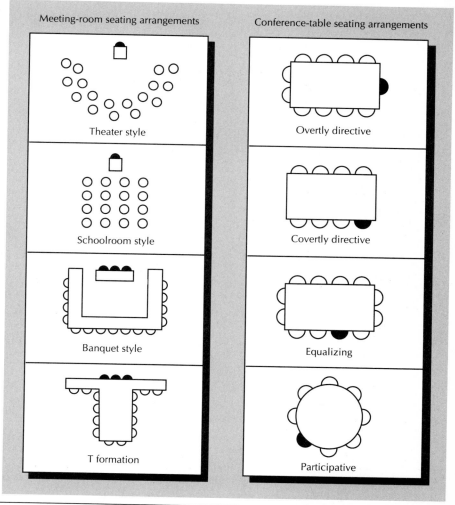

Meeting-room seating arrangements

Theater style

Schoolroom style

Banquet style

T formation

Conference-table seating arrangements

Overtly directive

Covertly directive

Equalizing

Participative

SOURCE: Susan Dellinger and Barbara Deane, *Communicating Effectively: A Complete Guide For Better Managing* (Radnor, Pa.: Chilton Book Co., 1982), pp. 158–159.

the formality of the seating arrangements minimizes group interaction. This style is appropriate for a medium to large group meeting when the purpose is to disseminate information with a minimum of interaction.

The banquet style has the leader or leaders sitting at a separate table in the middle of the U-shaped participants' seating area. This style is useful when participants need to spread out worksheets and other materials. As for interaction, the setting focuses attention squarely on the leaders as the large space in the middle effectively isolates members from one another.

There are eight basic seating arrangements.

In the T formation the head table is attached to the end of the main participants' table. Participants have more face-to-face contact with each other, the only major exception being the people on either end of the head table who have their backs to everyone else. Attention is focused on the leaders who are clearly set off from the rest of the group.

All four styles can be effective for informational meetings. However, they have limited value for problem-solving meetings, which tend to rely on the conference table seating arrangements suggested in the last four frames of Figure 14.1.

The overtly directive arrangement has the chairperson presiding over one end of the table. This focuses the attention on the Chair and gives him or her the option of retaining tight control over the agenda and the meeting. This seating arrangement remains one of the most popular.

The covertly directive arrangement pays some lip service to shared power. It appears to be more democratic while enabling the chairperson to maintain control — provided no one is sitting at either end of the table!

The equalizing pattern is appropriate when the leader truly wants participation. It is particularly effective when the leader knows what he or she thinks about the problem and wants to establish an environment in which others can be creative while he or she maintains a low profile, deliberately not leading others with his or her own opinion.

The participative pattern uses a round table. Nothing so minimizes status and power differences as does a circular conference table. In this arrangement everyone is equal and encouraged to participate as a full partner.

After reflecting on the purpose and objectives of the meeting, the manager can then choose the type of seating arrangement that will best serve the situation. The individual must be careful not to overlook the effect of proxemics on the outcome of the meeting.

8. How Should the Agenda Be Formulated and Distributed?

Notice that we did not ask, "Should there be an agenda?" The answer to that question is "yes." The agenda lets everyone know beforehand what topics will be discussed. This allows people to prepare themselves prior to the meeting and to bring with them whatever documents are needed, thus greatly cutting down on the number of times items have to be tabled for later consideration.

The agenda should be arranged logically.

The ordering of agenda items can be done in several ways. A frequent strategy is to list first all those items that can be brought to closure quickly and easily, leaving the rest of the meeting to discuss lengthier items. The agenda in Figure 14.2 is an example of this format; note how it starts with a review of the last meeting's minutes. It then proceeds through several other brief topics, leaving the balance of the meeting to discuss items 5 and 6, which are expected to take considerably more time. Notice that item 7,

Figure 14.2

An example of an
agenda.

Building & Grounds   September 7, 1990
Committee

AGENDA

1. Acceptance of minutes
2. Welcome new members
3. Calendar of 1990-1991 meetings (information)
4. Election of new chairperson
5. Analysis of adequacy of campus security (status report)
6. Set recommended campus housing rates for 90-91 (decision)
7. Other business

other business, has been deliberately left vague. Even if the manager fails to schedule some time for miscellaneous discussion, it will happen and will likely be disruptive to the planned sequence of topics. If participants see an open discussion topic included on the agenda, however, they will more likely hold their comments until that time.

Another way to order the agenda is to group items according to some natural interrelationship of topics. This is especially important if the manager is planning to cycle people in and out of the meeting as they are needed. An agenda organized in this way might have two or three main topics. Those invited to the first part of the meeting could reasonably be asked to leave before the second set of topics got underway.

Still another way is to reverse the order found in Figure 14.2 and get to the involved topics first. Leaving the easier, short topics for last has the benefit of avoiding the possibility of getting stuck on low-payoff topics and not having enough time to get to important things. After holding a few meetings, managers are usually able to tell what works best for them. Yet, regardless of the format of the agenda, certain important communication strategies should be kept in mind.

1. *Keep the agenda specific.* Don't overgeneralize items so that people are unable to adequately prepare. Referring to Figure 14.2, simply listing "Security" for item number 5 really does not tell the participant anything.

2. *Let people know what items are open for discussion and which are purely informational.* Participants often come to a meeting expecting a decision to be made only to find out that they are merely receiving a status report on a given subject. The parenthetical remarks on our sample agenda let people know exactly what to expect. The calendar of 1990 meetings, for example, is not open for suggestions but will be presented as information to the participants. The item on housing rates, however, will be treated in a decision-making mode, and closure is expected at this meeting. The campus security item will likely be raised again and is being provided merely as a status report at this meeting.

The agenda should use these eight communication strategies.

3. *Consider including timing on the agenda.* Noting the amount of time allotted for specific agenda items can be very helpful in showing the relative importance of each topic.[17] By eliminating the open-endedness of such items, discussion is often shorter and more directed. Our agenda, for example, might note 30 minutes next to item 7.

4. *Include any background reading material with the agenda.* Nothing bores people faster than having massive handouts circulated during the meeting that they need to quickly skim before discussion can begin. This is a major time waster and an invitation for people to make decisions on faulty or poorly digested information. It is better to compile these handouts first and circulate them with the agenda. "Background papers and committee reports are an excellent resource if they are sent two weeks ahead of time. Only if they are brief will they be read, and only if they are read will they help to encourage discussions, focus issues, and provide the necessary background information on agenda items."[18]

5. *Alternate working items with reporting items.* Having a long list of reporting items tends to bore participants. It is better to sandwich them in with participating items so that members can be alternately actively involved and then listening. In our sample agenda, item 4, election of a new chairperson, is a working item, and the status report on campus security, item 5, is largely a reporting item. This is followed by item 6, housing rates, which gets everyone back into a decision-making mode. Another strategy is to schedule items first which require a lot of concentration.

   The early part of a meeting tends to be more lively and creative; therefore, it is often helpful to schedule items first that require mental energy. If one item holds great interest for everyone, wait until other useful work has been accomplished before introducing it. Then this key item can be used to bridge the attention gap that frequently occurs after the first 30 or 40 minutes of a meeting.[19]

6. *Keep the agenda and the meeting short.* A four-hour time frame and a 20-item agenda will not generate participant enthusiasm. It is better to schedule two or three shorter meetings and keep the number of items per meeting to five or six.

7. *Remember that people do not remember.* Circulate agendas two to three days before the meeting so they are fresh in everyone's minds. Too much lead time results in people putting off their advance work or forgetting the meeting altogether. Too little lead time is a good excuse for not doing the advance work at all and for arriving at the meeting unprepared.

8. *Anticipate conflicts and sandwich those items in between more harmonious ones.* Scheduling explosive issues at the beginning of the meeting often results in the agenda never progressing beyond item 1. On the other hand, scheduling these items for the end of the meeting will inevitably result in conflict with everyone leaving in a spirit of disharmony. Noncontroversial items both before and after the dissension-producers can lead to better interpersonal relations and a feeling of unity rather than disharmony. Some leaders like to tackle these controversial issues right away. "However, unless the meeting leader is deliberately trying to minimize the time available for controversial items, it is probably best to put the most complex and important items near the top of the agenda so that they are discussed while the participants are fully alert and enthusiastic."[20]

CONDUCTING THE MEETING

After carefully planning the meeting, the manager must switch his or her attention to conducting an effective session. Good planning greatly increases chances of success, but there also are a number of important areas to know about in chairing a meeting. If all physical arrangements are satisfactory, the room is an appropriate size, and the seating arrangement is suitable and comfortable, the leader must now focus on the five major steps in conducting a meeting.

Set the Stage

Put everyone at ease.

The manager's first job is to put people at ease with his or her opening remarks. A good way to begin is by thanking everyone for coming and then clearly stating the purpose of the meeting. This gets everyone focused on the business at hand. Before beginning, however, the leader should offer copies of the agenda to anyone who might have forgotten to bring his or hers along.

Stick to the Agenda

Next, the manager should get to the agenda and waste very little time starting on item 1. The trick is neither to overdirect nor to underdirect the meeting. Meetings can easily be too structured or too informal. The highly structured leader, more common than the highly unstructured one, often unintentionally curtails participation in an effort to move quickly and stay on schedule. Participants do not feel free to speak up. Kiechel puts it this way: "Set the discussion rolling. Then, for the rest of the meeting, say as little as you can while still discharging your duties as master of the revels. Listen intently. Sit up and look directly at whoever is speaking. Remember that participants will take their cue on how to behave from you." [21]

Be Aware of Participant Dynamics

Meeting leaders should know that there are three general categories of meeting participants: (1) positive participants, (2) negative participants, and (3) nonparticipants. [22]

Positive participants are eager to get involved, but sometimes they tend to dominate meetings. Leaders should nurture their enthusiasm but urge them to yield to other members when necessary. Negative participants are at the meeting for a variety of nonproductive reasons. Some want to criticize; some want to be heard; some don't think the meeting is important and openly do their paperwork or write memos and letters.

A number of other dysfunctional behaviors may appear among group members, including blocking, personal power plays, joking, and dominating.

Blocking may be conscious or unconscious, but it effectively stops the progress of the meeting. The blocker leads the group off on a tangent, continues to make objections at every possible point, and generally succeeds in focusing attention on himself or herself rather than on the issue.

Learn to control dysfunctional behavior.

Personal power plays are equally disruptive to a meeting. Here the hidden agenda of the offender is to gain power at the expense of the leader. He or she often does this by polarizing the group or splitting off a clique around a specific issue.

Joking behavior is another dysfunctional phenomenon if it occurs frequently. Here the person(s) shows that the agenda is really not to be taken seriously; on the contrary, the meeting is merely an opportunity to clown around and have a good time.

Dominating attention-seeking behavior by one or more members can quickly serve to disinterest the rest of the group. The dominator has the "last word" on every item and keeps many of the more passive members from speaking up. Why make the effort to talk when the loudmouth would only interrupt them anyway?

Bradford has offered some general guidelines in handling these dysfunctional behaviors and regaining control of the meeting.[23] The first is to confront the participant in a caring way that is conducive for the individual to examine his or her behavior and the consequences it is having on the meeting.

Second, the leader should be careful to concentrate on the dysfunctional behavior and not on the person. For example, telling the constant interruptor, "Charlie, I really get frustrated at all the interruptions when I'm trying to make a point," is likely to get a better response than saying, "Charlie, I've had it with you! You're keeping me from getting anything accomplished!"

Third, the leader should be careful to point out the effects that the dysfunctional behavior is having on the meeting. The individual may be unaware of the effect he or she is causing.

Finally, it is helpful to suggest alternative behaviors that might be more satisfying for all concerned such as telling Charlie, "Why don't you jot down all your questions and I'll get to them as soon as I've completed my presentation." This confrontation of dysfunctional behavior helps build the effective functioning of the group and fosters open lines of communication.

Encourage Participation

Most people enjoy belonging to groups where individual participation is high. If the leader is too dogmatic or only a few members do all the talking, less aggressive participants are likely to fade into the background and become apathetic. Assuming that the leader has invited only those who have the ability to contribute to the meeting, he or she should encourage each individual to participate. Some ways of doing so are as follows:

1. Consider calling a brainstorming session where everyone in turn is asked for an idea and no criticism is allowed. This often gets people actively involved and interested.

2. Break the group into subgroups to discuss the agenda item, with a spokesperson for each subgroup reporting back to the overall group.

3. If the situation is serious, ask the subgroups to discuss ways to get the whole group to participate more, thus directly involving everyone in the problem.

Ways of encouraging participation

4. Show rewarding verbal and nonverbal behavior for participation, being courteous and thanking people for their ideas, even when you don't agree with them.

5. Try to sidestep the comments of the dominator by saying, "Charlie, we've benefited a lot from your comments, but I'd like to hear what Marty has to say."

6. Ask specific questions to specific people to encourage them to get involved. Before

opening up the discussion to anyone ask, for example, "Jean, do you feel you can live with these budget figures?"

7. Resist the temptation to give anyone your informed opinion up front. This will immediately cause reluctance by some to disagree. Instead, keep a low profile on issues where you want the honest opinions of others.

Bring the Meeting to Closure

Finish on time.

The leader should keep an eye on the clock and try to end the meeting close to the expected time. Before doing so, a summation should be presented of what has been accomplished, and all participants should know what to expect next. When is the next meeting? Will the minutes be circulated? What assignments are people responsible for and when are they due? Remember, a successful meeting will leave both leaders and participants with a feeling of accomplishment.

POST-MEETING FOLLOWUP

When the meeting is over, the leader should undertake a post-meeting followup by reflecting on what has transpired. Were the goals of the meeting met? Did everyone participate adequately? Were the physical arrangements satisfactory? Could anything have been done better? What should be done differently in future meetings? What actions must the leader take now to follow up on decisions made in the meeting? The individual should be absolutely sure that he or she follows through on whatever personal promises were made and do so in a timely fashion.

Implications for Management

1. Be able to clearly state the objectives of the committee. What are you trying to accomplish? These objectives can serve as a guide in planning the rest of the committee's activities.

2. When choosing people to attend, make the mistake of inviting too many people rather than too few. If people are there who feel their time is being wasted or they do not want to participate, they can always excuse themselves. It is those who are not invited who create the biggest problems.

3. Always have an agenda and make sure that everyone who is attending the meeting is given one. In fact, unless it is a special meeting where the topic is confidential, share the agenda with anyone who asks you about it. This lets everyone know that your meetings are democratically run and you are not trying to hide anything. It also encourages people to agree to serve on your committees because they know they have nothing to fear from others in the organization who believe that the committee is up to some secret work.

4. Make it a point to do post-meeting followup. This helps you look at things in perspective. Sometimes you will realize that something happened that needs to be addressed before the next meeting. Other times you will realize that the group is beginning to come together as a cohesive unit and you can be moving at a faster pace. This type of followup is very useful in helping you plan for the next meeting of the group.

C A S E   I N   P O I N T

Revisited

The major issue is that no one can really get ready for the meeting because Adrian fails to provide them with sales data. Everyone is kept in the dark until the last moment. From the case we know that the data are available by the end of the previous week. If nothing else, Adrian could provide the sales managers this information on Friday afternoon or early Monday morning and reschedule the meeting for later that day or the next day.

Why is Adrian not giving them the sales data in advance? Several answers are possible. One is that he enjoys having power over them, and when no one but he has the data, this is exactly what happens. Another is that he feels insecure dealing with the managers, so he wants to know something they don't know. A third is that he feels this approach will motivate them to push their people harder and higher sales will result.

In any event, Adrian is going to have to change his ways. The president will not allow the situation to continue, and Adrian will have to redesign the way the meetings are run. The best thing he can do now is to visit with the executive who walked out of the meeting and work out a plan of action that is agreeable to him. In this way he will be obeying the order from the president and, at the same time, have a strategy for ensuring that the problem does not recur. Undoubtedly, Adrian will have to start giving out the sales figures in advance. However, he must then decide how to run the meeting. One idea is to discuss these figures, and, working as a team, the sales managers could brainstorm regarding ways low-sales performance areas could be brought up to par. By getting the executive to help him manage the meeting, Adrian is going to be much more effective than he has been with his previous approach.

YOU BE THE CONSULTANT

Dom's Impending Decision

The Dominick Company is a medium-sized consumer goods firm. The company manufactures and sells hardware products throughout the United States. When the company started out it had a small manufacturing facility and a team of five salespeople. The owner and founder, Dom Dominick, would spend three days a week on the road talking to the owners of small hardware stores. He would find out what types of new hardware products were needed. Then back at the company, he would discuss these ideas with his son, Tony, who was in charge of new product development.

In the beginning, Dominick's produced standard hardware products: hammers, screwdrivers, ladders, and so on. However, they designed the products so that they were lighter and easier to use than the competition's. Beginning in the mid-1960s, the firm started turning out portable, handheld tools. Dominick's caught the market at just the right time and sales soared.

During the 1970s the firm continued to grow, expanding its coverage from east of the Mississippi to all 48 contiguous states. However, one thing did not change. The company continued to use an outside transportation firm to handle all its shipping. The company was owned by Dom's cousin. The two men had grown up together, and when Dominick's needed a company to deliver its merchandise to the wholesalers and retailers, there was never any doubt as to who would get the business.

Last month Dom's cousin came to visit him. The cousin had decided to retire and, having no children who wanted to take over the business, he offered the company to Dom. His argument was as follows, "Your firm will save money by running its own transportation system. Why give these profits to someone else? You helped me get started and become one of the biggest truckers in the region. The whole business is geared exclusively to handling your operations. We can have both of our accountants sit down and work out an arrangement that is to our mutual benefit."

At first Dom resisted the offer. However, after his accountant and lawyer talked to him, he changed his mind.

The problem now confronting Dom is how should the acquisition be integrated into the overall corporation? The head of the production department has come by to see Dom and encourage him to put the shipping firm under the direct control of the production area. "It's a natural extension of what we do now," the vice president told Dom. The head of the marketing department made a similar pitch for putting the shipping firm in the marketing area. "We take over from production as soon as the products leave the assembly line. Transportation is one of our responsibilities." The head of the finance department has argued that the new acquisition should remain a separate entity, thereby creating a new functional area. "These people can work independently of production or marketing. They know how to coordinate things with these departments, and putting them into someone else's area is a waste of time and effort."

Dom is not sure what to do. He respects the judgment of all three senior-level executives but realizes he cannot make a decision that will accommodate all their recommendations. So he decided to head a committee to look into the matter and formulate recommendations. He intends to have his outside consultant advise him regarding the specifics of using a committee to make this decision.

Assume you are the consultant. What recommendation would you make to Dom regarding committee size and composition? Also, what does he need to know regarding how to conduct committee meetings? Be as practical as possible in your advice.

Key Points in This Chapter

1. The ten major characteristics of meetings are participants; purpose; special logistics; atmosphere; cost; time frame; advance preparation; program and agenda; start, middle, and finish; and followup. Each was described in the chapter.

2. The popular myths about meetings include the beliefs that (a) the leader has to be totally responsible for the success of the meeting; (b) the individual needs to exercise tight control; (c) group participation is always appropriate; (d) if everyone in the group is courteous, the meeting is bound to succeed; and (e) touching base with everyone is good management. The problems with these lines of reasoning were explained in the chapter.

3. A number of pros and cons are associated with meetings. In the chapter both were discussed. The manager needs to take advantage of the benefits while sidestepping the drawbacks.

4. The four basic criteria that can be used in evaluating committees are objectives, size, sessions, and orientations. This type of analytical breakdown allows a better understanding of how and why committees function as they do.

5. In planning for the meeting, the chairperson has to answer eight key questions. These were presented in Figure 14.1 and discussed in the chapter. If the leader can adequately address each of these, he or she will greatly increase the chances of having a successful meeting.

6. After the meeting is over, the leader should engage in post-meeting followup. This involves an evaluation of what happened and a followthrough on any decisions that were made. This also serves as a basis for preparing for the next meeting.

Questions for Discussion and Analysis

1. All meetings share ten characteristics. What are they? Describe each.

2. What are the five popular myths about meetings? Explain each and then debunk it.

3. What are four advantages of meetings? Describe each.

4. What are four of the major disadvantages of meetings? Describe each.

5. Committees can be analyzed in terms of four criteria: objectives, size, sessions, and orientations. What does this statement mean? Be complete in your answer.

6. In setting up a meeting, what does the leader need to know about the purpose, objectives, and type of meeting? Explain.

7. In setting up a meeting, what does the leader need to determine regarding who should attend and where the meeting should be held? Be complete in your answer.

8. What does a committee chairperson need to know about how the meeting room should be arranged? Incorporate Figure 14.2 into your answer.

9. Should all meetings have an agenda? Explain.

10. In conducting a meeting, what five major steps must the chairperson carry out? What does the individual have to know about each? Explain.

Exercises

1. Assume that you work for New American University and have been asked to plan an annual meeting for all adjunct (part-time) faculty. You estimate there are about 100 such faculty members and the meeting should be held in two months. Prepare a comprehensive planning checklist to guide your efforts.

2. You have received a letter from Dr. Randolph, an adjunct faculty member in the humanities department. He is not planning to attend the meeting and states that he feels his attendance is unimportant because so many people will be there that nothing will be accomplished. Prepare a letter to Dr. Randolph outlining the benefits of this meeting as you see them.

3. Assume that the above meeting has been held. In all, 72 people attended and information was disseminated on a variety of subjects. New faculty were introduced and welcomed, and the dean brought everyone up to date on the university building plans and new policies. You now are preparing a followup memo listing a summary of items discussed. In addition, you are preparing a short evaluation questionnaire to be mailed to all attendees to get their assessment of the meeting and suggestions for the next meeting. In small groups, draft the questionnaire.

References

1. "Successful Meetings: Management's Ongoing Challenge," *Small Business Report*, January 1987, p. 75.

2. Eva Schindler-Rainman, and Ronald Lippitt, in collaboration with Jack Cole, *Taking Your Meetings out of the Doldrums* (San Diego, Calif.: University Associates, 1975), pp. 17–18.

3. Richard J. Dunsing, "You and I Have Got to Stop Meeting This Way," *Supervisory Management*, October 1976, pp. 11–14.

4. *Ibid.*, pp. 12–13.

5. "Successful Meetings," p. 75.

6. *Ibid.*

7. Andrew S. Grove, "How (and Why) to Run a Meeting," *Fortune*, July 11, 1983, p. 132.

8. Antony Jay, "How to Run a Meeting," *Harvard Business Review*, March–April 1976, p. 46.

9. *Ibid.*

10. Grove, *op. cit.*, pp. 132–133.

11. Glenn W. Soden, "Avoid Meetings or Make Them Work," *Business Horizons*, March–April 1984, p. 48

12. Norman B. Sigband and Arthur H. Bell, *Communication for Management and Business*, 5th ed. (Glenview, Ill.: Scott, Foresman, 1989), p. 443.

13. *Ibid., p. 325.*

14. Waldron Berry, "Making a Contribution to Meetings," *Management Solutions*, September 1988, p. 22.

15. James D. Kimes, "Making Your Meetings Count," *Management Accounting*, January 1987, p. 56.

16. William Fotsch, "Small Groups, Interacting Skills, and Conflict Resolution," in John Louis DiGaetani, ed., *The Handbook of Executive Communication* (Homewood, Ill.: Dow Jones-Irwin, 1986).

17. "Successful Meetings," p. 77.

18. Richard Cassell, "Using Action Items to Facilitate Meetings," in DiGaetani, ed., *The Handbook of Executive Communication*, p. 605.

19. *Ibid.*, p. 605.

20. Ralph Anderson and Bert Rosenbloom, "Conducting Successful Sales Meetings," in DiGaetani, ed., *The Handbook of Executive Communication*, p. 620.

21. Walter Kiechel III, "How to Lead a Meeting," *Fortune*, August 29, 1988, p. 98.

22. "Successful Meetings," p. 78.

23. Leland Bradford, *Make Meetings Work* (San Diego, Calif.: University Associates, 1976), pp. 49–50.

Annotated Bibliography

Callahan, Joseph A., *Communicating: How to Organize Meetings and Presentations* (New York: Franklin Watts, 1984).

Callahan's work is a traditional, serious approach to meetings. Although the Gordon book described below makes many points through witty examples, Callahan relies on guidelines, lists of suggestions, and self-tests. This is a comprehensive book on organizing and conducting meetings, but it also includes several chapters on conducting speeches and oral presentations.

Doyle, Michael, and David Straus, *How to Make Meetings Work* (New York: The Berkley Publishing Group, 1985).
  Doyle and Straus describe their model for effective meetings. Called the interaction method, it is designed to stop wasting time and to get things done at meetings. The book gives helpful hints on how to handle problem people at meetings as well as how to develop agendas and arrange meeting rooms.

Gordon, Myron, *How to Plan & Conduct a Successful Meeting*, New York: Sterling Publishing Co., 1985.
  This easy-to-read book is full of useful advice starting with the premise that the reader is the most important ingredient of any meeting. Practical techniques are provided to plan and lead effective meetings.

Part Six

EMERGING CHALLENGES

The purpose of Part Six is to focus on the future and what will surely be the increasing demands for effective organizational communication at all levels. In the future, more even than today, good managers will have to be good communicators.

Chapter 15 is a totally new chapter on the subject of international communication. Increased levels of international investment, the sociopolitical changes in Eastern Europe, and the newly defined business arena brought forth by changes in the European Common Market all make it vitally important that managers are able to communicate in the international business environment as well as in the national market. Chapter 15 takes a detailed look at the cultural differences among countries and the impact these differences have on communication between people in those countries. Specific challenges of international communication are analyzed so that you may begin to be sensitized as to how to be an effective part of the international business world.

Chapter 16 examines things that we must do in the near future to improve organizational communication. The chapter begins with a description of the communication audit and then proceeds to explain how such an audit is conducted. The focus of attention then switches to the topic of communication training. Some of the most common forms of communication training techniques are described. The chapter ends by relating how posttraining communication evaluation should be carried out.

CHAPTER 15

The Challenge of International Communication

"Communication takes on special importance in international management because of the difficulties in conveying meanings between parties from different countries."

Richard M. Hodgetts and Fred Luthans, *International Management* (New York: McGraw-Hill, 1991, in press).

Objectives

1. To explain the emerging communication challenge that is being created by the increasing amount of world trade and international investment.

2. To identify and describe the four cultural dimensions that help explain behavioral differences between countries.

3. To explain the importance of understanding country clusters when communicating with people from other nations.

4. To discuss some of the major communication challenges confronting managers doing business internationally, including external and internal communication, explicit and implicit communication, perception, language, and communication flows.

5. To present suggestions and guidelines that can be helpful in dealing with communication problems in the international arena.

C A S E   I N   P O I N T

It's Not Like Back Home

For the last three years Joel Kindrel's company has had a manufacturing plant in the Philippines. Three months ago Joel learned that he would be transferred to the plant for a one-year stint. Joel looked forward to the assignment because he knows that every individual who has been promoted into top management has spent at least one year abroad.

Joel arrived at his new assignment six weeks ago. Unfortunately, things do not seem to be going as well as he had hoped. From what he can glean thus far, Joel seems to have made two mistakes. The first was a suggestion he made regarding the installation of an individual incentive payment plan. Productivity in the plant has not been very high and Joel believed that he could improve things by offering more money for more work. However, the idea seems to have backfired. During the two weeks that the plan was in effect, productivity dropped to its lowest level ever. Upon reviewing the results, Joel scrapped the plan and went back to paying the production personnel a weekly wage. The second problem relates to his discussions with other top managers regarding how to run the plant. Joel is accustomed to talking things over and seeing what other managers think before making decisions. However, Joel found that the other managers tend to rely heavily on him to tell them what to do, and they seem to resent being asked to give their opinion. "It's almost as if they did not want to participate in the decision-making process," he told his wife. "I'm trying to get them involved so that they feel like a part of the team, but they seem more interested in just sitting on the sidelines and letting me decide what should be done. I don't get it. Why aren't they willing to play a more active role in running the business?"

Earlier this week Joel was assigned a new assistant. The individual was born and raised in the Philippines but has spent the last five years working for the company stateside. The individual will be taking over Joel's job when his one-year assignment is up. Joel hopes that this person will be able to give him some advice and assistance regarding how he can manage the plant more effectively. "One thing is for sure," Joel told his wife. "He is unlikely to give me any bad advice. I think I made most of the mistakes that I am capable of making. What I need now is to find someone who can help me better understand how to adjust my approach to managing this plant. Quite obviously, I have a great deal to learn about communicating and leading these personnel."

Exactly what mistakes did Joel make? To what do you attribute these problems? Be specific in your answer. Also, in the future, how should Joel change his behavior? What specific suggestions would you give him regarding how to communicate and lead the personnel? Write down your analysis of the situation and then put it aside. We will return to it later.

INTRODUCTION

A number of international developments are occurring that promise to make the world of business during the 1990s a very interesting and challenging place. One of these developments is the growth of international investment. Another is the changing political philosophies of communist bloc and Third World countries. These changes are resulting in increased international trade, and as this increase occurs the need for an understanding of international communication will become more important.

INTERNATIONAL INVESTMENT

The United States is the favorite investment target of foreign firms.

The United States is currently the favorite investment target of foreign firms. They see the United States as highly stable and a safe haven for their money. By the end of 1988, as seen in Figure 15.1, foreigners had invested more money in the United States than America had invested abroad. Moreover, investments here are beginning to increase much faster than those being made overseas.

A large percentage of these foreign funds are being used to buy American businesses and to set up operations in the United States. Conversely, many of the American dollars invested abroad are going into buying businesses and establishing overseas operations. At the same time, billions more are being spent on importing and exporting activities. The United States, West Germany, Japan, South Korea, and Hong Kong are major exporters and importers.[1] This economic activity is important to the study of international business communication because if the United States is going to be doing business with foreign firms, an understanding of how these people communicate is critical.

ECONOMIC AND POLITICAL DEVELOPMENTS

A number of significant economic and political developments occurred during the late 1980s, and many others will be coming to fruition over the next decade. One of the most unexpected and important changes has been the movement by many communist bloc nations toward a semifree enterprise system. Poland[2] and the Soviet Union[3] are two good examples. Both nations understand the need for trade with the West, and in an effort to promote international business they are allowing entrepreneurs to set up private businesses and to profit from their efforts.

The most economically advanced countries in Europe belong to the Common Market.

Another important development is the Common Market, which consists of the largest and most economically developed countries in Europe including England, France, West Germany, Italy, and the Netherlands. The goal of the Common Market is to eliminate all trade barriers by 1992 and, in effect, turn these countries into one giant economic market that will have greater purchasing power than the United States.[4] This market is so important to U.S. businesses, that more and more of them are setting up and expanding operations in Europe every month.

A third important development is the emergence of Far Eastern countries as major economic powers. Primary examples include Japan and South Korea. The Japanese have made major inroads in the auto industry, in addition to buying American firms such as Dunlop Tire and most of Fairchild Semiconductor and setting up operations of their own.[5] The South Koreans have had great success with the production and sale of computers, automotive, and electronic goods.[6] China may also become a major market, although political considerations continue to be a major stumbling block in dealing with the government of Beijing. Nevertheless, in the future, more and more American firms will be doing business with Occidental companies located both here and abroad.

Figure 15.1

International investment.

$327 BILLION Total U.S. investment abroad		$329 BILLION Total foreign investment in the United States	
Countries where the United States invested most in 1988		**Countries with the biggest investment in the United States in 1988**	
Canada	$61 billion	Britain	$102 billion
Britain	$48 billion	Japan	$53 billion
West Germany	$22 billion	Netherlands	$49 billion
Bermuda	$20 billion	Canada	$27 billion
Switzerland	$19 billion	West Germany	$24 billion

DIRECT INVESTMENT

Direct foreign investment in the United States outpaced American investment abroad by $41 billion in 1988; the year before, the difference was just $2.7 billion. But Americans still collect nearly three times the income from their properties.

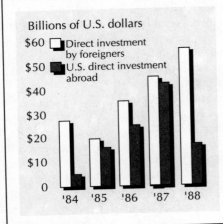

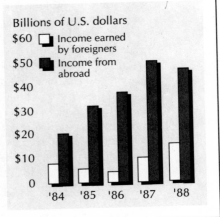

SOURCE: *Fortune*, as reported by the Commerce Department, July 32, 1989, p. 81.

Newly developed countries such as Brazil, Hong Kong, and Singapore are also becoming actively involved in the international arena. So are less developed countries such as Peru, Liberia, and Israel. These countries are active in the international arena as both exporters and importers. During the 1990s, the amount of business they do with the United States will likely increase substantially.

As the United States increases its business activities with other countries and vice versa, more and more managers will be communicating with foreign customers, partners, employees, and bosses. In understanding how to do this effectively, one of the primary areas of attention will be cultural considerations. Before examining this area, however, take Self-Assessment Quiz 15.1 and see how much you currently know about international communication.

Increasingly, managers will be communicating with foreign customers, partners, employees, and bosses.

SELF-ASSESSMENT QUIZ 15.1

What Do You Know About International Communication?

Answer each of the follow by placing a true (T) or false (F) before it.

———— 1. Far Eastern managers tend to use implied communication much more than Western managers do.

———— 2. Formal authority is very important in Japan.

———— 3. The value systems of people around the world are changing rapidly.

———— 4. Orientals never lose their temper when communicating.

———— 5. Korean managers put much more emphasis on downward communication than on upward communication.

———— 6. Australian managers are very humanistic and tend to communicate a genuine concern for their people.

———— 7. Delegation of authority and the promotion of upward communication are common among British managers.

———— 8. In Argentina, rapid decision making is often regarded as more important than slow, deliberate analysis and communication of the facts.

———— 9. French managers like people to go through channels as opposed to using informal communication channels to circumvent red tape.

———— 10. Scandinavian managers are much more likely to use two-way communication than are American managers.

Answers are in the Answer section at the back of the book.

Implications for Management

1. Remember that international operations are increasing in importance, and so managers are going to have to learn how to communicate with their counterparts throughout the world. This development is being compounded by the fact that many firms are now regarding the world as one large market, rather than a series of individual, small markets. This global view will intensify the need for effective international communication skills.

2. In learning how to communicate effectively, start by learning about the country's culture. How do people act? What is important to them? Do they work hard? Do they work fast? Do they work long hours? This information is useful in getting a basic understanding of how people regard business and the role it plays in their lives.

3. In order to communicate effectively with foreign business people, learn the language. A short course on how to say the most basic expressions or conduct a simple conversation can be very useful. Learning how to read basic information such as street signs and restaurant menus is also helpful. Remember that if you are sent overseas, you are not likely to have a colleague or an interpreter with you at all times, so it is wise to acquire some basic communication skill.

CULTURAL IMPLICATIONS

The U.S. and foreign approach to doing business differs.

The way business is conducted in the United States is not the same way it is conducted in many other countries. For example, most Americans work from 9 A.M. to 5 P.M., Monday through Friday. In Japan many people work on Saturdays as well. In Latin cultures such as Spain, Portugal, Mexico, and South American countries, people take an afternoon siesta and then go back to work until evening. In Arabian countries, Thursday and Friday are days off, which means that foreign companies with major customers in the Middle East often work seven days a week or adjust the work schedules of their people to reflect those of their overseas client. In addition, the values and beliefs of people around the world are different. These differences can be explained in terms of cultural dimensions.

Cultural Dimensions

Culture is acquired knowledge used to interpret experience.

Culture is acquired knowledge that people use to interpret experience and to generate social behavior.[7] Researchers have found that culture can be examined by looking at its subparts or dimensions. The four dimensions of culture that are of most value in understanding international business communication are (1) power distance, (2) uncertainty avoidance, (3) individualism, and (4) masculinity.

POWER DISTANCE   Power distance is the extent to which less powerful members of an institution or organization are able to accept the fact that power is unequally distributed.[8] In countries where people unquestioningly obey the orders of their supe-

Power distance is the extent to which the less powerful accept unequal power distribution.

riors, high power distance exists. In nations where lower level personnel do not feel threatened by their bosses and they sometimes question authority, there is low power distance. Latin American countries tend to have high power distance, as do nations in the Far East and Mideast. In Europe, France, Belgium, and Italy have been found to have high power distance. This is in contrast to Anglo countries such as the United States, Great Britain, Ireland, and Australia which have low power distance. Other low power distance countries include the Scandinavian countries, the Netherlands, West Germany, and Switzerland.

Countries with high power distance tend to have tall organizational structures, and all communication goes through channels. It takes longer to get things done, but the integrity of managerial positions and formal power is protected. Countries with low power distance tend to have flatter organizational structures and make wide use of informal communication. Authority is often based on expertise, knowledge, and negotiation skills as well as the formal authority of the position. Communication in an organization in a high power distance country is strikingly different from that in a low power distance country.

Uncertainty avoidance is the extent to which people try to avoid ambiguous situations.

UNCERTAINTY AVOIDANCE Uncertainty avoidance is the extent to which people feel threatened by ambiguous situations and have created beliefs and institutions that try to avoid these situations.[9] Organizations in countries that do not like uncertainty make heavy use of written job descriptions and policy manuals. They have written rules for handling just about every situation, and employees are taught to do things "by the book." Managers are low risk takers, and workers stay with their organization for a long time because they are afraid to change jobs and take on different responsibilities with another firm. Examples include Latin American nations such as Uruguay, Venezuela, and Argentina, those in the Mideast and Far East such as Iran, Pakistan, Egypt, Kuwait, Korea, and Japan, and some in Europe including Italy, Yugoslavia, Belgium, and Greece.

Companies in countries that have low uncertainty avoidance have a minimum of written rules and low structuring of tasks. Managers are moderate-to-high risk takers, there is high labor turnover as workers seek to improve their situation by changing jobs, and employees tend to be fairly ambitious. Examples include the Anglo and European countries such as the United States, Canada, Ireland, Great Britain, Denmark, Sweden, and the Netherlands, and some newly industrialized countries in the Far East such as Singapore, Hong Kong, Indonesia, and the Philippines.

Individualism is the tendency to look after yourself and your immediate family.

INDIVIDUALISM Individualism is the tendency of people to look after themselves and their immediate family only.[10] This cultural value can be examined on a continuum with individualism on one end and collectivism on the other. Collectivism is the tendency of people to belong to groups or collectives and to look after each other in exchange for loyalty. Countries with high individualism promote self-independence and individual initiative and achievement. Importance is given to autonomy, variety of lifestyle, individual security, and the belief in one's personal abilities. Examples of countries with high individualism include the United States, Australia, Great Britain, the Netherlands, Switzerland, West Germany, Norway, and Denmark. Research shows that in many cases countries with high national wealth tend to encourage high individualism.

Countries with high collectivism tend to promote group harmony and interdependence among people. Teamwork is given high priority, with each member of the team being treated as an equal. Even if someone does outstanding work, the individual is given no more recognition than any other member of the group. Importance is given to order, duty, expertise, and security provided by the organization. Examples of countries with high collectivism include Japan, Saudi Arabia, Kuwait, Mexico, Korea, Singapore, Venezuela, and Ecuador.

MASCULINITY Masculinity is defined as "a situation in which the dominant values in society are success, money, and things." [11] This dimension is often measured on a continuum with the opposite extreme being femininity, which is "a situation in which the dominant values in society are caring for others and the quality of life." [12] Countries with a high masculinity index place great importance on earnings, recognition, advancement, and challenge. Individuals are encouraged to be independent decision makers, and achievement is defined in terms of recognition and wealth. The workplace is often characterized by high job stress, and many managers believe their workers dislike work and have to be kept under some degree of control. Companies in this type of culture tend to favor large-scale enterprises, and economic growth is considered more important than conservation of the environment. The school system promotes high performance, and students are encouraged to be career oriented. Examples of countries with a high masculinity index include Japan, Venezuela, Mexico, and, to a somewhat lesser degree, Great Britain, the United States, and Canada.

> Masculinity is a situation in which success, money, and things are dominant values.

Countries that have a low masculinity index (high femininity) tend to place a great deal of importance on cooperation, a friendly atmosphere, and job security. Individuals are encouraged to be group decision makers, and achievement is defined in terms of human contacts and the living environment. The workplace tends to be characterized by low stress, and managers give their employees more credit for being responsible and allow them more freedom. These societies tend to favor small-scale enterprise and place great importance on conservation of the environment. The school system teaches social adaptation, and there is fairly low job stress in the workplace. Examples of countries with a low masculinity index include Sweden, Norway, Denmark, the Netherlands, Finland, and Yugoslavia.

INTEGRATING THE DIMENSIONS A description of these four cultural dimensions is useful in helping to explain the differences in the work environment and communication practices of different countries. These dimensions also help identify country clusters that are characterized by nations with similar values and behaviors. For example, Hofstede has combined these dimensions by examining them in pairs. Figure 15.2 provides an example. (Also see Table 15.1 for a list of all the countries in the figure.) The figure shows that some countries have high power distance and individualism; others are low on both dimensions; and the remainder are high on one and low on the other. The United States is in the southwest quadrant of the figure. Americans have extremely high individualism and moderately low power distance. They like to achieve

> Cultural dimensions help explain differences in the work environment and communication practices.

Figure 15.2

A power distance X individualism—collectivism plot for 50 countries and 3 regions.

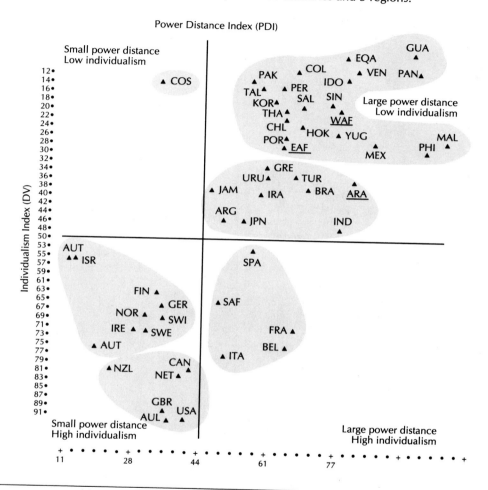

Power Distance Index (PDI)

SOURCE: Geert Hofstede, "The Cultural Relativity of Organizational Practices and Theories," *Journal of International Business Studies,* Fall 1983, p. 79.

things on their own, and they do not get upset when others have more power than they do. Because Americans are taught to believe that everyone is equal, they are not overawed by individuals with important titles or jobs. Australians, Canadians, British, Dutch, and New Zealanders have similar beliefs. This is in contrast to the Japanese who have moderately high power distance and moderately low individualism. They are group oriented. Panama, Ecuador, and Venezuela have high power distance and high collectivism. They are even more group oriented and hierarchical in their approach.

Table 15.1

THE COUNTRIES AND REGIONS

ARA	Arab countries (Egypt, Lebanon, Lybia, Kuwait, Iraq, Saudi Arabia, United Arab Emirates)	ITA	Italy
		JAM	Jamaica
		JPN	Japan
		KOR	South Korea
ARG	Argentina	MAL	Malaysia
AUL	Australia	MEX	Mexico
AUT	Austria	NET	Netherlands
BEL	Belgium	NOR	Norway
BRA	Brazil	NZL	New Zealand
CAN	Canada	PAK	Pakistan
CHL	Chile	PAN	Panama
COL	Colombia	PER	Peru
COS	Costa Rica	PHI	Philippines
DEN	Denmark	POR	Portugal
EAF	East Africa (Kenya, Ethiopia, Zambia)	SAF	South Africa
		SAL	Salvador
EQA	Equador	SIN	Singapore
FIN	Finland	SPA	Spain
FRA	France	SWE	Sweden
GBR	Great Britain	SWI	Switzerland
GER	Germany	TAI	Taiwan
GRE	Greece	THA	Thailand
GUA	Guatemala	TUR	Turkey
HOK	Hong Kong	URU	Uruguay
IDO	Indonesia	USA	United States
IND	India	VEN	Venezuela
IRA	Iran	WAF	West Africa (Nigeria, Ghana, Sierra Leone)
IRE	Ireland		
ISR	Israel	YUG	Yugoslavia

SOURCE: Geert Hofstede, "The Cultural Relativity of Organizational Practices and Theories," *Journal of International Business Studies,* Fall 1983, p. 79.

Figure 15.3 provides another example of how these cultural dimensions can be combined. This figure shows masculinity–femininity and uncertainty avoidance. Notice that the United States has a moderately high masculinity index (money, power, and acquisition of wealth is important) and moderately low uncertainty avoidance (risk taking is encouraged and bureaucratic red tape is discouraged). This is in contrast to Yugoslavia, for example, where the quality of work life is given a high degree of importance but uncertainty is discouraged (low risk taking, things are done by the book). Notice that many of the Scandinavian countries are in the northwest quadrant (low uncertainty avoidance and low masculinity).

Certain patterns of behavior are similar between various countries.

These cultural clusters illustrate that certain patterns of behavior are similar between various countries. In recent years researchers have taken these ideas and analyzed them

Figure 15-3

A masculinity-
femininity *X*
uncertainty
avoidance plot for
50 countries and 3
regions.

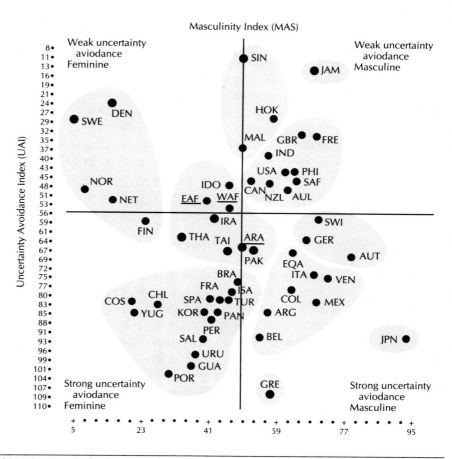

Masculinity Index (MAS)

SOURCE: Geert Hofstede, "The Cultural Relativity of Organizational Practices and Theories," *Journal of International Business Studies,* Fall 1983, p. 79.

on an overall basis.[13] The result has been a synthesis of country clusters as presented in Figure 15.4. This figure reveals eight basic clusters of countries with similar cultures and values. Companies operating in the countries within one of these clusters find a great deal of similarity within the cluster. However, when a firm moves from one cluster to another, the attitudes, beliefs, values, and methods of doing business are often different. In addition, the farther one moves away from a particular cluster, the greater the change. For example, a firm doing business in Canada would have very little problem with culture. If the firm were to set up operations in a Germanic or Latin European cluster, the challenge would be much greater. However, it would not be as difficult as if the firm set up operations in a Latin American or Nordic country. The

Figure 15-4

Country clusters.

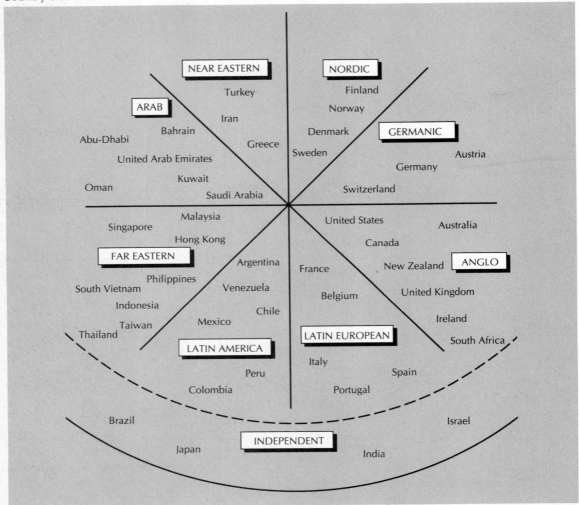

SOURCE: Simcha Ronen and Obed Shenkar, "Clustering Countries on Attitudinal Dimensions: A Review and Synthesis," *Academy of Management Journal,* September 1985, p. 449.

farther away one moves from a particular cluster in Figure 15.4, the greater the cultural differences one faces. This finding is particularly applicable in the case of communication, a topic addressed in the next section. Before continuing, take Self-Assessment Quiz 15.2 and see how much you currently know about Japanese management and communication practices.

SELF-ASSESSMENT QUIZ 15.2

What Do You Know About Japanese Management and Communication Practices?

Answer each of the following by placing a T (true) or F (false) to the left of it.

———— 1. In Japan, workers are guaranteed lifelong employment, and this is why so many of them work until they are well into their seventies.

———— 2. Japanese management has proven so effective that today this country's productivity is the highest in the world.

———— 3. Research shows that the Japanese are the hardest working people in the world.

———— 4. Many Japanese are not participative managers; they are autocratic.

———— 5. Loyalty among many Japanese workers is low.

———— 6. Most Japanese work long hours because they enjoy the work.

———— 7. Japanese communication systems are much more participative and humanistic than those in the United States.

———— 8. Japanese sent to the United States to run operations here are quick to adopt American methods of communicating and leading.

———— 9. Most Japanese firms reserve top management positions in their overseas subsidiaries for Japanese nationals.

———— 10. Most young Japanese college graduates entering the workforce express a desire to stay with their firm for a lifetime, but after only a few years on the job these attitudes change and only about one-third of them feel this way.

Answers are in the Answer section at the back of the book.

Implications for Management

1. Know that countries in the same cultural cluster tend to have similar values and ways of doing things, including their use of formal and informal organizational communication patterns. Countries in other clusters tend to do things differently, such as make greater or less use of informal communications, employ benevolent autocratic or participative leadership styles, and place high or low value on organizational position as opposed to job knowledge or expertise. By understanding the values of the particular cluster, it is possible to overcome common cultural barriers and communicate more effectively.

2. Remember that within each cultural cluster there are basic values to which most of the countries subscribe. These values also influence communication patterns and styles. For example, the Americans are highly pragmatic and place great importance on high achievement, drive, and competence. They value success, efficiency, and high productivity. Communicating with them in terms of these values is likely to find a receptive audience. The Japanese believe in many of the same ideas, but they are more group oriented. Therefore, although individual incentive plans work well with American workers, group incentive plans tend to be more effective among the Japanese. In addition, personnel are often rewarded on the basis of seniority and not merit, and there is a great deal of paternalism in Japan.

3. Keep in mind that some clusters put great emphasis on the quality of working life. They give their workers a great deal of authority and control over the workplace. Scandinavian managers, especially those in Sweden, fall into this category. In communicating with these people, quality of work life must be given greater attention than profit and productivity because people are regarded as more important than things.

4. Remember that some countries within a cluster will have different value orientations than the others. For example, in the Anglo cluster, most countries are similar to the Americans. However, the Australians tend to be a mix of the Anglo and Nordic cultures. They place a high value on morality and humanism and a low value on achievement, success, competition, and risk. So when communicating with them and doing business "down under," managers have to be sure they are in step with local values.

COMMUNICATION CHALLENGES

Cultural differences in the international arena are often reflected in communication challenges. The following examines five of the major challenges confronting managers doing business in this arena.

External and Internal Communication

Managers doing business overseas quickly realize that communications and directives external to their operations often have a significant effect on how successful they will be. A good example is the governmental effort to regulate international trade.[14] For some time the United States has been engaged in discussions regarding reciprocal trade agreements with Japan. The U.S. government is encouraging Japan to open its markets and American companies to enter this market. However, the Japanese perspective is that America is much stronger than she wants others to realize and that the trade imbalance between the two countries is not a major issue. The director of the International Economic Affairs Department of the Japan Federation of Economic Organizations explained the Japanese viewpoint as follows:

Communication external to operations can affect success.

American competitiveness cannot be measured by the balance-of-payments table. Many U.S. companies are producing a host of goods abroad and sending them back home. Such companies are already among the most competitive and integrating elements in the European economic scene. U.S. companies in Japan show much higher profit rates than Japanese companies in the States.

The United States is not hallowing, it is replenishing. It is not deindustrializing, it is only shedding a set of outgrown clothing. During the process, it looks off guard and sometimes vulnerable, and now that it has realized a fairly extensive currency devaluation, now that competitiveness has again captured its attention, American dynamism will surely rise to the challenge.[15]

Other external communication is more one way, not directly involving all parties affected by the message. A good example centers on Common Market rules designed to ensure that European firms are not forced out of their home markets. Recently, the Common Market's Competition Directorate has been empowered to approve mergers between large European firms.[16] The objective of this rule is to ensure that American and Japanese firms do not dominate the European market. Another example of external communication is the recent Common Market decision to place a floor on the price of computer chips. The Europeans have complained that other countries have produced chips and dumped them in Europe at below-cost prices. This is unlikely to happen in the future. During the 1990s only European-made chips will be sold in the Common Market.[17]

Internal Communication is also influenced by cultural differences.

Internal communication is also influenced by cultural differences. For example, Pascale investigated the communication techniques used by American and Japanese managers operating both in their home country and in each other's home country. He found that in some ways the two national groups used similar techniques. For example, American managers in the United States made an average of 37 phone calls daily, and American managers in Japan averaged 34 calls a day. Japanese managers in the United States made 30 calls a day, and their counterparts in Japan made 35 calls a day. Whereas the use of the phone to convey information did not vary between the two groups, Pascale did find some other important communication differences. Japanese managers in Japan made much greater use of face-to-face contacts than did American or Japanese managers in the United States. He also found greater use of upward and lateral communication in Japanese-based Japanese firms, whereas managers in U.S.-based Japanese firms used communication patterns similar to those of American firms.[18] With regard to the quality of decision making among the various groups of managers, Pascale found no differences. Each group gave itself a high score on decision making. However, the Japanese-based Japanese firms perceived the quality of decision implementation as higher than that of the other three groups.[19]

Explicit and Implicit Communication

In some countries, managers use implicit directions and in other countries explicit.

Another major difference between domestic and internal communication is the use of explicit and implicit communication. In some countries of the world, managers are very explicit in their directives and communiques, whereas in others they are very implicit. In the United States, for example, managers are taught to be explicit. When they set objectives with subordinates, they relate what they want done, by when it should be accomplished, the way in which progress will be measured, and what the final outcome should be. For example, they may direct a subordinate to increase encyclopedia sales in the New York Metropolitan area by 12 percent over last year. Half of this increase should occur during the months of September to December of this year, and the other 6 percent during the remaining eight months of next year.

In many other countries, communication is much more implicit. Rather than telling people what to do, managers make suggestions and discuss approaches that might be employed in solving a particular problem. The subordinate picks up these cues and uses them as a guide in making a final decision. This approach is so prevalent in Japan that it is even a part of their legal system. Only in recent years, for example, have the courts allowed spectators to take notes during a trial. Newspaper reporters were expected to listen, get the gist of what was going on, and then write their story from memory. It took a lawsuit by an American lawyer to change this practice![20]

Perception

American perceptions often differ from foreign perceptions.

The way Americans perceive things is often different from the way people in other countries perceive them. For example, in the United States individual incentive payment plans are becoming very popular. The more work someone does, the greater the person's pay. These plans are not popular in Japan because they clash with the country's collectivist approach. In Japan group incentive plans are used because in the Japanese culture to single any one out for special attention is considered embarrassing or rude.

Another example of perceptual difficulty is created by the way foreigners do business. Americans are accustomed to conducting business meetings behind closed doors with no interruptions. In many countries of the world, however, privacy is not provided for these types of meetings. Here is an example.

> A Canadian conducting business in Kuwait is surprised when his meeting with a high ranking official is not held in a closed office and is constantly interrupted. Using the Canadian-based cultural assumptions that (a) important people have large private offices with secretaries to monitor the flow of people into the office, and (b) important business takes precedence over less important business and is therefore not interrupted, the Canadian interprets the Kuwaiti's open office and constant interruptions to mean that the official is neither as high ranking nor as interested in conducting the business at hand as he had previously thought. The Canadian's interpretation of the office environment leads him to lose interest in working with the Kuwaiti.[21]

As a third example, H. C. Triandis describes a situation in which an American supervisor who favored employee participation was interacting with a Greek subordinate who both expected and wanted a dominant boss to take charge. The behaviors and interpretations of both parties are presented in Table 15.2.

Another example of perception problems faced by American executives overseas has to do with how the translation of advertising messages into the local language can totally change the meaning of the message.

> Ford . . . introduced a low cost truck, the "Fiera," into some of the less-developed countries. Unfortunately, the name meant "ugly old woman" in Spanish. Needless to say, this name did not encourage sales. Ford also experienced slow sales when it introduced a top-of-the-line automobile, the "Comet" in Mexico under the name "Caliente." The puzzling low sales were finally understood when Ford discovered that "caliente" is slang for a street walker.[22]

Table 15.2

BEHAVIOR AND INTERPRETATION: AN INTERNATIONAL COMMUNICATION PROBLEM	
Behavior	Attribution
American: How long will it take you to finish this report?''	**American:** I asked him to participate. **Greek:** His behavior makes no sense. He is the boss. Why doesn't he tell me?
Greek: ''I don't know. How long should it take?''	**American:** He refuses to take responsibility. **Greek** I asked him for an order.
American: ''You are in the best position to analyze time requirements.''	**American:** I press him to take responsibility for his actions. **Greek:** What nonsense: I'd better give him an answer.
Greek: ''10 days.''	**American:** He lacks the ability to estimate time; this time estimate is totally inadequate.
American: ''Take 15. Is it agreed? You will do it in 15 days?''	**American:** I offer a contract. **Greek:** These are my orders: 15 days.
In fact, the report needed 30 days of regular work. So the Greek worked day and night, but at the end of the 15th day, he still needed to do one more day's work.	
American: ''Where is the report?''	**American:** I am making sure he fulfills his contract. **Greek:** He is asking for the report.
Greek: ''It will be ready tomorrow.''	(Both attribute that it is not ready.)
American: ''But we agreed it would be ready today.''	**American:** I must teach him to fulfill a contract. **Greek:** The stupid, incompetent boss! Not only did he give me the wrong orders, but he doesn't even appreciate that I did a 30-day job in 16 days.
The Greek hands in his resignation.	The American is surprised. **Greek:** I can't work for such a man.

SOURCE: Adapted from H. C. Triandis, *Interpersonal Behavior* (Monterey, Calif.: Brooks/Cole, 1977), p. 248, and reported in Simcha Ronen, *Comparative and Multinational Management* (New York: John Wiley & Sons, 1986), pp. 101–102.

One laundry detergent company certainly wishes now that it had contacted a few locals before it initiated its promotional campaign in the Middle East. All of the company's advertisement pictured soiled clothes on the left, its box of soap in the middle, and clean clothes on the right. But, because in that area of the world people tend to read from the right to the left, many potential customers interpreted the message to indicate the soap actually soiled the clothes.[23]

Language

Often translations only approximate the message.

Language is another common barrier. Part of this problem was illustrated above in the use of advertising copy which is translated directly from one language to another. A complementary problem is the ability to capture the literal meaning of the message. Quite often translations are only approximations of what is actually being conveyed.

Hildebrandt, for example, found that among American subsidiaries he studied in Germany, language was a major problem when sending written messages to the home office. In an effort to reduce communication problems, the subsidiaries used a rather elaborate translation process. Typical steps in this process included: (1) holding a staff conference to determine what to include in the written message to the home office; (2) writing the initial draft in German; (3) rewriting the draft in German; (4) translating the material into English; (5) consulting with bilingual staff members regarding the translation; and (6) rewriting the English draft a number of additional times until the paper was judged acceptable for transmission. Even after all these steps were taken, the German staff personnel admitted they felt uncomfortable with the message being sent. They were sure that it did not contain totally accurate material. Moreover, when English experts reworked the material and put it into final form, the Germans admitted they were not sure whether the message captured the substantive intent or included editorial alterations.[24]

The significance of this translation barrier was made even clearer by Schermerhorn who recently conducted research among 153 Hong Kong Chinese bilinguals enrolled in an undergraduate management course at a major local university.[25] The students were given two scenarios written in either English or Chinese. One scenario involved a manager who was providing information or assistance to a subordinate. The other involved a manager who was giving personal support or praise to a subordinate. A careful translation and back-translation method was followed to create the Chinese-language versions of the research instruments. Two bilingual Hong Kong Chinese, both of whom were highly fluent in English and had expertise in the field of management, shared roles in the process. First, each translated one scenario and the evaluation questions into Chinese. Then they translated each other's Chinese versions back into English, and they discussed and resolved translation differences in group consultation with the researcher. Finally, a Hong Kong professor read and interpreted the translations correctly as a final check of equivalency. The participants were then asked to answer eight evaluation questions about the scenarios.

A significant difference was found between the two sets of responses. Those who were queried in Chinese gave different answers from those queried in English. Schermerhorn therefore concluded that language plays a key role in conveying information between cultures and that in conducting cross-cultural management research, bilingual individuals should not be queried in their second language.

Communication Flows

Communication flows are the same in international and domestic organizations. The two most important are upward and downward communication. However, some important differences exist in terms of emphasis. In addition, as seen in "International Communication in Action: Organizational Epigrams," certain stereotypes of communication flows help capture the flavor of upward and downward communication throughout the world.

DOWNWARD COMMUNICATION Organizations use downward communication primarily to convey orders and information. In Oriental countries, this channel is less direct than in the United States because of the implicitness of the communication

INTERNATIONAL COMMUNICATION IN ACTION

Organizational Epigrams

An epigram is a terse, witty statement. The following organizational epigrams are designed to poke fun at the way communication flows in international organizations; they were created by individuals with experience in each of these countries. Each epigram is accompanied by a brief explanation.

Americans believe they have a link to the top of the organization, regardless of their location in the hierarchy. Even personnel at the lowest level believe they can talk directly to the president.

American

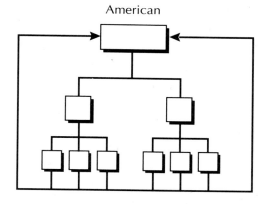

In England top managers and workers communicate among themselves, but there is no communication link between the two groups.

British

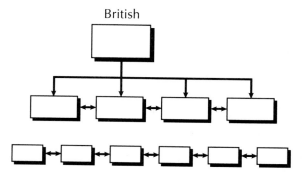

In China everyone is a small cog in a giant machine. The hierarchy is bureaucratic, with everyone having only a few subordinates. The hierarchy

Continued on next page

contains a large number of levels designed to accommodate, no doubt, the massive numbers of people in the organization.

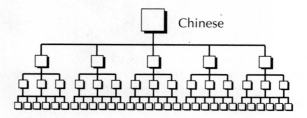

In Saudi Arabia no one coordinates their activities with anyone else. The structure consists of individual entities who operate alone.

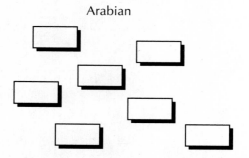

In Albania the person who is second in command is completely left out of the chain of command.

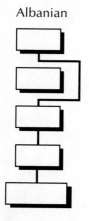

In Norway the chain of command runs from the top through to middle management. The people at the bottom do not receive information from their boss; instead, communication comes from the chief executive officer who violates the chain of command and comes down the line. The person to whom this individual speaks then passes the information along to all the other workers.

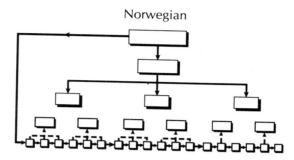

Norwegian

These epigrams illustrate that all communication flows throughout the world are much less efficient than the enterprise would like.

SOURCE: Adapted from Simcha Ronen, *Comparative and Multinational Management* (New York: John Wiley & Sons, 1986), pp. 313–319.

Downward communication is less direct in Oriental countries.

process. In Germanic countries, downward communication consists of strict orders that are to be obeyed without question. Meanwhile, in France downward communication is not only direct but also extends beyond business matters. For example, Inzerelli has found that French managers use organizational communication to influence their subordinates in nonwork-related matters, including the type of spouse the subordinate should marry, how many children they should have, and whether the wife should work.[26] Simply put, in some countries communication incorporates more than just work-related issues.

UPWARD COMMUNICATION Organizations use upward communication to transfer information from subordinate to superior. The primary purpose of this communication flow is to provide feedback and to ask questions or obtain assistance from higher level management. In the United States there is a strong effort to promote upward communication. In other countries such as those in the Far East, upward communication has long been used. Managers in the Orient make extensive use of suggestion systems and quality circles to obtain employee input, and they are usually available to listen to their people's concerns. Commenting on Matsushita's approach to dealing with employee suggestions, Pascale and Athos have reported:

The United States promotes upward communication.

> Matsushita views employee recommendations as instrumental to making improvements on the shop floor and in the marketplace. He believes that a great many little people, paying attention each day to how to improve their jobs, can accomplish more than a whole headquarters full of production engineers and planners.
>
> Praise and positive reinforcement are an important part of the Matsushita philoso-

phy. . . . Approximately 90 percent of . . . suggestions receive rewards; most only a few dollars per month, but the message is reinforced constantly: "Think about your job; develop yourself and help us improve the company." The best suggestions receive company-wide recognition and can earn substantial monetary rewards. Each year, many special awards are also given, including presidential prizes and various divisional honors.[27]

The company has used the same approach wherever it has established plants worldwide, and it has proven very successful. Each employee sees himself or herself as an important member of a successful team and is willing to do whatever is necessary to ensure the success of the group.

Outside the Far East upward communication is not as popular. For example, in Latin America many managers believe employees should follow orders and not ask a lot of questions. In Germany much less use is made of this form of communication. In most cases, however, the evidence shows that employees prefer to at least supplement downward communication with upward channels. The biggest obstacle to this effort is that the manager's cultural values often encourage a greater one-way than two-way emphasis and many employees come to accept this communication pattern. American firms operating overseas are often oriented toward two-way communication.[28] This approach can be helpful as long as it is acceptable to the employees. For example, in Germany most workers are accustomed to downward communication from the management, and some feel that a two-way process is inappropriate. In these cases, management often finds that a one-way process is more effective.

Implications for Management

1. Remember that the most effective communication process will be a reflection of the culture. If the personnel are accustomed to participating in decision making, two-way communication channels must be developed and nurtured. If the personnel are accustomed to being told what to do, one-way channels are more important, and attempts to incorporate worker input into the decision will be seen as a sign of management weakness.

2. Keep in mind that one of the most important ways of improving international communication is through language training. Most non-English-speaking managers who come to the United States have English-language training or get it here. Most Americans, on the other hand, who do business in non-English-speaking countries are not trained in that language. This is true for both the written and spoken language.

3. Obtain some cultural training about the country with which you will be doing business. There are important differences between the United States and most other countries. Moreover, often the customs of the subcultures in the country and the region where you are doing business may be unique to that area. Learning about these subcultures can be very helpful in knowing what to do and what to avoid doing. If you are being sent overseas, at the very least read a book on the culture and customs of that country.

C A S E   I N   P O I N T

Revisited

Now that you have had a chance to read the chapter, you should realize that Joel's mistakes were a result of his failure to understand the culture of the Philippines. Figure 15.1 shows that the Philippines are characterized by low individualism and high power distance. People are group oriented, and they feel comfortable in situations where one person has a great deal of power in contrast to the others. This attitude is in direct contrast to the United States (again see Figure 15.1) where individualism and low power distance are operative. Joel was accustomed to doing business the way he did in the United States. His new assistant should be particularly helpful in familiarizing Joel with the culture of the country and showing him how to communicate and interact more effectively with the personnel.

YOU BE THE CONSULTANT

Going International

Shuling & Whisler Inc. (S&W) is a successful high-tech computer firm located in a southwestern state. The firm is nonunionized and is well known for the quality of its products. One of its latest offerings is a medical computer scanner that helps doctors monitor the flow of blood through the body. Another of its medical-type computers is widely used by brain surgeons in helping to detect cerebral blockages and to identify the best way to surgically correct the situation. A third machine (the company's best-selling medical computer) helps identify cardiac problems and provides the surgeon with a three-dimensional color picture of the heart action. S&W has been so successful in developing state-of-the-art medical technology that currently there is a six-month backlog on orders. Some of these machines are being ordered from as far away as China and the Soviet Union.

Last month the company was approached by two firms, one from London and another from Tokyo. They would like the right to build these machines in their country and distribute them in specific geographic locales. The British firm would like exclusive production and distribution rights for Europe and the Middle East. The Japanese firm would like production and distribution rights for all of Asia including the entire Soviet Union. S&W believes that it can increase its worldwide sales by almost 100 percent if it grants these exclusive manufacturing and distribution rights to the two companies. At the same time, the firm is concerned about the quality of the product. "We build our machines to precise specifications," the president noted. "There is no room for production or assembly error. If these machines do not perform flawlessly, the patient's life could be in danger. If we were to grant anyone the right to manufacture these machines, we would need to have control over the operation to ensure that things are done exactly the way they are in our local plant."

The British and Japanese companies are willing to allow S&W to oversee their production operations, and they are willing to make any changes S&W wants made. "We are just as anxious as they are," noted the spokesperson for the British firm, "to ensure that these machines perform flawlessly. No one knows how to manufacture these computers better than S&W and we are willing to allow them to exercise complete production control in our plant. If the machines do not pass their inspection parameters, we won't ship them." A Japanese executive has expressed similar feelings. However, the top managers at S&W are still concerned about the difficulty associated with overseeing the control process. Here is the viewpoint of one of them.

> If we're going to enter into an agreement with these two firms, we're going to have to send people to London and to Tokyo to oversee the control process. This means that we are going to have all types of communication problems. We don't really know how the British work. Sure we're related by customs, but they probably have a lot of ways of doing things that will be strange to us. The Japanese present an even bigger challenge. We don't speak Japanese and we don't know much about how they do business. Yet the responsibility for overseeing the final product will be ours. I think we're getting in over our heads. I think we should just keep manufacturing locally and use these guys as our overseas distributors.

Assume that you have been asked to provide the president of S&W with your input regarding the challenges the firm will face if it signs an agreement with the British and/or Japanese. What communication problems might the firm face? What would you recommend the company do? Explain.

Key Points in This Chapter

1. There are two major reasons why international business communication is becoming an important area of interest. One is that more and more countries are investing in other nations. A second is that countries are importing and exporting more goods to each other. This increase in international trade means that during the 1990s companies will be doing more business with overseas customers both here and in other foreign locations.

2. The way business is conducted in the United States is not the same way it is conducted in many other countries. These differences can be explained in terms of four cultural dimensions: (a) power distance, (b) uncertainty avoidance, (c) individualism, and (d) masculinity.

3. Power distance is the extent to which less powerful members of an institution or organization are able to accept the fact that power is unequally distributed. Uncertainty avoidance is the extent to which people feel threatened by ambiguous situations and have created beliefs and institutions that try to avoid these situations. Individualism is the tendency of people to look after themselves and their immediate

family only. In contrast, collectivism is the tendency of people to belong to groups or collectives and to look after each other in exchange for loyalty. Masculinity is a situation in which the dominant values in society are success, money, and things. In contrast, femininity is a situation in which the dominant values in society are caring for others and the quality of life.

4. These four cultural dimensions help explain some of the differences in the work environment and communication practices of different countries. These dimensions also help identify country clusters that are characterized by nations with similar values and behaviors. Figure 15.3 provides a good example.

5. Cultural differences in the international arena are often reflected in communication challenges. These include external and internal communication, explicit and implicit communication, perception, language, and communication flows. Each of these challenges was discussed in the chapter, along with steps that can be taken to help deal with them.

Questions for Discussion and Analysis

1. If international trade between nations continues to increase, how will this development impact on the need to study international business communication? Explain.

2. Based on the data in Figure 15.1, what conclusions can you draw regarding the likelihood of American managers doing business with foreign firms during the 1990s? Defend your answer.

3. What is meant by the term *culture?* What are the four dimensions of culture? Identify each?

4. If a country has high power distance, what type of communication flow would you expect to be most prevalent in organizations, upward or downward? Why? Would you expect communication to be faster or slower, when contrasted with organizations in low power distance countries? Why?

5. If a country has a high uncertainty avoidance, would you expect communication to flow smoothly and quickly, or would there be a great deal of red tape and bureaucratic procedure to overcome? Defend your answer.

6. If a country is characterized by high individualism, would you expect people to take the initiative in communicating and getting things done, or would you expect them to wait for guidance and direction from management? Why?

7. If a country has a high masculinity index, would you expect there to be more or less two-way communication when contrasted with an organization in a country with a low masculinity index? Explain.

8. Figure 15.3 provides a series of country clusters based on the four cultural dimensions. What conclusion can you draw regarding the likely differences in communication styles between the United States and Denmark? Would your answer be

markedly different if you were examining the differences in communication styles between the United States and Saudi Arabia? Why or why not?

9. In what way is implicit communication a barrier to American firms doing business overseas? Explain.

10. Why is perception so important to effective international business communication? Use an example in your answer.

11. Can international communication problems be resolved through the use of interpreters? Why or why not? Defend your answer.

12. How do communication flows in overseas firms differ from those in the United States? Of what importance is this difference? Explain, using French and Japanese firms as your examples.

Exercises

1. Andy Carvallo is being transferred from the New York City branch of a major computer firm to its Tokyo office. Andy would like get an idea of the cultural differences he is likely to confront in his new locale. Using the four cultural dimensions discussed in this chapter, explain what these cultural differences will be? Describe them for Andy.

2. Joanne Cleffer has been a bank manager in Toronto for the last five years. She is now going to be transferred to a new position in Mexico City. Will there be many cultural differences in the way business is done? How will communication patterns be affected? Based on your answer, offer her three guidelines or suggestions regarding how to communicate effectively in this new environment.

3. Form a team of seven people and have each choose one of the non-Anglo clusters in Figure 15.3. Then go to the library and gather information on how business communication occurs in this cluster. Compare the countries in this cluster to the United States. Then have each person, in round-robin fashion, report his or her findings to the others.

References

1. "Surging Investment," *Fortune*, July 31, 1989, pp. 80–81; and "Shifting Trade Patterns," *Fortune*, July 31, 1989, pp. 88–89.

2. Bill Javetski and Sylwester Kruppa, "For a Jump-Start, Poland Tries a Jolt of Capitalism," *Business Week*, August 8, 1988, pp. 38–39.

3. Peter Galuszka et al., "Reforming the Soviet Economy," *Business Week*, December 7, 1987, pp. 76–88.

4. Steven Greenhouse, "Europe's Big 1992 Goal: Truly Common Market," *New York Times*, March 14, 1988, pp. 21, 25.

5. William J. Holstein et al., "Japan's Bigger and Bolder Forays into the U.S.," *Business Week*, November 17, 1986, pp. 80–81.

6. Laxmi Nakarmi, Larry Armstrong, and William J. Holstein, "Korea," *Business Week*, September 5, 1988, pp. 44–50.

7. For still other definitions, see Geert Hofstede, "Culture and Organizations," *International Studies of Management & Organization*, Winter 1980, pp. 23–26.

8. Geert Hofstede and Michael Bond, "The Need for Synergy Among Cross-Cultural Studies," *Journal of Cross-Cultural Psychology*, December 1984, p. 419.

9. Geert Hofstede, *Culture's Consequences: International Differences in Work-Related Values* (Beverly Hills, Calif.: Sage Publications, 1980).

10. *Ibid.*

11. *Ibid.*, pp. 419–420.

12. *Ibid.*, p. 420.

13. Simcha Ronen and Oded Shenkar, "Clustering Countries on Attitudinal Dimensions: A Review and Synthesis," *Academy of Management Journal*, September 1985, pp. 435–454.

14. Robert Neff, Paul Magnusson, and William J. Holstein, "Rethinking Japan," *Business Week*, August 7, 1989, pp. 44–52.

15. Kazuo Nukazawa, "Japan & the U.S.A. Wrangling Toward Reciprocity," *Harvard Business Review*, May–June 1988, p. 44.

16. Jonathan Kapstein, "Writing the New Rules for Europe's Merger Game," *Business Week*, February 6, 1989, pp. 48–49.

17. Thane Peterson, "The EC Just Says No to Japan's Cheap Chips," *Business Week*, January 30, 1989, pp. 46–47.

18. Richard Tanner Pascale, "Communication and Decision Making Across Cultures: Japanese and American Comparisons," *Administrative Science Quarterly*, March 1978, pp. 91–110.

19. *Ibid.*, p. 103.

20. David E. Sanger, "U.S. Lawyer Makes Japan Sit Up and Take Note," *New York Times*, March 17, 1989, p. 24.

21. Nancy J. Adler, *International Dimensions of Organizational Behavior* (Boston: Kent Publishing Co., 1986), p. 61.

22. David A. Ricks, *Big Business Blunders: Mistakes in Multinational Marketing* (Homewood, Ill.: Dow Jones-Irwin, 1983), p. 39.

23. *Ibid.*, p. 55.

24. H. W. Hildebrandt, "Communication Barriers Between German Subsidiaries and Parent American Companies," *Michigan Business Review*, July 1973, p. 9.

25. John R. Schermerhorn, "Language Effects in Cross-Cultural Management Research: An Empirical Study and a Word of Caution," *National Academy of Management Proceedings*, 1987, pp. 102–105.

26. Giorgio Inzerilli, "The Legitimacy of Managerial Authority—A Comparative Study," *National Academy of Management Proceedings*, 1980, pp. 58–62.

27. Richard Tanner Pascale and Anthony G. Athos, *The Art of Japanese Management* (New York: Warner Books, 1981), pp. 82–83.

28. William K. Brandt and James M. Hulbert, "Patterns of Communications in the Multinational Corporation: An Empirical Study," *Journal of International Business Studies*, Spring 1976, pp. 57–64.

Annotated Bibliography

Adler, Nancy J., *International Dimensions of Organizational Behavior* (Boston: Kent Publishing, 1986).

> This book provides important insights into the area of international business behavior including culture and communication. The examples are easy to follow, and the overall approach is both comprehensive and interesting.

Haire, Mason, Edwin E. Ghiselli, and Lyman W. Porter, *Managerial Thinking: An International Study* (New York: John Wiley & Sons, 1966).

> This is still the most comprehensive study available on the managerial attitudes and beliefs of international managers. The results of the study are based on research conducted among 3,641 managers from 14 countries on four continents and contain both profiles and conclusions of country clusters throughout the world.

Hodgetts, Richard M., and Fred Luthans, "Japanese HR Management Practices: Separating Fact from Fiction," *Personnel*, April 1989, pp. 42–45.

> This article identifies and describes critical human resources management practices of the Japanese and explodes some of the popular myths regarding how they are able to achieve such high productivity. For those looking for insights regarding Japanese management, this is must reading.

Hodgetts, Richard M., and Fred Luthans, *International Management* (New York: McGraw-Hill, 1991).

> This book examines international management practices from both a research-based and a practical, hands-on approach. Particular attention is given to culture and communication styles of managers throughout the world.

Neff, Robert, Paul Magnusson, and William J. Holstein, "Rethinking Japan," *Business Week*, August 7, 1989, pp. 44–52.

> This article provides some of the most up-to-date information regarding why the

United States is having such a difficult time negotiating with Japan and why during the 1990s this country is likely to continue to be one of the most difficult for U.S. firms to break into.

Ohmae, Kenichi, "Managing in a Borderless World," *Harvard Business Review*, May-June 1989, pp. 152–161.
This article by one of the leading international consultants in the world points out the importance of viewing the marketplace as one without national borders. Some of the most important steps in attaining this objective are discussed. Strong focus is placed on thinking and communicating from a global perspective.

CHAPTER 16

Improving Organizational Communication

" . . . The key to all successful organization management — is effective communication."

Human Resource Management: The Manager's Communication Responsibility, a brochure published by the Xerox Corporation, p. 1.

Objectives

1. To describe the nature of the communication audit.

2. To explain how a communication audit is conducted.

3. To discuss the main phases in a communication training program.

4. To describe some of the most well-known forms of communication training techniques.

5. To relate how post-training communication evaluation should be carried out.

C A S E   I N   P O I N T

The Training Program

The management of J. B. Williams knows that it has a great many communication problems. A communication audit that was conducted two months ago revealed that, among other things, the firm's upward communication channels are viewed by the employees as totally ineffective. After giving the matter a great deal of thought, top management decided to approve communication training for all departments.

Judith Cornwell is in charge of one of the firm's largest departments. When she learned of management's decision she was very pleased. "I've had lots of problems in my department," she told her boss, "because my people are ineffective listeners. I'm going to shop around and find a seminar that will help them improve their listening skills."

Since the firm does not have an in-house training department, Judith began talking to some of her fellow managers. From the conversation, she realized that they too intended to rely on outside training. Judy knew just the person she was going to get. Professor Henry Valzone is a professor in the Management Department at a large local university. Judy had been a student in Henry's strategic planning course, and she had enjoyed it very much. Henry does quite a bit of training and consulting, and when Judy called him up, he was delighted to hear from her.

"I've got something of a problem," she told Henry. "I need to get my people some training in the area of upward communication channels. Our communication audit revealed that most of our personnel do not feel comfortable communicating with their boss. Do you do much work along the lines of opening upward communication channels?" Henry answered that communication was one of his major training areas. "I've been working with a number of different firms over the past year on just this type of

problem. Why don't I drop by and talk to you about it?"

The following Tuesday Judy and Henry had lunch. During the meal Henry mentioned a dozen firms for whom he had conducted communication seminars. Judy recognized the names of over half the firms. Henry then explained how he would go about addressing her problem. It all sounded very good, and the two of them quickly agreed on a price for the one-day seminar.

Earlier this week Henry conducted the workshop. He began by discussing the importance of upward communication and having each person list the two major problems that confronted them on a daily basis. Later in the day he listed some of the problems on the board and offered general guidelines for dealing with them. The rest of the seminar was focused on three specific areas: understanding barriers to communication, learning how to identify informal groups, and understanding why feedback is vital to effective communication.

When the conference was over, Judy thanked Henry for his work. She then asked the participants to fill our a questionnaire regarding the value of the seminar. The most frequent response was, "interesting and enjoyable but I received very little specific help in how to open upward communication channels for my people." When Judy's boss read the reviews, he was not pleased. "What happened during this seminar?" he asked her. "Apparently most people didn't get much out of it. I'd like you to write me a memo regarding what went wrong."

What did go wrong? Why? How could it have been avoided? Write down your answers and then put them aside. We will return to them later.

INTRODUCTION

This book has constantly made the point that effective management is almost synonymous with good organizational communication. We feel there can be little dispute of this point. Why then are so many organizations still plagued by poor communication systems and what can be done about it? An in-house Xerox Corporation publication put it best, "It's one thing to *say* that good communication is vital; it's another to make it happen . . . . Managers said that they didn't see communication as a business priority and they didn't really have time for it. But then they added that they believed good communication is important and that if they ever got the time, they would do something about it because it did seem to make a difference." [1]

We assert that the time is now and that nothing is more important in terms of long-term organizational health. Where can an organization start? By assessing the current organizational communication system. For a number of years, communication audits have been available for that purpose. This chapter looks at the purpose and procedures of communication audits and then investigates training models appropriate for organizational communication needs. Finally, general conclusions for managers who wish to improve their communication climate are suggested.

THE COMMUNICATION AUDIT

The word "audit" often conjures up accounting and its accompanying procedures and practices. Communication audits, though different in makeup, have similar goals: a determination of what is happening, an identification of organizational strengths and weaknesses—all geared toward creating a more effective overall communication climate. Like an accounting audit, a communication audit alerts the organization to possible problems before they occur. As such, it is an excellent diagnostic tool.

Benefits of the Audit

The *communication audit* is a complete analysis of an organization's internal and external communication systems. Depending on the mandate and interests of top management, it can range from consideration of a single division to the entire organization. In any case, top management involvement and support are necessary if the effort is to be meaningful.

Audit data may be beneficial to the organization in at least seven ways.

1. To use premeasurement and postmeasurement data to determine the impact of new communication programs.

Communication audits have these benefits.

2. To assess the impact of on-going programs such as the Employee Retirement Income Security Act which required employers to make information available to employees about all benefit programs.

3. To assess the impact of organizational changes such as restructuring, computerization, and new training programs.

4. To chart the current organizational structure as an aid to reorganizational efforts.

5. To identify key communication groups prior to restructuring. This is especially important for multinational corporations that make overseas assignments.

6. To detail major communication costs associated with expansion into other areas or countries. (These include telephone, postage, and meetings.)

7. To develop new communication training programs geared to solve problems identified by the communication audit.[2]

Communication audits touch on many aspects of an organization's communication activity. Table 16.1 provides a list of questions to which a typical audit provides answers.

Table 16.1

COMMUNICATION AUDIT QUESTIONS

1. What environmental factors affect the organization's communication system?
2. What structural factors affect the organization's communication system?
3. What is the impact of stress and fear on the effectiveness of communication activities in the organization?
4. What is the relationship between mechanization and communication activity?
5. How can computers be used better to simulate organizational communication problems and activities?
6. What nonverbal communication variables exist within the organization?
7. What is the effect of change on communicative interaction and behavior?
8. How can formal and informal communication patterns be identified and standardized?
9. What are the differences between intershift and intrashift communication patterns within the organization?
10. What is the effect of isolation on such variables as organizational interaction? Morale? Productivity?
11. What are the most effective communication media under specific conditions?
12. What are the communication preferences of individuals concerning superiors? Subordinates? Peers?
13. What is the relationship between the levels of the organization and the amount of information received at these levels?
14. What is the effect of timing (opportune/inopportune) of communication of important events on morale and productivity?
15. What is the effect of intergroup relationships on the decision-making process in the organization?
16. How much change in the organization is realistic? Attainable? Practical?
17. What is the effect of changing values and value systems on the communication system of the organization?
18. What are the role and function of power groups in the organization?
19. What standards or norms should be developed to assess the effectiveness of the organizational communication system?
20. What is the cost (time and/or money) expended to process efficiency of information sources?

SOURCE: Gerald M. Goldhaber, *Organizational Communication* (Dubuque, Iowa: William C. Brown, 1986), pp. 400–401.

Among the companies that have conducted communication audits, many meaningful recommendations have been made and implemented. Some of them are as follows:

Past audits have
made other
recommendations.

1. Adding new formal channels of communication to make up for reported communication gaps.

2. Instituting an open communication system reference to communication goals and policies and other items of information.

3. Hiring or shifting personnel to improve the communication flow within the organization.

4. Establishing communication training programs for personnel.

5. Allowing better tracking of the company's external image as perceived by consumers, stockholders, and so on.

6. Providing additional communication about career opportunities within the organization.[3]

Conducting the Audit

There are perhaps as many specific methods of conducting a communication audit as there are people who conduct them. Nevertheless, most organizations follow some typical steps. Often, the first entails hiring an outside consultant to head up the project. Although many large companies carry out their own audits without outside help, external consultants often add much to the process. Quite often they have more experience and training in conducting these audits. They also tend to be more objective than their internal counterparts and are able to give their full attention to the project.

Joseph Kopec, a senior communication consultant, notes that regardless of who conducts the project, most audits go through six stages: holding the planning meeting; conducting top management interviews; collecting and analyzing the communication material; conducting employee interviews; preparing, administering, and analyzing the survey; and communicating the results. The following examines each of these steps.[4]

HOLDING THE PLANNING MEETING   The first objective is to establish the purposes of the audit. Generally, the purposes are prevention, investigation and correction, and innovation. Organizations that maintain a proactive posture use the preventive audit as a means of assuring that the communication system is "healthy," much like an annual medical exam assures one of good physical health. Investigation with the goal of correction takes place when it is recognized that communication problems do exist. Innovative audits take place when an organization is contemplating a major change and wants to increase its ability to adapt.[5] During this meeting the focus of the audit also is determined. Three different subsystem levels can be concentrated on: (1) interpersonal: those matters or problems that are the domain of a single individual and over which complete or primary control is possible; (2) interpersonal: those matters or problems that are outside the control of any one person, and are affected by the interaction of two or more persons; and (3) organizational: those matters or problems that may stem from the

The audit has six
major stages.

particular idiosyncrasies, structures, policies, and procedures of a given organization (department, division, firm).[6]

During this stage time also is devoted to establishing audit objectives, planning a general timetable, and identifying specific communication activities and variables for audit purposes. Table 16.2 shows a number of these variables.

The focus, objectives, and activities must be determined.

CONDUCTING TOP MANAGEMENT INTERVIEWS In this stage, an assessment of top management's attitudes about communication, as well as its perceptions of specific communication strengths and weaknesses, is made. Typically the president, vice president(s), and heads of functional departments such as personnel, finance, communication, and marketing are interviewed. This step is critical because it not only pinpoints areas for additional research, but also provides insight into individual managers' styles of communication.[7]

Management attitudes must be assessed.

COLLECTING AND ANALYZING COMMUNICATION MATERIAL At the same time that the top management interviews are being conducted, a wide variety of communication material is collected, inventoried, and analyzed so as to judge its

Table 16.2

AUDIT VARIABLES	
Authority, responsibility	Message
Channels, networks	Content
Linkage	Direction
Propinquity	Distortion
Status differences	Distribution
Interpersonal attraction	Speed
Satisfaction	Rate
Sense of achievement	Internal noise
Traffic density	External noise
Load, people	Redundancy
Load, time	Efficiency
Efficiency	Modes
Environmental contact	Verbal, oral
Expectations	Verbal, written
Interaction	Nonverbal
Ability	Motivation
Retention	Objectives
Comprehension	Operational functions
Satisfaction	Organizational structure
Sense of achievement	Skills
Status differences	Communication
Interpersonal attraction	Perceptual

SOURCE: Dale A. Level, Jr. and William P. Galle, Jr. *Business Communications: Theory and Practice* (Dallas, Tex. Business Publications, 1988), p. 405.

Internal and external documents are examined.

communication effectiveness. This material includes such internal documents as memos, newsletters, bulletin board notices, benefit plan descriptions, procedures manuals, and orientation materials. It also includes external materials such as advertisements and news releases. The review is conducted in accord with the overall goals as well as the perceived strengths and weaknesses that were identified earlier.

CONDUCTING EMPLOYEE INTERVIEWS "Focus" groups of employees are identified within each functional area, and these groups then are interviewed. The purpose of these interviews is to obtain opinions across demographic lines as well as to solicit ideas free from the influence of others. As a result supervisors are kept out of groups with their own employees and vice versa.[8]

PREPARING, ADMINISTERING, AND ANALYZING THE SURVEY Next project leaders draft a survey instrument for general distribution. This is a particularly critical part of the procedure because poorly structured questions will, at best, gather little valuable information and will, at worst, elicit erroneous responses. Before using the questionnaire in the organization at large it will be tested on a pilot group, providing the opportunity to rewrite the instrument and eliminate any problem areas.

Next the questionnaire is distributed. At this point the object is to get as broad a coverage as possible. Employees at all levels of the study will be surveyed. If it is possible the surveys will be passed out in person. Otherwise, they will be sent through the mail. Research reveals that audit surveys mailed to the office rather than home are more likely to be returned.

Then the data must be analyzed.

The last part of this phase is the tabulation and summarization of the responses. The actual calculations often are handled by the computer. However, it is very important that operational people understand the critical nature of this step. As Kopec warns, "Be sure you have some way to professionally and expeditiously handle this volume of material. And be sure if you use your internal data processing personnel that they understand and agree to the high priority this information should have. Be sure you can also guarantee privacy of data. This is critical given current court cases."[9]

Finally, the results must be communicated to the personnel.

COMMUNICATING THE RESULTS The results are analyzed in conjunction with the analysis of the printed material already collected. Interpretations of the audit material are then developed and put into an audit report, which is sent to management. This report also includes recommendations for action. At the same time the employees are given feedback in order to let them know that their responses have served as a basis for recommended action.

Additional Data Treatment Methods

In addition to the survey methodology presented above, organizations can make use of other methods of collecting and/or treating audit information. These include content analysis, readability tests, and semantic differential, ECCO analysis, interaction analysis, Odiorne's communication audit, the communication log, and shadowing.

CONTENT ANALYSIS Content analysis looks at messages according to specific measurable units such as sentence length, vocabulary usage, and level of abstraction.

Key words or phrases often are studied and subtle meanings revealed. For example, management's real attitude toward its open-door policy may be revealed by log accounts of impromptu meetings with employees such as "Ralph Smith interrupted my budget planning to complain about his supervisor." Both "interrupted" and "complain" reveal a negative bias on the part of the manager.

READABILITY TESTS Written material has "readability" when it can be read one time and comprehended. This often is measured by answering the question: Is the person writing at the level of the reader's understanding? Many times what is perfectly clear to the writer is confusing and uncertain to the reader.

There are a number of commonly used audit techniques.

SEMANTIC DIFFERENTIAL This technique uses a scale of paired adjectives such as good and bad, honest and dishonest. There is usually a continuum between the two extremes on which the respondent can identify his or her feelings about the variable being measured. Figure 16.1 illustrates a partial questionnaire designed around an open-door policy and using the semantic differential.

ECCO ANALYSIS ECCO (Episodic Communication Channels in Organizations) is a rather complicated technique that puts a trace on messages as they move through the organization systems. The objective is to determine which messages flow through which channels, the time involved, and the distortion caused by such movement. This

Figure 16.1

Open-door policy.

Promotes honest communication	1 2 3 4 5 6 7 8	Promotes dishonest communication
Is encouraged by management	1 2 3 4 5 6 7 8	Is not encouraged by management
Leads to increased trust and confidence in management	1 2 3 4 5 6 7 8	Does not lead to increased trust and confidence in management
Allows one to air personal gripes	1 2 3 4 5 6 7 8	Does not allow one to air personal gripes
Allows one to air job-related gripes	1 2 3 4 5 6 7 8	Does not allow one to air job-related gripes
Overall, it is an effective policy	1 2 3 4 5 6 7 8	Overall, it is not an effective policy

analysis requires quite a bit of time and expertise on the part of the observer/tracer, but if properly done it can provide important feedback on communication activities.

INTERACTION ANALYSIS The reader is referred back to Chapter 10 and the information on network analysis. Interaction analysis typically depends on sociometric data designed to compare the informal system with the formal system.

ODIORNE'S COMMUNICATION AUDIT This technique is typical of a number of questionnaire approaches that query superior groups and subordinate groups separately and then compare the results to pinpoint discrepancies and identify potential communication hazards.

COMMUNICATION LOG In this self-reporting technique individuals are asked to record their communication activities. They often are asked to note the medium used, the subject covered, the time used, and a host of other related items. A great deal of descriptive material can be gathered with this technique, but analysis and interpretation are usually difficult. In addition, one is constrained by the degree of cooperativeness and ability of the log keepers.

SHADOWING This technique is very similar to the communication log. However, with shadowing a trained observer literally follows the subjects around and makes the notations for them. Shadowing is a much more complete way of gathering information on communication patterns and habits than is the communication log. On the other hand, it is also a very expensive approach.

Implications for Management

1. Don't underestimate the value of communication audits. They provide insights regarding communication problems and their causes. These audits should be carried out at least every couple of years. They are one of the best ways of finding out how effective the organizational communication system is working.

2. Remember that a communication audit is only as good as the information it collects. Unless people from all levels of the hierarchy are polled and they feel free to give objective responses, the audit is unlikely to produce useful information.

3. Once the data are collected and analyzed, answer the question: now what? Unless something is done to address the problems, there is likely to be little success with future audits. Everyone will ask themselves why they should participate when nothing happens as a result of their efforts. You must be serious not only about finding out if there are communication problems but in doing something about them. Remember, the buck stops with you!

COMMUNICATION TRAINING

When the communication audit has been completed, management should know where the organization's communication weaknesses are. For example, the final audit report may indicate weaknesses in such skill areas as providing feedback to employees, running effective meetings, and problem solving. Training seems to be called for, but setting up an effective training program to specifically address these problems can be a complicated job. Far too often, a firm simply will purchase a standard training package that addresses a communication area in general but does not take into account the unique problems that face this particular firm. In fact, the organization should seek a tailor-made program that focuses on its particular needs. This calls for a four-step approach as described in Figure 16.2.

Pretraining analysis is important.

Phase one, the pretraining analysis, can be done with a communication audit such as that already described, or through the use of a less rigorous investigation such as a questionnaire or a series of meetings with managers for the purpose of identifying organizational communication problems that warrant attention. Phase two, formulation of training objectives, looks at both planning and informational goals. How will the program be run and how will its effectiveness be evaluated? The third phase includes all of the actual training. The fourth phase is a post-training evaluation. During this phase the organization will use a variety of evaluation instruments in determining how well the training objectives have been met. This evaluation feedback is firmly linked to all phases of the communication training. The following examines phases two, three, and four in greater detail.

Formulation of Training Objectives

Objectives should be specific and measurable.

The first step in an effective communication training program is a clear statement of the objectives. These objectives should be written in specific, measurable terms. Often referred to as behavioral objectives, they should be specifically designed for each particular program and should clearly spell out what the trainee will be able to do when

Figure 16.2

A communication training model.

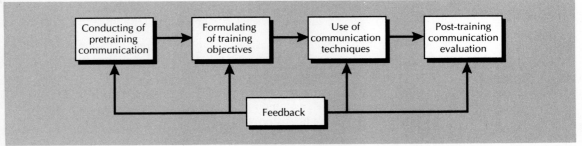

the training has been completed. For example, the behavioral objectives for an effective listening seminar might be as follows:

By the end of this six-hour seminar, the trainee will be able to:

1. Explain the ten most important reasons for ineffective listening and analyze his or her own use of these pitfalls.

2. Differentiate between active and passive listening and relate the pros and cons of each.

3. Demonstrate active listening responses to a variety of typical work-related situations.

4. Give examples of neutral probes designed to keep the speaker thinking and talking through his or her concerns.

Can you recognize sound objectives? Take a minute and assess the objectives listed in Self-Assessment Quiz 16.1. When you are done, check your answers with those at the end of the book.

SELF-ASSESSMENT QUIZ 16.1

Can You Recognize Good Behavior Objectives?

Directions: Assume that the purpose of a particular training workshop is to improve superior–subordinate communication. The following ten training objectives have been set by the trainer. Rate each of them as P (poor), S (satisfactory), or G (good).

_____ 1. Be a better listener.

_____ 2. Read training materials and handouts.

_____ 3. Demonstrate effective performance appraisal interviewing techniques.

_____ 4. Deliver nonthreatening but specific feedback on employee performance.

_____ 5. Understand feedback techniques.

_____ 6. Be a good example to the employees.

_____ 7. Be able to assess the information needs of the employees.

_____ 8. Assess the nonverbal content of superior–subordinate communication for confirming or conflicting cues.

_____ 9. Be able to set a good example by being more self-disclosing in superior–subordinate communication.

_____ 10. Communicate better.

Answers are in the Answer section at the back of the book.

When the training is over, trainees can review the behavioral objectives and see if they are able to perform as expected. Trainers, in turn, can assess the program, the trainees, and the objectives themselves based on the results. In sum, training objectives provide a map for reaching an overall goal by breaking it down into a series of manageable components or building blocks. Many training programs are sabotaged from the outset because of inadequate or inaccurate training objectives — or the absence of them. Their absence is almost a certain promise of failure, for a haphazard approach to training serves only to frustrate trainers and contribute to an attitude that training is "soft" nonsense and a waste of time.

Use of Communication Training Techniques

A number of training models are particularly suited to communication training. These include role playing, games and structured experiences, case studies, and lectures/discussions. Before examining these representative techniques, it is wise to heed Goldhaber's warning that "Too often, companies purchase training programs without regard for both current and future needs of the organization . . . training, especially communication training, fulfills an important need within an organization and that need can be assessed *prior* to development and/or purchase of a training program and the results can be evaluated *after* such a program is administered."[10]

The choice of the technique should be based on the answers to three questions: Which technique will meet the specific behavioral objectives desired? Which technique will provide a meaningful growth experience for the trainee and result in enhanced skills that can be directly transferred to the job? Which technique will actively engage the trainer in the most appropriate learning structure? In regard to the last question, a participative simulation may well provide a better learning environment than a more traditional lecture, although more actual theory is communicated in the lecture format.

ROLE PLAYING   Role playing involves an acting out of a real-life situation. Typically, the facilitator or trainer will set the scene by assigning general role descriptions to various participants. For example, one person may be assigned the role of a supervisor who is to discipline a worker for breaking a company rule. The other person is assigned the role of the worker. Once started, the simulation allows the trainees the latitude to interpret their roles freely. Much can be learned from the results. At the end of the role play, general discussion is held about what has transpired, pinpointing both weaknesses and strengths. Typical criticisms include lack of eye contact, interrupting behavior, nonverbal messages, talking too much or too little, biased listening, and judgmental behavior. Subsequent role plays will incorporate lessons as they are learned, thus providing the trainees with realistic experience. Often these sessions are videotaped so participants can watch themselves and better understand their own behavior as they process input from observers. In addition, "before" and "after" videotapes can graphically illustrate progress in training objectives.

Role playing provides for personal insights.

GAMES AND STRUCTURED EXPERIENCES   Games are competitive exercises that pit individuals or groups against others. An example of a communication game used by the authors is groups charged with building a square out of 20 pieces of cardboard

Games develop interpersonal skills.

provided to each of the four- to six-member teams. The first group to complete its square is the winner. Typically, some teams designate an authoritarian leader whereas others try to be very participative. Predictably, in a stressful, compressed time exercise the groups with an autocratic leader tend to have the edge. When the game is over, there is an in-depth discussion of observations, feeling, and, most importantly, meanings derived from the experience. In the process, interpersonal skills are developed.

Structured experiences are noncompetitive.

Structured experiences are similar to games except that they are not competitive and the learning objectives are specified in advance. One example, often used by the authors, is an exercise for illustrating the pros and cons of one-way versus two-way communication. A trainer volunteer is placed behind the group and asked to describe a series of geometric shapes that the group is to draw to specifications. Participants are not allowed to ask questions or to indicate their progress in any way. Placement of the "boss" behind the group limits the individual's ability to read the group's nonverbal messages. When the exercise is complete, the "boss" then faces the group and describes another set of shapes for them to draw. This time two-way communication is illustrated by the group's being allowed to ask any questions it wishes, slow down the "boss," ask for a repeat of a direction, and so forth. Results then are compared and general discussion ensues. As with games, this discussion phase is the key part of the training. Needless to say, it usually results in the participants admitting that they were better able to complete the task with two-way than with one-way communication.

CASE STUDIES Case studies use written documents and stories that relate actual job situations. The trainees are given time to read the case, usually before the meeting, and are asked to come up with tentative answers to case-related questions. For example, the participants may be given a case that relates a productivity problem that was caused by a manager's failure to properly handle the introduction of computers into the workplace. Typical case questions would include:

Case studies allow for analysis of written documents.

1. What is the problem in this case?

2. How did the problem arise?

3. What could have been done to avoid this problem?

4. Given the situation, what should be done now?

Extensive discussion then follows as the trainees explore their varied answers to the case questions.

LECTURES/DISCUSSIONS Lecture/discussion is the most widely used training technique, and in the case of communication training, among the least effective. It is a good vehicle for one-way delivery of information to a large group, but it is deficient in providing an effective transmission of meaning. Feedback and interaction are lacking.

The lecture is a very popular approach.

One author has criticized the approach by noting, "It would also appear that paperback books and copy machines are relatively inexpensive means of providing trainees with whatever information the lecturer would present live. Then, with the free time, the group can interact and discuss the readings. Another substitute for the live lecture is to use video cassette information recorded in advance."[11]

Post-Training Communication Evaluation

Regardless of the training techniques chosen, post-training evaluation and feedback is a very important final step. Did the training adequately meet the stated objectives? Were the problems correctly diagnosed and treated? Did the training point out other problem areas that need to be addressed? Many companies spend a great deal of time and money organizing and running a training program but virtually no money evaluating the results. No wonder so many employees view these programs as a waste of time. In overcoming this problem, management should ask six post-training questions:

1. Were the trainees adequately prepared for the program? Were the training objectives compatible with organizational goals?

2. Were the trainees adequately motivated to learn the material in the program?

3. Were the training techniques valid and professionally administered?

Post-training questions must be asked.

4. Did the training techniques actually result in the objectives being met?

5. Were the trainees sufficiently trained so that their behavioral change will positively affect organizational goals?

6. Did the training results transfer to on-the-job activities?[12]

MANAGEMENT IS COMMUNICATION

As we reach the end of this book we hope each reader will reflect on his or her personal organizational communication skills. If you will remember the following important guidelines for communication, your job will be easier and more enjoyable and so will that of your employees and co-workers.

Give Positive Reinforcement Whenever Possible

Remember that what you "stroke" is usually what you get. Far too often managers look up from their paperwork only to note an undesirable behavior or deviation from objectives. Have a positive attitude with your employees. Workers avoid communicating with many managers because they see them as scolding clockwatchers who are always out to "catch" them doing something wrong. Remember that, with today's value systems, employees are as interested in how they are treated as they are with salary benefits. The classical manager described in Chapter 2 does not do very well with today's increasingly professional and independent workforce. Praise costs nothing but a few moments of time, and its potential positive benefit is incalculable.

Be Open and Honest

Honest communication with employees often is a neglected art. People like to know where they stand and what expectations their managers have for them. When employees sense a less-than-honest communication climate between themselves and their managers, the informal channels proliferate and the error contained in the grapevine

ETHICS IN COMMUNICATION

Limiting the Right of Privacy

In managing effectively, many firms are finding that one area in particular demands a great deal of consideration: drug and alcohol testing. In recent years, firms have been developing on-site drug testing programs, and this practice is likely to increase during the 1990s. On the one hand, critics claim that these programs violate the right of personal privacy and are unethical. On the other hand, supporters claim that the issue is so critical to the survival of businesses that such testing is totally justified.

It has been estimated that drug and alcohol abuse cost American businesses about $100 billion annually in lost productivity, increased absenteeism, and higher health care costs. As a result, many employers require drug tests of incoming employees as well as periodic tests of current workers. Do these tests violate the individual's right to privacy? The courts have held that they do not because, if the person were to be a drug abuser and later injure someone as a consequence of drug-influenced behavior, the firm could be held liable. Thus the company has a right to protect itself from the outset. At the same time the courts have said that the employer cannot communicate the results of these tests to anyone who does not have a need to know them. Otherwise the employee can sue the employer for violation of privacy.

One of the biggest problems that many firms face is convincing unions of the need for drug testing. The courts have held that companies cannot unilaterally decide to implement a drug testing program if the workforce is covered by a union contract. This matter must be negotiated with the union. For example, research shows that many unions will agree to drug testing for new job applicants and when there is reasonable suspicion that a current employee is a substance abuser. However, the unions will not agree to random drug testing. This issue will continue to be a focal point of attention during the 1990s.

Where there is no union, management has greater leeway in deciding how to handle the drug testing issue. However, even here there is strong opposition to random testing, and most firms are looking for alternative approaches. The most acceptable approach is for companies to develop a series of procedures that will ensure both the reliability of the tests and the confidentiality of the results. One expert has the following comment:

> Every employer should have a substance abuse program which includes a testing component. Drug and alcohol abuse in the workplace is too widespread and grave a problem to ignore. Employers who do so needlessly throw away money and expose themselves to substantial tort liability. At the same time, however, designing and implementing a substance abuse program is not an exercise to be

Continued on next page

taken on casually. A poorly designed, haphazardly implemented program will expose the employer to substantial liability, costing the employer more money than it will save. Fortunately, liability is largely avoidable if the program is developed and implemented with experienced guidance.

SOURCE: James R. Redeker and Jonathan A. Segal, "Profits Low? Your Employees May Be High!" *Personnel Journal*, June 1989, pp. 72–78.

increases. Trust between managers and subordinates is a major characteristic of a healthy communication climate. Today this trust is more difficult to foster in the midst of problems such as substance abuse. Does the employer have the right to interfere when an employee is suspected of being a substance abuser? What about drug testing? See "Ethics in Communication: Limiting the Right of Privacy." Generally if a substance abuse problem manifests itself in the workplace, confrontation of the issue by the employer is a must. Most managers are supportive but firm and require the employee to seek organizational or community resources for help.

Solicit Employee Feedback

Do not be satisfied with your own honest communication with employees. If it remains strictly a one-way street, the manager will soon think his or her efforts are futile and put less effort into maintaining an honest system. Ask employees what they think. Encourage them to brainstorm and otherwise to participate. Pay attention and demonstrate that you understand their concerns and appreciate their input even if you cannot do as they suggest.

Take a Genuine Interest in Your Employees

Valuable guidelines for improving managerial communications

Every employee likes to be treated as a human being, not as a secretary, a nurse, or an engineer. For too long we have learned not to get involved in people's personal lives, yet report after report shows that employees equate job satisfaction at least partially with their supervisors' "caring" about them as persons. Take the time to ask your subordinates about their interests, their health, their family, or whatever else seems to concern them. Make sure, however, that your interest is genuine because an insincere "how's your family?" is seen as a trivial courtesy, nothing more.

Communicate Goals and Objectives

One of the foremost reasons why employees do not identify more closely with their companies is that they are not apprised of its goals and objectives. Simply understanding where their job fits within the overall plan often can be very motivational. Understanding the direction of the company both in the short run and the long run helps the employee identify with a meaningful job. Remember from the chapter on formal communication that studies conclusively show that employees *do* want more and better information from upper levels in the hierarchy. They want to learn about goals and objectives from the source and not from the grapevine.

Listen to Complaints

Active listening is an extremely important managerial concern. An area in which this concern is especially important is in listening to employee problems and complaints. These problems may merely be symptoms of more complex problems within the organizational system, and treating symptoms does nothing but momentarily assuage the pain. So try to get at the cause of the employee's concern and address it; otherwise, you will have to deal with it over and over again.

Reward Effective Communication Efforts

Like anything else, something that is rewarded in meaningful ways tends to be repeated. Employees work with more enthusiasm when their efforts are equitably rewarded. If you really want open multidirectional communication, you must reward those who make a true effort to do so. This reward may be as simple as paying full attention to the employee who is sharing her concerns with you. Appreciation and acknowledgment of effort are rewards that are intrinsically motivating for many but that managers tend to overlook.

Above All, Set a Good Example!

Employees tend to look to managers to set the communication climate. If you are always too busy to take the time to communicate effectively, employees will not make the effort to use formal channels. If, however, you conscientiously and consistently strive to improve your personal communication habits and noticeably appreciate employee efforts to do the same, you will see a much improved climate. However, do not expect to see dramatic change overnight. Improving the organizational communication climate is a slow process. Old habits must be replaced by new habits; organizational communication processes must be examined and made more effective.

To a very large extent, management is communication, and effective communication skills are the number one requirement of the successful manager. The evidence is all around us if we but choose to look. Even a relatively small effort to improve organizational communication can put a company at a competitive advantage. As Roger D'Aprix says,

> In fact, there is a host of potential gains for the organization from a small investment in more effective communication. It may be possible to create a climate in which people honestly feel that they can speak out without fear of retribution. It may be possible to motivate people to give management their best suggestions on cost effectiveness and improved ways of doing things. It may make it easier for people to accept difficult decisions because they understand their necessity. It may permit earlier identification of mistaken policy or inappropriate practice. And, finally, it may improve the organization's chances of outdistancing its principal competitors in employee climate, thereby improving its ability to recruit, train, and retrain people and improving its overall effectiveness in the marketplace.[13]

C A S E   I N   P O I N T

Revisited

Judy made a number of mistakes. The primary one was that she did not get Henry to design a program geared directly to her needs. He offered a general communication program. Notice that not all the topics he covered were geared directly toward upward communication. How could this have been prevented? One way is by having Henry submit a detailed training program including objectives (what the participants are going to learn) and content (the specific topics, tools, and techniques that will be included). On the positive side, Judy's mistake was not original. Many managers commit this error because they lack experience regarding what to look for in training programs. Judy needs to become more familiar with how to evaluate a program prior to its presentation. Much of the information in the second part of this chapter could be of value to her.

Implications for Management

1. Remember that every successful management training program must begin with a plan. What is to be done and why? Many firms buy or sponsor general communication programs that are not specifically designed to address their particular needs. The result is a program that is interesting and sometimes entertaining, but not one that helps them cope with communication problems that are affecting organizational productivity. Your programs should be tailor-made.

2. Before the program begins, know how you are going to evaluate the effort. This means writing measurable, specific behavioral objectives that are directly tied to the program content. It will take some time to get good at this, but your efforts will pay off in better programs.

3. Keep in mind that you can use many different types of communication training techniques. It helps to use more than just one or two, because this enlivens the program and keeps the participants interested. On the other hand, if the program is only one day in duration, do not use too many different techniques. This detracts from the participants' ability to digest and analyze what they are learning. Pick a handful and work with these.

4. Be aware that post-training communication evaluation is a must. It is better to find out that the program did not go well and work on improving it the next time than it is to remain in the dark regarding its success or failure. When the program is over, get objective feedback and use this to help you design even better programs the next time.

YOU BE THE CONSULTANT

Planning the Project

A large insurance company recently completed a communication audit. The audit was conducted by its in-house personnel department and covered all levels of the hierarchy. The results were compiled into a 54-page study entitled "Communication Practices," and sent to managers throughout the organization.

Many communication problems are highlighted in the study. One is the apparent failure of the company's open-door policy. Over 80 percent of the employees feel that their boss discourages them from coming by to discuss problems or get advice. A second is the perception that each hierarchical group has of its own behavior and of the behavior of the level above it. For example, when it comes to willingness to communicate change in advance, give praise and encouragement, and follow through on promises, the data in Table 1 show the perceptual gaps. A third is the failure of management to understand how to effectively use the informal organization in getting things done.

On an overall basis, the report concludes that management at all levels of the structure needs communication training. In fact, notes the audit, most managers are surprised that management has not provided such training in the past.

After reading the report and holding a meeting with the top management staff, the president has decided to call in a training and consulting group to provide management the assistance it needs. A number of consulting groups would like to bid on the job, and the president has decided to make the final choice on the basis of the proposal that is submitted. Each is to examine the data in Tables 1 – 3 and spell out the type of training it will offer. The firm with the best proposal will get the job.

Assume you are the member of your consulting firm who has been charged with this assignment. What behavioral objectives would you set for your program? Identify them and then spell out the type of training you would recommend. Describe the specific approaches you would take. How would you go about conducting a post-training evaluation? Be complete in your writeup.

Table 1

HOW OFTEN DOES YOUR BOSS COMMUNICATE CHANGE IN ADVANCE?
(HOW OFTEN DO YOU?)

	Often	Usually	Sometimes	Seldom	Never
Vice presidents	5(45)	15(45)	20(10)	30	30
General managers	4(52)	13(43)	19(5)	36	28
Foremen	3(57)	10(41)	18(2)	39	30
Supervisors	2(63)	9(37)	16	41	32
Workers	1	7	15	45	32

Table 2

HOW OFTEN DOES YOUR BOSS GIVE PRAISE AND ENCOURAGEMENT TO YOU? (HOW OFTEN DO YOU?)

	Often	Usually	Sometimes	Seldom	Never
Vice presidents	25(60)	35(35)	30(5)	10	—
General managers	20(70)	45(30)	25	10	—
Foremen	15(78)	30(22)	20	15	20
Supervisors	14(87)	21(13)	33	23	9
Workers	1	6	22	35	36

Table 3

HOW OFTEN DOES YOUR BOSS FOLLOW THROUGH ON PROMISES? (HOW OFTEN DO YOU?)

	Often	Usually	Sometimes	Seldom	Never
Vice presidents	32(60)	28(38)	20(2)	15	5
General managers	26(67)	24(30)	15(3)	20	15
Foremen	21(75)	22(24)	27(1)	23	7
Supervisors	10(95)	18(5)	30	28	14
Workers	5	15	34	30	16

Key Points in This Chapter

1. The communication audit is a complete analysis of an organization's internal and external communication systems. The purpose of the audit is to identify where communication is effective and where it is not.

2. The six stages in a communication audit are these: holding the planning meeting; conducting top management interviews; collecting and analyzing communication material; conducting employee interviews; preparing, administering, and analyzing the survey; and communicating the results. Each was discussed in the chapter.

3. In addition to the survey methodology, the other methods of collecting and/or treating audit information include content analysis, readability tests, the semantic differential, ECCO analysis, interaction analysis, Odiorne's communication audit, the communication log, and shadowing. Each of these was discussed in the chapter.

4. Communication training has four important phases: a pretraining communication analysis, the formulation of training objectives, the use of communication training

techniques, and post-training communication evaluation. The first and last phases tie everything together and ensure that the objectives are attained.

5. In communicating effectively managers need to remember eight points: give positive reinforcement whenever possible; be open and honest; solicit employee feedback; take genuine interest in the employees; communicate goals and objectives; listen to complaints; reward effective communication efforts; and, above all, set a good example.

Questions for Discussion and Analysis

1. Before undertaking a communication audit, seven factors should be given consideration. What are they? Identify them.

2. There are six steps in conducting a communication audit. What takes place in each step? Describe each.

3. A number of data treatment methods are used in collecting and/or treating audit information. Some of these include content analysis, readability tests, the semantic differential, ECCO analysis, and interaction analysis. How do each of these contribute to the analysis of the audit information?

4. How does a communication log differ from shadowing? Compare and contrast the two.

5. What is the first stage in communication training? Identify and describe it.

6. What do managers need to know about training objectives? In your answer identify and describe three such objectives being sure to explain the difference between a poorly stated and a well-stated objective.

7. What are some of the most common communication training techniques? Identify and describe four of them.

8. Why is post-training communication evaluation so important? Explain.

9. What are some useful important communication guidelines that managers should follow? Identify and describe five.

Exercises

1. Reynolds Toy Corporation has called you in to study their internal communication system. At the initial meeting with the top managers you suggested a communication audit as a diagnostic tool. This idea was accepted with enthusiasm by Reynolds. Tomorrow there will be a planning meeting between yourself and the management team. Prepare an agenda for the meeting including a list of questions you will want answered during the planning session.

2. In small groups, draft a survey instrument that you can use with Reynolds employees to uncover communication problem areas.

3. The CEO of Reynolds Toy Corporation has called you in to say that he has decided you should provide standard training programs in decision making, listening, and performance appraisal. With a classmate, role play your meeting, being sure to bring out in the process the benefits of tailor-made communication training.

References

1. *Human Resource Management: The Manager's Communication Responsibility*, a brochure published by the Xerox Corporation, n.d., p. 1.

2. Gerald M. Goldhaber, *Organizational Communication* (Dubuque, Iowa: William C. Brown, 1986), pp. 400–401.

3. Raymond L. Falcione, "Auditing Organizational Communication" in John Louis DiGaetani, *The Handbook of Executive Communication* (Homewood, Ill.: Dow Jones-Irwin, 1986), p. 780.

4. Joseph A. Kopec, "The Communication Audit," *Public Relations Journal*, May 1982, pp. 25–26.

5. Dale A. Level, Jr. and William P. Galle, Jr., *Business Communications: Theory and Practice* (Dallas, Tex.: Business Publications, 1988), p. 402.

6. *Ibid.*, p. 319.

7. Kopec, *op. cit.*, p. 25.

8. *Ibid.*

9. *Ibid.*, p. 26.

10. Goldhaber, *op. cit.*, p. 451.

11. *Ibid.*, p. 461.

12. *Ibid.*, p. 474.

13. Roger D'Aprix, *Communicating for Productivity* (New York: Harper & Row, 1982), p. 95.

Annotated Bibliography

D'Aprix, Roger, *Communicating for Productivity* (New York: Harper & Row, 1982). D'Aprix combines the wisdom of his years as a manager of employee communication at the Xerox Corporation, and now as president of Organizational Communication Services, into a practical discourse on the state of organizational communication and how to improve it. He puts the onus squarely on the shoulders of senior management and warns that, "It is always a disaster when they try to delegate by hiring a sort of tribal medicine man to do the communicating in their stead."

John Louis DiGaetani, ed., *The Handbook of Executive Communication* (Homewood, Ill.: Dow Jones-Irwin, 1986).

This compilation of essays is designed as a basic reference source about all the important aspects of communication in business such as writing, listening, speaking, interviewing, and interpersonal skills. The essays are written in a variety of styles by major communication authors. This is a great reference book!

Answers to Self-Assessment Quizzes

Self-Assessment Quiz 1.1: What Do These Words Mean?

1. **c.** Biweekly means every other week.

2. **d.** Mandatory means required.

3. **a.** Relinquish means to give up or to cede.

4. **a.** In the business world, a liquid position is characterized by a firm that has a great deal of cash on hand.

5. **d.** Tardy means late.

6. **a.** In the business world, bears are investors who believe the stock market will go down; hence, they are sellers.

7. **a.** In technical business jargon, burning the blueprints means making a photocopy of them. (New employees who are unfamiliar with the term have been known to destroy original copies.)

8. **d.** Conceptual skills are possessed by individuals with the ability to integrate ideas and see them all as part of a composite. As a result, they are excellent strategic planners.

9. **c.** Tacit means implied or understood, rather than written or spoken.

10. **b.** Solvent means being able to pay one's bills.

How well did you do? Most people get seven right. Regardless of your score, however, remember that managers who use words that others do not understand have done a very poor job of coding their messages.

Self-Assessment Quiz 2.1: Are You a Classical Management Person?

1. True	6. True	
2. False	7. False	
3. True	8. False	
4. False	9. True	
5. True	10. False	

The higher your score, the greater your support for classical management practices. A score of eight or more indicates strong support for scientific and administrative management thinking. Hopefully, by the time you have finished reading this chapter, your score will be down in the range of two to three.

Self-Assessment Quiz 2.2: Are You a Human Relations Management Person?

1.	True	6.	True
2.	True	7.	False
3.	False	8.	True
4.	False	9.	False
5.	True	10.	False

The higher your score, the greater your support for human relations management practices. A score of eight or more is very high and indicates strong support for this philosophy. Hopefully, by the time you have finished reading this chapter, your score will be down in the range of two to three.

Self-Assessment Quiz 2.3: Are You a Human Resources Management Person?

1.	False	6.	False
2.	True	7.	True
3.	False	8.	False
4.	True	9.	False
5.	False	10.	False

The higher your score, the greater your support for human resources management practices. A score of eight or more is very good and indicates strong support for this philosophy. Hopefully, by the time you have finished reading this chapter, your score will be up to the eight or nine range.

Self-Assessment Quiz 3.1: What Do You Know About Listening? An Initial Inquiry

1. True. As you will learn in this chapter, research studies show that about 45 percent of a manager's communication time is spent listening. This is more than the time spent speaking (30 percent), writing (16 percent), or reading (9 percent).

2. False. This is a popular myth. Naturally a hearing handicap will impact on listening efficiency, but merely having perfect hearing in no way ensures that a person is a good listener.

3. False. Many people believe that intelligent individuals are also effective listeners. In truth, no such correlation has been found.

4. False. Like effective reading and writing, listening *is* a teachable skill.

5. True. If you really "tune in" to someone, and listen actively, you will find yourself exerting energy and effort. You may also hear things you would prefer to ignore. Effective listening can be both physically and psychologically draining.

6. False. As discussed in depth in this chapter, such a probing response mode serves the needs of the listener better than those of the speaker.

7. False. Studies reveal this percentage to be about 25 percent.

8. False. Outlining often distracts listeners and causes them to miss many of the main points the speaker is making.

9. False. Another common myth. There is no known correlation between these two modes of communication.

10. False. Active listening takes energy. An effective listener must concentrate complete attention on the speaker and resist distractions. It is hard work!

How well did you do? The average person gets only three to five right. If you did not do as well as you would have liked, remember that effective listening habits can be taught. By the time you have finished studying all the material in this chapter, you should be able to score at least a 9 on this quiz.

Self-Assessment Quiz 3.2: Identify Your Response Style

Answers: Count up how many checks you had for each letter: A, B, C, D, and E. The one with the most checks is your dominant response mode. The title or word that describes each of these response modes is as follows:

A = Directing

B = Judgmental

C = Probing

D = Smoothing

E = Active/Empathic

Interpretations for Figure 4.2

(a)-(c). These are examples of sensory reality. There is a right answer for each. In (a) the circle is round; in (b) the two center circles are identical in size; and in (c) the length and width of the hat are equal.

(d) and (e). These are examples of normative reality. There is interpretation involved. The most common answer to (d) is that it is the face of a man with a beard (perhaps Christ). Other common responses include an abstract painting and a map of a particular area of the world. The most common answer to (e) is that it is a bird with a large beak, although if you have the animal look in the opposite direction it becomes a rabbit (the bird's beak becomes the rabbit's ears). Another common response is that it is an island surrounded by water with birds or clouds above.

Self-Assessment Quiz 4.1: How Do You Feel About Self-Disclosure?

Answers seen as indicating comfortableness with self-disclosure behavior are as follows.

1. False. Office politics and gossip will flourish when information is restricted and guarded.

2. False. While initially this may be perceived as the case by some employees, long-term authentic, open relationships can be fostered only by the manager setting an example.

3. True. Employees like to know where they stand and where they are headed. Trying to "figure out" the boss is both nonproductive and time consuming.

4. False. Though a commonly held belief, "familiarity breeds contempt" has not been proven. Open, comfortable, interpersonal relationships foster a good working climate.

5. True. Why spend time trying to guess what the other folks you relate to are thinking? The best way to gain accurate knowledge is directly from them!

6. False. Privacy is read as secrecy by others and they will try to figure out your motives — usually incorrectly!

7. False. Failure to confront issues may lead to fewer arguments now but substantially bigger problems later on. When you finally explode, people will not understand because it will appear as though you have gone along with everything previously.

8. False. Disclosure may be time consuming, but in the long run it is far less so than operating on erroneous assumptions and partial knowledge.

9. False. Just as disclosure works at home, it will work to promote healthier professional relationships as well.

10. False.   This is a tough one and particularly problematic with supervisors who are secretive themselves. They may indeed see you as a little eccentric. Nevertheless, they will have more knowledge of who you really are and how to motivate and reward you. Hopefully, you'll set a good example.

Scoring   Count up your numbers of self-disclosure answers. The higher the number, the more you believe in self-disclosure as a personal style. The lower the score, the more secretive you tend to be.

Self-Assessment Quiz 4.2: Fact or Inference?

Let us review the quiz you just took:

1. "I am 23 years old" is a pure and simple fact. Of course, I might be lying about my age, but no inference is evident.

2. "Ralph makes a good salary as a mechanic" implies that we know what constitutes a "good salary." It is inferential rather than factual.

3. "Roger ran 5 miles after work today" sounds like fact, but unless you actually followed behind and clocked him, it's probably inference. Also, it is likely that he did not run the whole way.

4. "My husband always comes home early" tells us very little. What's early? Early from what? Do you really mean *always?* This is, of course, inference.

5. "Sally liked my chocolate cake." The inference here is "liked." What does it mean on a scale of one to ten? Was Sally telling the truth? Fact would be, "Sally said she liked my cake."

6. "She is a middle-aged woman" is inference. What does "middle-aged" mean? 30? 40? 55? 60?

7. "It snowed yesterday in Philadelphia" is fact verifiable by observation, newspaper, and TV reports.

8. "It's going to be a sunny day tomorrow" is inference whether it is based on the weatherman's educated guess or your notice of a red sun at sunset.

9. "In the winter, the water is too cold for swimming" is an inference. What does "too cold" mean? "Too cold" where? In my heated, indoor pool?

10. "Sam always does well on his math tests" is inference. What does "well" mean? Does he always perform the same? "Well" as compared to what? Fact would be "Sam has never scored less than 82 percent on a math test."

Self-Assessment Quiz 5.1: What Do You Know About Kinesics?

At the beginning of the section on kinesics, you answered a self-assessment quiz. Let us review the answers to each question.

1. False.   The hands are far less expressive in nonverbal communication than are the eyes or the face.

2. False.   The employee is likely to be confused. He or she may discount the scolding totally or conclude that it is a good-natured, mild warning. The seriousness of the situation is frustrated by the smile.

3. False.   Single body movements are often misleading. Gesture clusters should be sought and congruence checked between gestures, facial expressions, and words.

4. False.   In some societies shaking your head from left to right means "yes."

5. False.   Nonverbal behavior may be calculated, but in more instances it is automated and unconscious.

6. False.   Just the opposite. Women invariably hold eye contact longer and more often than men.

7. False.   In some societies being late is expected. Even in America, coming late to a party is considered more important than being on time.

Self-Assessment Quiz 5.2: How Territorial Are You?

10–25 points: *Highly territorial.* Your instincts of staking out and protecting what you consider yours are high. You believe in your territorial rights in others. The lower the score, the more territorial you are.

26–39 points: *Ambiguous about territoriality.* You may act territorial in some circumstances and not in others. Your behavior is not consistent with the theory of territoriality. You are somewhat unsure of how you feel about these issues.

40–50 points: *Not territorial.* You disagree, perhaps ethically, with the entire concept of territoriality. You dislike possessiveness, protectiveness, and jealousy. The concept of private ownership is not central to your philosophy of life.

Self-Assessment Quiz 6.1: What Type of Group Do You Prefer?

The 10 items that you were asked to rank in terms of personal preference contain factors related to lower-level need satisfaction and upper-level satisfaction. Column A total reveals your preference for, or the importance of, lower-level need satisfiers. Notice that job security, wages, working conditions, job descriptions, and benefit plans are all geared to help you meet your physiological and safety needs. Column B total reveals your preference for, or the importance of, upper-level need satisfiers. Advancement, responsibility, a chance to succeed, recognition, and interesting work all help satisfy esteem and self-actualization needs.

Since you placed a "1" next to the most important factor and a "10" next to the least important factor, the column with the *lowest* total represents the one that is most important to you. If the two totals are almost identical, it indicates that you would seek to satisfy both lower-level and upper-level need satisfaction equally. (Most people have higher totals in Column A and lower totals in Column B.)

If you are more interested in lower-level need satisfaction, this means that you would seek groups where survival and security are extremely important. The group would put a great deal of attention on protecting members from dismissal. Work output might not be very high, but there would be a high concern for group unity and togetherness. Such groups are more common at the worker (as opposed to the manager) level.

If you are more interested in upper-level need satisfaction, you are more likely to find comfort in management-oriented groups where individual success is often given as much importance as group success. You would be more concerned with doing things well than you would be with keeping your job. This attitude is quite common among people who feel secure about themselves. They believe that even if they are dismissed or laid off, they can always find work elsewhere. Their motto is: "You can't keep a good person down!"

Self-Assessment Quiz 6.2: How Word-Creative Are You?

The answers, along with explanations where needed, are as follows:

1. green: village green, green light, golf green.

2. cover: cover up, hard cover, book cover.

3. foot: foot loose, club foot, football.

4. light: flashlight, starlight, limelight.

5. floor: floor show, dance floor, ground floor.

6. ball: ballgame, high ball, fast ball.

7. blood: blue blood (old, rich family), blood pressure, blood line.

8. blue: sky blue, blue blood, blue point (a type of oyster).

9. high: high priest, high proof (liquor with a high alcohol content), high tide.

10. Dutch: Dutch door (a door that is divided horizontally so that part of it can be opened and part of it closed), Dutch oven, Dutch cheese.

How well did you do? Most people get five right when working individually and seven right when working with a group. Remember, however, that creativity can be developed but you have to work at it!

Self-Assessment Quiz 7.1: Identifying Your Personal Philosophy of Management

The statements in this quiz are all related to Theory X. If you are unclear as to what is meant by this statement, read the next couple of pages of the text following the quiz before continuing with this explanation.

The lower your score, the greater your tendency to subscribe to Theory Y tenets. The higher your score, the greater your tendency to subscribe to Theory X tenets. A score of more than 40 indicates that you are basically a Theory X manager. A score of less than 20 indicates that you are solidly in the Theory Y camp. Most effective leaders today are Theory Y people. On occasion, they will subscribe to a particular Theory X belief. For example, if they are having a great deal of difficulty with a particular employee they may, indeed, use close control with the individual. However, in the main they use loose control and place a great deal of confidence and trust in their people. As you read the beliefs of Theory X and Theory Y leaders, keep in mind that, although Theory Y sounds very good, most managers, in practice, tend to lean somewhat toward Theory X in their orientation.

Self-Assessment Quiz 7.2: Least Preferred Co-Worker Scale

Interpretation of Scores

Individuals with high LPC scores are relationship-motivated people. Those with a score of 64 or more fit into this category. These people tend to accomplish tasks through good interpersonal relations with the group. Once their primary task has been accomplished, however, they may become brusque or authoritarian in nature. On the other hand, in tense, anxiety-arousing situations, they may become so concerned with interpersonal relationships that they fail to accomplish their assigned task.

Individuals with low LPC scores (57 or less) are highly motivated to accomplish tasks to which they have committed themselves. They tend to do so through clear and standardized work procedures. They commonly employ a no-nonsense approach to the job. They will care about the feelings, attitudes, and opinions of their subordinates but not if these get in the way of goal attainment.

Regardless of which group you fall into, your ability to get things done is going to depend on how well your individual personality and leadership style fit the requirements of the leadership situation. Your LPC score will not help you one way or the other.

Self-Assessment Quiz 8.1: What Do You Know About Formal Organizational Communication?

1. True	6. True
2. False	7. True
3. False	8. True
4. False	9. True
5. False	10. True

These answers are explained in the chapter. Before reading the chapter most people answer only five right. After reading the chapter, they answer all ten correctly. If you missed any, take the quiz again after you have finished with the chapter. If you still miss some, check your mistakes by rereading that portion of the material.

Self-Assessment Quiz 9.1: What Do You Know About the Grapevine?

1. False.   Studies show that the majority of information carried by the grapevine is factual in nature.

2. False.   See the answer above.

3. False.   Effective management will use the grapevine in constructive ways. By improving the communication climate, management can greatly reduce the rumor factor of the grapevine.

4. False.   The grapevine is a fact of life and should be respected as a valuable part of the total communication system.

5. False.   Formal and informal channels serve different purposes.

6. False.   If a rapid answer is needed, the grapevine is the preferred source.

7. False.   In times of stress, the grapevine becomes unusually active.

8. False.   Everybody participates in the informal system.

9. False.   The opportunity for informal communication is positively correlated with job satisfaction.

10. False.   A healthy grapevine indicates organizational interest and activity. It has the potential to relieve stress and motivate employees.

Most people answer no more than seven correctly. How well did you do?

Self-Assessment Quiz 9.2: How Well Do You Understand Network Forms?

1. W   6. W

2. AC   7. W

3. AC   8. AC

4. C   9. Ch

5. AC

Self-Assessment Quiz 10.1: What Do You Know About Organizational Communication Barriers?

1. True.   Studies show that when messages are repeatedly passed through numerous channels distortion occurs.

2. False.   This can lead to bypassing levels and its accompanying problems.

3. False.   Studies show that the more distance there is between employees, the less effective communication patterns tend to be.

4. False.   Horizontal channels are often jammed with rumors and gossip.

5. False.   People tend to make up information whenever it is not otherwise available.

6. True.   Employees tend to positively bias information regarding themselves.

7. False.   Information ownership refers to the hoarding of information by people who think it will give them a competitive edge.

8. True.   Messages become distorted and feelings are often hurt as a result of bypassing.

9. False.   A trusting climate is critical to candid, effective communication.

10. False.   Not necessarily so! High aspirers often carefully select their communication messages so as to advance their own agendas.

11. False.   Studies show that most employees do indeed want more downward communication.

12. False.   The more often a message is repeated, the more likely it is to be distorted.

13. False.   There are many communication "isolates" suffering from underload in today's organizations.

14. True.   There is less demand for high-quality and quantity information processing in routine, self-contained jobs.

How well did you do? On average, most people get 9 right. After studying the material in this chapter, you should get all 14 right.

Self-Assessment Quiz 10.2: Are You A Victim of Communication Overload?

Answers: "Yes" answers on any of these questions indicates an overload condition. If you answered "yes" to five or more questions, you are already experiencing serious overload problems.

Self-Assessment Quiz 11.1: Power and You

This quiz provides you with some initial insights regarding the types of power you prefer to use. Although there are only three situations, this is enough for our purposes. Notice that columns (a) – (e) relate to reward, coercive, legitimate, referent, and expert power, respectively. Your lowest number indicates your favorite choice and vice versa. On the basis of your answers, now go back and review the first section of the chapter and compare your favorite choices with your least preferred ones. How do you go about wielding power? What type of person are you? Your answers should provide you with some insights to these questions.

Self-Assessment Quiz 11.2: Your Approach to Persuasion and Negotiation

The nine alternatives in this self-assessment quiz can be divided into three categories. The first three alternatives relate to the use of power; the second three relate to the use of time; and the last three to the use of information. Since you put a "1" next to your favorite alternative on down to a "9" next to your last choice, the column with the lowest total represents the variable that you most prefer to use. As you read the section related to these three variables, notice how we have incorporated them into the self-assessment quiz. Also keep in mind which variable you most preferred and see if you can determine why as you read that particular section.

Self-Assessment Quiz 12.1: What Is Your Attitude Toward Conflict?

The statements on the left are labeled T for traditional; those on the right are labeled C for current. Count the number of check marks you had on each side. If you had seven or more on one side, that side reflects your attitude toward conflict. If you had a 6–4 or 5–5 division, you have no strong beliefs in either approach, although you are probably in a transition stage of moving from one side to the other. Retake this quiz when you have finished reading the chapter and see if your responses have changed.

Answers to Self-Assessment Quiz 13.1: Can You Recognize a Leading Question?

1. Leading question. Puts the person on the spot and almost forces a "yes" answer.

2. Leading question. Obviously there's something wrong with you if you don't answer yes.

3. Neutral question.

4. Neutral question.

5. Leading question. Clearly the interviewer has indicated her bias with the word "ridiculous."

6. Neutral question.

7. Neutral question.

8. Neutral question.

9. Leading question. Apparently the interviewer is not a union proponent.

10. Leading question. Anything but a "no" is obviously unacceptable; why bother even to ask the question?

Self-Assessment Quiz 13.2: Are These Legal Questions?

1. Illegal.   You may be accused of discriminating if she answers yes.

2. Illegal.   Marital status is not a legitimate occupational qualification.

3. Legal.   This is a legitmate question to see whether the applicant's background matches the skills and knowledges required by the job.

4. Legal.   This is a legitimate occupational qualification *if* the person would need to be bonded for the job.

5. Illegal.   A person's age is not a legitimate occupational qualification.

6. Legal.   Agreement to travel is a legitimate occupational qualification.

7. Illegal.   This is no concern of the employer.

8. Illegal.   This hints of sexual harassment and could lead the applicant straight to the EEOC.

9. Illegal.   Religion is not a legitimate occupational qualification unless the person is applying for a position within a church.

10. Legal.   This is a legitimate concern if the employer has some feeling that he or she may not be able to meet the applicant's needs.

Self-Assessment Quiz 14.1: How Much Do You Know About Effective Meetings?

Here are the answers to the quiz. Note how well you did. After you have finished reading the chapter, take the quiz again and compare your progress. If you miss any the second time around, reread that material. For the moment, use your answers as a gauge to measure what you know currently about the use of committees.

1. True	6. True	11. True
2. False	7. False	12. True
3. False	8. True	13. False
4. False	9. True	14. False
5. True	10. False	15. True

Self-Assessment Quiz 15.1: What Do You Know About International Communication?

1. True.   Managers in the Orient put much heavier reliance on implicit communication than do Western managers.

2. True.   The Japanese rely very heavily on formal authority.

3. False.   Surprisingly, value systems are not changing very slowly.

4. False.   Orientals often lose their temper when things do not go well.

5. True.   Korean managers, as most managers in the Far East, rely heavily on downward, one-way communication.

6. True.   Of all Anglo groups, the Australians tend to be the most humanistic and caring of all.

7. True.   British managers, unlike many European managers, encourage upward communication.

8. True.   The Argentineans often place more emphasis on the speed with which decisions are made than on the effectiveness of these decisions.

9. True.   The French place strong emphasis on the hierarchy and like the system and order it brings to the workplace.

10. False.   American managers tend to give greater importance to two-way communication than any other nation.

Self-Assessment Quiz 15.2: What Do You Know About Japanese Management and Communication Practices?

1. False.   In some companies workers are guaranteed lifetime employment, but this is true for only about 30 percent of the entire workforce.

2. False.   U.S. productivity is the highest.

3. False.   Most people who are polled on this question say the Americans are the hardest working.

4. True.

5. True.

6. False.   They work long hours because they need the money for living expenses.

7. False.   They are much more one-way and autocratic.

8. False.   They are slow to do so and often prefer to use methods that have worked well in Japan.

9. True.

10. True.

Self-Assessment Quiz 16.1: Can You Recognize Good Behavioral Objectives?

1. Satisfactory, but barely, unless it is tied to specific behaviors that are measurable at the beginning and end of the training.

2. Poor. This is not really a behavioral objective. It is merely an assumption of participation in the training session.

3. Good, although it might well be augmented by identifying what those techniques are.

4. Good. This objective clearly states what the participant should be able to do by the end of the session.

5. Satisfactory, but again just barely so. "Understanding" is not an action verb in the sense that "doing" or "demonstrating" are. Nor does it automatically translate into desired behavior.

6. Poor. Be a good example at what? How?

7. Good. Assessing needs is an important skill, although the method of assessment is not stated.

8. Good. This clearly indicates what skill is expected.

9. Good. It lists the specific behavior that is expected.

10. Poor. Better by whose standards? By what measure?

How well did you do? Most people answer only half of them correctly the first time through. However, after you have read the section on setting behavioral objectives you should answer all of them correctly. If you do not, go back and reread the objective in the quiz and the answer given above until you understand why the latter evaluation is correct.

Name Index

Subject Index